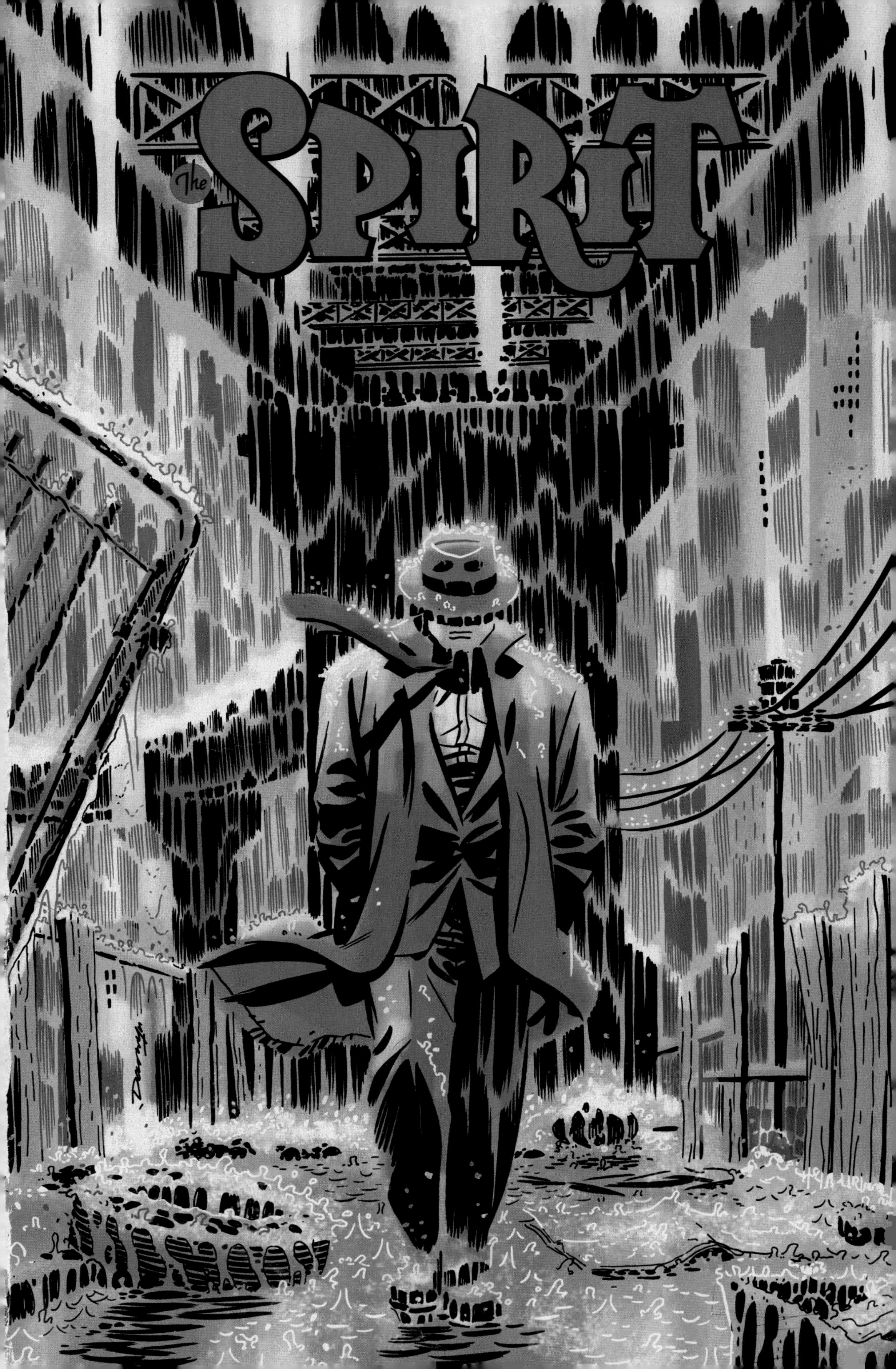
The SPIRIT

Writers
Darwyn Cooke
Walter Simonson
Kyle Baker
Glen David Gold
Gail Simone
Denny O'Neil

Artists
Darwyn Cooke & J. Bone
Chris Sprouse & Karl Story
Kyle Baker
Eduardo Risso
Phil Hester & Andy Parks
Ty Templeton

Colors by Dave Stewart, Alex Sinclair
and Jim Charalampidis
Letters by Jared K. Fletcher

Original series covers and Collected Edition cover by Darwyn Cooke

The Spirit created by Will Eisner

The SPIRIT

Dan DiDio, Senior VP–Executive Editor / Ben Abernathy and Scott Dunbier, Editors–Original Series
Kristy Quinn, Assistant Editor–Original Series / Bob Joy, Editor–Collected Edition
Robbin Brosterman, Senior Art Director / Paul Levitz, President & Publisher
Georg Brewer, VP–Design & DC Direct Creative / Richard Bruning, Senior VP–Creative Director
Patrick Caldon, Executive VP–Finance & Operations / Chris Caramalis, VP–Finance
John Cunningham, VP–Marketing / Terri Cunningham, VP–Managing Editor
Alison Gill, VP–Manufacturing / David Hyde, VP–Publicity / Hank Kanalz, VP–General Manager, WildStorm
Jim Lee, Editorial Director–WildStorm / Paula Lowitt, Senior VP–Business & Legal Affairs
MaryEllen McLaughlin, VP–Advertising & Custom Publishing / John Nee, Senior VP–Business Development
Gregory Noveck, Senior VP–Creative Affairs / Sue Pohja, VP–Book Trade Sales
Steve Rotterdam, Senior VP–Sales & Marketing / Cheryl Rubin, Senior VP–Brand Management
Jeff Trojan, VP–Business Development, DC Direct / Bob Wayne, VP–Sales

THE SPIRIT Book Two, published by DC Comics, 1700 Broadway, New York, NY 10019. Cover and compilation Copyright © 2008 Will Eisner Studios, Inc. All Rights Reserved.
THE SPIRIT and images of Denny Colt, Commissioner Dolan and Ebony are registered trademarks owned by Will Eisner Studios, Inc.
Originally published in single magazine form as THE SPIRIT #7-13 © 2007, 2008 DC Comics and Will Eisner Studios, Inc.

DC Comics, a Warner Bros. Entertainment Company.

HC ISBN: 978-1-4012-1920-8
SC ISBN: 978-1-4012-2220-8

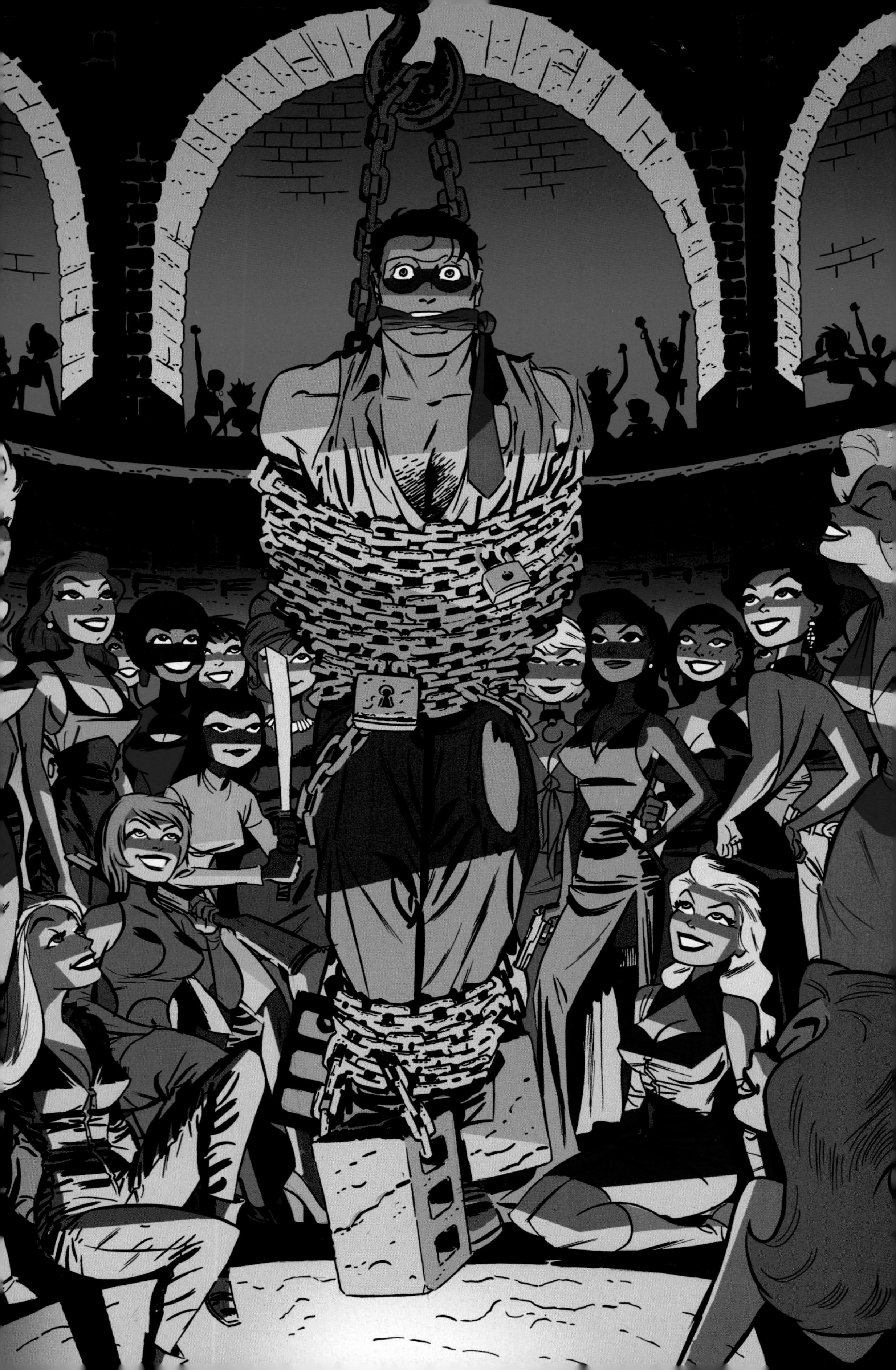

1

ACTION · Mystery · ADVENTURE

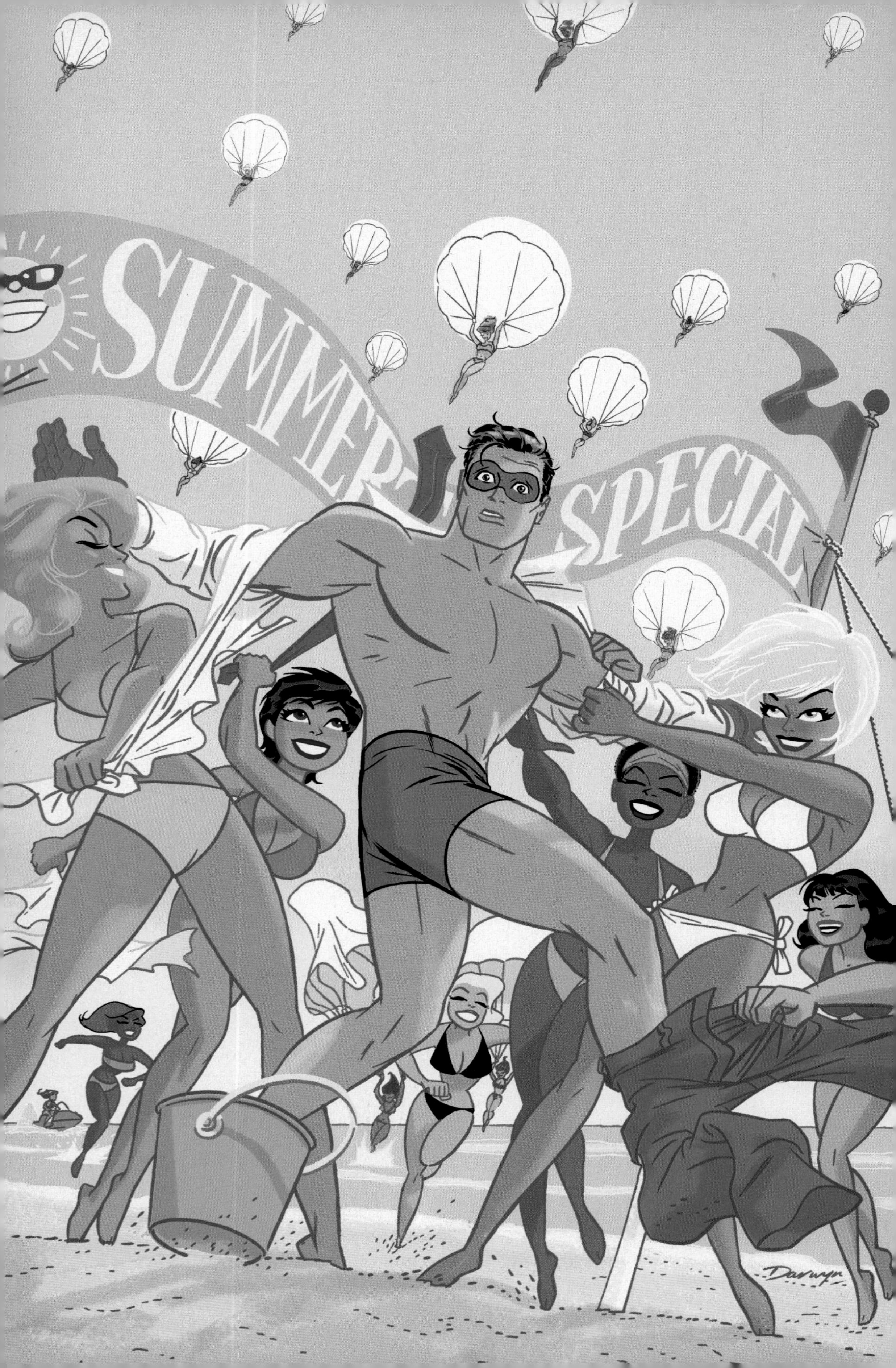
SUMMER
SPECIAL
Darwyn

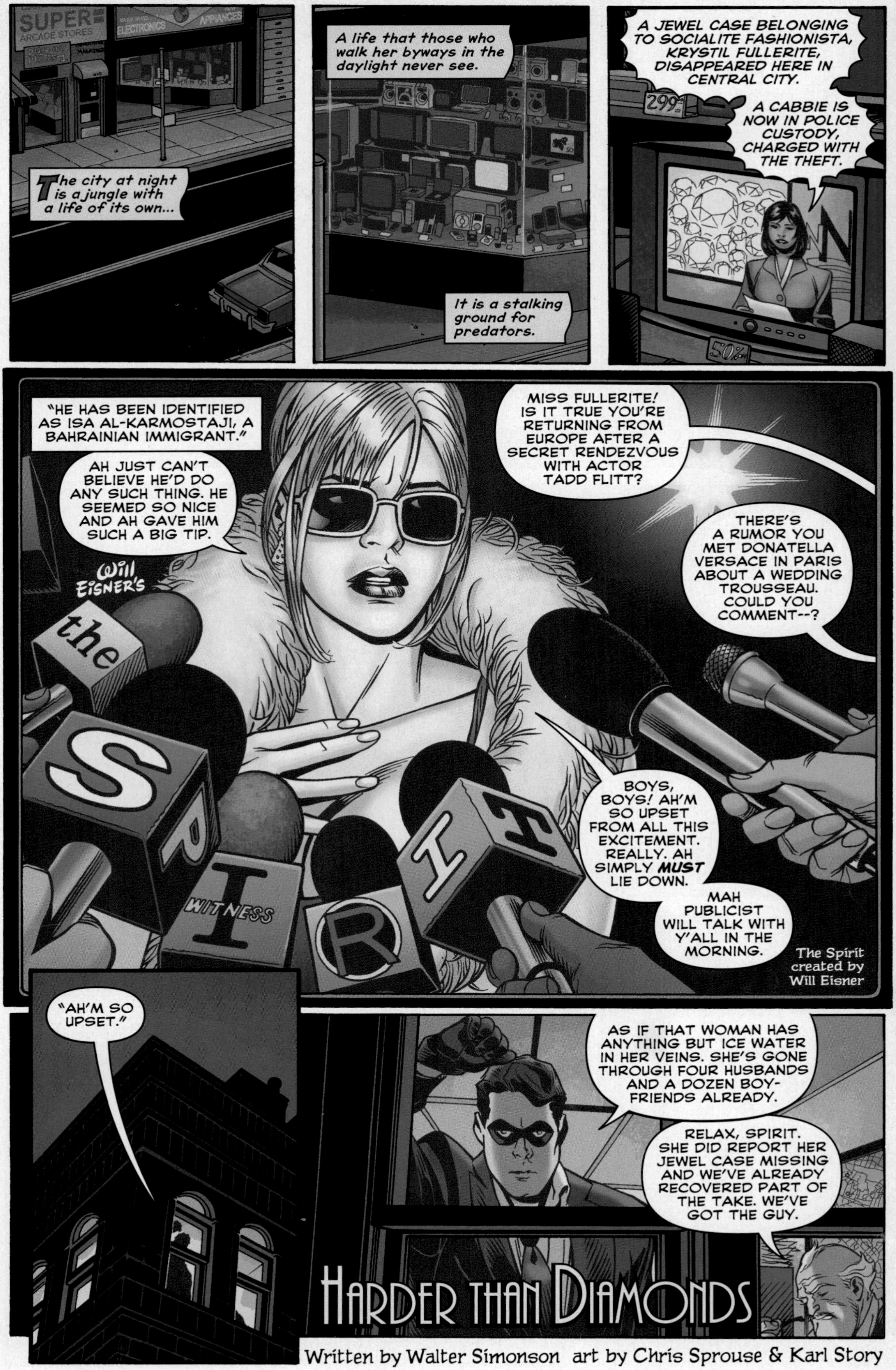
SUPER
ARCADE STORES
ELECTRONICS
APPLIANCES
The city at night is a jungle with a life of its own...
A life that those who walk her byways in the daylight never see.
It is a stalking ground for predators.
A JEWEL CASE BELONGING TO SOCIALITE FASHIONISTA, KRYSTIL FULLERITE, DISAPPEARED HERE IN CENTRAL CITY.
299
A CABBIE IS NOW IN POLICE CUSTODY, CHARGED WITH THE THEFT.
50%
"HE HAS BEEN IDENTIFIED AS ISA AL-KARMOSTAJI, A BAHRAINIAN IMMIGRANT."
AH JUST CAN'T BELIEVE HE'D DO ANY SUCH THING. HE SEEMED SO NICE AND AH GAVE HIM SUCH A BIG TIP.
MISS FULLERITE! IS IT TRUE YOU'RE RETURNING FROM EUROPE AFTER A SECRET RENDEZVOUS WITH ACTOR TADD FLITT?
THERE'S A RUMOR YOU MET DONATELLA VERSACE IN PARIS ABOUT A WEDDING TROUSSEAU. COULD YOU COMMENT--?
Will Eisner's
the
SPIRIT
WITNESS
BOYS, BOYS! AH'M SO UPSET FROM ALL THIS EXCITEMENT. REALLY. AH SIMPLY MUST LIE DOWN.
MAH PUBLICIST WILL TALK WITH Y'ALL IN THE MORNING.
The Spirit created by Will Eisner
"AH'M SO UPSET."
AS IF THAT WOMAN HAS ANYTHING BUT ICE WATER IN HER VEINS. SHE'S GONE THROUGH FOUR HUSBANDS AND A DOZEN BOY-FRIENDS ALREADY.
RELAX, SPIRIT. SHE DID REPORT HER JEWEL CASE MISSING AND WE'VE ALREADY RECOVERED PART OF THE TAKE. WE'VE GOT THE GUY.
HARDER THAN DIAMONDS

Written by Walter Simonson art by Chris Sprouse & Karl Story
Color by Dave Stewart Letters by Jared Fletcher Ass't Editor Kristy Quinn Editor Scott Dunbier

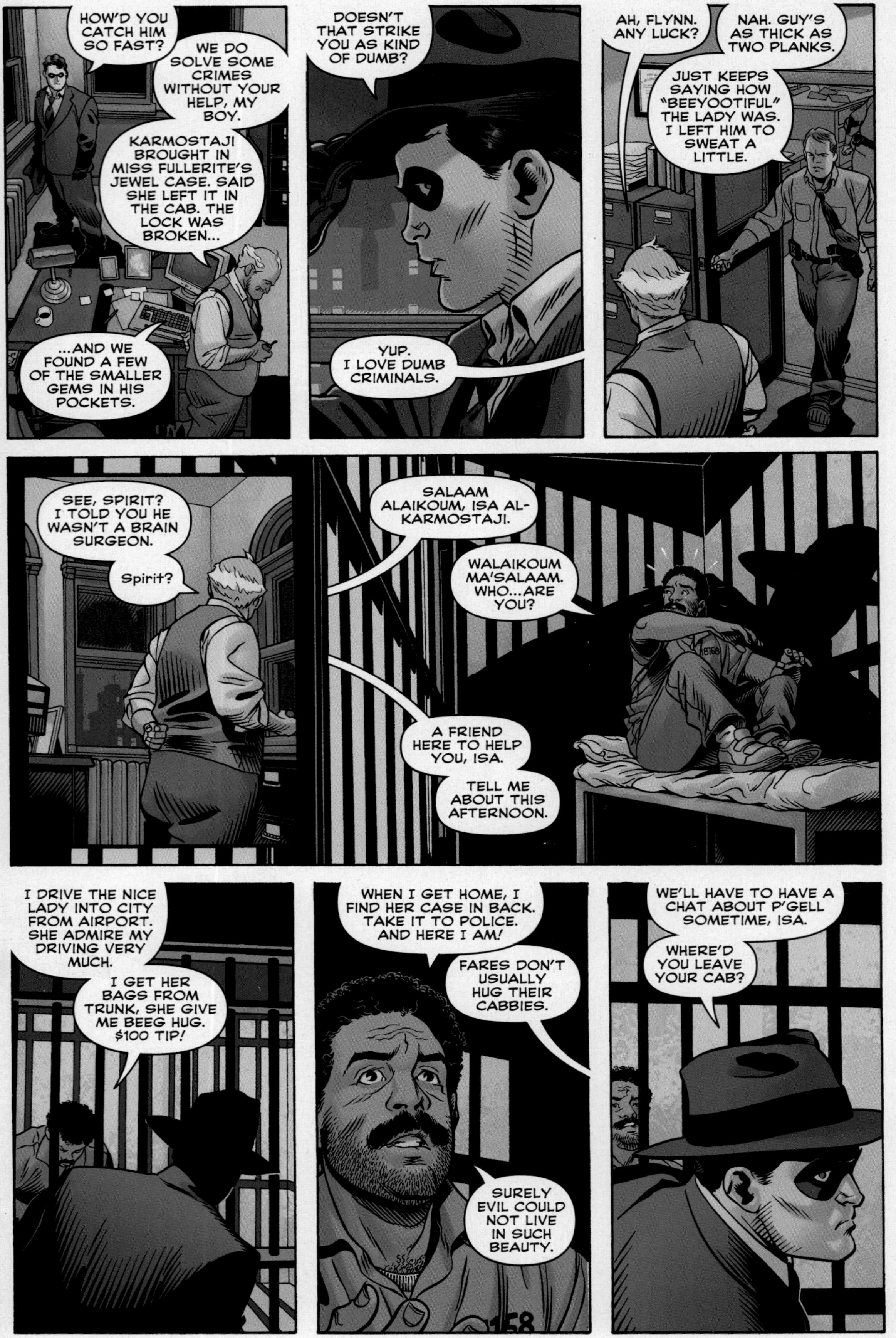
HOW'D YOU CATCH HIM SO FAST?
WE DO SOLVE SOME CRIMES WITHOUT YOUR HELP, MY BOY.
KARMOSTAJI BROUGHT IN MISS FULLERITE'S JEWEL CASE. SAID SHE LEFT IT IN THE CAB. THE LOCK WAS BROKEN...
...AND WE FOUND A FEW OF THE SMALLER GEMS IN HIS POCKETS.
DOESN'T THAT STRIKE YOU AS KIND OF DUMB?
YUP. I LOVE DUMB CRIMINALS.
AH, FLYNN. ANY LUCK?
NAH. GUY'S AS THICK AS TWO PLANKS.
JUST KEEPS SAYING HOW "BEEYOOTIFUL" THE LADY WAS. I LEFT HIM TO SWEAT A LITTLE.
SEE, SPIRIT? I TOLD YOU HE WASN'T A BRAIN SURGEON.
Spirit?
SALAAM ALAIKOUM, ISA AL-KARMOSTAJI.
WALAIKOUM MA'SALAAM. WHO...ARE YOU?
A FRIEND HERE TO HELP YOU, ISA.
TELL ME ABOUT THIS AFTERNOON.
I DRIVE THE NICE LADY INTO CITY FROM AIRPORT. SHE ADMIRE MY DRIVING VERY MUCH.
I GET HER BAGS FROM TRUNK, SHE GIVE ME BEEG HUG. $100 TIP!
WHEN I GET HOME, I FIND HER CASE IN BACK. TAKE IT TO POLICE. AND HERE I AM!
FARES DON'T USUALLY HUG THEIR CABBIES.
SURELY EVIL COULD NOT LIVE IN SUCH BEAUTY.
WE'LL HAVE TO HAVE A CHAT ABOUT P'GELL SOMETIME, ISA.
WHERE'D YOU LEAVE YOUR CAB?

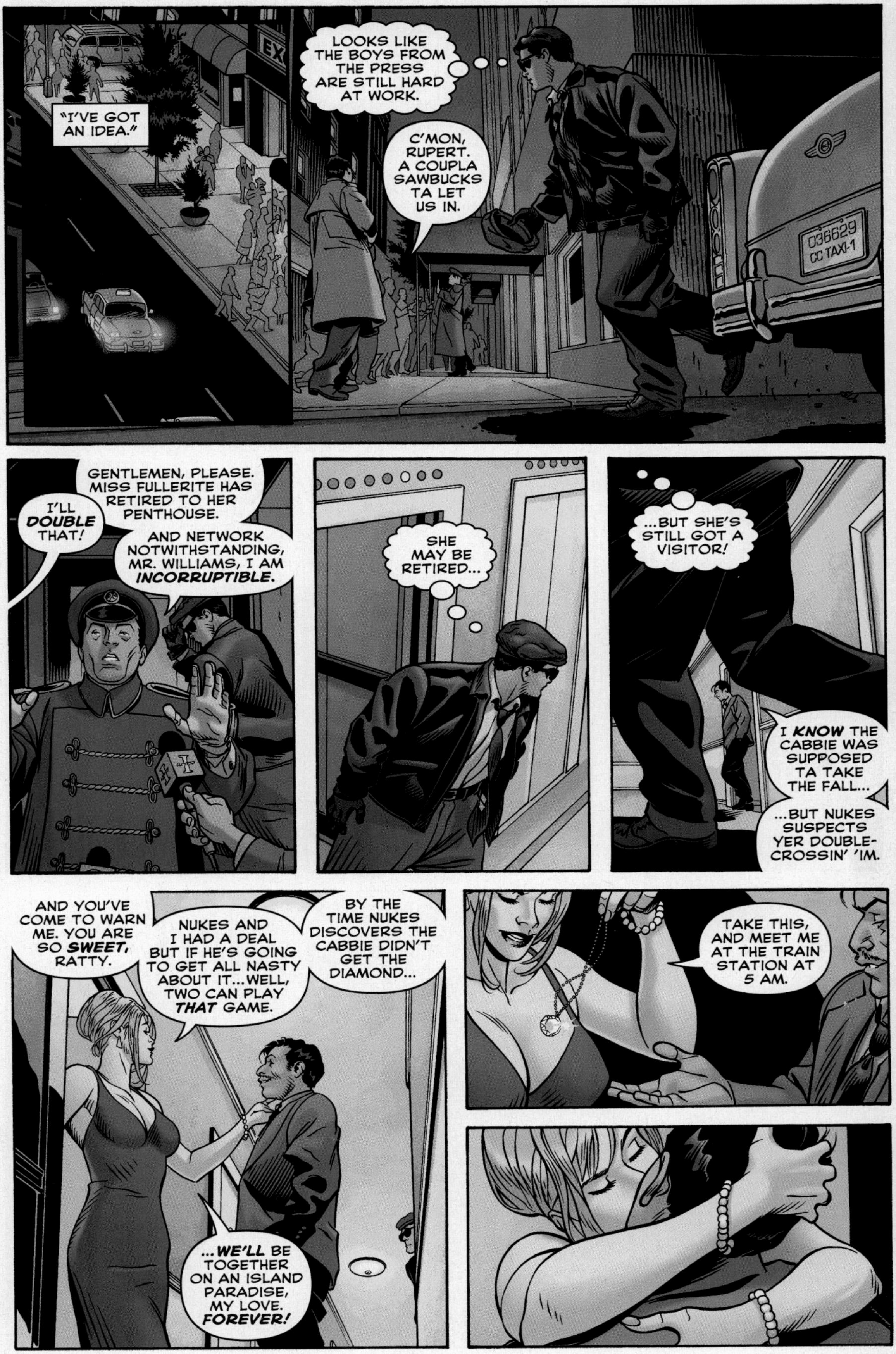
"I'VE GOT AN IDEA."
EX
LOOKS LIKE THE BOYS FROM THE PRESS ARE STILL HARD AT WORK.
C'MON, RUPERT. A COUPLA SAWBUCKS TA LET US IN.
036629 CC TAXI-1
GENTLEMEN, PLEASE. MISS FULLERITE HAS RETIRED TO HER PENTHOUSE.
I'LL DOUBLE THAT!
AND NETWORK NOTWITHSTANDING, MR. WILLIAMS, I AM INCORRUPTIBLE.
SHE MAY BE RETIRED...
...BUT SHE'S STILL GOT A VISITOR!
I KNOW THE CABBIE WAS SUPPOSED TA TAKE THE FALL...
...BUT NUKES SUSPECTS YER DOUBLE-CROSSIN' 'IM.
AND YOU'VE COME TO WARN ME. YOU ARE SO SWEET, RATTY.
NUKES AND I HAD A DEAL BUT IF HE'S GOING TO GET ALL NASTY ABOUT IT...WELL, TWO CAN PLAY THAT GAME.
BY THE TIME NUKES DISCOVERS THE CABBIE DIDN'T GET THE DIAMOND...
...WE'LL BE TOGETHER ON AN ISLAND PARADISE, MY LOVE. FOREVER!
TAKE THIS, AND MEET ME AT THE TRAIN STATION AT 5 AM.

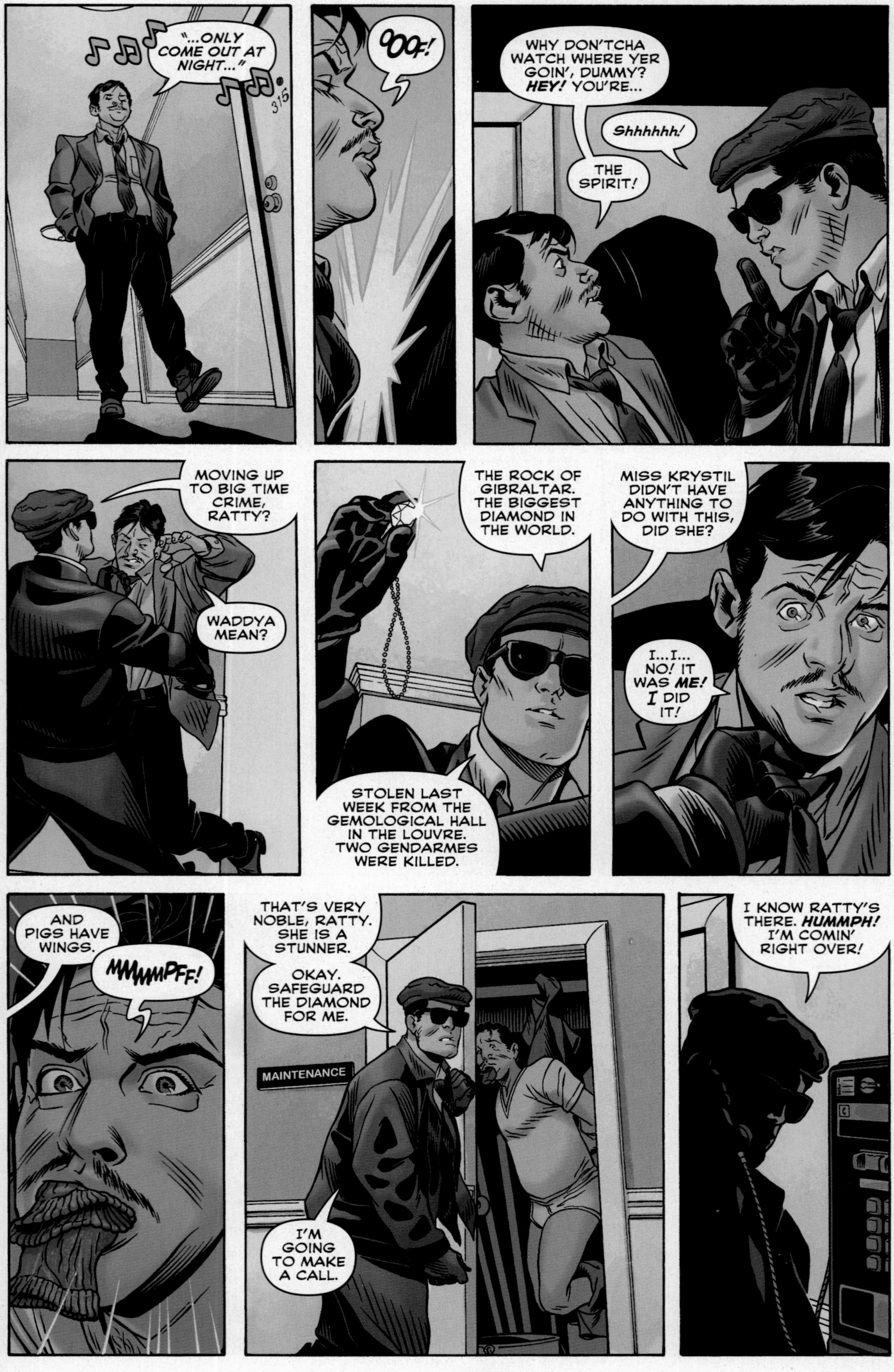
"...ONLY COME OUT AT NIGHT..."
315
OOF!
WHY DON'TCHA WATCH WHERE YER GOIN', DUMMY? **HEY!** YOU'RE...
Shhhhhh!
THE SPIRIT!
MOVING UP TO BIG TIME CRIME, RATTY?
WADDYA MEAN?
THE ROCK OF GIBRALTAR. THE BIGGEST DIAMOND IN THE WORLD.
STOLEN LAST WEEK FROM THE GEMOLOGICAL HALL IN THE LOUVRE. TWO GENDARMES WERE KILLED.
MISS KRYSTIL DIDN'T HAVE ANYTHING TO DO WITH THIS, DID SHE?
I...I... NO! IT WAS **ME!** **I** DID IT!
AND PIGS HAVE WINGS.
MMMMPFF!
THAT'S VERY NOBLE, RATTY. SHE IS A STUNNER.
OKAY. SAFEGUARD THE DIAMOND FOR ME.
MAINTENANCE
I'M GOING TO MAKE A CALL.
I KNOW RATTY'S THERE. **HUMMPH!** I'M COMIN' RIGHT OVER!

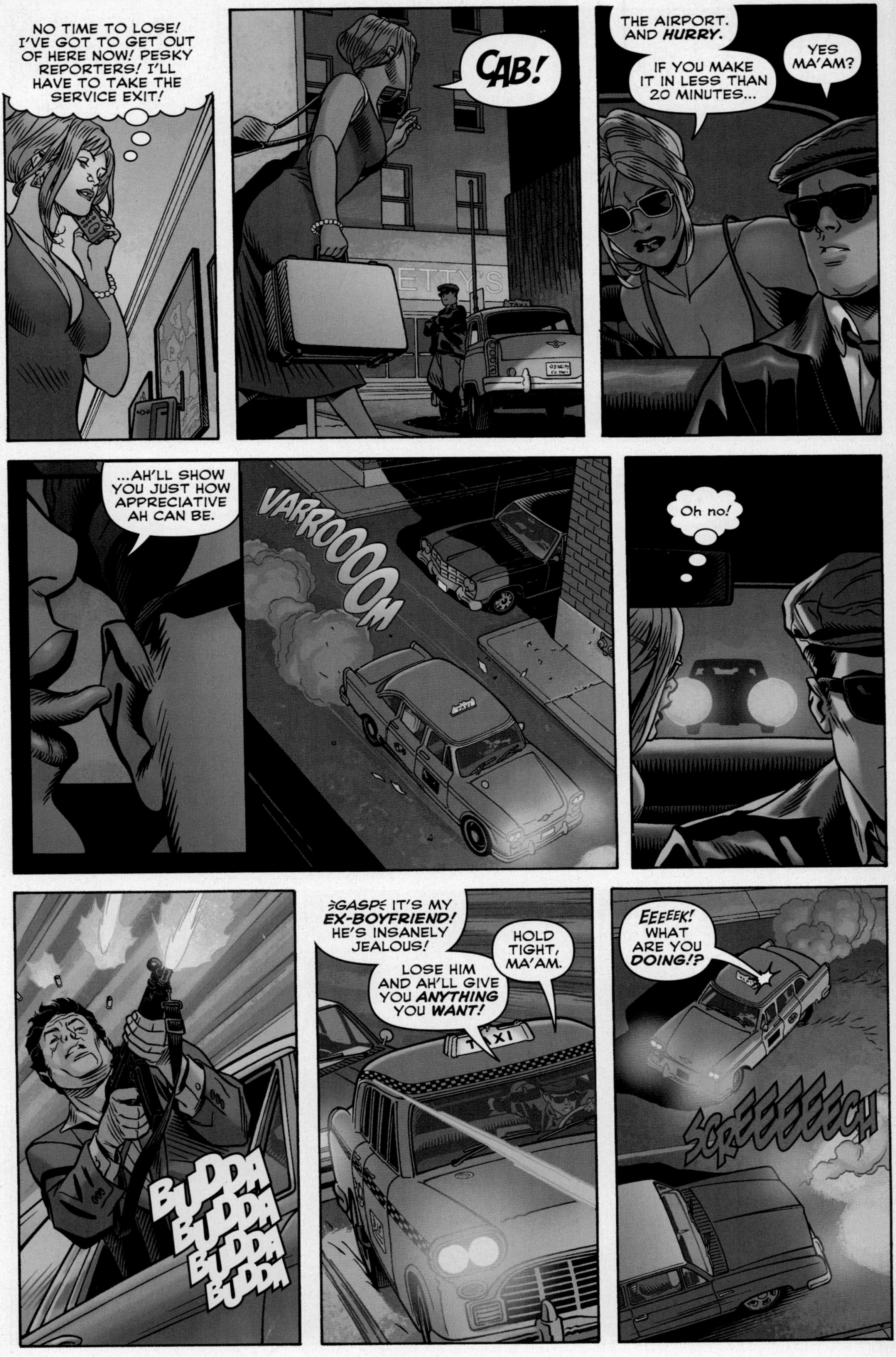
NO TIME TO LOSE! I'VE GOT TO GET OUT OF HERE NOW! PESKY REPORTERS! I'LL HAVE TO TAKE THE SERVICE EXIT!
CAB!
ETTY'S
TAXI
THE AIRPORT. AND HURRY.
YES MA'AM?
IF YOU MAKE IT IN LESS THAN 20 MINUTES...
...AH'LL SHOW YOU JUST HOW APPRECIATIVE AH CAN BE.
VARROOOOM
TAXI
Oh no!
BUDDA BUDDA BUDDA BUDDA
GASP IT'S MY EX-BOYFRIEND! HE'S INSANELY JEALOUS!
HOLD TIGHT, MA'AM.
LOSE HIM AND AH'LL GIVE YOU ANYTHING YOU WANT!
TAXI
EEEEEK! WHAT ARE YOU DOING!?
SCREEEEECH

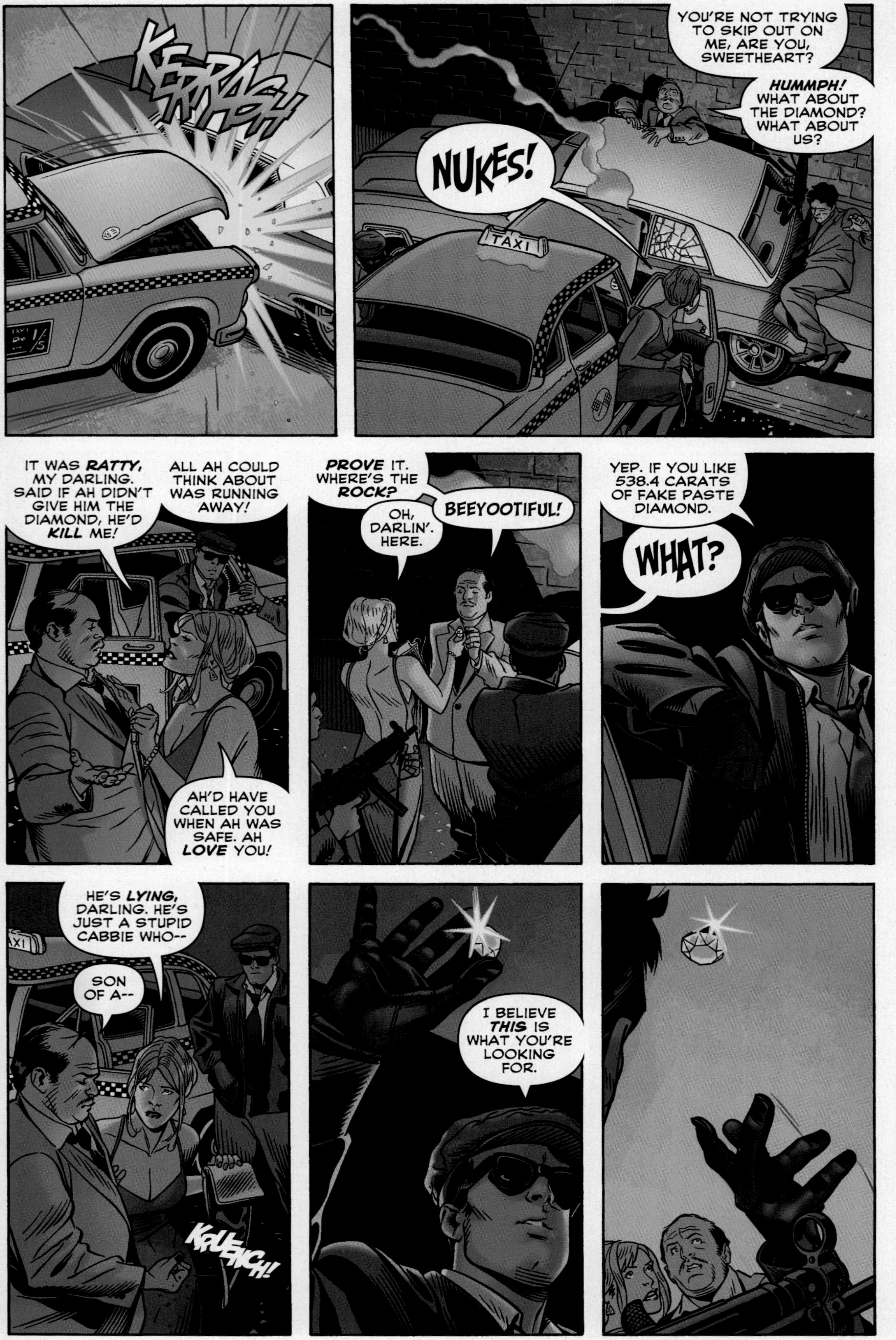
KERRASH
YOU'RE NOT TRYING TO SKIP OUT ON ME, ARE YOU, SWEETHEART?
HUMMPH! WHAT ABOUT THE DIAMOND? WHAT ABOUT US?
NUKES!
TAXI
IT WAS RATTY, MY DARLING. SAID IF AH DIDN'T GIVE HIM THE DIAMOND, HE'D KILL ME!
ALL AH COULD THINK ABOUT WAS RUNNING AWAY!
AH'D HAVE CALLED YOU WHEN AH WAS SAFE. AH LOVE YOU!
PROVE IT. WHERE'S THE ROCK?
OH, DARLIN'. HERE.
BEEYOOTIFUL!
YEP. IF YOU LIKE 538.4 CARATS OF FAKE PASTE DIAMOND.
WHAT?
HE'S LYING, DARLING. HE'S JUST A STUPID CABBIE WHO--
SON OF A--
KRUNCH!
I BELIEVE THIS IS WHAT YOU'RE LOOKING FOR.

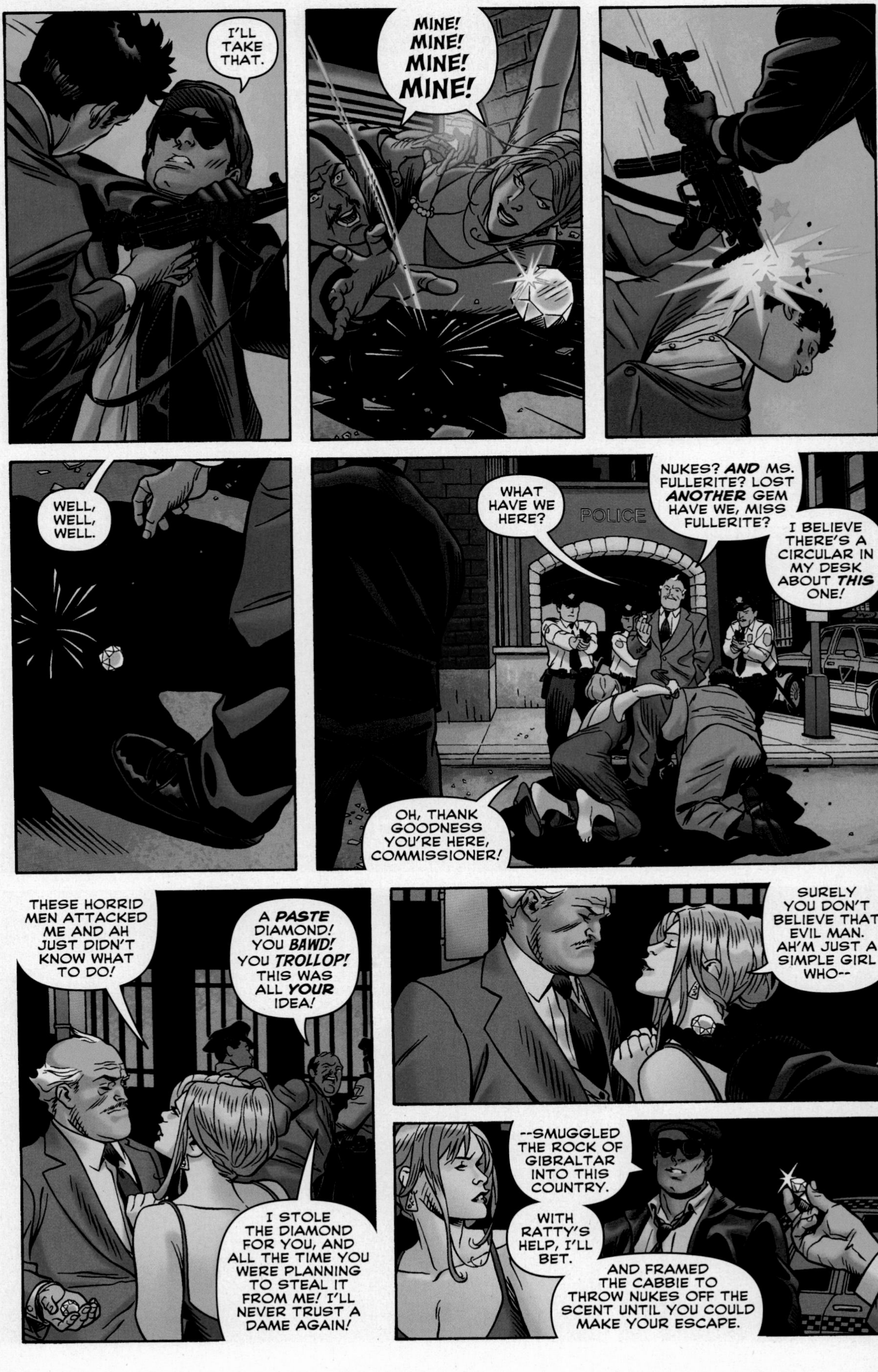
I'LL TAKE THAT.
MINE! MINE! MINE! MINE!
WELL, WELL, WELL.
WHAT HAVE WE HERE?
POLICE
NUKES? AND MS. FULLERITE? LOST ANOTHER GEM HAVE WE, MISS FULLERITE?
I BELIEVE THERE'S A CIRCULAR IN MY DESK ABOUT THIS ONE!
OH, THANK GOODNESS YOU'RE HERE, COMMISSIONER!
THESE HORRID MEN ATTACKED ME AND AH JUST DIDN'T KNOW WHAT TO DO!
A PASTE DIAMOND! YOU BAWD! YOU TROLLOP! THIS WAS ALL YOUR IDEA!
I STOLE THE DIAMOND FOR YOU, AND ALL THE TIME YOU WERE PLANNING TO STEAL IT FROM ME! I'LL NEVER TRUST A DAME AGAIN!
SURELY YOU DON'T BELIEVE THAT EVIL MAN. AH'M JUST A SIMPLE GIRL WHO--
--SMUGGLED THE ROCK OF GIBRALTAR INTO THIS COUNTRY.
WITH RATTY'S HELP, I'LL BET.
AND FRAMED THE CABBIE TO THROW NUKES OFF THE SCENT UNTIL YOU COULD MAKE YOUR ESCAPE.

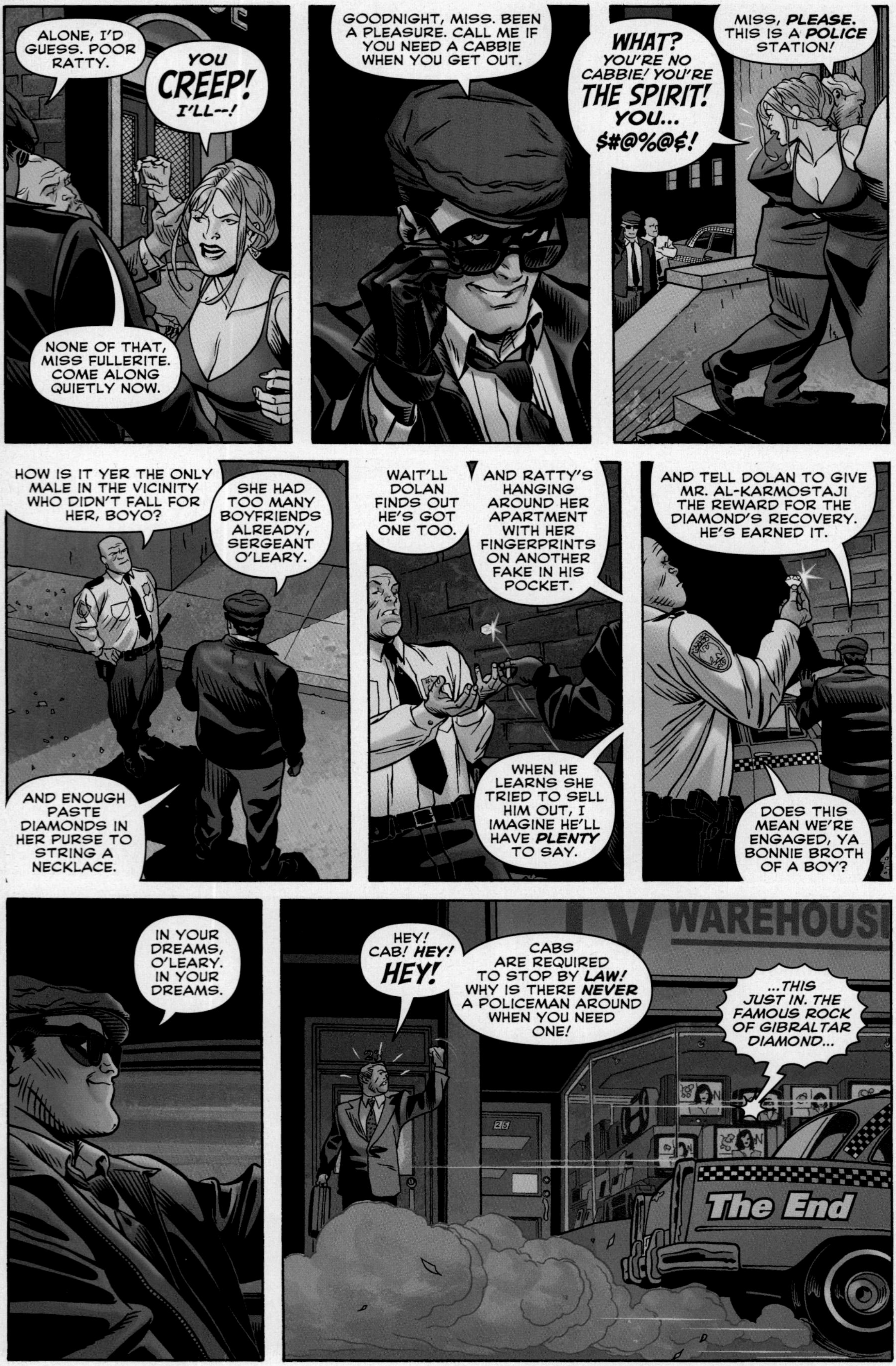
ALONE, I'D GUESS. POOR RATTY.
YOU CREEP! I'LL--!
NONE OF THAT, MISS FULLERITE. COME ALONG QUIETLY NOW.
GOODNIGHT, MISS. BEEN A PLEASURE. CALL ME IF YOU NEED A CABBIE WHEN YOU GET OUT.
WHAT? YOU'RE NO CABBIE! YOU'RE THE SPIRIT! YOU... $#@%@¢!
MISS, PLEASE. THIS IS A POLICE STATION!
HOW IS IT YER THE ONLY MALE IN THE VICINITY WHO DIDN'T FALL FOR HER, BOYO?
SHE HAD TOO MANY BOYFRIENDS ALREADY, SERGEANT O'LEARY.
AND ENOUGH PASTE DIAMONDS IN HER PURSE TO STRING A NECKLACE.
WAIT'LL DOLAN FINDS OUT HE'S GOT ONE TOO.
AND RATTY'S HANGING AROUND HER APARTMENT WITH HER FINGERPRINTS ON ANOTHER FAKE IN HIS POCKET.
WHEN HE LEARNS SHE TRIED TO SELL HIM OUT, I IMAGINE HE'LL HAVE PLENTY TO SAY.
AND TELL DOLAN TO GIVE MR. AL-KARMOSTAJI THE REWARD FOR THE DIAMOND'S RECOVERY. HE'S EARNED IT.
DOES THIS MEAN WE'RE ENGAGED, YA BONNIE BROTH OF A BOY?
IN YOUR DREAMS, O'LEARY. IN YOUR DREAMS.
WAREHOUS
HEY! CAB! HEY! HEY!
CABS ARE REQUIRED TO STOP BY LAW! WHY IS THERE NEVER A POLICEMAN AROUND WHEN YOU NEED ONE!
...THIS JUST IN. THE FAMOUS ROCK OF GIBRALTAR DIAMOND...
25
The End

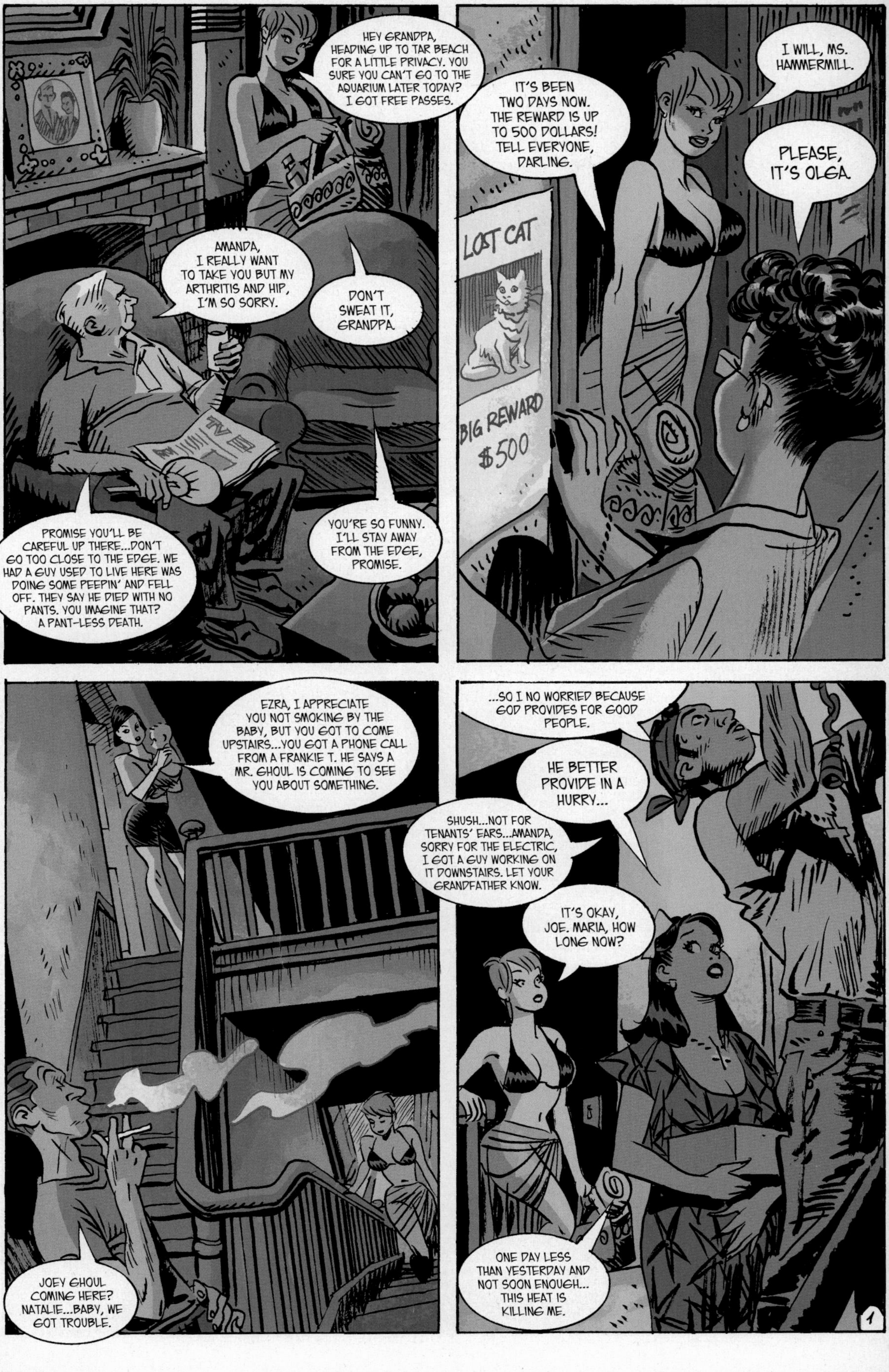
HEY GRANDPA, HEADING UP TO TAR BEACH FOR A LITTLE PRIVACY. YOU SURE YOU CAN'T GO TO THE AQUARIUM LATER TODAY? I GOT FREE PASSES.
AMANDA, I REALLY WANT TO TAKE YOU BUT MY ARTHRITIS AND HIP, I'M SO SORRY.
DON'T SWEAT IT, GRANDPA.
PROMISE YOU'LL BE CAREFUL UP THERE...DON'T GO TOO CLOSE TO THE EDGE. WE HAD A GUY USED TO LIVE HERE WAS DOING SOME PEEPIN' AND FELL OFF. THEY SAY HE DIED WITH NO PANTS. YOU IMAGINE THAT? A PANT-LESS DEATH.
YOU'RE SO FUNNY. I'LL STAY AWAY FROM THE EDGE, PROMISE.
IT'S BEEN TWO DAYS NOW. THE REWARD IS UP TO 500 DOLLARS! TELL EVERYONE, DARLING.
I WILL, MS. HAMMERMILL.
PLEASE, IT'S OLGA.
LOST CAT
BIG REWARD $500
EZRA, I APPRECIATE YOU NOT SMOKING BY THE BABY, BUT YOU GOT TO COME UPSTAIRS...YOU GOT A PHONE CALL FROM A FRANKIE T. HE SAYS A MR. GHOUL IS COMING TO SEE YOU ABOUT SOMETHING.
JOEY GHOUL COMING HERE? NATALIE...BABY, WE GOT TROUBLE.
...SO I NO WORRIED BECAUSE GOD PROVIDES FOR GOOD PEOPLE.
HE BETTER PROVIDE IN A HURRY...
SHUSH...NOT FOR TENANTS' EARS...AMANDA, SORRY FOR THE ELECTRIC, I GOT A GUY WORKING ON IT DOWNSTAIRS. LET YOUR GRANDFATHER KNOW.
IT'S OKAY, JOE. MARIA, HOW LONG NOW?
ONE DAY LESS THAN YESTERDAY AND NOT SOON ENOUGH... THIS HEAT IS KILLING ME.

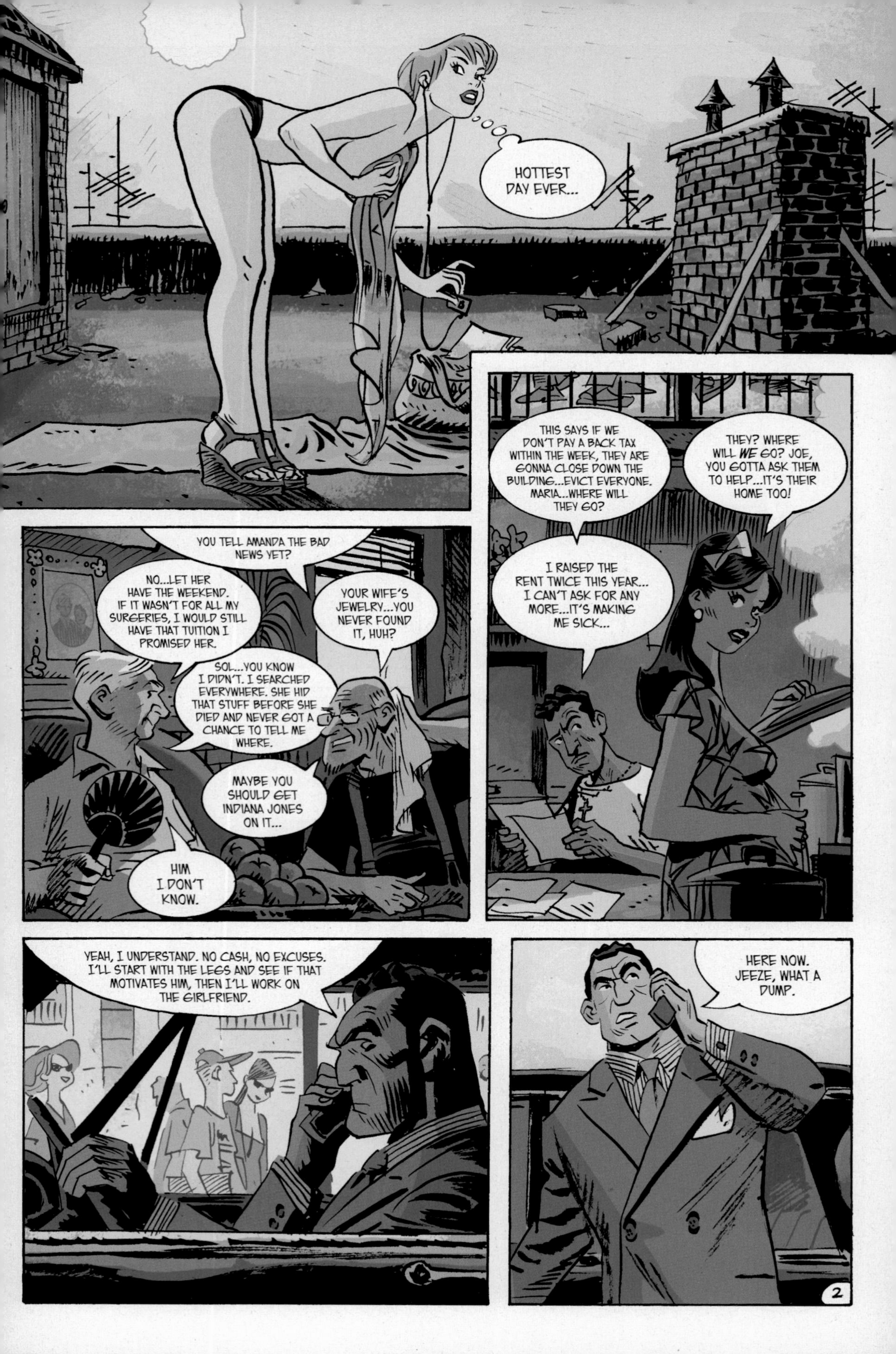
HOTTEST DAY EVER...
YOU TELL AMANDA THE BAD NEWS YET?
NO...LET HER HAVE THE WEEKEND. IF IT WASN'T FOR ALL MY SURGERIES, I WOULD STILL HAVE THAT TUITION I PROMISED HER.
YOUR WIFE'S JEWELRY...YOU NEVER FOUND IT, HUH?
SOL...YOU KNOW I DIDN'T. I SEARCHED EVERYWHERE. SHE HID THAT STUFF BEFORE SHE DIED AND NEVER GOT A CHANCE TO TELL ME WHERE.
MAYBE YOU SHOULD GET INDIANA JONES ON IT...
HIM I DON'T KNOW.
THIS SAYS IF WE DON'T PAY A BACK TAX WITHIN THE WEEK, THEY ARE GONNA CLOSE DOWN THE BUILDING...EVICT EVERYONE. MARIA...WHERE WILL THEY GO?
THEY? WHERE WILL *WE* GO? JOE, YOU GOTTA ASK THEM TO HELP...IT'S THEIR HOME TOO!
I RAISED THE RENT TWICE THIS YEAR... I CAN'T ASK FOR ANY MORE...IT'S MAKING ME SICK...
YEAH, I UNDERSTAND. NO CASH, NO EXCUSES. I'LL START WITH THE LEGS AND SEE IF THAT MOTIVATES HIM, THEN I'LL WORK ON THE GIRLFRIEND.
HERE NOW. JEEZE, WHAT A DUMP.
2

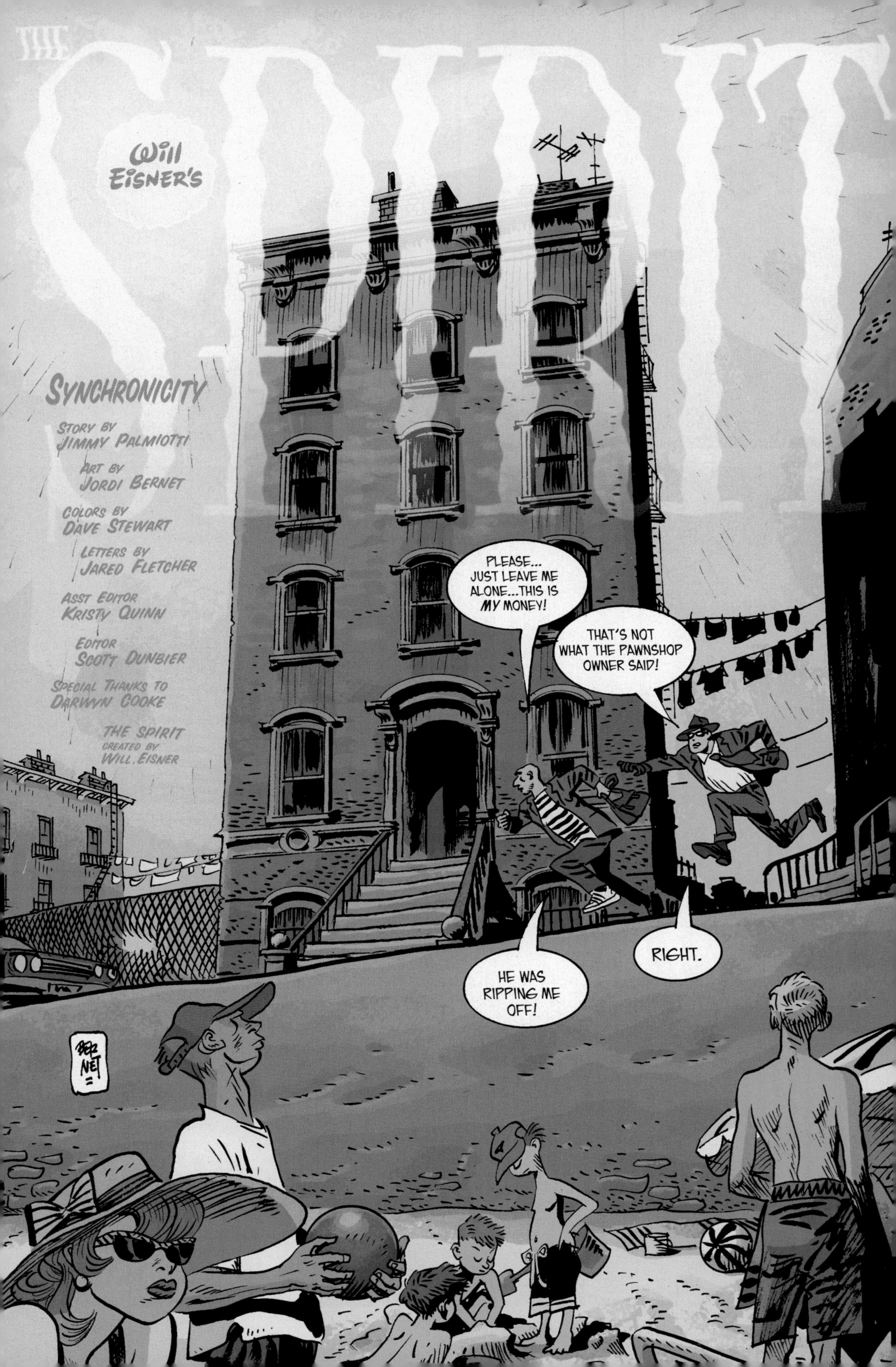
THE SPIRIT
Will Eisner's
SYNCHRONICITY
STORY BY JIMMY PALMIOTTI
ART BY JORDI BERNET
COLORS BY DAVE STEWART
LETTERS BY JARED FLETCHER
ASST EDITOR KRISTY QUINN
EDITOR SCOTT DUNBIER
SPECIAL THANKS TO DARWYN COOKE
THE SPIRIT CREATED BY WILL EISNER
PLEASE... JUST LEAVE ME ALONE...THIS IS MY MONEY!
THAT'S NOT WHAT THE PAWNSHOP OWNER SAID!
HE WAS RIPPING ME OFF!
RIGHT.
BERNET

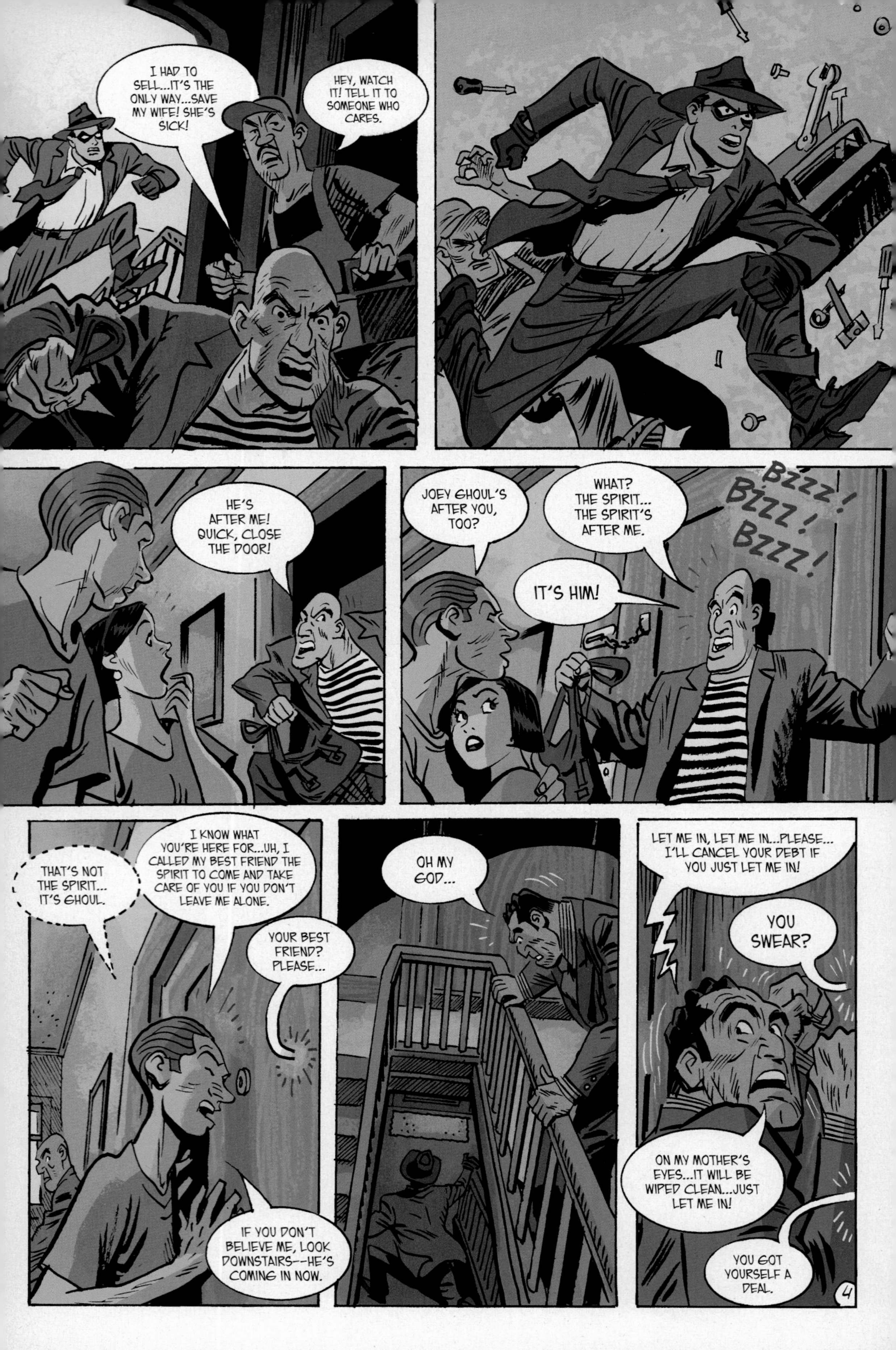
I HAD TO SELL...IT'S THE ONLY WAY...SAVE MY WIFE! SHE'S SICK!
HEY, WATCH IT! TELL IT TO SOMEONE WHO CARES.
HE'S AFTER ME! QUICK, CLOSE THE DOOR!
JOEY GHOUL'S AFTER YOU, TOO?
WHAT? THE SPIRIT... THE SPIRIT'S AFTER ME.
BZZZ! BZZZ! BZZZ!
IT'S HIM!
THAT'S NOT THE SPIRIT... IT'S GHOUL.
I KNOW WHAT YOU'RE HERE FOR...UH, I CALLED MY BEST FRIEND THE SPIRIT TO COME AND TAKE CARE OF YOU IF YOU DON'T LEAVE ME ALONE.
YOUR BEST FRIEND? PLEASE...
IF YOU DON'T BELIEVE ME, LOOK DOWNSTAIRS--HE'S COMING IN NOW.
OH MY GOD...
LET ME IN, LET ME IN...PLEASE... I'LL CANCEL YOUR DEBT IF YOU JUST LET ME IN!
YOU SWEAR?
ON MY MOTHER'S EYES...IT WILL BE WIPED CLEAN...JUST LET ME IN!
YOU GOT YOURSELF A DEAL.
4

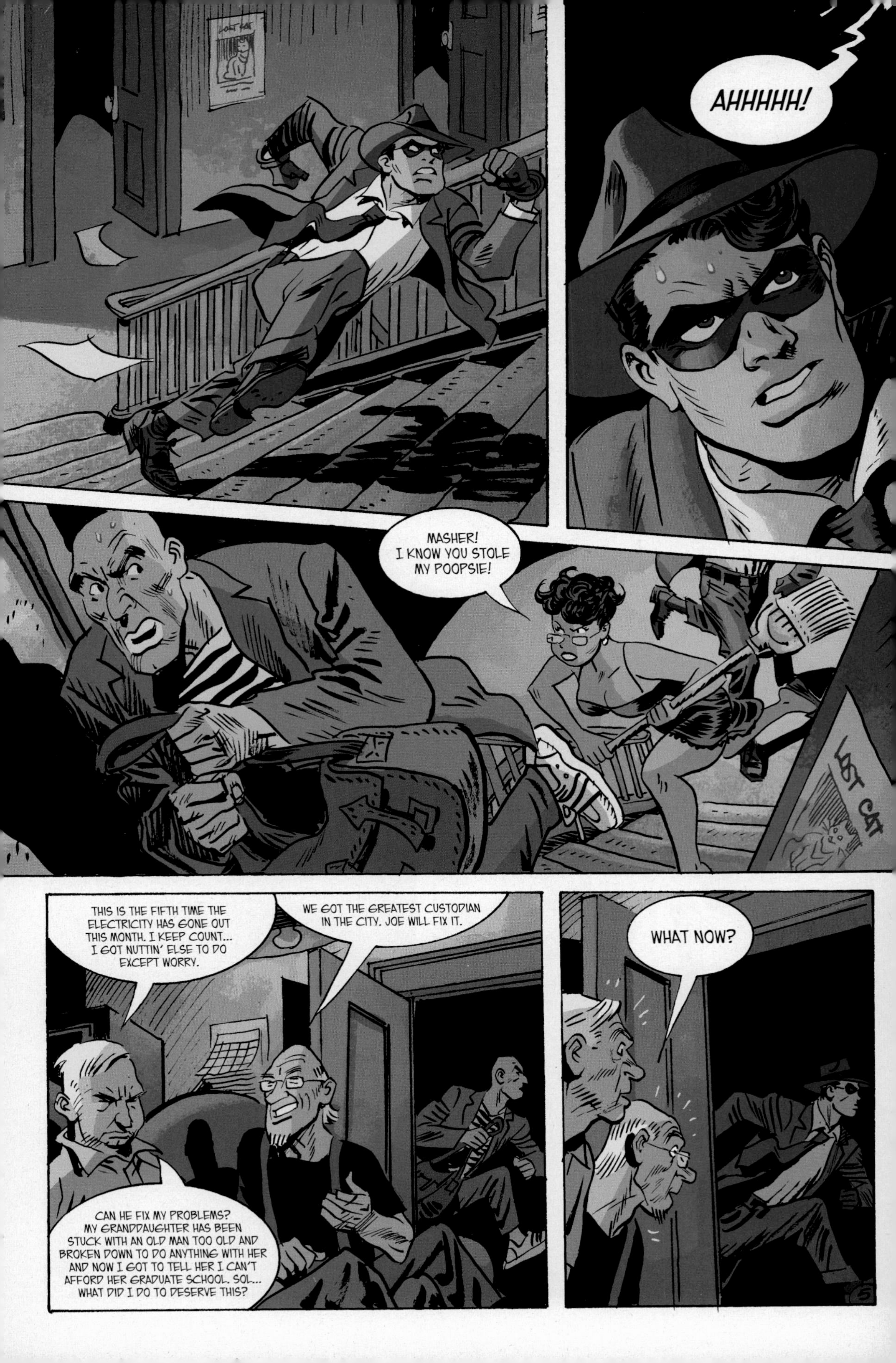

LOST CAT
AHHHHH!
MASHER! I KNOW YOU STOLE MY POOPSIE!
LOST CAT
THIS IS THE FIFTH TIME THE ELECTRICITY HAS GONE OUT THIS MONTH. I KEEP COUNT... I GOT NUTTIN' ELSE TO DO EXCEPT WORRY.
WE GOT THE GREATEST CUSTODIAN IN THE CITY. JOE WILL FIX IT.
CAN HE FIX MY PROBLEMS? MY GRANDDAUGHTER HAS BEEN STUCK WITH AN OLD MAN TOO OLD AND BROKEN DOWN TO DO ANYTHING WITH HER AND NOW I GOT TO TELL HER I CAN'T AFFORD HER GRADUATE SCHOOL. SOL... WHAT DID I DO TO DESERVE THIS?
WHAT NOW?

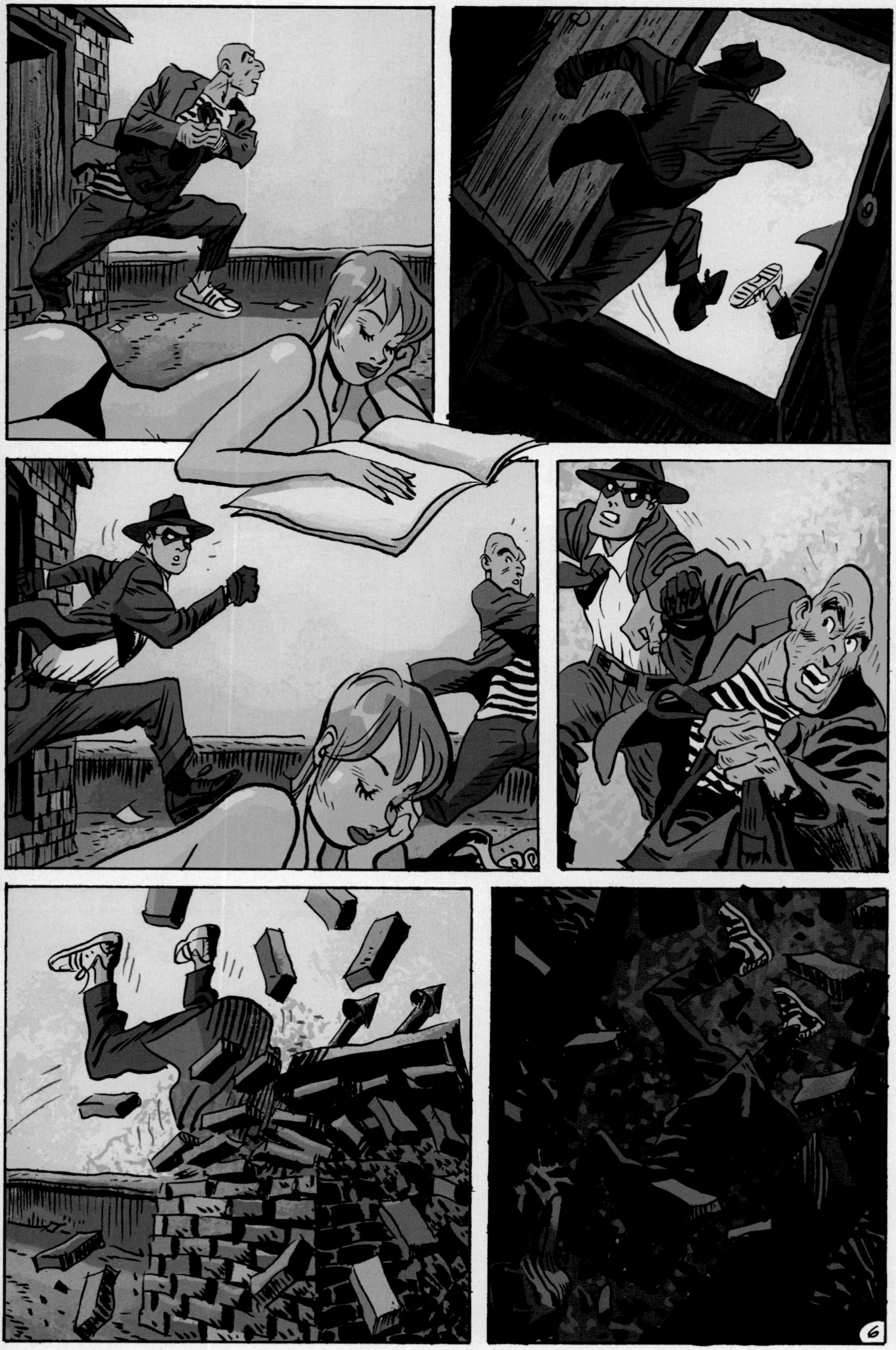

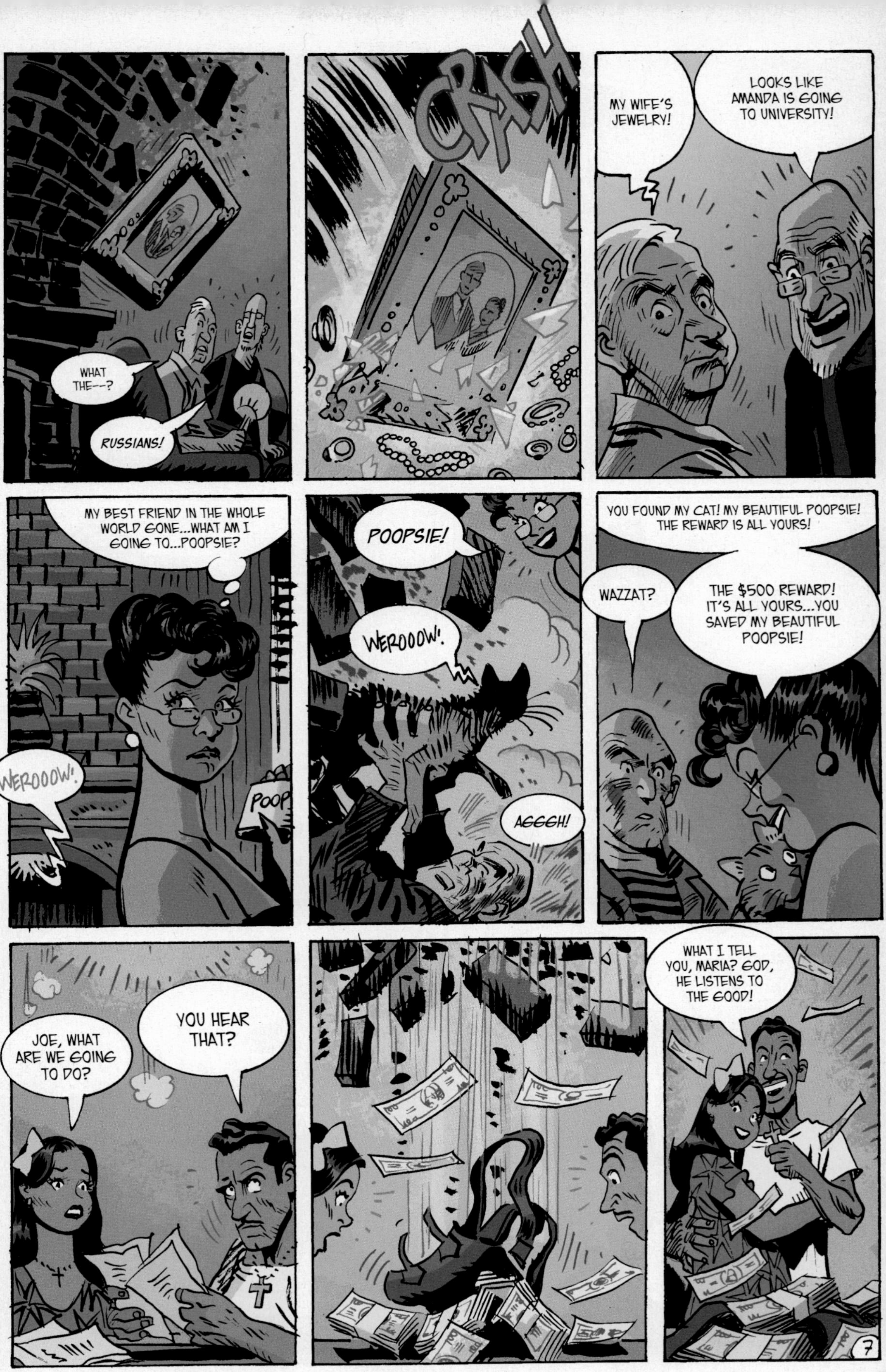

WHAT THE--?
RUSSIANS!
CRASH
MY WIFE'S JEWELRY!
LOOKS LIKE AMANDA IS GOING TO UNIVERSITY!
MY BEST FRIEND IN THE WHOLE WORLD GONE...WHAT AM I GOING TO...POOPSIE?
WEROOOW!
POOP
POOPSIE!
WEROOOW!
AGGGH!
YOU FOUND MY CAT! MY BEAUTIFUL POOPSIE! THE REWARD IS ALL YOURS!
WAZZAT?
THE $500 REWARD! IT'S ALL YOURS...YOU SAVED MY BEAUTIFUL POOPSIE!
JOE, WHAT ARE WE GOING TO DO?
YOU HEAR THAT?
WHAT I TELL YOU, MARIA? GOD, HE LISTENS TO THE GOOD!

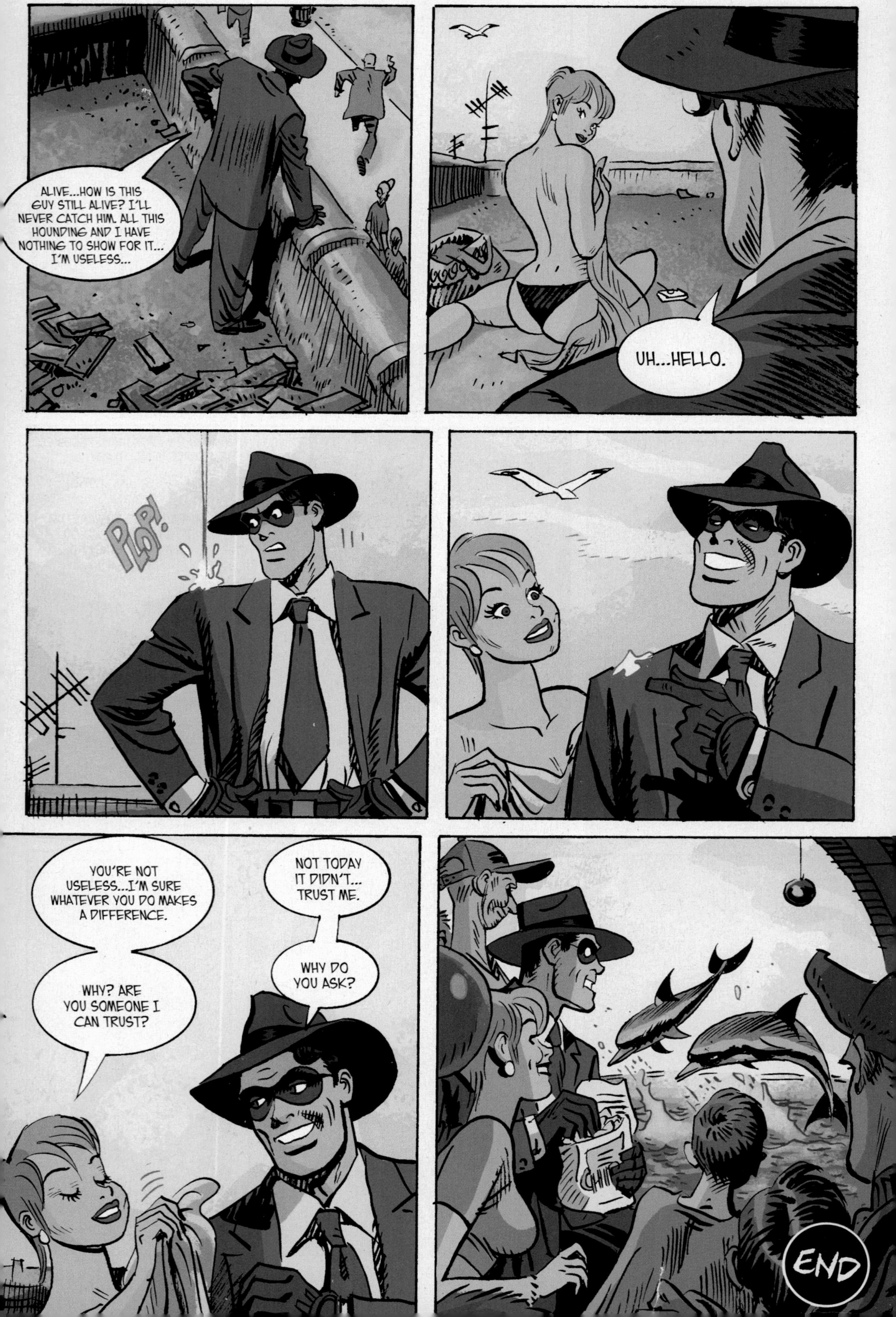
ALIVE...HOW IS THIS GUY STILL ALIVE? I'LL NEVER CATCH HIM. ALL THIS HOUNDING AND I HAVE NOTHING TO SHOW FOR IT... I'M USELESS...
UH...HELLO.
PLOP!
YOU'RE NOT USELESS...I'M SURE WHATEVER YOU DO MAKES A DIFFERENCE.
NOT TODAY IT DIDN'T... TRUST ME.
WHY? ARE YOU SOMEONE I CAN TRUST?
WHY DO YOU ASK?
END

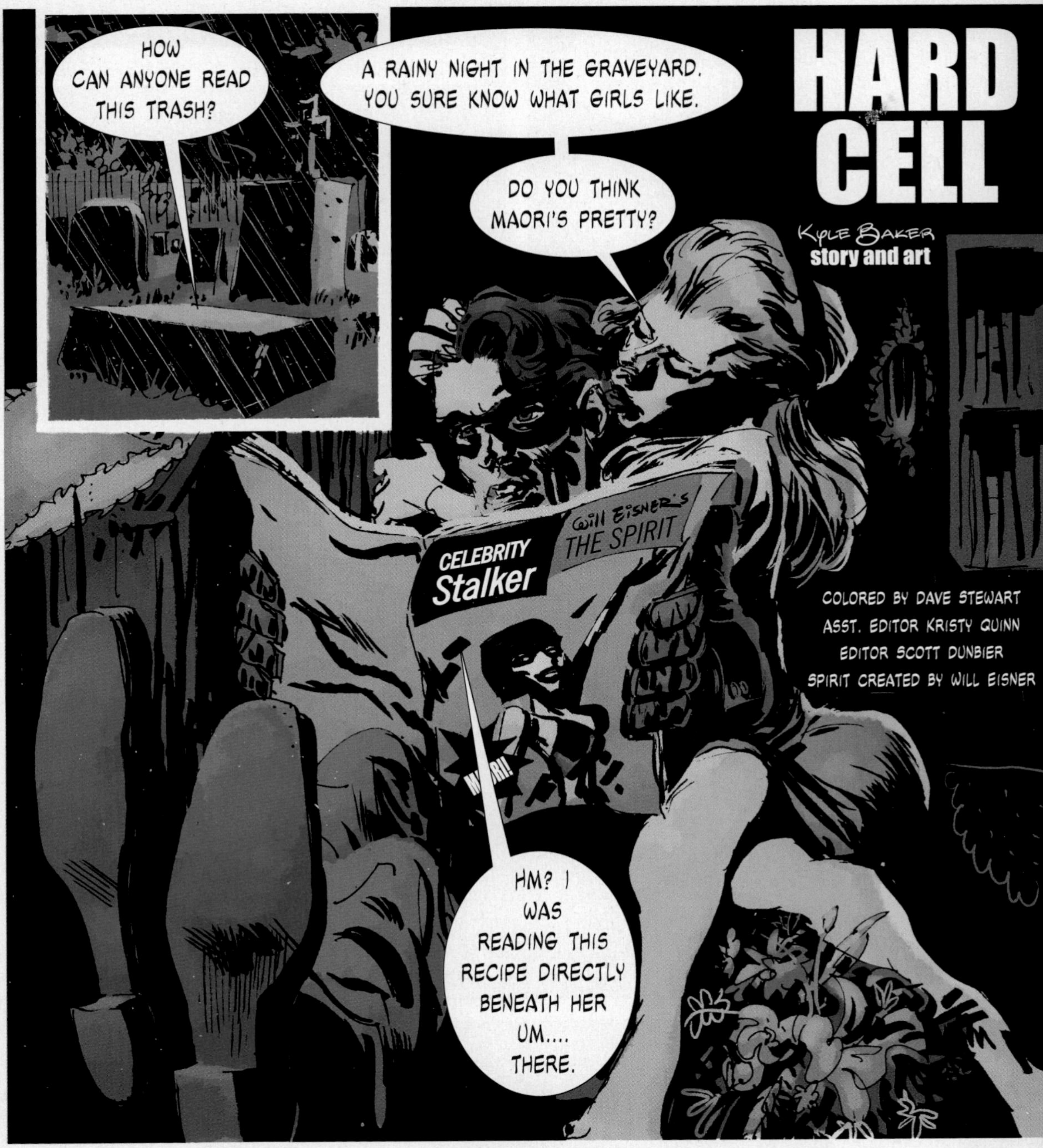
HARD CELL
KYLE BAKER
story and art
HOW CAN ANYONE READ THIS TRASH?
A RAINY NIGHT IN THE GRAVEYARD. YOU SURE KNOW WHAT GIRLS LIKE.
DO YOU THINK MAORI'S PRETTY?
WILL EISNER'S THE SPIRIT
CELEBRITY Stalker
MAORI!
COLORED BY DAVE STEWART
ASST. EDITOR KRISTY QUINN
EDITOR SCOTT DUNBIER
SPIRIT CREATED BY WILL EISNER
HM? I WAS READING THIS RECIPE DIRECTLY BENEATH HER UM.... THERE.

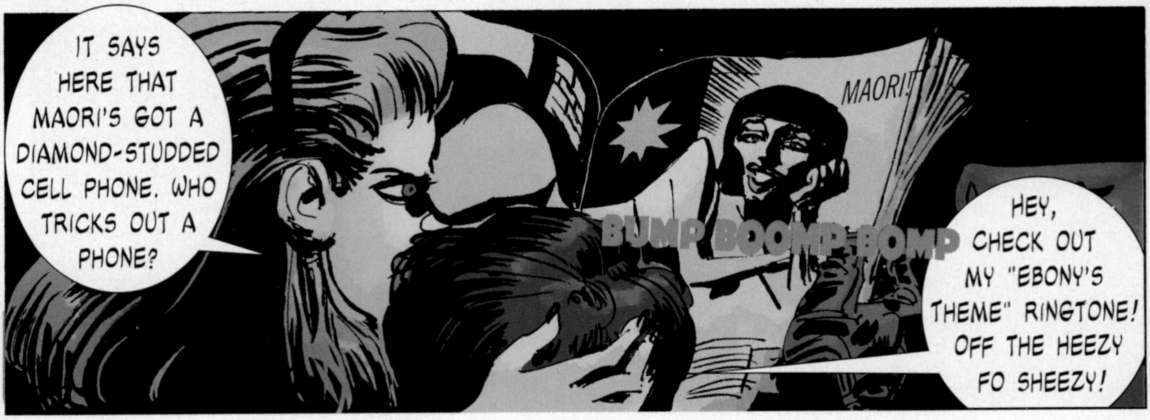
IT SAYS HERE THAT MAORI'S GOT A DIAMOND-STUDDED CELL PHONE. WHO TRICKS OUT A PHONE?
MAORI!
BUMP BOOMP BOMP
HEY, CHECK OUT MY "EBONY'S THEME" RINGTONE! OFF THE HEEZY FO SHEEZY!

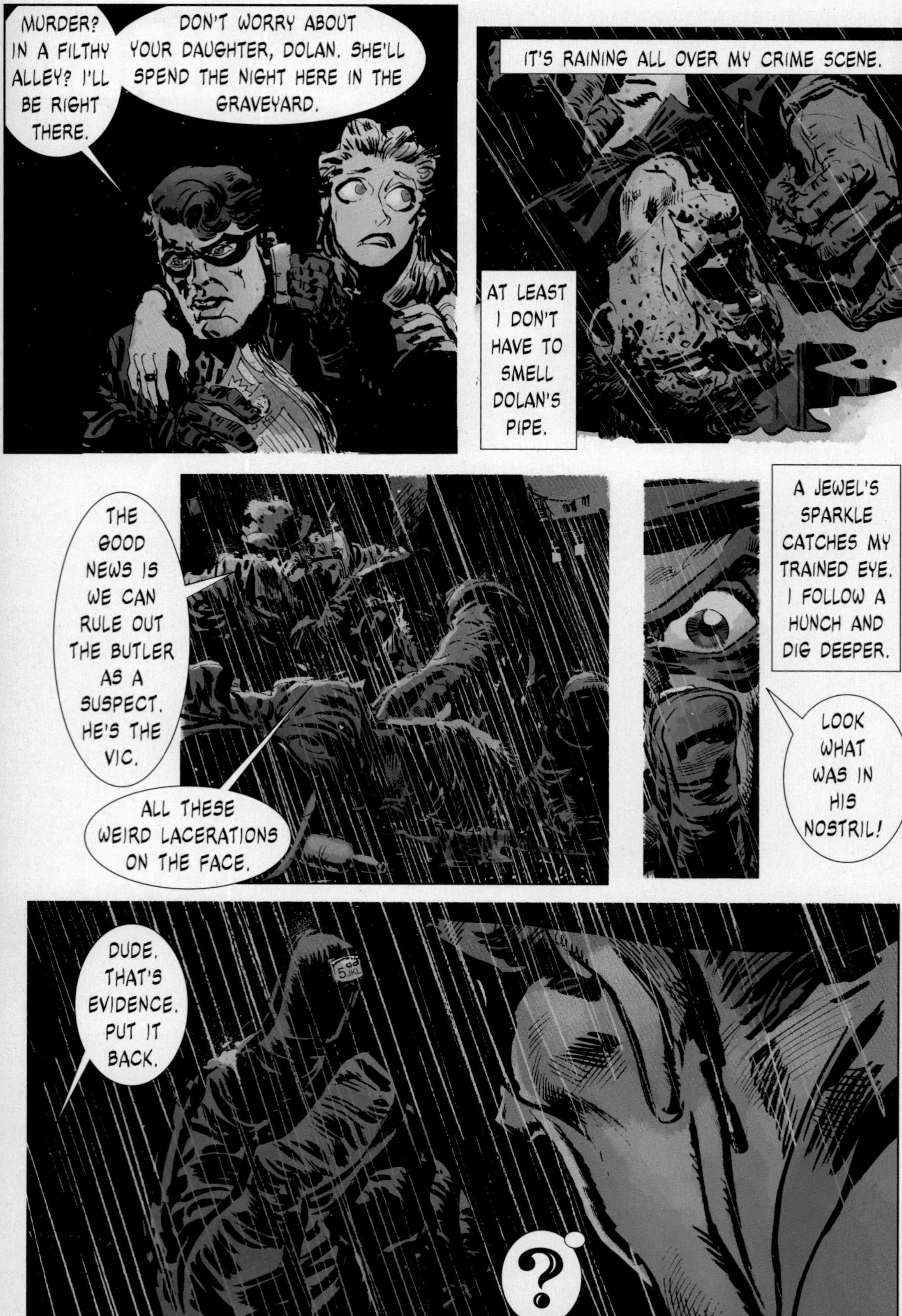
MURDER? IN A FILTHY ALLEY? I'LL BE RIGHT THERE.
DON'T WORRY ABOUT YOUR DAUGHTER, DOLAN. SHE'LL SPEND THE NIGHT HERE IN THE GRAVEYARD.
IT'S RAINING ALL OVER MY CRIME SCENE.
AT LEAST I DON'T HAVE TO SMELL DOLAN'S PIPE.
THE GOOD NEWS IS WE CAN RULE OUT THE BUTLER AS A SUSPECT. HE'S THE VIC.
ALL THESE WEIRD LACERATIONS ON THE FACE.
A JEWEL'S SPARKLE CATCHES MY TRAINED EYE. I FOLLOW A HUNCH AND DIG DEEPER.
LOOK WHAT WAS IN HIS NOSTRIL!
DUDE. THAT'S EVIDENCE. PUT IT BACK.
?

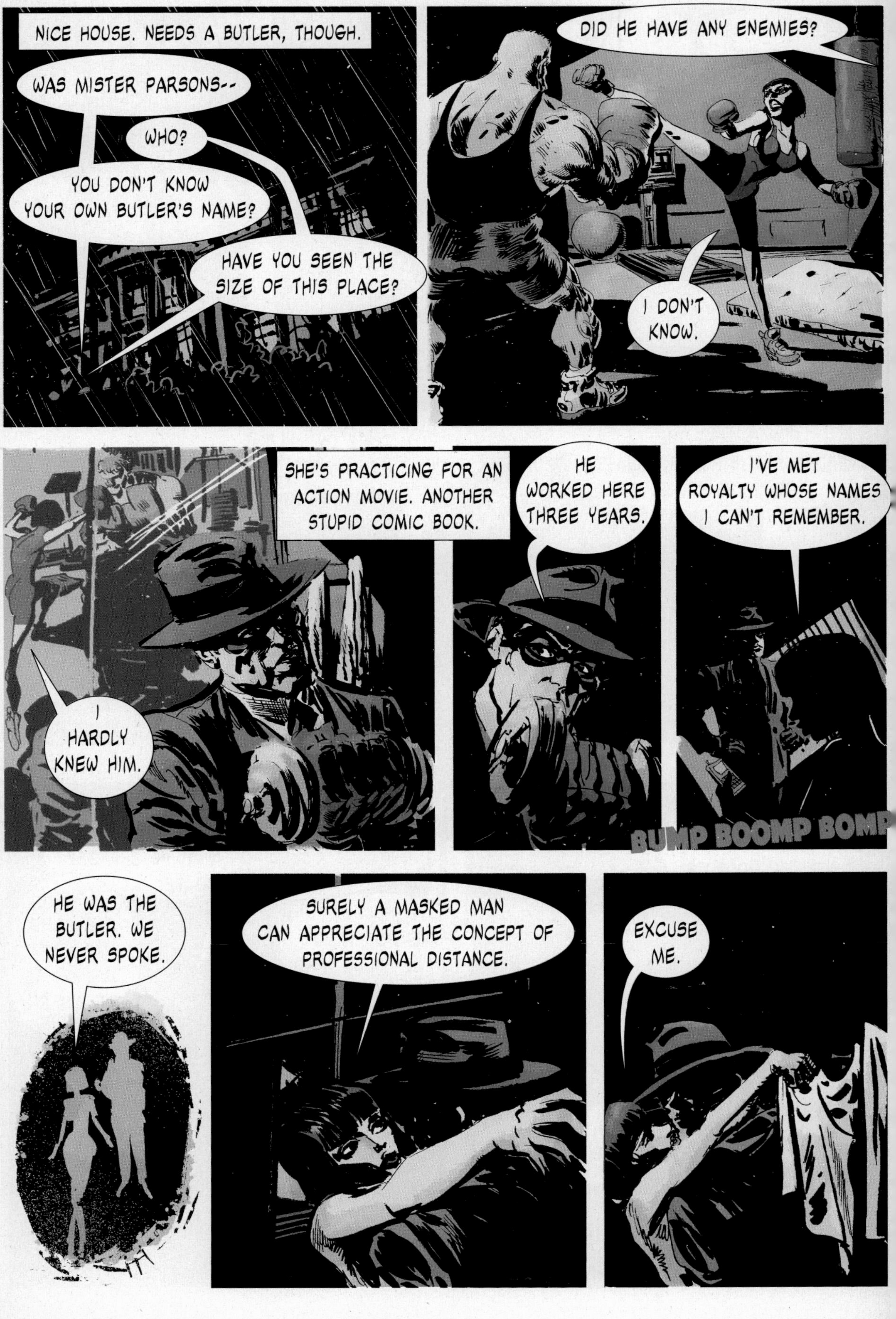

NICE HOUSE. NEEDS A BUTLER, THOUGH.
WAS MISTER PARSONS--
WHO?
YOU DON'T KNOW YOUR OWN BUTLER'S NAME?
HAVE YOU SEEN THE SIZE OF THIS PLACE?
DID HE HAVE ANY ENEMIES?
I DON'T KNOW.
SHE'S PRACTICING FOR AN ACTION MOVIE. ANOTHER STUPID COMIC BOOK.
I HARDLY KNEW HIM.
HE WORKED HERE THREE YEARS.
I'VE MET ROYALTY WHOSE NAMES I CAN'T REMEMBER.
BUMP BOOMP BOMP
HE WAS THE BUTLER. WE NEVER SPOKE.
SURELY A MASKED MAN CAN APPRECIATE THE CONCEPT OF PROFESSIONAL DISTANCE.
EXCUSE ME.

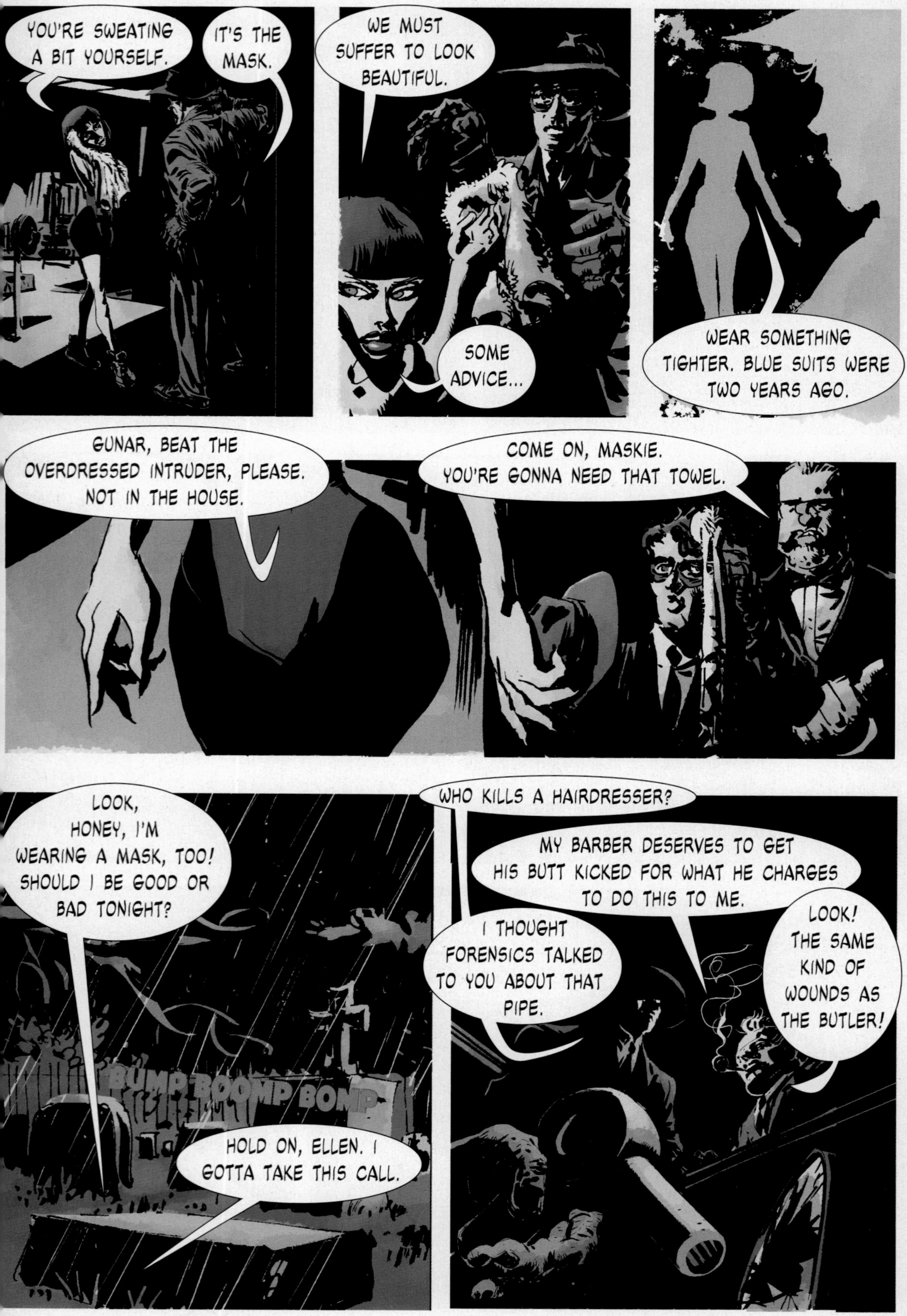
YOU'RE SWEATING A BIT YOURSELF.
IT'S THE MASK.
WE MUST SUFFER TO LOOK BEAUTIFUL.
SOME ADVICE...
WEAR SOMETHING TIGHTER. BLUE SUITS WERE TWO YEARS AGO.
GUNAR, BEAT THE OVERDRESSED INTRUDER, PLEASE. NOT IN THE HOUSE.
COME ON, MASKIE. YOU'RE GONNA NEED THAT TOWEL.
LOOK, HONEY, I'M WEARING A MASK, TOO! SHOULD I BE GOOD OR BAD TONIGHT?
BUMP BOOMP BOMP BOMP
HOLD ON, ELLEN. I GOTTA TAKE THIS CALL.
WHO KILLS A HAIRDRESSER?
MY BARBER DESERVES TO GET HIS BUTT KICKED FOR WHAT HE CHARGES TO DO THIS TO ME.
I THOUGHT FORENSICS TALKED TO YOU ABOUT THAT PIPE.
LOOK! THE SAME KIND OF WOUNDS AS THE BUTLER!

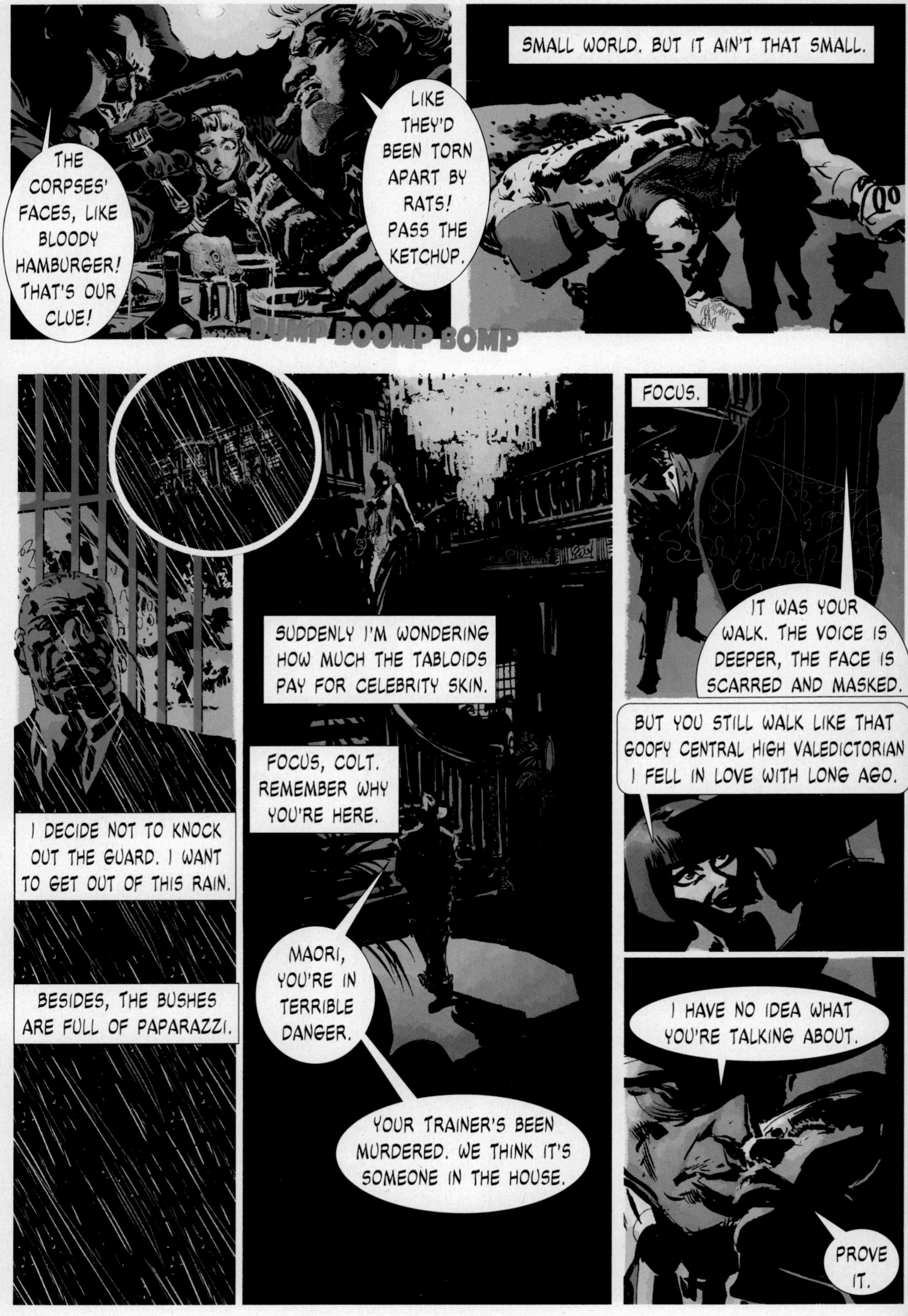
THE CORPSES' FACES, LIKE BLOODY HAMBURGER! THAT'S OUR CLUE!
LIKE THEY'D BEEN TORN APART BY RATS! PASS THE KETCHUP.
BUMP BOOMP BOMP
SMALL WORLD. BUT IT AIN'T THAT SMALL.
I DECIDE NOT TO KNOCK OUT THE GUARD. I WANT TO GET OUT OF THIS RAIN.
BESIDES, THE BUSHES ARE FULL OF PAPARAZZI.
SUDDENLY I'M WONDERING HOW MUCH THE TABLOIDS PAY FOR CELEBRITY SKIN.
FOCUS, COLT. REMEMBER WHY YOU'RE HERE.
MAORI, YOU'RE IN TERRIBLE DANGER.
YOUR TRAINER'S BEEN MURDERED. WE THINK IT'S SOMEONE IN THE HOUSE.
FOCUS.
IT WAS YOUR WALK. THE VOICE IS DEEPER, THE FACE IS SCARRED AND MASKED.
BUT YOU STILL WALK LIKE THAT GOOFY CENTRAL HIGH VALEDICTORIAN I FELL IN LOVE WITH LONG AGO.
I HAVE NO IDEA WHAT YOU'RE TALKING ABOUT.
PROVE IT.

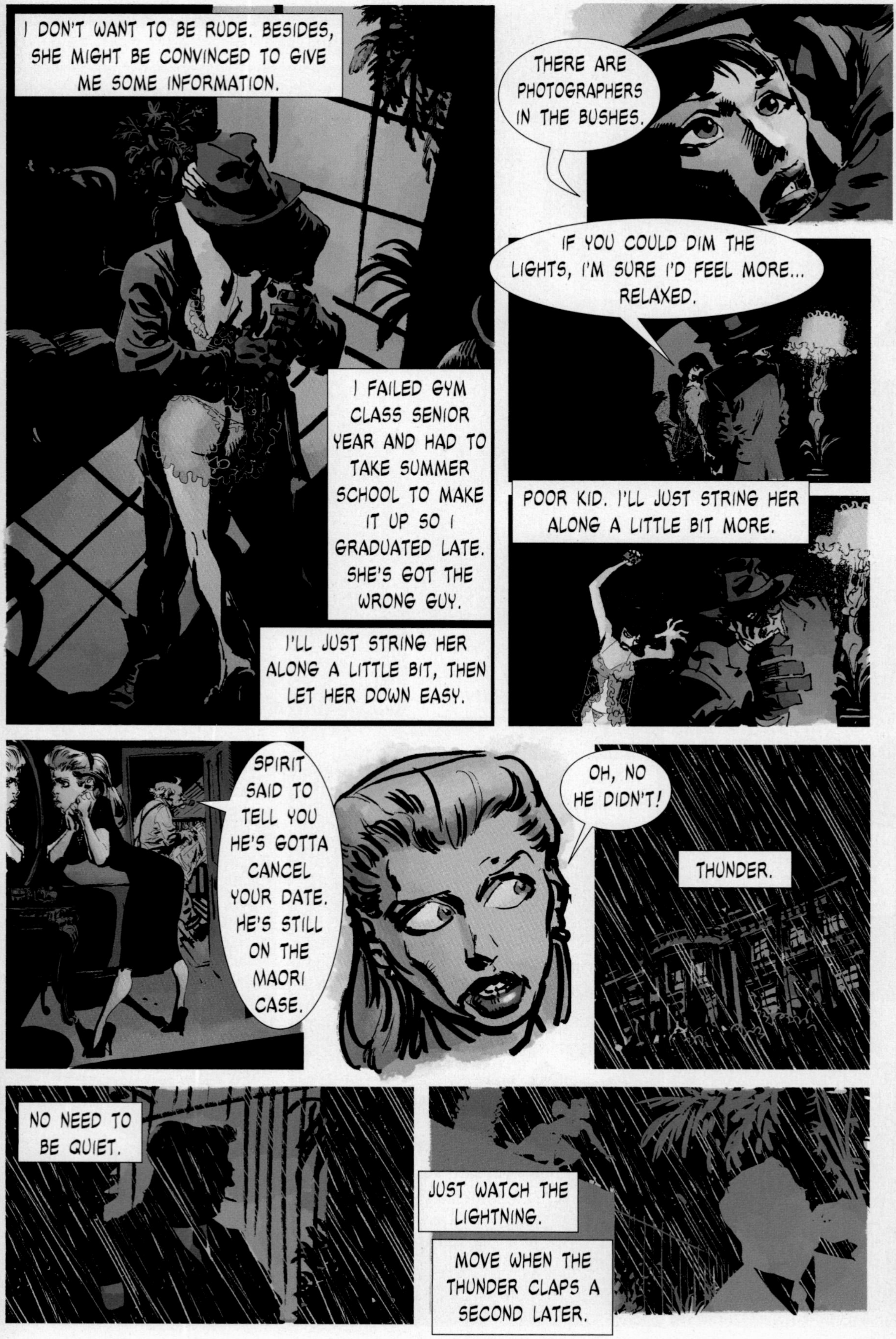
I DON'T WANT TO BE RUDE. BESIDES, SHE MIGHT BE CONVINCED TO GIVE ME SOME INFORMATION.
I FAILED GYM CLASS SENIOR YEAR AND HAD TO TAKE SUMMER SCHOOL TO MAKE IT UP SO I GRADUATED LATE. SHE'S GOT THE WRONG GUY.
I'LL JUST STRING HER ALONG A LITTLE BIT, THEN LET HER DOWN EASY.
THERE ARE PHOTOGRAPHERS IN THE BUSHES.
IF YOU COULD DIM THE LIGHTS, I'M SURE I'D FEEL MORE... RELAXED.
POOR KID. I'LL JUST STRING HER ALONG A LITTLE BIT MORE.
SPIRIT SAID TO TELL YOU HE'S GOTTA CANCEL YOUR DATE. HE'S STILL ON THE MAORI CASE.
OH, NO HE DIDN'T!
THUNDER.
NO NEED TO BE QUIET.
JUST WATCH THE LIGHTNING.
MOVE WHEN THE THUNDER CLAPS A SECOND LATER.

SHE DOESN'T BREAK HIS NECK.

HER PULSE RACING, HER SENSES HEIGHTENED, EVERYTHING SEEMS MORE VIVID. SHE HEARS EVERY RAINDROP.

THE CELL PHONE FEELS LIKE A WRECKING BALL.

SHE WAKES IN THE POOL.

THEIR GLISTENING LIMBS THRASH POWERFULLY. CHESTS HEAVING, THEIR SUPPLE, WET BOSOMS ACHE AND BURN FOR AIR'S CARESS.

STOP IT, OLD MAN. YOU'RE HALLUCINATING. FOCUS.

ELLEN'S NOT HERE.

YOU ALWAYS DO THIS!

SHE'S DRY. AND NAGGING. I MUST BE AWAKE.

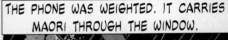

HOW COME EVERY TIME THERE'S A PRETTY GIRL IN THE CASE, ALL THE OTHER COPS GET TO GO HOME EARLY?

THE PHONE WAS WEIGHTED. IT CARRIES MAORI THROUGH THE WINDOW.

MY EYES WARN ELLEN.

SHE DUCKS JUST IN TIME.

YOU CAN TELL THOSE ARE REAL DIAMONDS BY THE WAY THEY CUT GLASS.

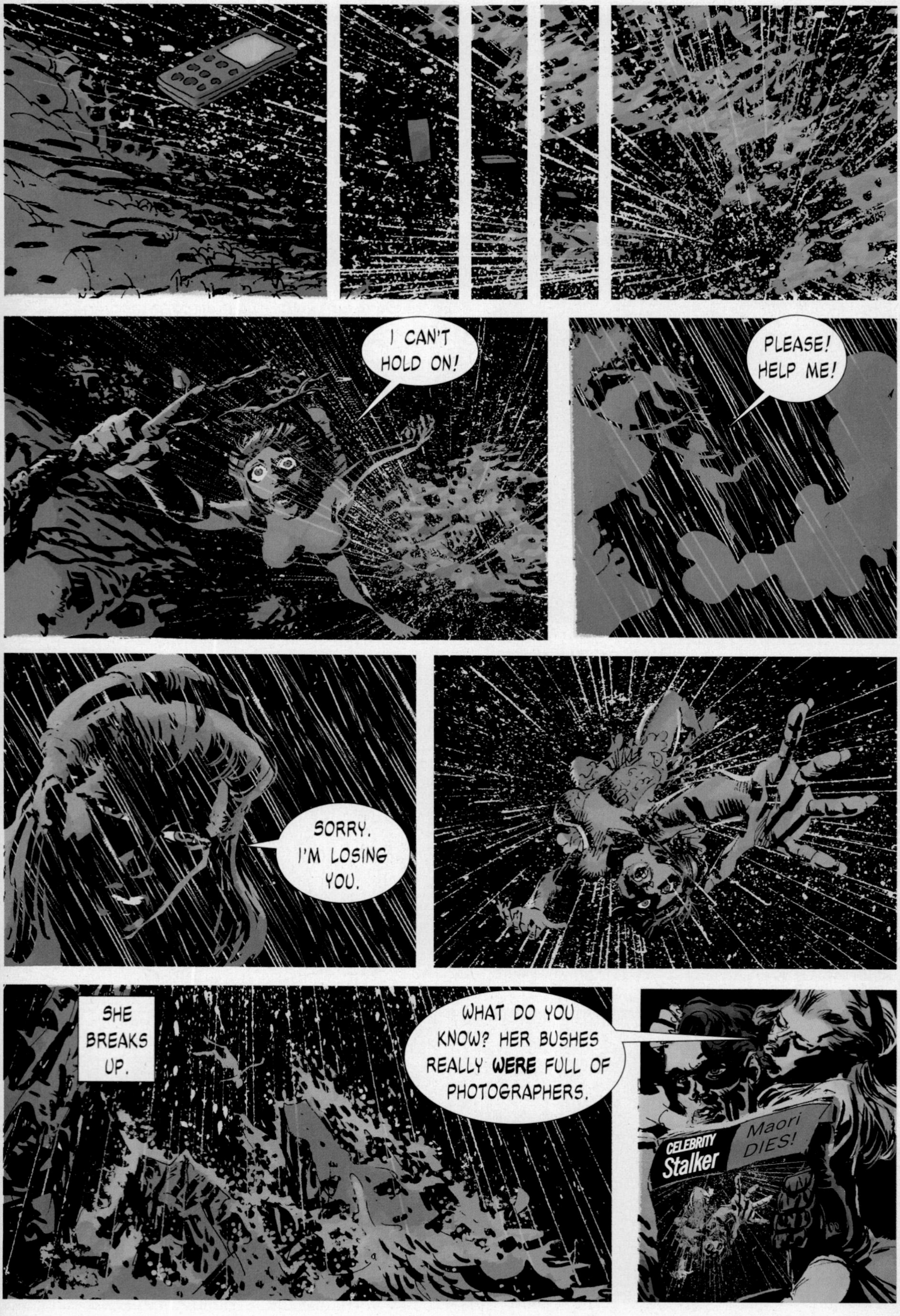
I CAN'T HOLD ON!
PLEASE! HELP ME!
SORRY. I'M LOSING YOU.
SHE BREAKS UP.
WHAT DO YOU KNOW? HER BUSHES REALLY **WERE** FULL OF PHOTOGRAPHERS.
CELEBRITY Stalker
Maori DIES!

2

ACTION • Mystery • ADVENTURE

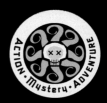

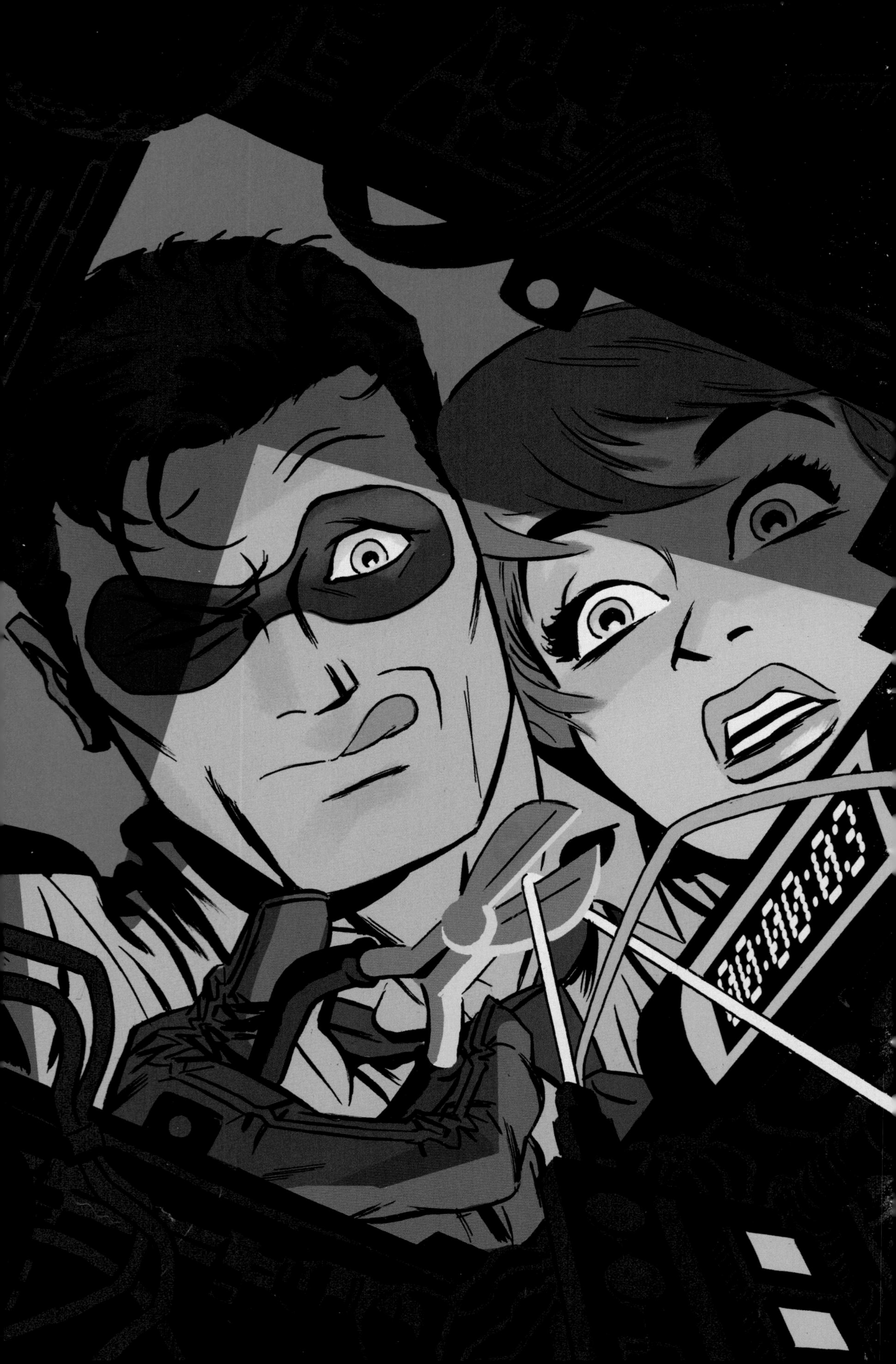
00:00:03

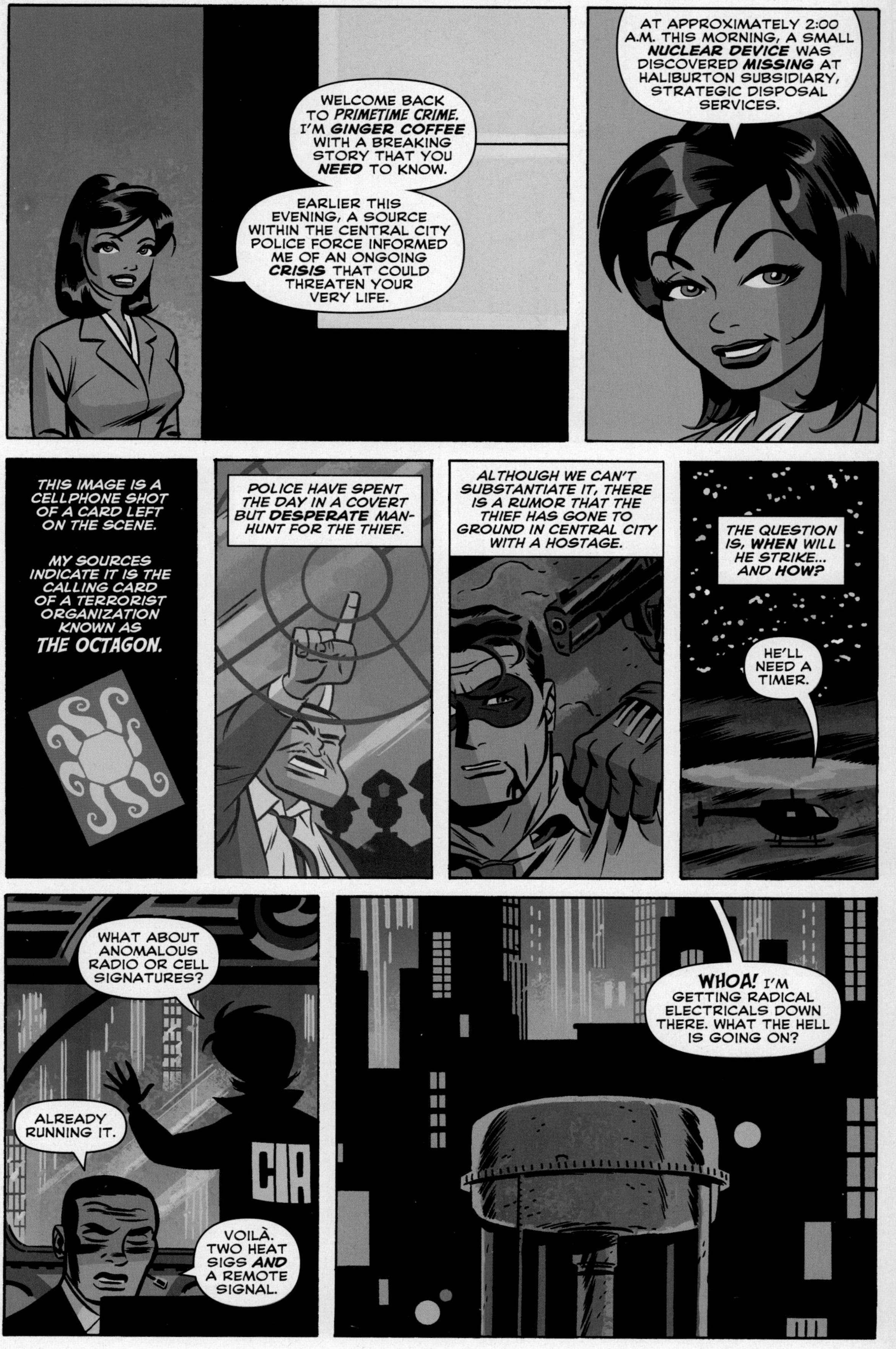
WELCOME BACK TO PRIMETIME CRIME. I'M GINGER COFFEE WITH A BREAKING STORY THAT YOU NEED TO KNOW.
EARLIER THIS EVENING, A SOURCE WITHIN THE CENTRAL CITY POLICE FORCE INFORMED ME OF AN ONGOING CRISIS THAT COULD THREATEN YOUR VERY LIFE.
AT APPROXIMATELY 2:00 A.M. THIS MORNING, A SMALL NUCLEAR DEVICE WAS DISCOVERED MISSING AT HALIBURTON SUBSIDIARY, STRATEGIC DISPOSAL SERVICES.
THIS IMAGE IS A CELLPHONE SHOT OF A CARD LEFT ON THE SCENE.
MY SOURCES INDICATE IT IS THE CALLING CARD OF A TERRORIST ORGANIZATION KNOWN AS THE OCTAGON.
POLICE HAVE SPENT THE DAY IN A COVERT BUT DESPERATE MAN-HUNT FOR THE THIEF.
ALTHOUGH WE CAN'T SUBSTANTIATE IT, THERE IS A RUMOR THAT THE THIEF HAS GONE TO GROUND IN CENTRAL CITY WITH A HOSTAGE.
THE QUESTION IS, WHEN WILL HE STRIKE... AND HOW?
HE'LL NEED A TIMER.
WHAT ABOUT ANOMALOUS RADIO OR CELL SIGNATURES?
ALREADY RUNNING IT.
CIA
VOILÀ. TWO HEAT SIGS AND A REMOTE SIGNAL.
WHOA! I'M GETTING RADICAL ELECTRICALS DOWN THERE. WHAT THE HELL IS GOING ON?

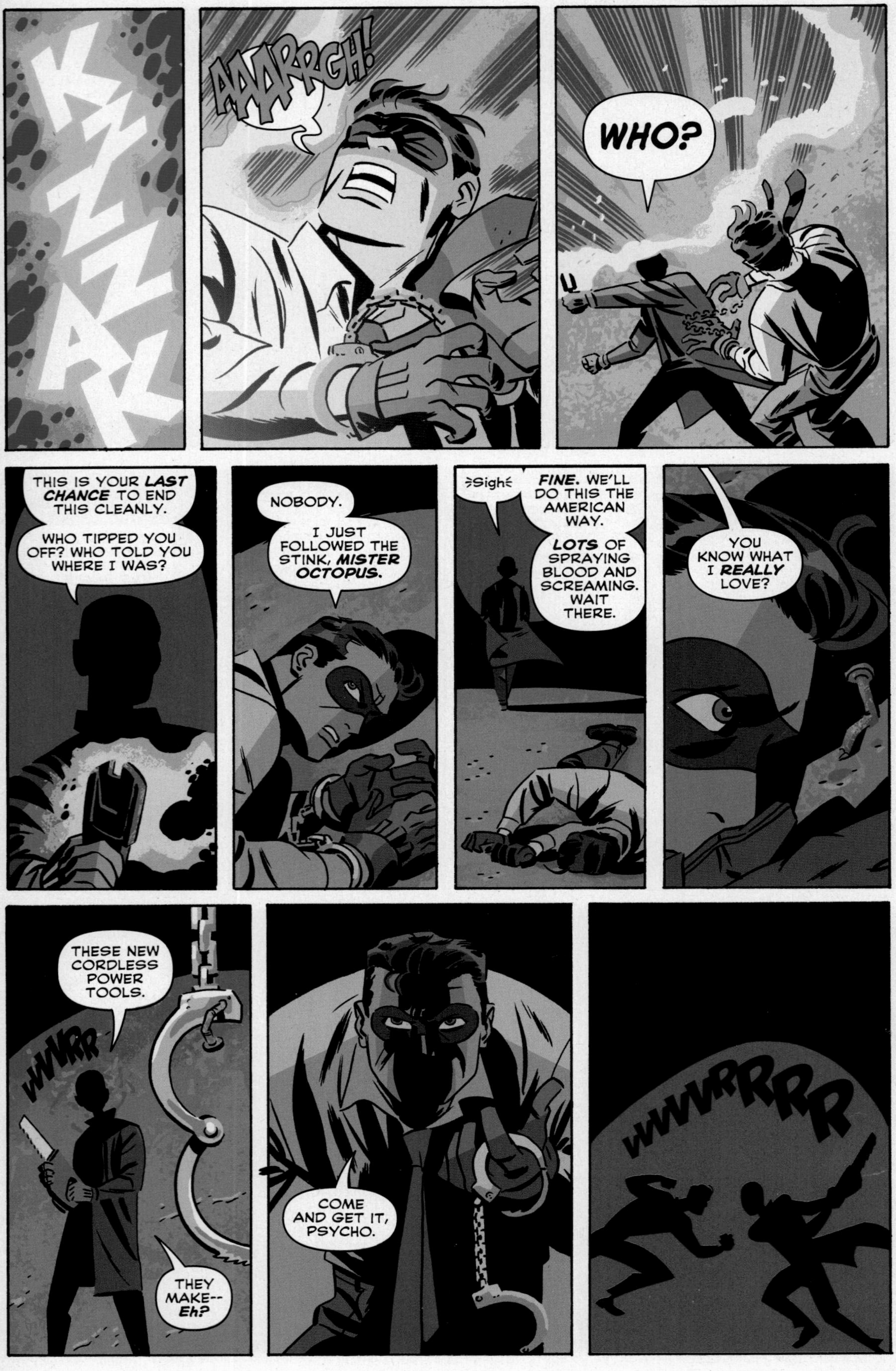

KZZAK
AAARRGH!
WHO?
THIS IS YOUR LAST CHANCE TO END THIS CLEANLY.
WHO TIPPED YOU OFF? WHO TOLD YOU WHERE I WAS?
NOBODY.
I JUST FOLLOWED THE STINK, MISTER OCTOPUS.
Sigh
FINE. WE'LL DO THIS THE AMERICAN WAY.
LOTS OF SPRAYING BLOOD AND SCREAMING. WAIT THERE.
YOU KNOW WHAT I REALLY LOVE?
THESE NEW CORDLESS POWER TOOLS.
WVRR
THEY MAKE-- Eh?
COME AND GET IT, PSYCHO.
WWVRRRR

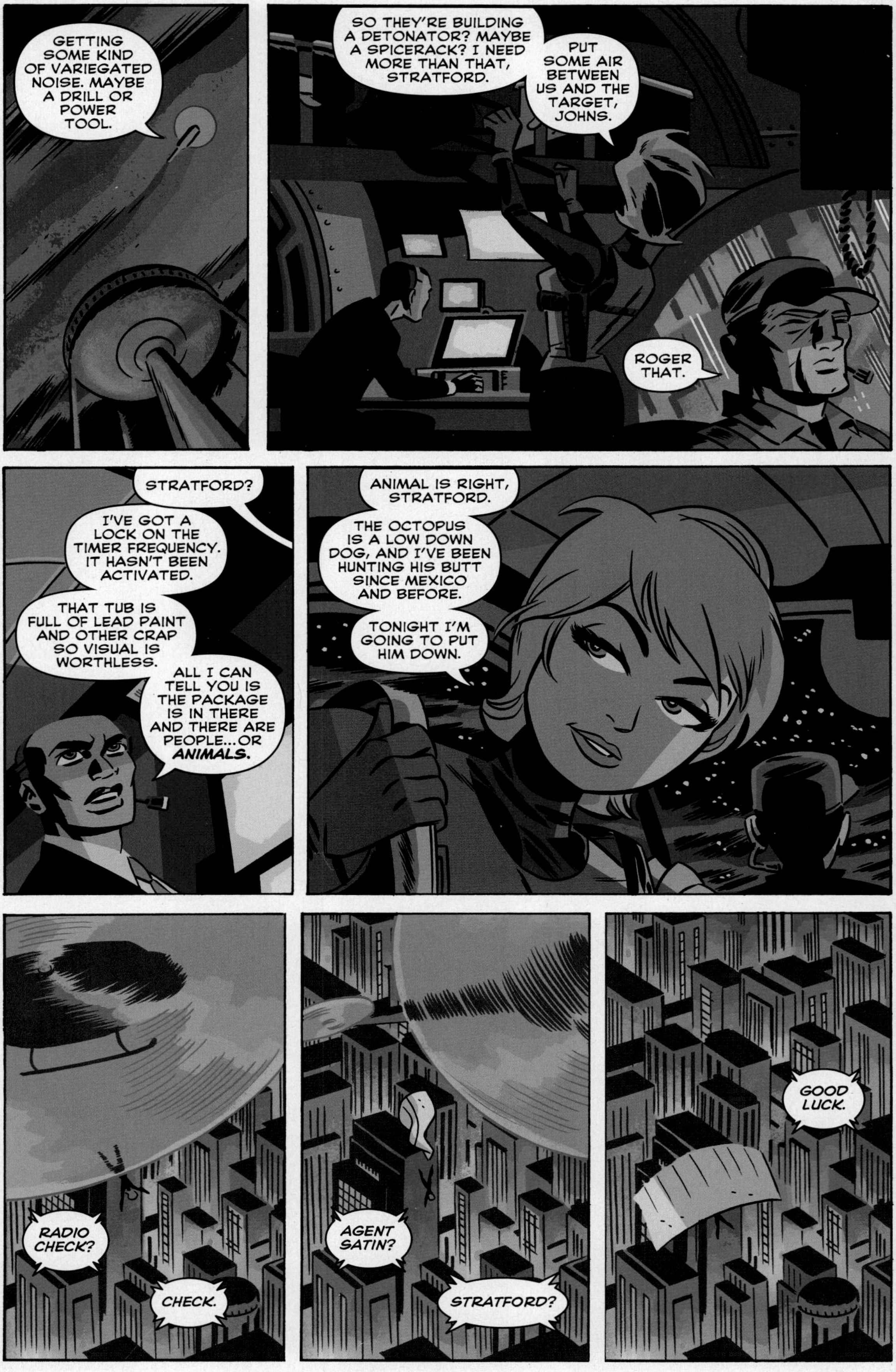
GETTING SOME KIND OF VARIEGATED NOISE. MAYBE A DRILL OR POWER TOOL.
SO THEY'RE BUILDING A DETONATOR? MAYBE A SPICERACK? I NEED MORE THAN THAT, STRATFORD.
PUT SOME AIR BETWEEN US AND THE TARGET, JOHNS.
ROGER THAT.
STRATFORD?
I'VE GOT A LOCK ON THE TIMER FREQUENCY. IT HASN'T BEEN ACTIVATED.
THAT TUB IS FULL OF LEAD PAINT AND OTHER CRAP SO VISUAL IS WORTHLESS.
ALL I CAN TELL YOU IS THE PACKAGE IS IN THERE AND THERE ARE PEOPLE...OR ***ANIMALS.***
ANIMAL IS RIGHT, STRATFORD.
THE OCTOPUS IS A LOW DOWN DOG, AND I'VE BEEN HUNTING HIS BUTT SINCE MEXICO AND BEFORE.
TONIGHT I'M GOING TO PUT HIM DOWN.
RADIO CHECK?
CHECK.
AGENT SATIN?
STRATFORD?
GOOD LUCK.

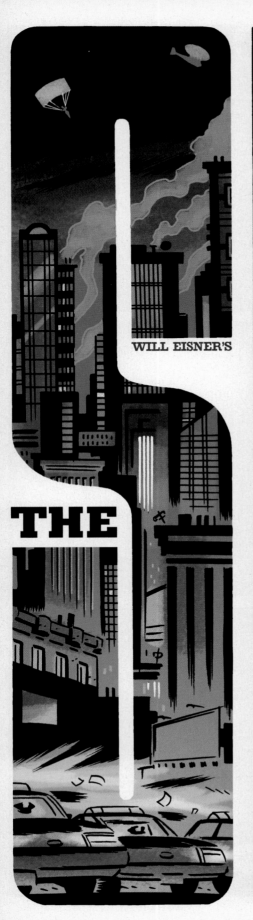

WILL EISNER'S

THE

BY
DARWYN COOKE
FINISHED ART
J. BONE
COLOR
DAVE STEWART
LETTERING
JARED K. FLETCHER
ASS'T EDITOR
KRISTY QUINN
EDITOR
SCOTT DUNBIER
THE SPIRIT CREATED BY
WILL EISNER

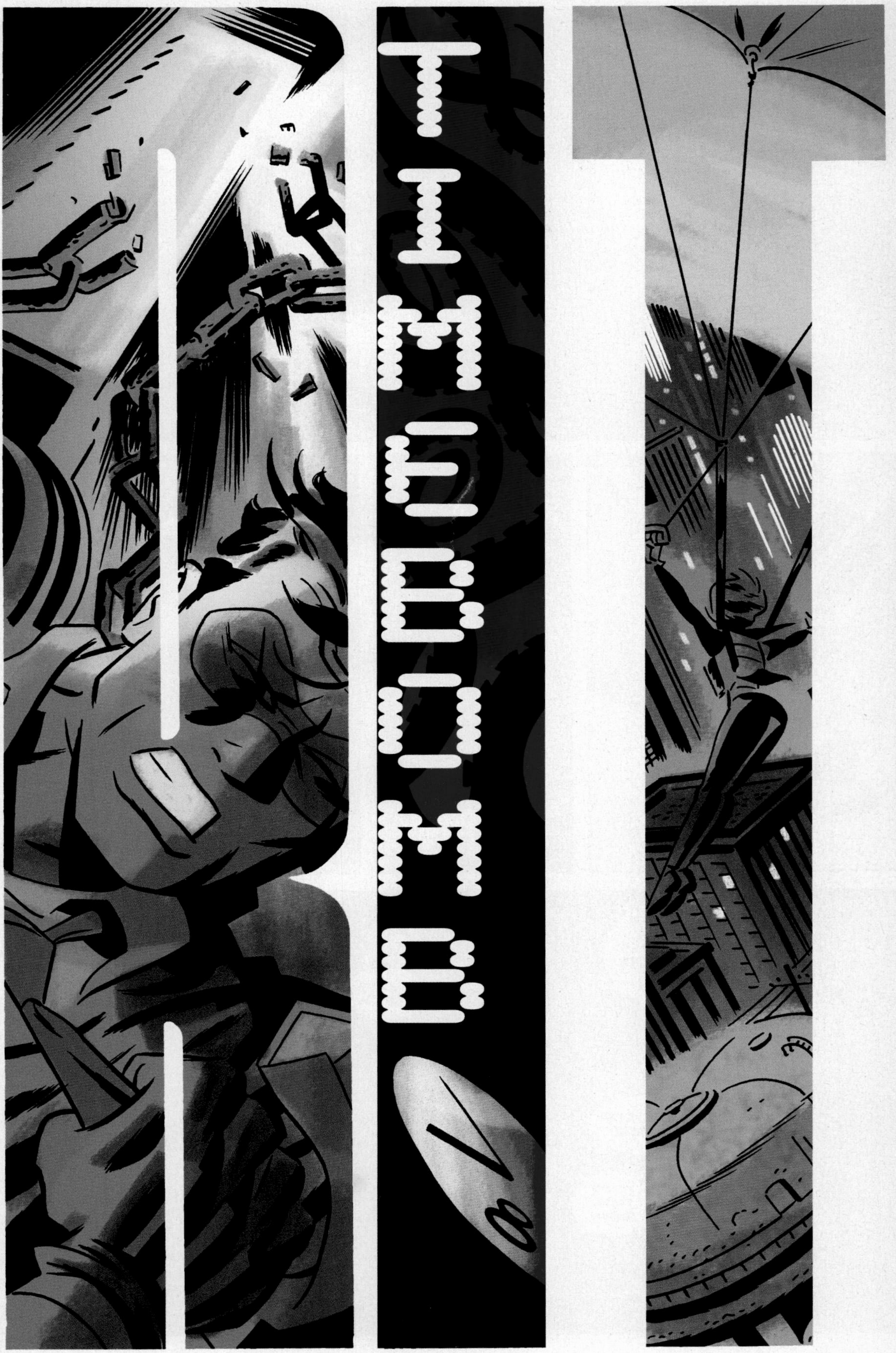
TIME BOMB

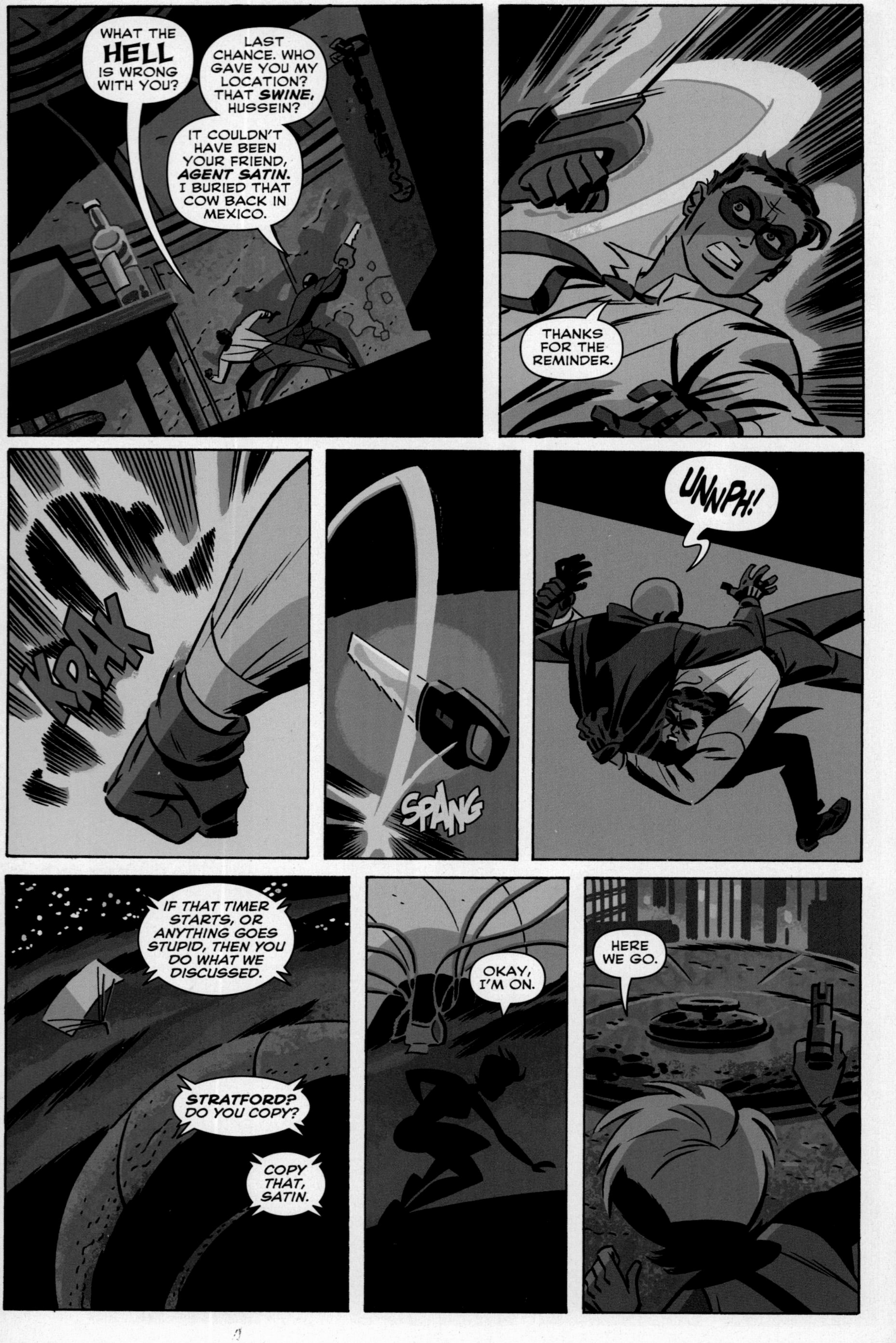
WHAT THE HELL IS WRONG WITH YOU?
LAST CHANCE. WHO GAVE YOU MY LOCATION? THAT SWINE, HUSSEIN?
IT COULDN'T HAVE BEEN YOUR FRIEND, AGENT SATIN. I BURIED THAT COW BACK IN MEXICO.
THANKS FOR THE REMINDER.
KRAK
SPANG
UNNPH!
IF THAT TIMER STARTS, OR ANYTHING GOES STUPID, THEN YOU DO WHAT WE DISCUSSED.
STRATFORD? DO YOU COPY?
COPY THAT, SATIN.
OKAY, I'M ON.
HERE WE GO.

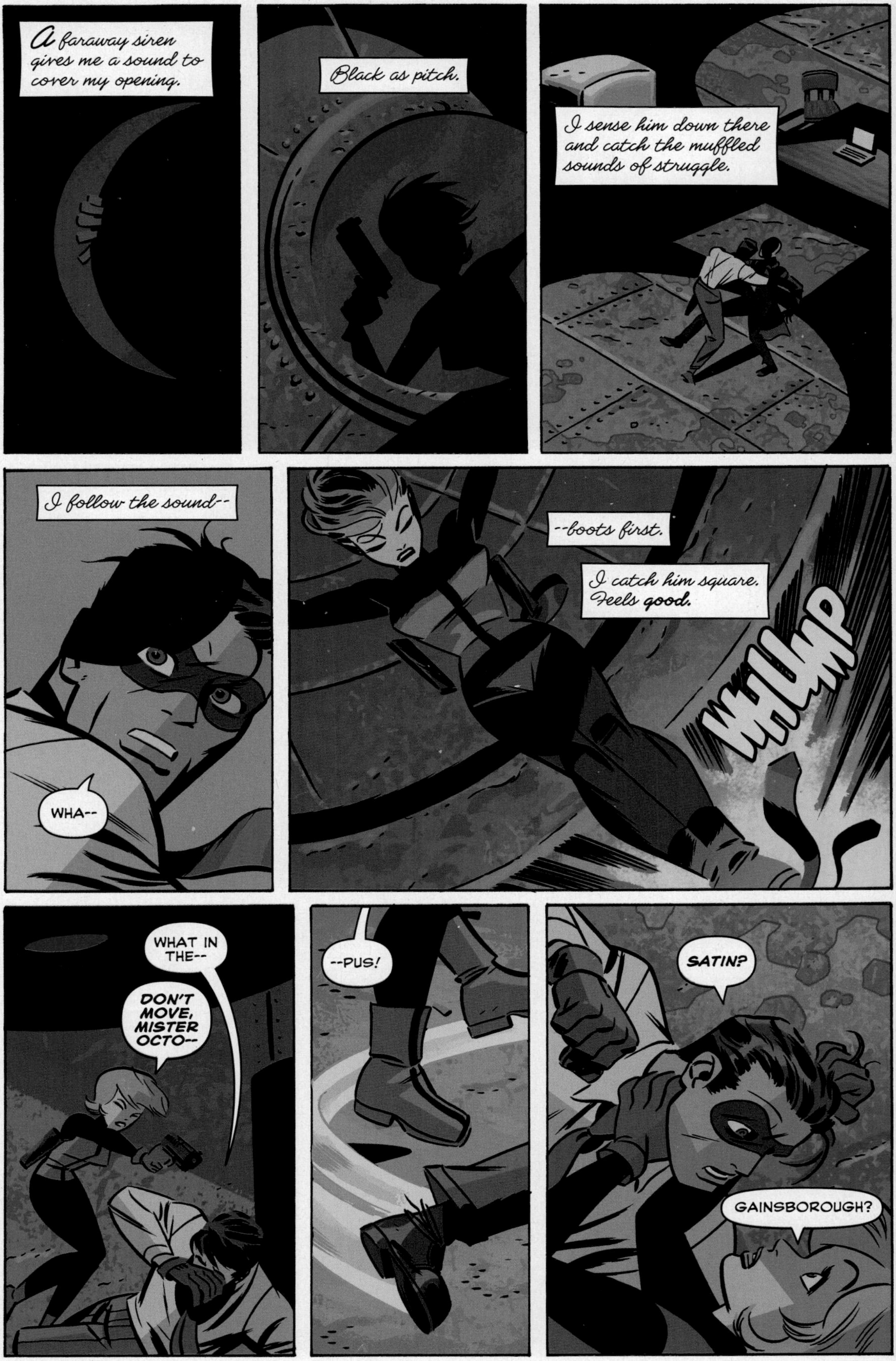
A faraway siren gives me a sound to cover my opening.
Black as pitch.
I sense him down there and catch the muffled sounds of struggle.
I follow the sound--
WHA--
--boots first.
I catch him square. Feels good.
WHUMP
WHAT IN THE--
DON'T MOVE, MISTER OCTO--
--PUS!
SATIN?
GAINSBOROUGH?

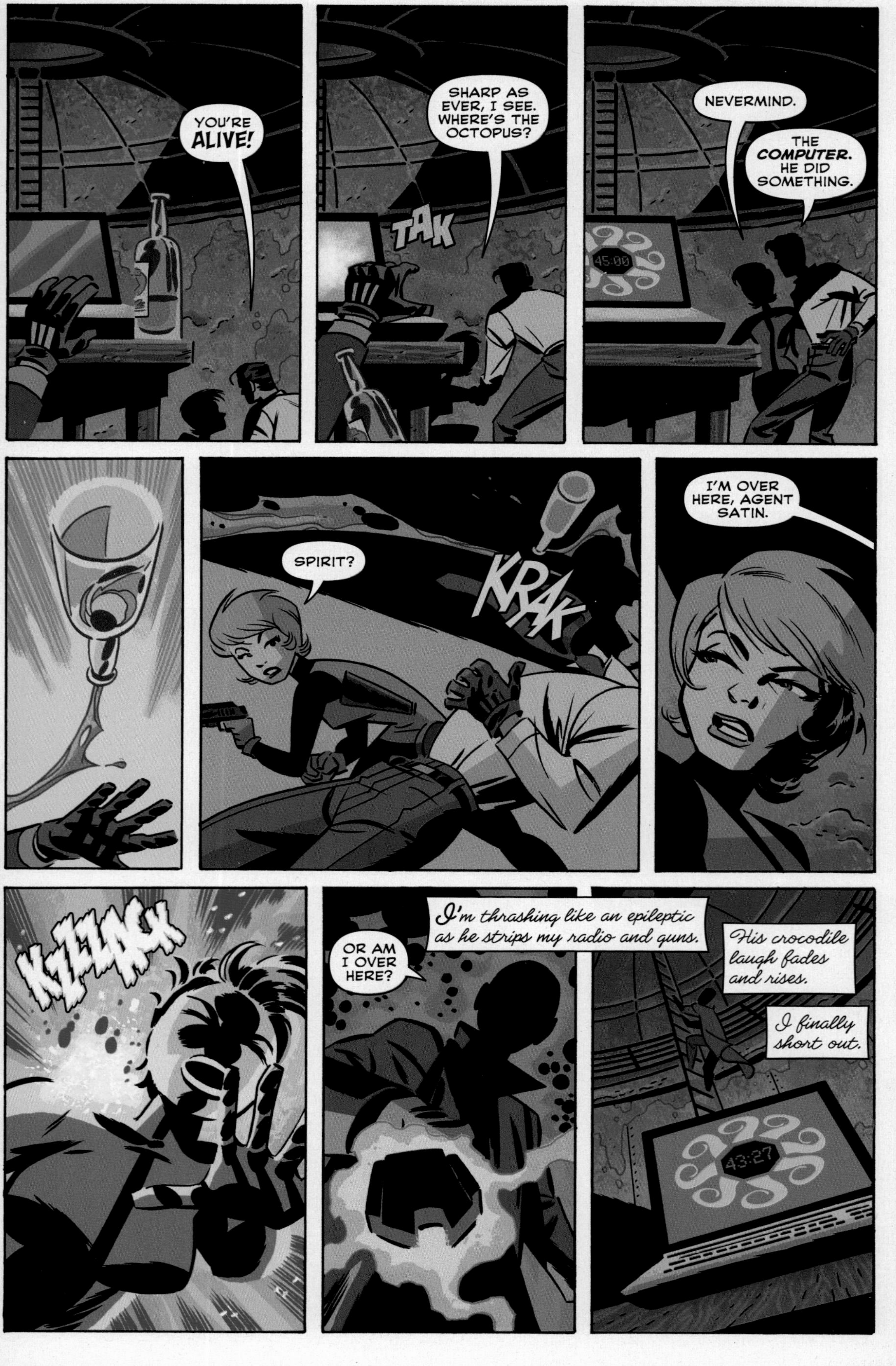
YOU'RE ALIVE!
TAK
SHARP AS EVER, I SEE. WHERE'S THE OCTOPUS?
NEVERMIND.
THE COMPUTER. HE DID SOMETHING.
45:00
SPIRIT?
KRAK
I'M OVER HERE, AGENT SATIN.
KZZZLACK
I'm thrashing like an epileptic as he strips my radio and guns.
OR AM I OVER HERE?
His crocodile laugh fades and rises.
I finally short out.
43:27

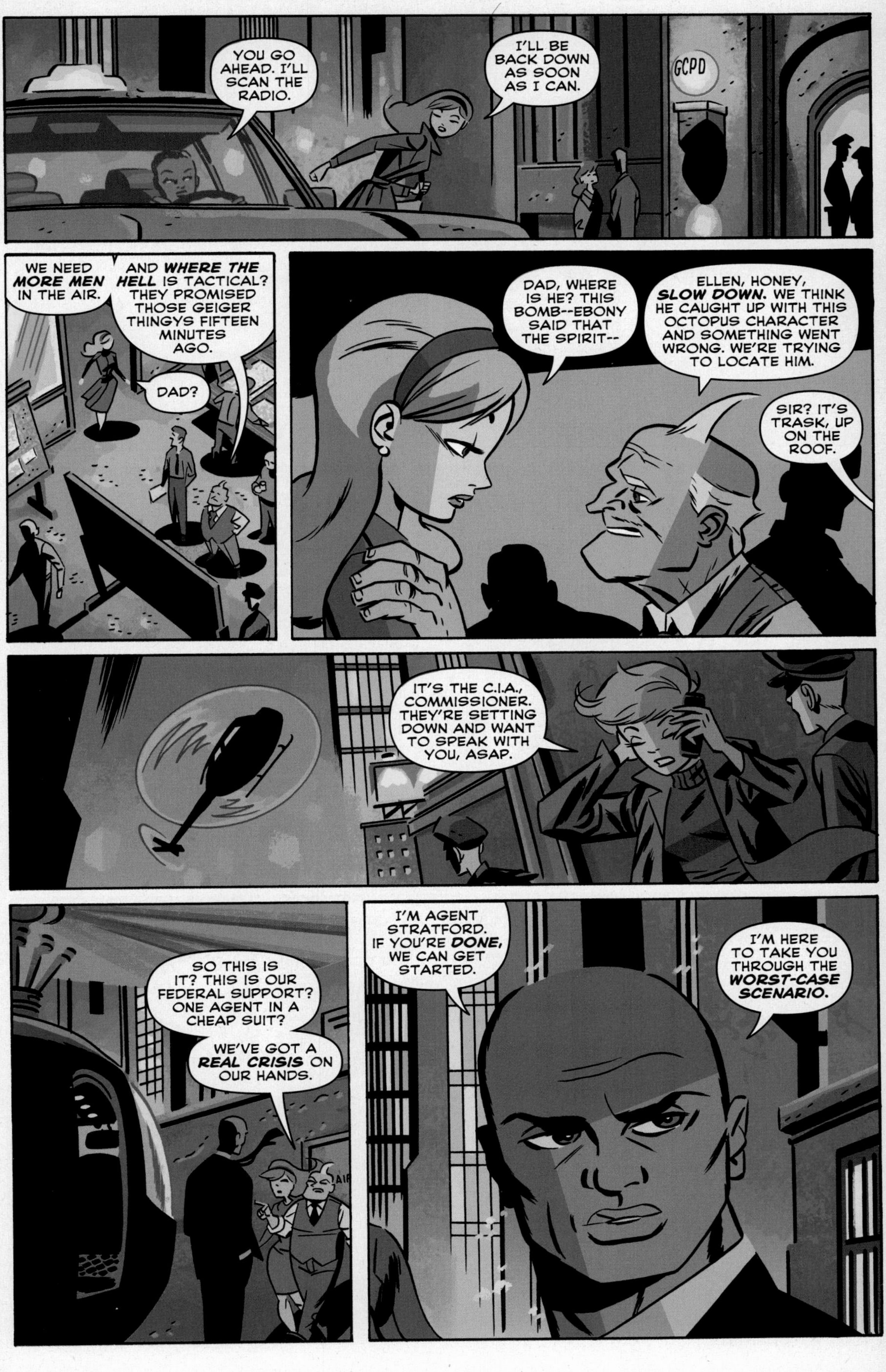
YOU GO AHEAD. I'LL SCAN THE RADIO.
I'LL BE BACK DOWN AS SOON AS I CAN.
GCPD
WE NEED MORE MEN IN THE AIR.
AND WHERE THE HELL IS TACTICAL? THEY PROMISED THOSE GEIGER THINGYS FIFTEEN MINUTES AGO.
DAD?
DAD, WHERE IS HE? THIS BOMB--EBONY SAID THAT THE SPIRIT--
ELLEN, HONEY, SLOW DOWN. WE THINK HE CAUGHT UP WITH THIS OCTOPUS CHARACTER AND SOMETHING WENT WRONG. WE'RE TRYING TO LOCATE HIM.
SIR? IT'S TRASK, UP ON THE ROOF.
IT'S THE C.I.A., COMMISSIONER. THEY'RE SETTING DOWN AND WANT TO SPEAK WITH YOU, ASAP.
SO THIS IS IT? THIS IS OUR FEDERAL SUPPORT? ONE AGENT IN A CHEAP SUIT?
WE'VE GOT A REAL CRISIS ON OUR HANDS.
I'M AGENT STRATFORD. IF YOU'RE DONE, WE CAN GET STARTED.
I'M HERE TO TAKE YOU THROUGH THE WORST-CASE SCENARIO.

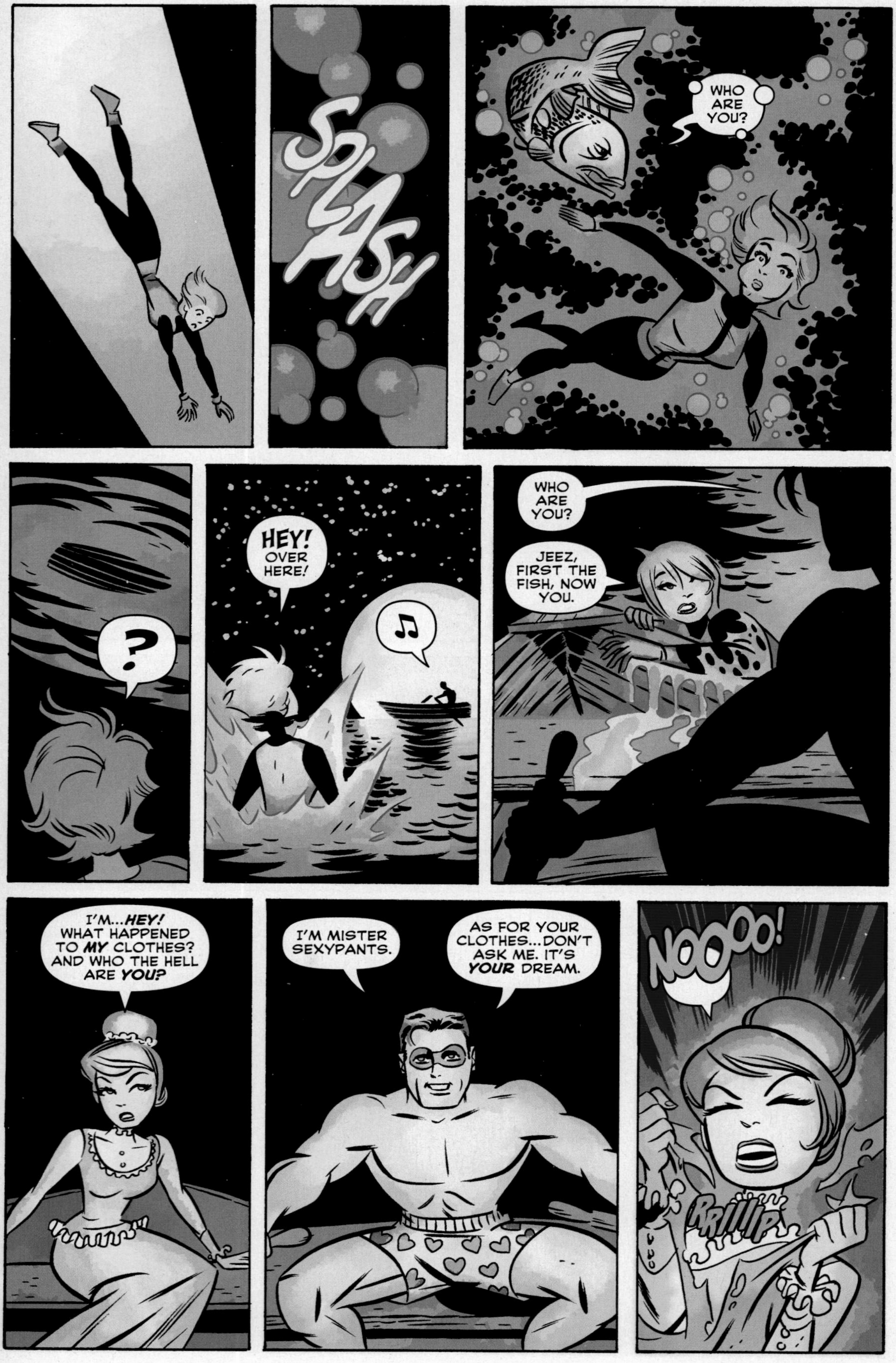
SPLASH
WHO ARE YOU?
?
HEY! OVER HERE!
♫
WHO ARE YOU?
JEEZ, FIRST THE FISH, NOW YOU.
I'M...HEY! WHAT HAPPENED TO MY CLOTHES? AND WHO THE HELL ARE YOU?
I'M MISTER SEXYPANTS.
AS FOR YOUR CLOTHES...DON'T ASK ME. IT'S YOUR DREAM.
NOOOO!
RRIIIIP

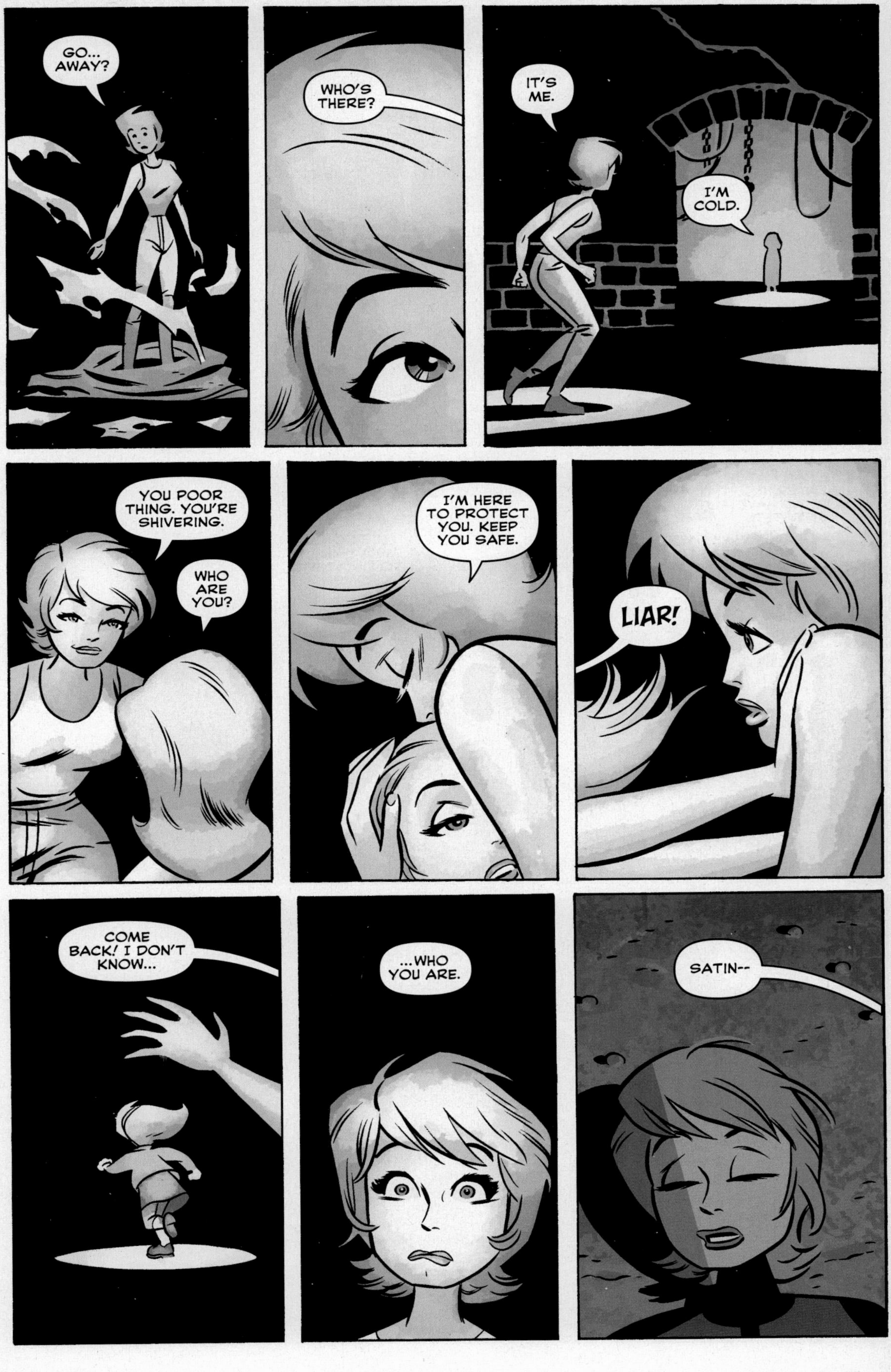
GO... AWAY?
WHO'S THERE?
IT'S ME.
I'M COLD.
YOU POOR THING. YOU'RE SHIVERING.
WHO ARE YOU?
I'M HERE TO PROTECT YOU. KEEP YOU SAFE.
LIAR!
COME BACK! I DON'T KNOW...
...WHO YOU ARE.
SATIN--

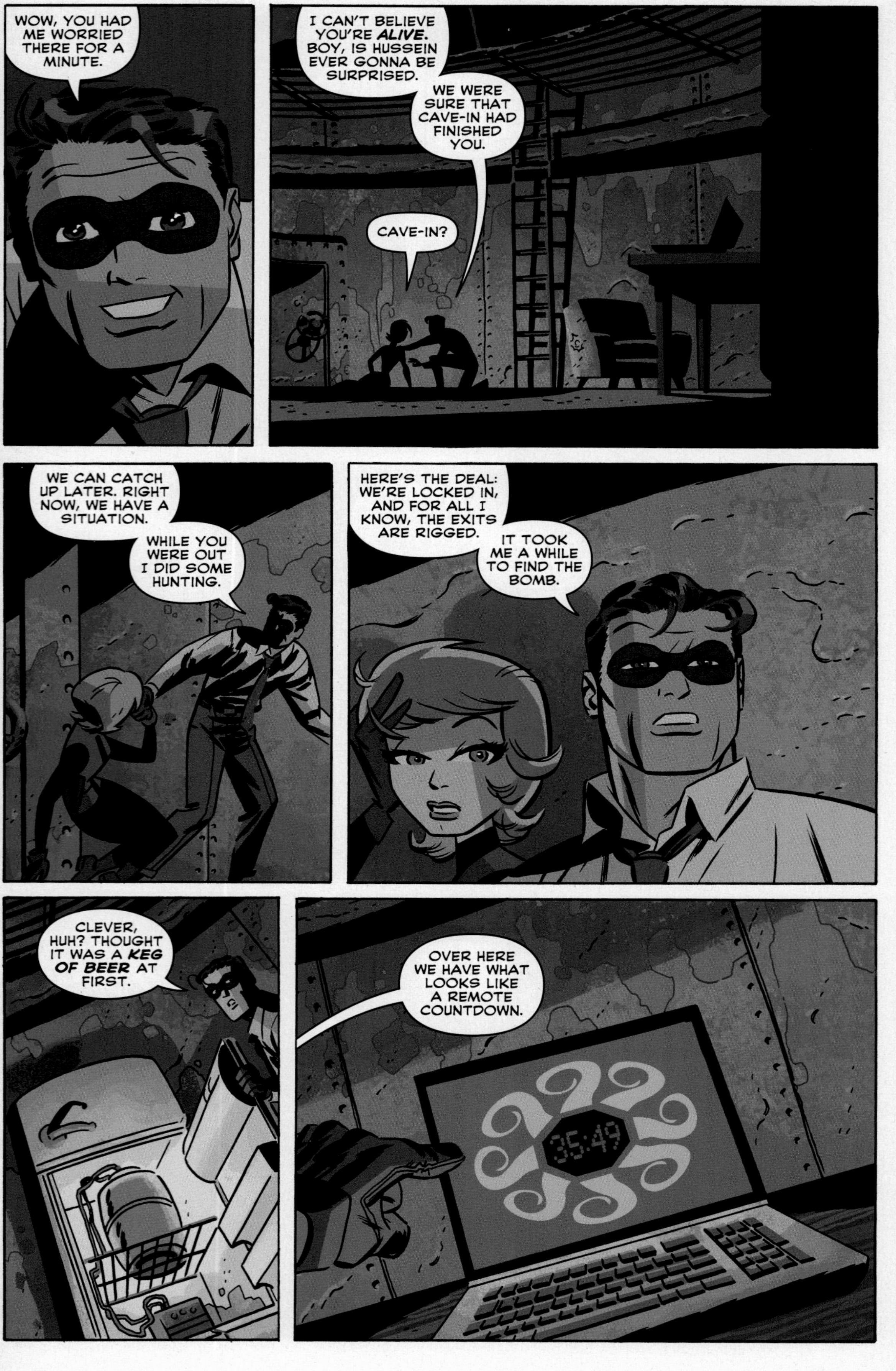
WOW, YOU HAD ME WORRIED THERE FOR A MINUTE.
I CAN'T BELIEVE YOU'RE **ALIVE.** BOY, IS HUSSEIN EVER GONNA BE SURPRISED.
WE WERE SURE THAT CAVE-IN HAD FINISHED YOU.
CAVE-IN?
WE CAN CATCH UP LATER. RIGHT NOW, WE HAVE A SITUATION.
WHILE YOU WERE OUT I DID SOME HUNTING.
HERE'S THE DEAL: WE'RE LOCKED IN, AND FOR ALL I KNOW, THE EXITS ARE RIGGED.
IT TOOK ME A WHILE TO FIND THE BOMB.
CLEVER, HUH? THOUGHT IT WAS A **KEG OF BEER** AT FIRST.
OVER HERE WE HAVE WHAT LOOKS LIKE A REMOTE COUNTDOWN.
35:49

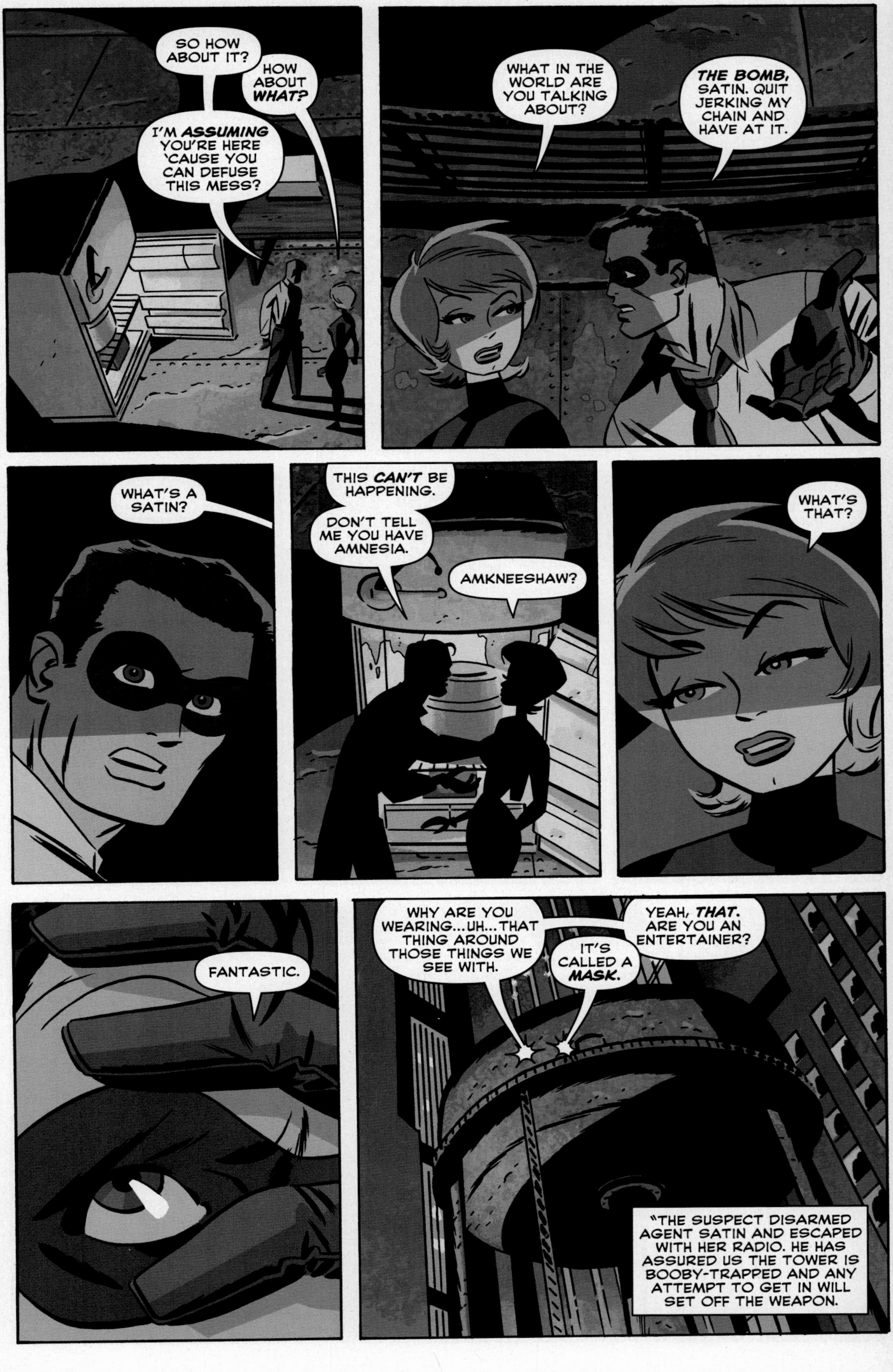
SO HOW ABOUT IT?
HOW ABOUT WHAT?
I'M ASSUMING YOU'RE HERE 'CAUSE YOU CAN DEFUSE THIS MESS?
WHAT IN THE WORLD ARE YOU TALKING ABOUT?
THE BOMB, SATIN. QUIT JERKING MY CHAIN AND HAVE AT IT.
WHAT'S A SATIN?
THIS CAN'T BE HAPPENING.
DON'T TELL ME YOU HAVE AMNESIA.
AMKNEESHAW?
WHAT'S THAT?
FANTASTIC.
WHY ARE YOU WEARING...UH...THAT THING AROUND THOSE THINGS WE SEE WITH.
YEAH, THAT. ARE YOU AN ENTERTAINER?
IT'S CALLED A MASK.
"THE SUSPECT DISARMED AGENT SATIN AND ESCAPED WITH HER RADIO. HE HAS ASSURED US THE TOWER IS BOOBY-TRAPPED AND ANY ATTEMPT TO GET IN WILL SET OFF THE WEAPON.

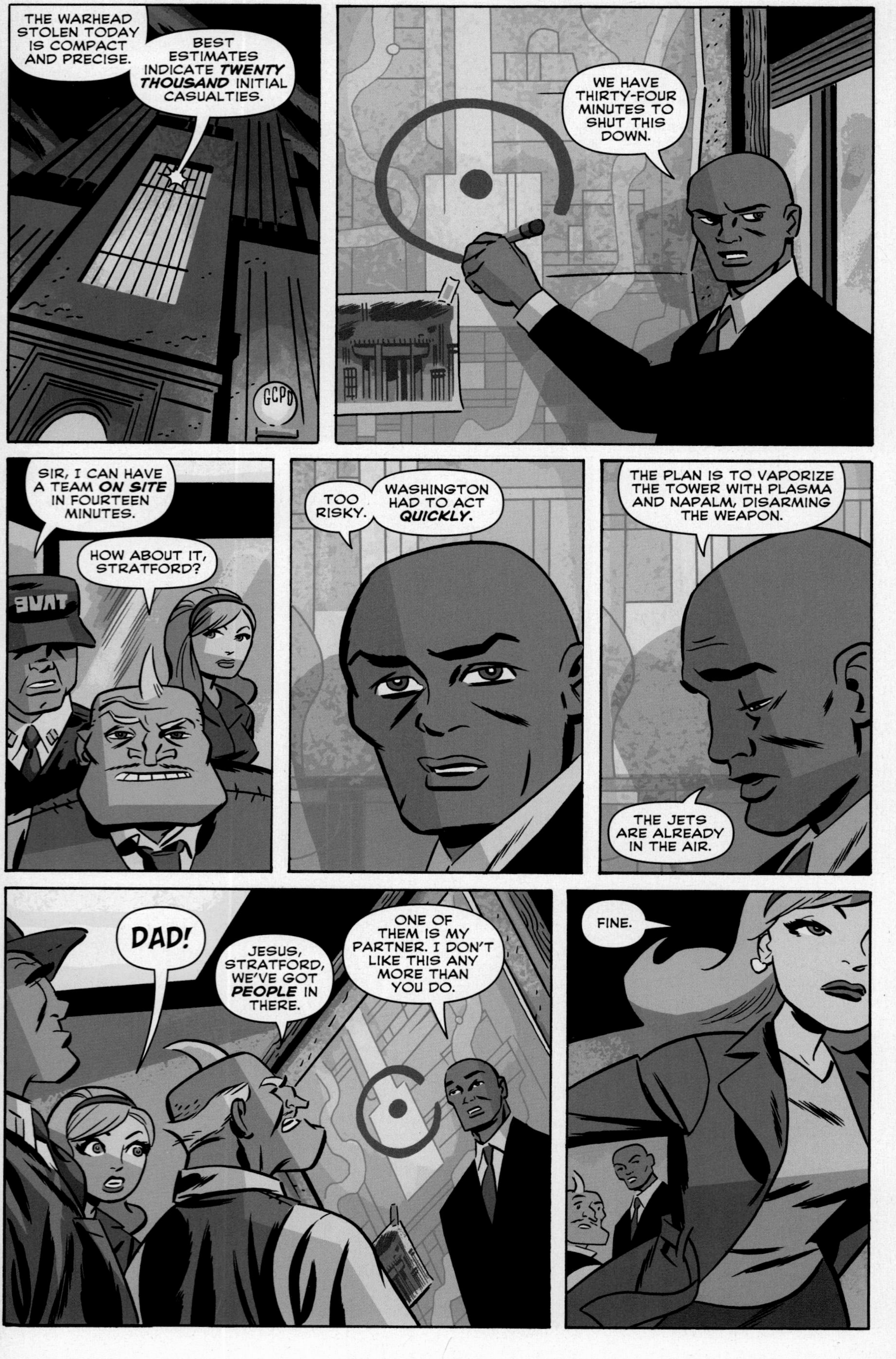
THE WARHEAD STOLEN TODAY IS COMPACT AND PRECISE.
BEST ESTIMATES INDICATE **TWENTY THOUSAND** INITIAL CASUALTIES.
GCPD
WE HAVE THIRTY-FOUR MINUTES TO SHUT THIS DOWN.
SIR, I CAN HAVE A TEAM **ON SITE** IN FOURTEEN MINUTES.
HOW ABOUT IT, STRATFORD?
TOO RISKY.
WASHINGTON HAD TO ACT **QUICKLY.**
THE PLAN IS TO VAPORIZE THE TOWER WITH PLASMA AND NAPALM, DISARMING THE WEAPON.
THE JETS ARE ALREADY IN THE AIR.
DAD!
JESUS, STRATFORD, WE'VE GOT **PEOPLE** IN THERE.
ONE OF THEM IS MY PARTNER. I DON'T LIKE THIS ANY MORE THAN YOU DO.
FINE.

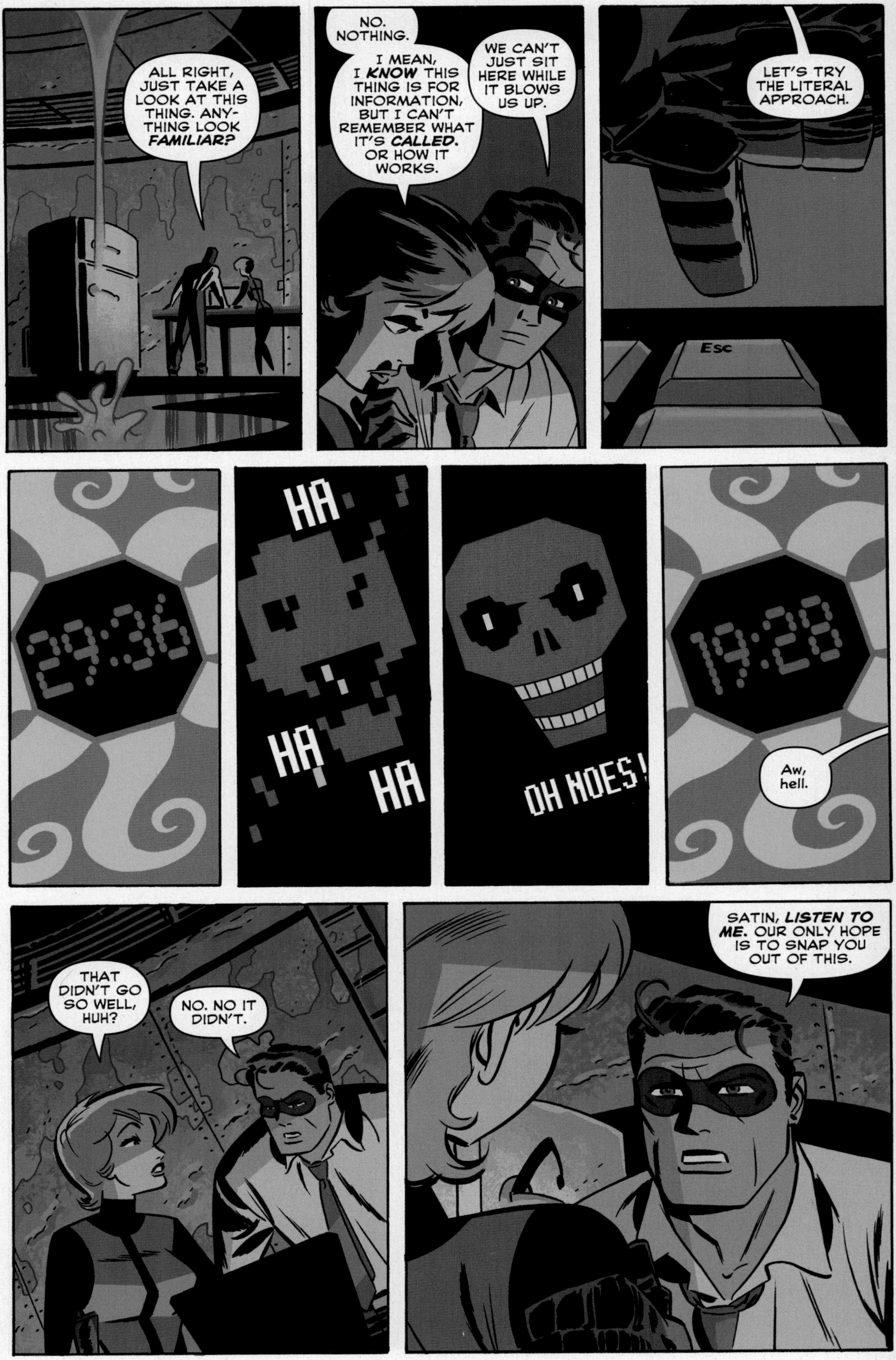
ALL RIGHT, JUST TAKE A LOOK AT THIS THING. ANYTHING LOOK FAMILIAR?
NO. NOTHING.
I MEAN, I KNOW THIS THING IS FOR INFORMATION, BUT I CAN'T REMEMBER WHAT IT'S CALLED. OR HOW IT WORKS.
WE CAN'T JUST SIT HERE WHILE IT BLOWS US UP.
LET'S TRY THE LITERAL APPROACH.
Esc
29:36
HA
HA
HA
OH NOES!
19:28
Aw, hell.
THAT DIDN'T GO SO WELL, HUH?
NO. NO IT DIDN'T.
SATIN, LISTEN TO ME. OUR ONLY HOPE IS TO SNAP YOU OUT OF THIS.

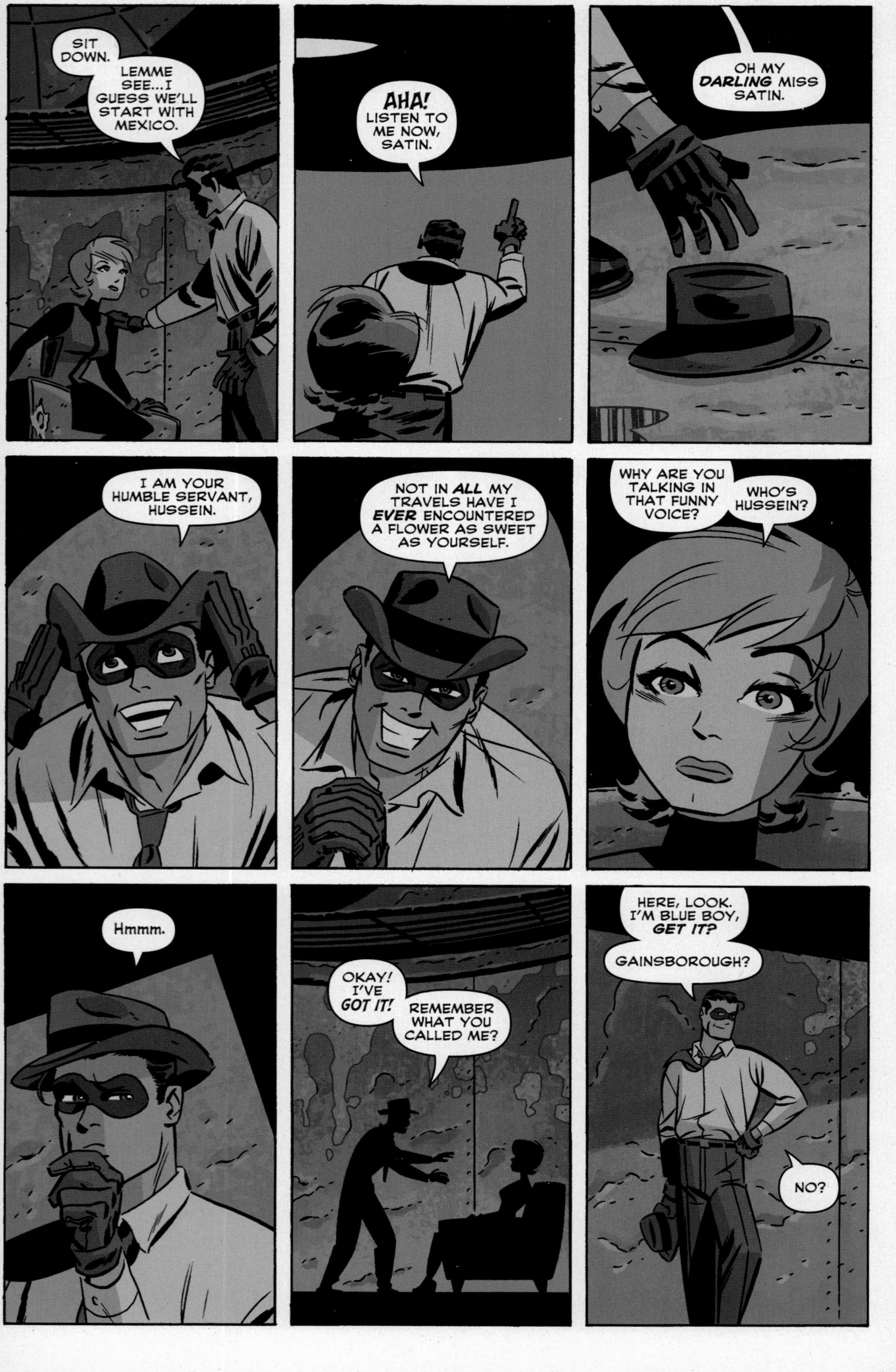
SIT DOWN.
LEMME SEE...I GUESS WE'LL START WITH MEXICO.
AHA! LISTEN TO ME NOW, SATIN.
OH MY DARLING MISS SATIN.
I AM YOUR HUMBLE SERVANT, HUSSEIN.
NOT IN ALL MY TRAVELS HAVE I EVER ENCOUNTERED A FLOWER AS SWEET AS YOURSELF.
WHY ARE YOU TALKING IN THAT FUNNY VOICE?
WHO'S HUSSEIN?
Hmmm.
OKAY! I'VE GOT IT!
REMEMBER WHAT YOU CALLED ME?
HERE, LOOK. I'M BLUE BOY, GET IT?
GAINSBOROUGH?
NO?

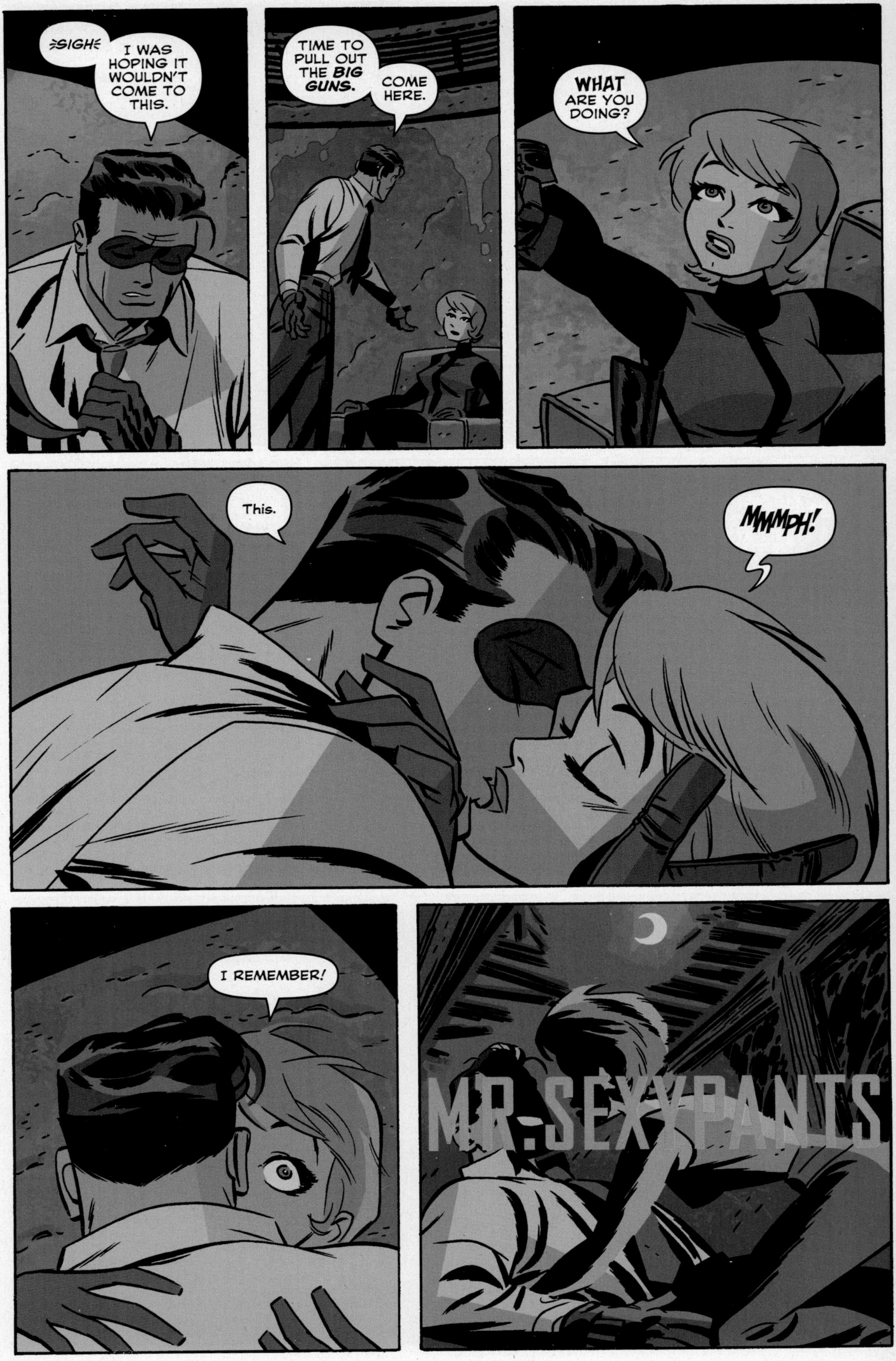

≶SIGH≶
I WAS HOPING IT WOULDN'T COME TO THIS.
TIME TO PULL OUT THE BIG GUNS.
COME HERE.
WHAT ARE YOU DOING?
This.
MMMPH!
I REMEMBER!
MR. SEXYPANTS

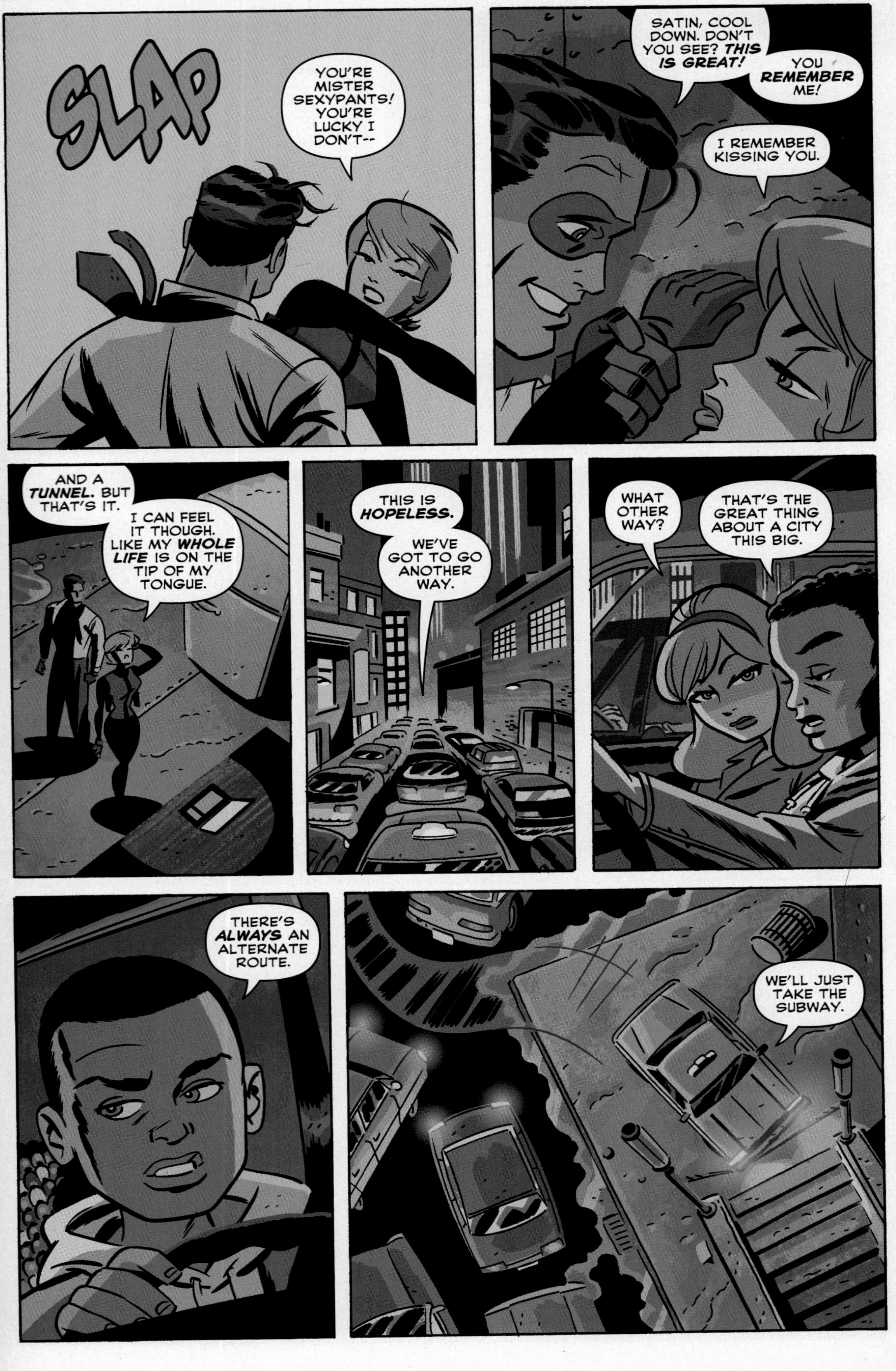
SLAP
YOU'RE MISTER SEXYPANTS! YOU'RE LUCKY I DON'T--
SATIN, COOL DOWN. DON'T YOU SEE? THIS IS GREAT!
YOU REMEMBER ME!
I REMEMBER KISSING YOU.
AND A TUNNEL. BUT THAT'S IT.
I CAN FEEL IT THOUGH. LIKE MY WHOLE LIFE IS ON THE TIP OF MY TONGUE.
THIS IS HOPELESS.
WE'VE GOT TO GO ANOTHER WAY.
WHAT OTHER WAY?
THAT'S THE GREAT THING ABOUT A CITY THIS BIG.
THERE'S ALWAYS AN ALTERNATE ROUTE.
WE'LL JUST TAKE THE SUBWAY.

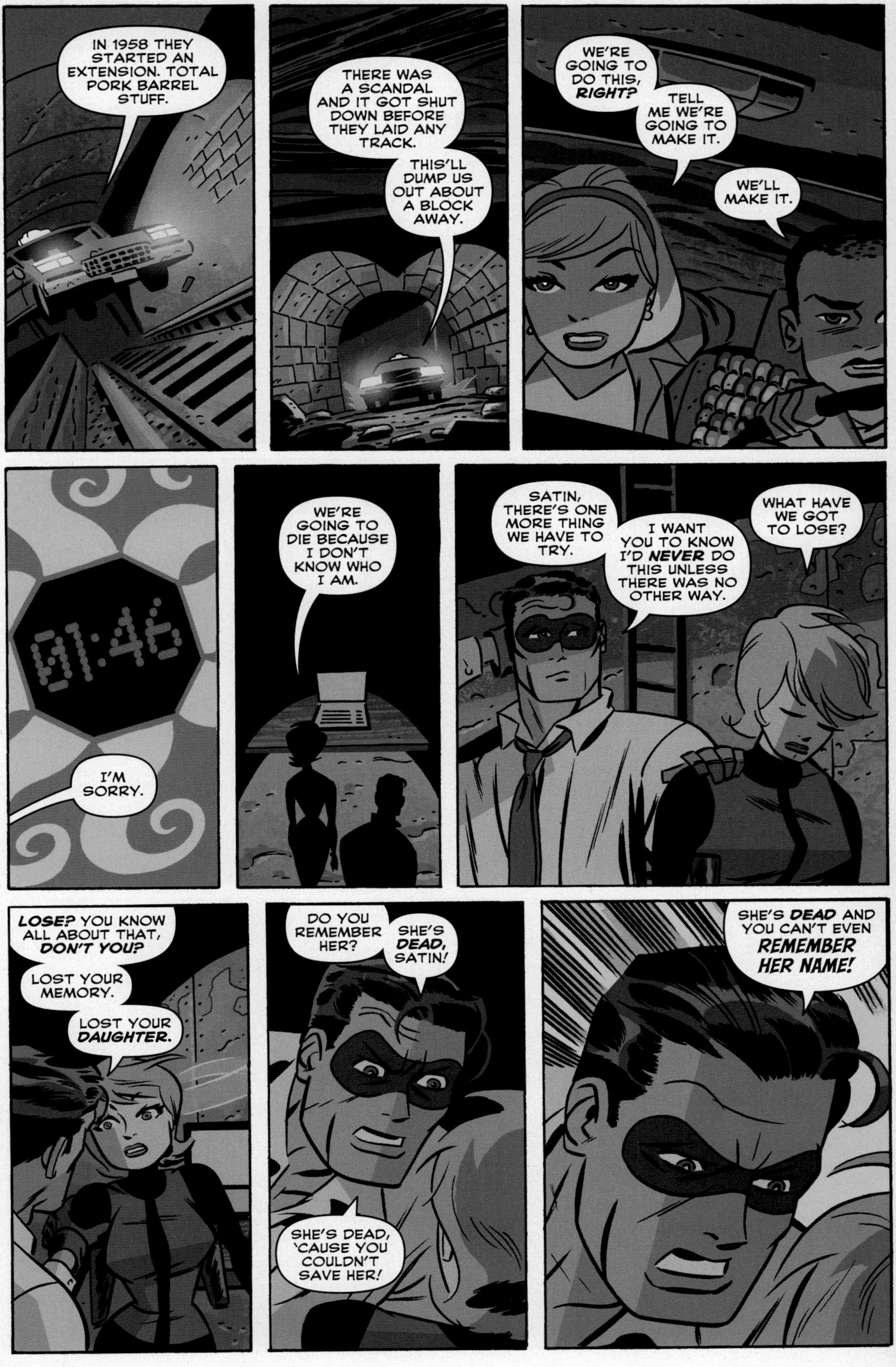
IN 1958 THEY STARTED AN EXTENSION. TOTAL PORK BARREL STUFF.
THERE WAS A SCANDAL AND IT GOT SHUT DOWN BEFORE THEY LAID ANY TRACK.
THIS'LL DUMP US OUT ABOUT A BLOCK AWAY.
WE'RE GOING TO DO THIS, RIGHT?
TELL ME WE'RE GOING TO MAKE IT.
WE'LL MAKE IT.
01:46
I'M SORRY.
WE'RE GOING TO DIE BECAUSE I DON'T KNOW WHO I AM.
SATIN, THERE'S ONE MORE THING WE HAVE TO TRY.
I WANT YOU TO KNOW I'D NEVER DO THIS UNLESS THERE WAS NO OTHER WAY.
WHAT HAVE WE GOT TO LOSE?
LOSE? YOU KNOW ALL ABOUT THAT, DON'T YOU?
LOST YOUR MEMORY.
LOST YOUR DAUGHTER.
DO YOU REMEMBER HER?
SHE'S DEAD, SATIN!
SHE'S DEAD, 'CAUSE YOU COULDN'T SAVE HER!
SHE'S DEAD AND YOU CAN'T EVEN REMEMBER HER NAME!

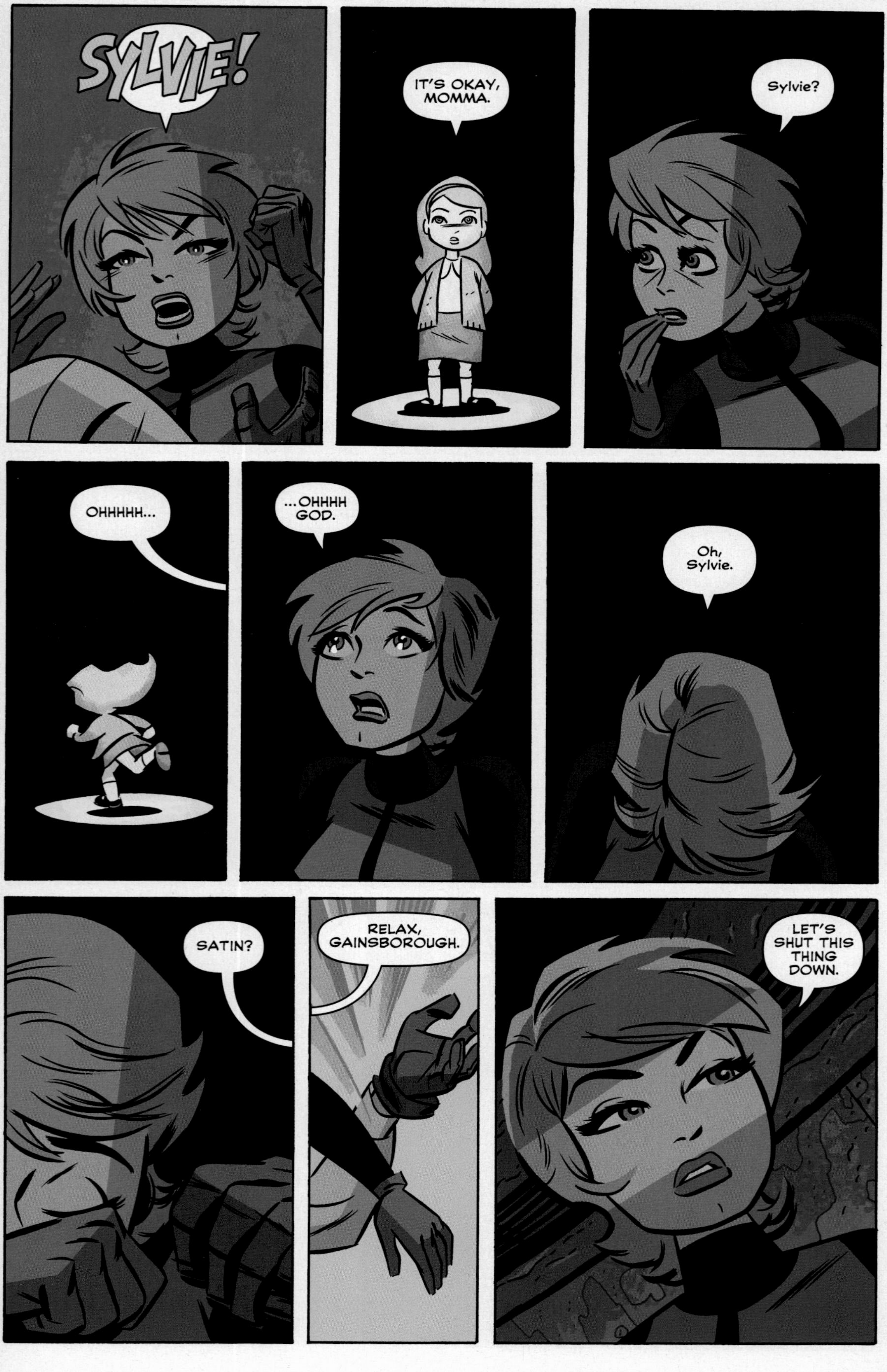
SYLVIE!
IT'S OKAY, MOMMA.
Sylvie?
OHHHHH...
...OHHHH GOD.
Oh, Sylvie.
SATIN?
RELAX, GAINSBOROUGH.
LET'S SHUT THIS THING DOWN.

THERE *IT IS*. WE'VE GOT TEN MINUTES TO GET THEM OUT AND GET CLEAR.

OKAY, LEADS FROM THE WEAPON TO A REMOTE RECEIVER.

THEY MENTIONED BOOBY TRAPS. WE HAVE TO BE CAREFUL.

BOOBY TRAPS? WHAT IS THIS, 1960?

RECEIVER PICKS UP SIGNAL FROM LAPTOP AND SENDS ELECTRICAL CHARGE TO WEAPON. *HENCE*, A POWER SOURCE.

SATIN...

NOTHING BACK HERE. NO BATTERIES, NO *NOTHING*.

IF THIS WAS BOOBY TRAPPED, IT WAS FIFTY YEARS AGO. THE THING IS RUSTED SHUT.

SON OF A BITCH. I THINK HE WENT *LOW TECH*.

BRILLIANT. NOBODY WOULD THINK TO CONSIDER IT.

UH, *SATIN?*

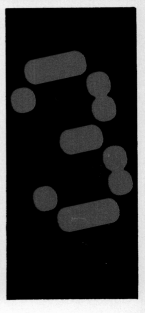

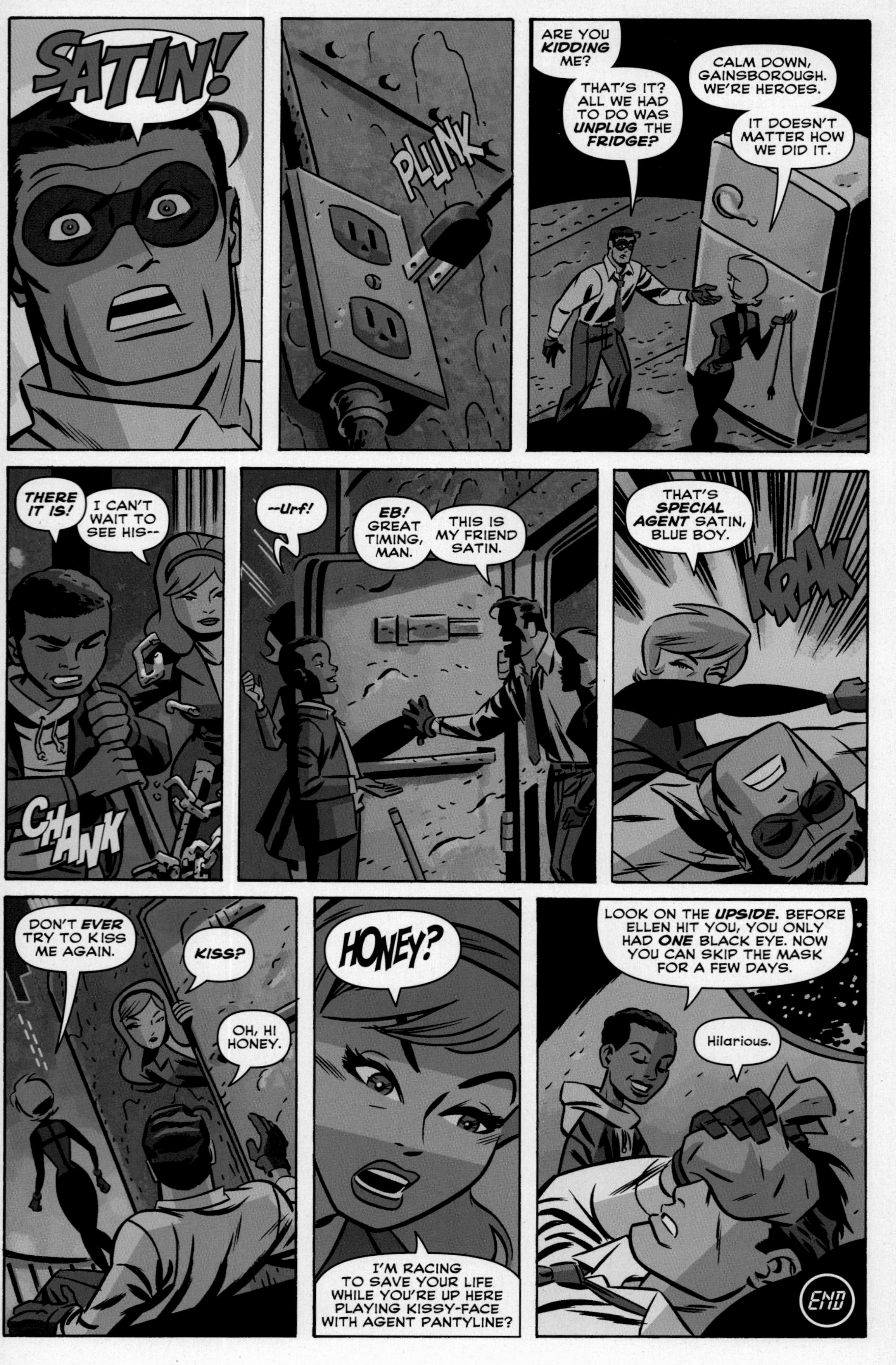

SATIN!
PLUNK
ARE YOU KIDDING ME?
THAT'S IT? ALL WE HAD TO DO WAS UNPLUG THE FRIDGE?
CALM DOWN, GAINSBOROUGH. WE'RE HEROES.
IT DOESN'T MATTER HOW WE DID IT.
THERE IT IS!
I CAN'T WAIT TO SEE HIS--
CHANK
--Urf!
EB! GREAT TIMING, MAN.
THIS IS MY FRIEND SATIN.
THAT'S SPECIAL AGENT SATIN, BLUE BOY.
KRAK
DON'T EVER TRY TO KISS ME AGAIN.
KISS?
OH, HI HONEY.
HONEY?
I'M RACING TO SAVE YOUR LIFE WHILE YOU'RE UP HERE PLAYING KISSY-FACE WITH AGENT PANTYLINE?
LOOK ON THE UPSIDE. BEFORE ELLEN HIT YOU, YOU ONLY HAD ONE BLACK EYE. NOW YOU CAN SKIP THE MASK FOR A FEW DAYS.
Hilarious.
END

3

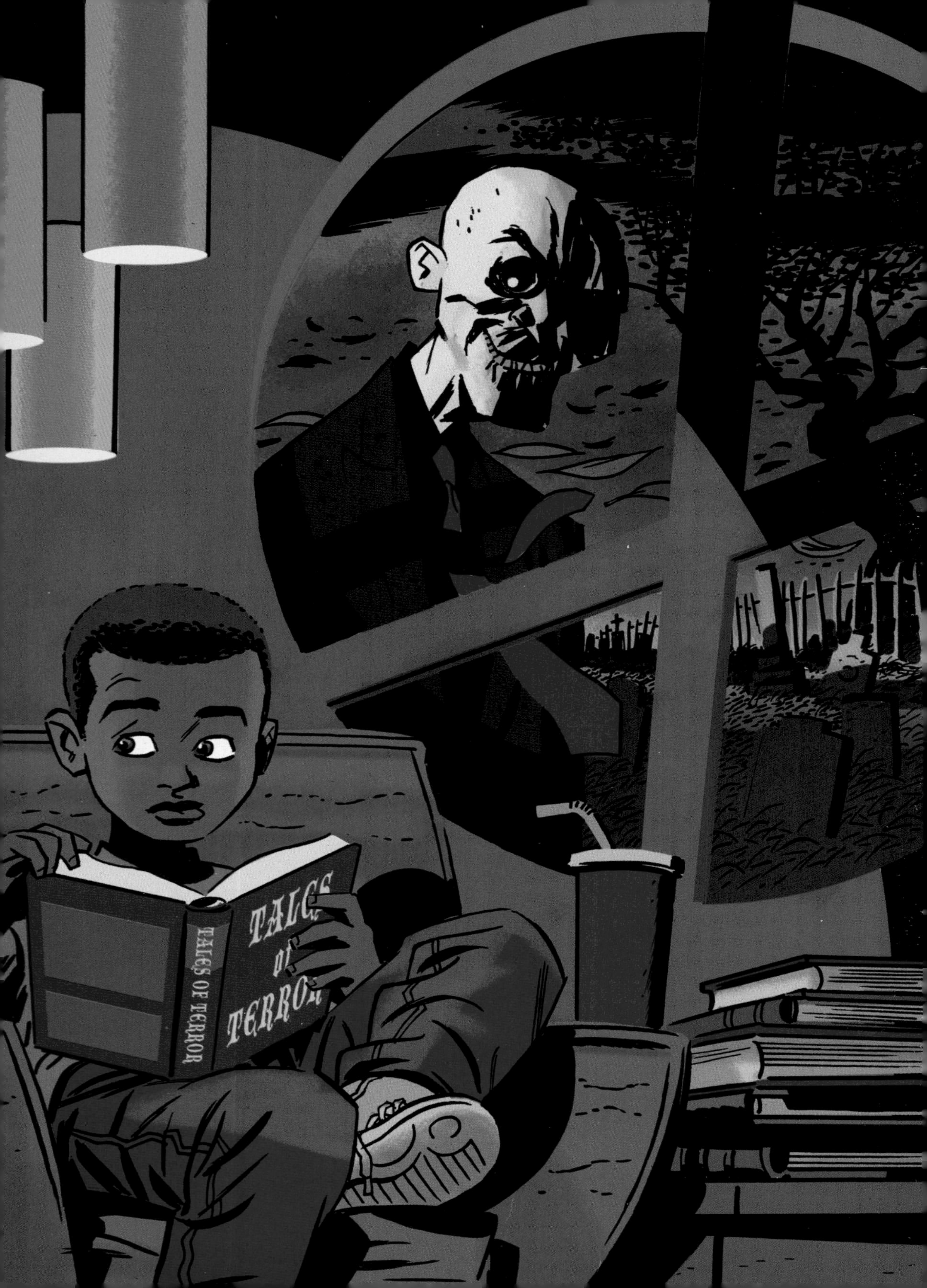

TALES of TERROR
TALES OF TERROR

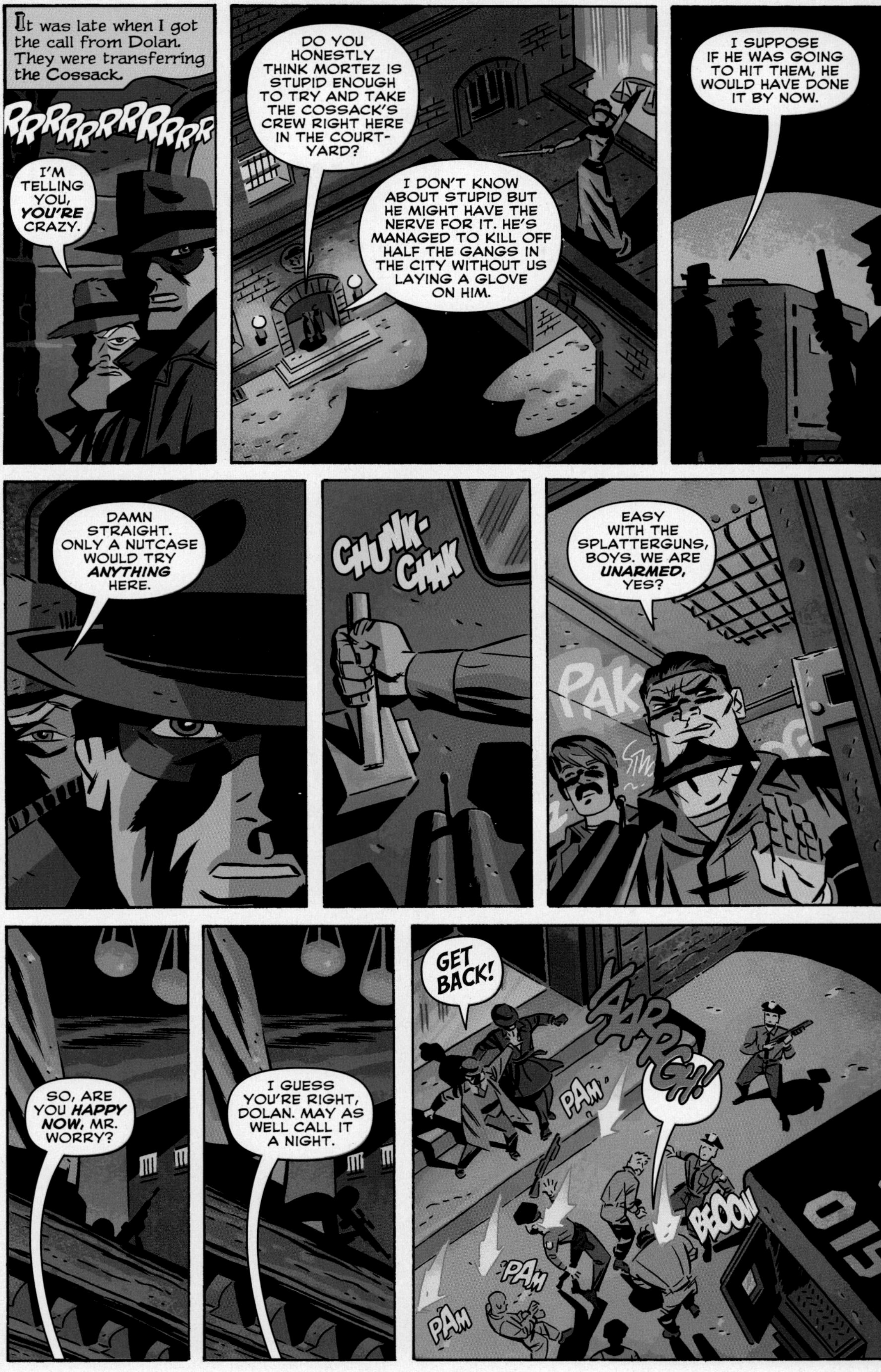
It was late when I got the call from Dolan. They were transferring the Cossack.
RRRRRRRRRRRR
I'M TELLING YOU, YOU'RE CRAZY.
DO YOU HONESTLY THINK MORTEZ IS STUPID ENOUGH TO TRY AND TAKE THE COSSACK'S CREW RIGHT HERE IN THE COURT-YARD?
I DON'T KNOW ABOUT STUPID BUT HE MIGHT HAVE THE NERVE FOR IT. HE'S MANAGED TO KILL OFF HALF THE GANGS IN THE CITY WITHOUT US LAYING A GLOVE ON HIM.
I SUPPOSE IF HE WAS GOING TO HIT THEM, HE WOULD HAVE DONE IT BY NOW.
DAMN STRAIGHT. ONLY A NUTCASE WOULD TRY ANYTHING HERE.
CHUNK-CHAK
EASY WITH THE SPLATTERGUNS, BOYS. WE ARE UNARMED, YES?
PAK
SO, ARE YOU HAPPY NOW, MR. WORRY?
I GUESS YOU'RE RIGHT, DOLAN. MAY AS WELL CALL IT A NIGHT.
GET BACK!
YAARGH!
PAM
BEOOW
PAM
PAM
015

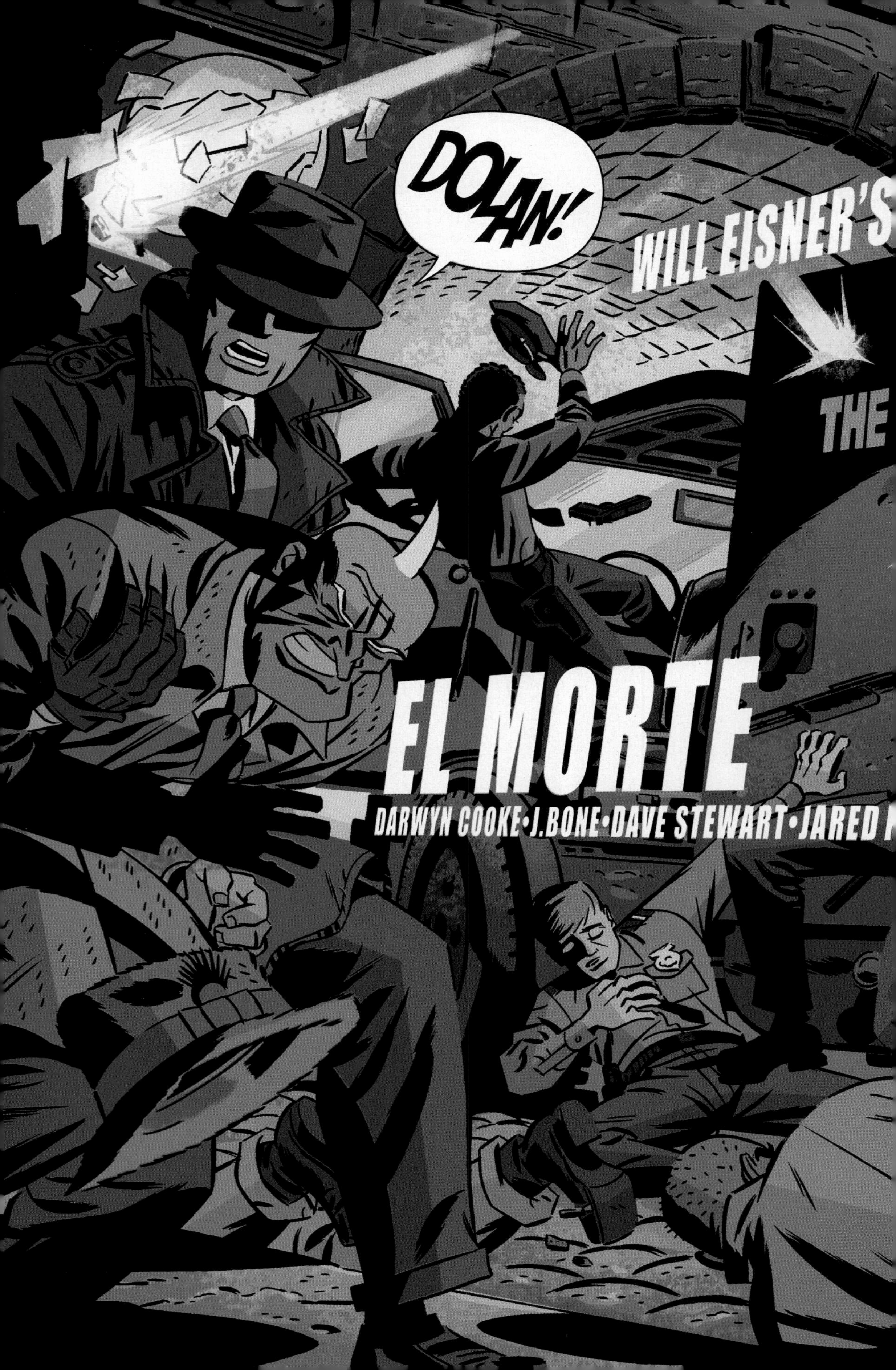
DOLAN!
WILL EISNER'S
THE
EL MORTE
DARWYN COOKE·J.BONE·DAVE STEWART·JARED

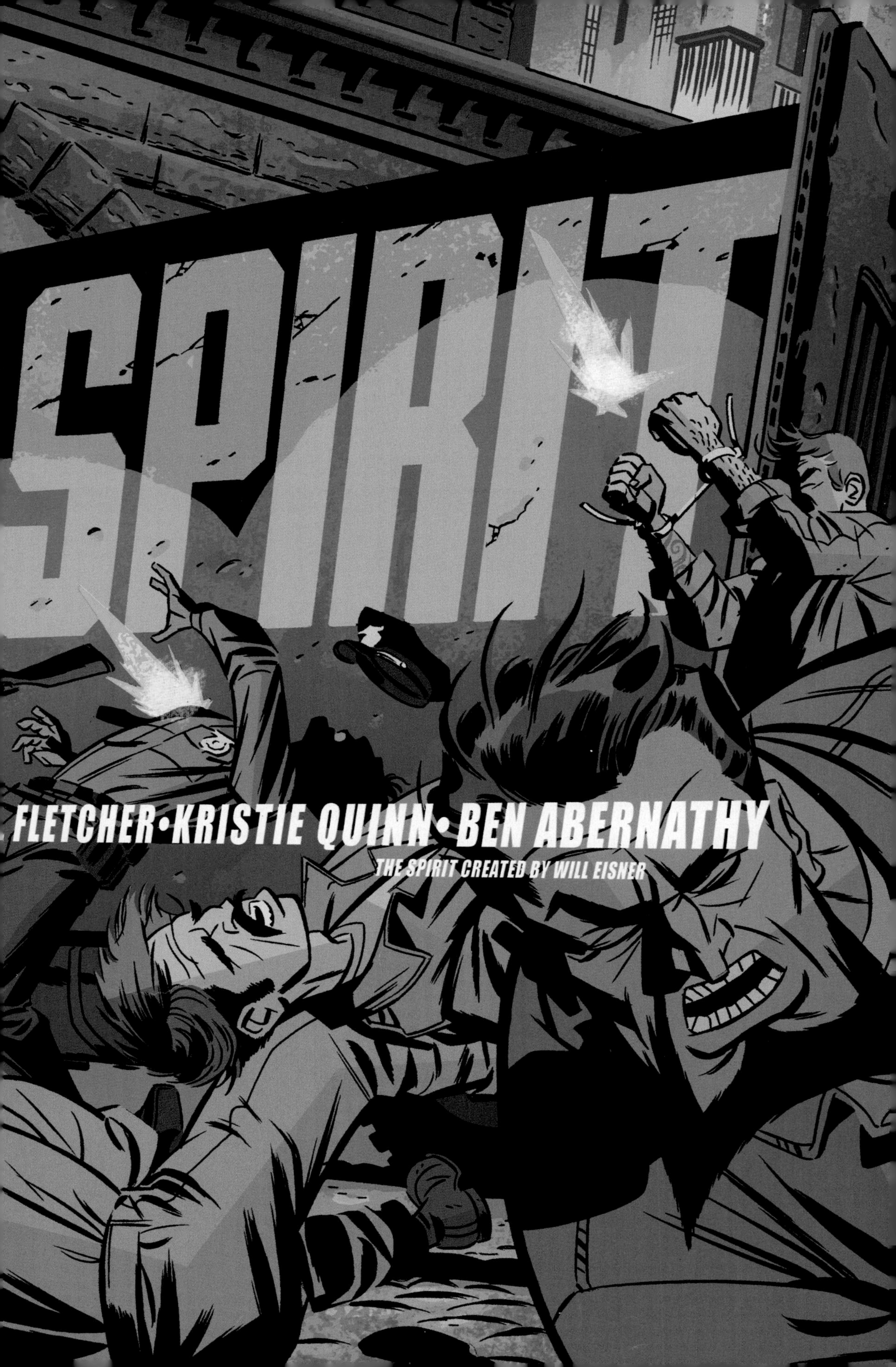
SPIRIT
FLETCHER•KRISTIE QUINN•BEN ABERNATHY
THE SPIRIT CREATED BY WILL EISNER

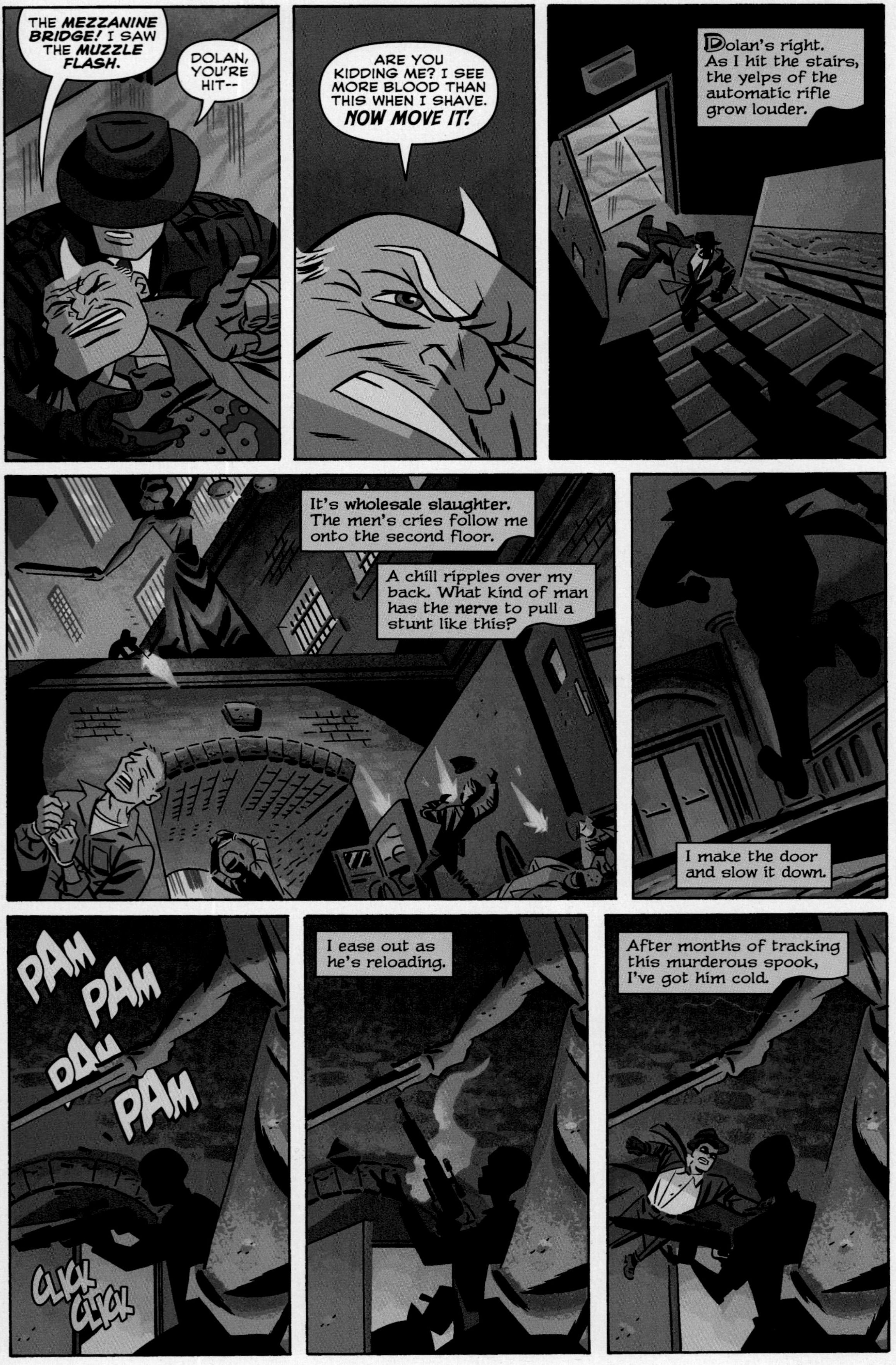
THE MEZZANINE BRIDGE! I SAW THE MUZZLE FLASH.
DOLAN, YOU'RE HIT--
ARE YOU KIDDING ME? I SEE MORE BLOOD THAN THIS WHEN I SHAVE. NOW MOVE IT!
Dolan's right. As I hit the stairs, the yelps of the automatic rifle grow louder.
It's wholesale slaughter. The men's cries follow me onto the second floor.
A chill ripples over my back. What kind of man has the nerve to pull a stunt like this?
I make the door and slow it down.
PAM PAM PAM PAM
CLICK CLICK
I ease out as he's reloading.
After months of tracking this murderous spook, I've got him cold.

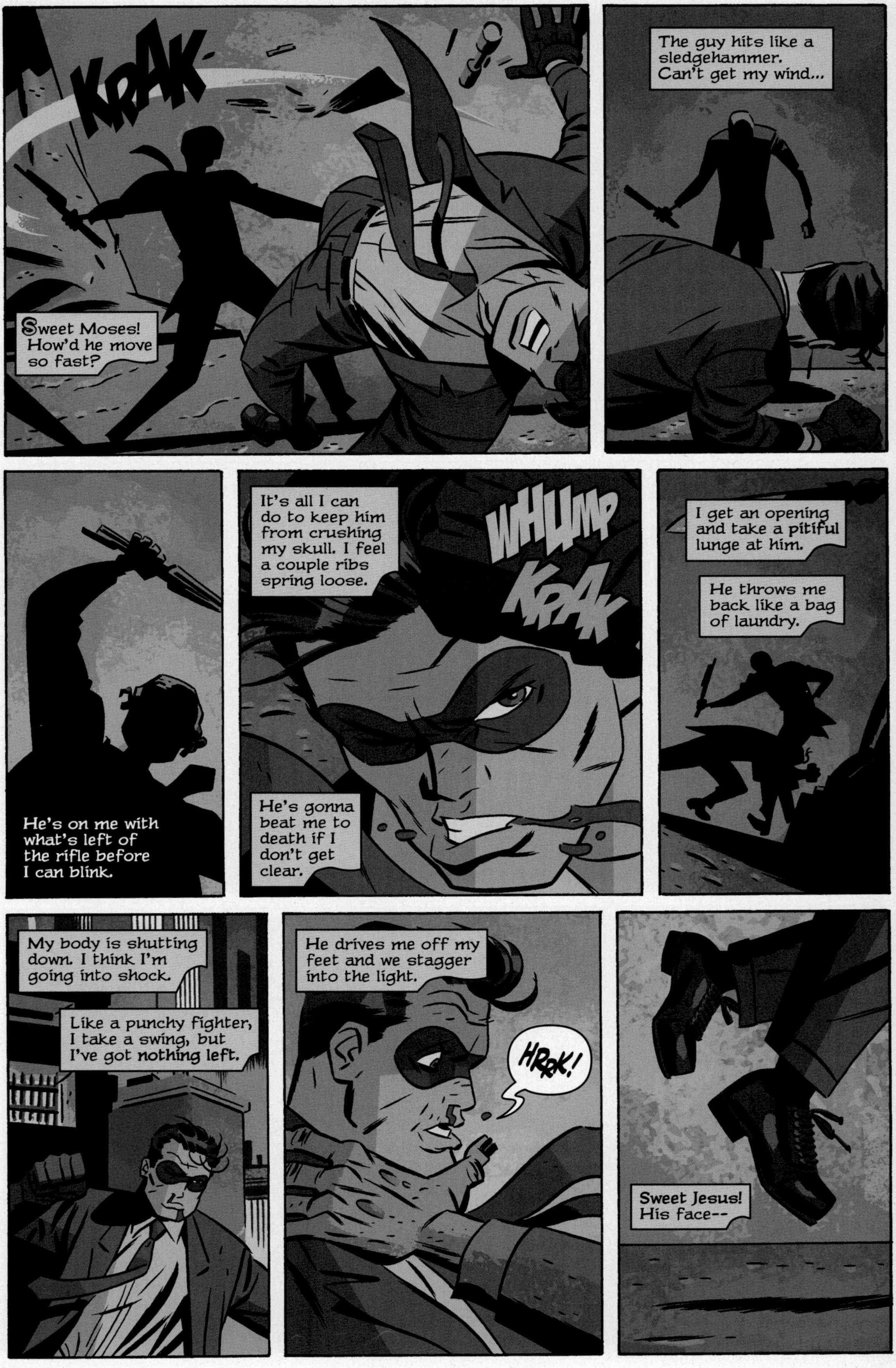
KRAK
Sweet Moses! How'd he move so fast?
The guy hits like a sledgehammer. Can't get my wind...
He's on me with what's left of the rifle before I can blink.
It's all I can do to keep him from crushing my skull. I feel a couple ribs spring loose.
WHUMP
KRAK
He's gonna beat me to death if I don't get clear.
I get an opening and take a pitiful lunge at him.
He throws me back like a bag of laundry.
My body is shutting down. I think I'm going into shock.
Like a punchy fighter, I take a swing, but I've got nothing left.
He drives me off my feet and we stagger into the light.
HRRK!
Sweet Jesus! His face--

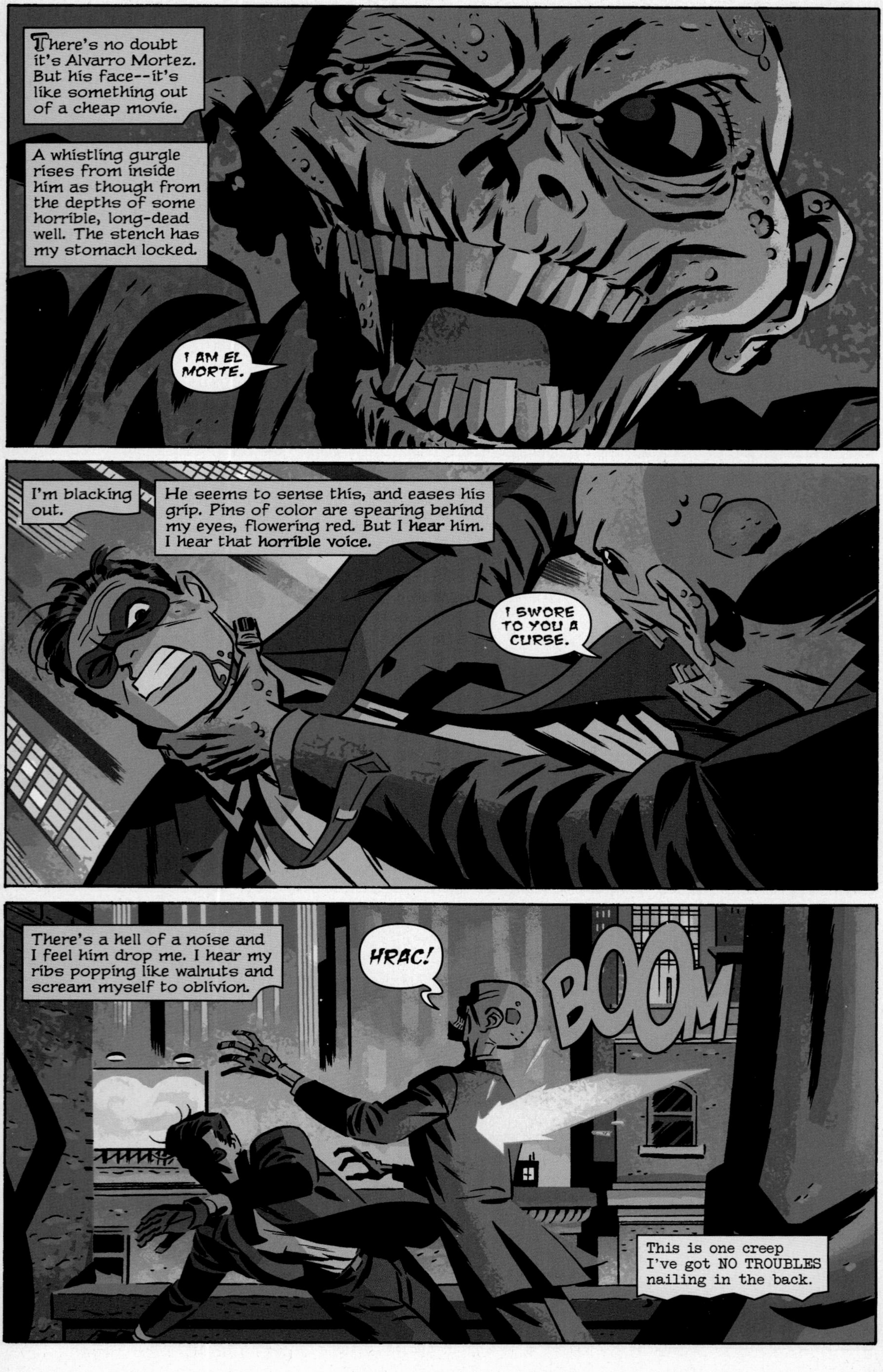
There's no doubt it's Alvarro Mortez. But his face--it's like something out of a cheap movie.
A whistling gurgle rises from inside him as though from the depths of some horrible, long-dead well. The stench has my stomach locked.
I AM EL MORTE.
I'm blacking out.
He seems to sense this, and eases his grip. Pins of color are spearing behind my eyes, flowering red. But I hear him. I hear that horrible voice.
I SWORE TO YOU A CURSE.
There's a hell of a noise and I feel him drop me. I hear my ribs popping like walnuts and scream myself to oblivion.
HRAC!
BOOM
This is one creep I've got NO TROUBLES nailing in the back.

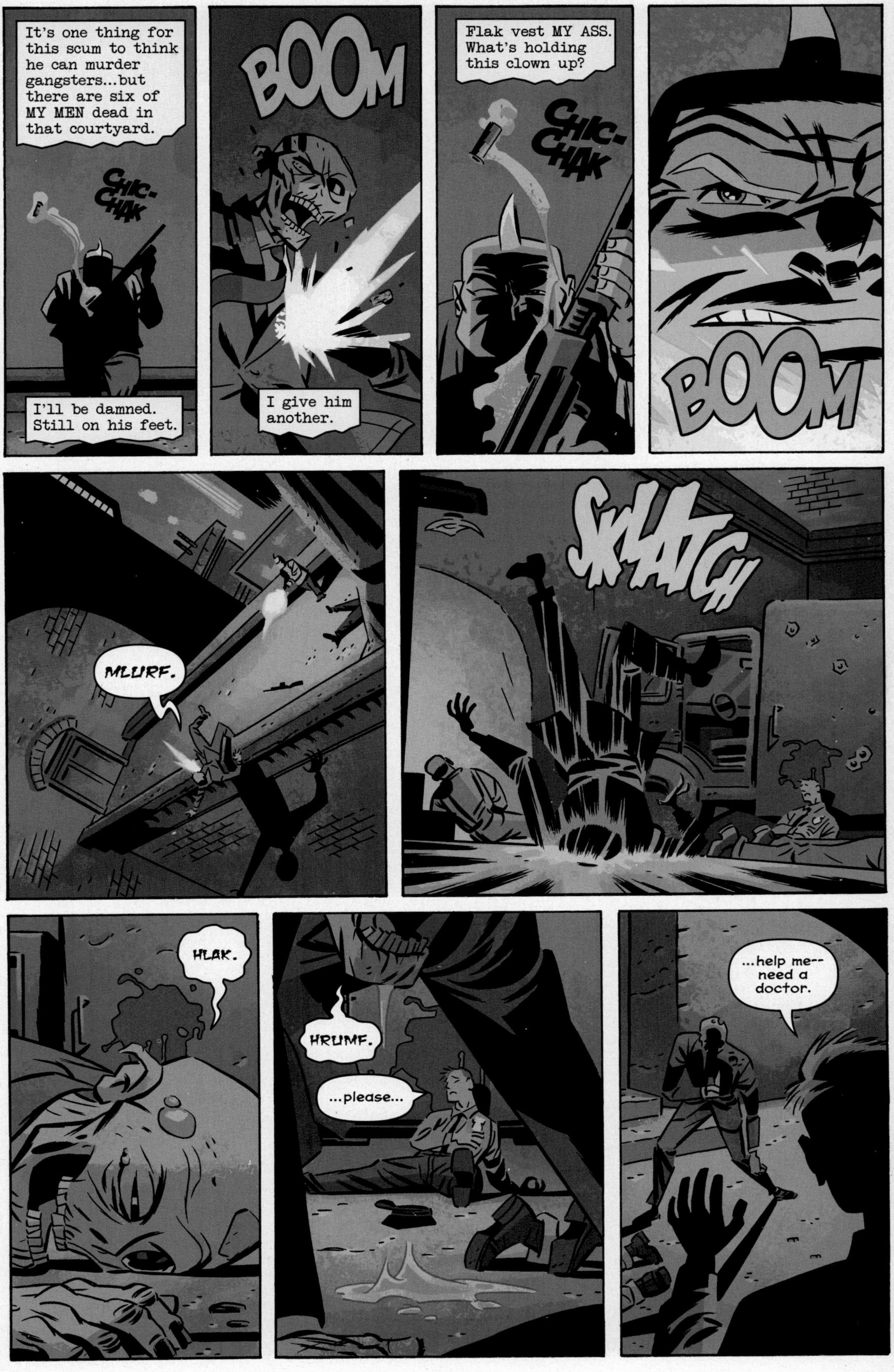
It's one thing for this scum to think he can murder gangsters...but there are six of MY MEN dead in that courtyard.
CHIC-CHAK
I'll be damned. Still on his feet.
BOOM
I give him another.
Flak vest MY ASS. What's holding this clown up?
CHIC-CHAK
BOOM
MLURF.
SKLATCH
HLAK.
HRUMF.
...please...
...help me--need a doctor.

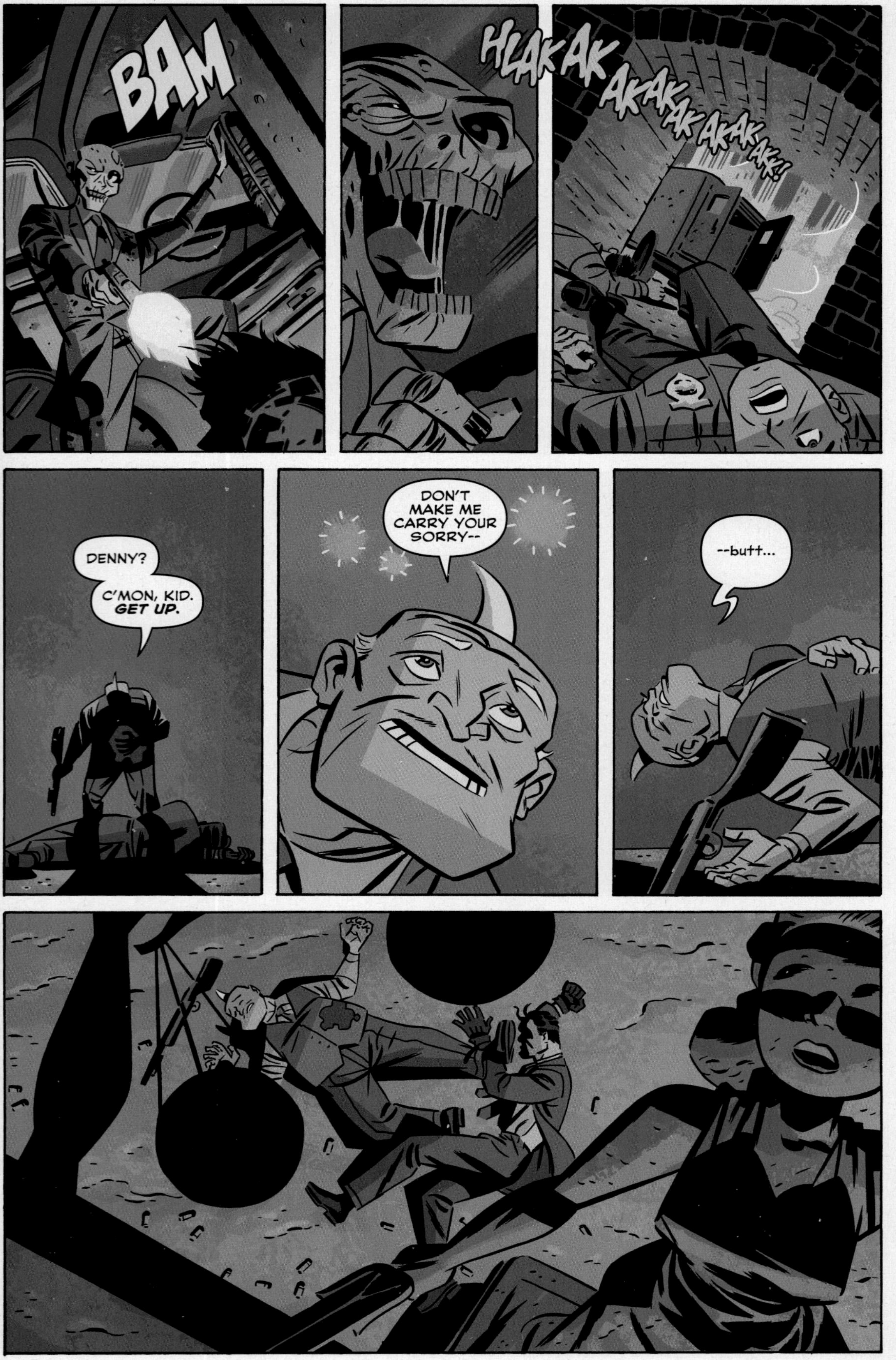
BAM
HLAKAK AKAKAK AKAKAKAK!
DENNY?
C'MON, KID. GET UP.
DON'T MAKE ME CARRY YOUR SORRY--
--butt...

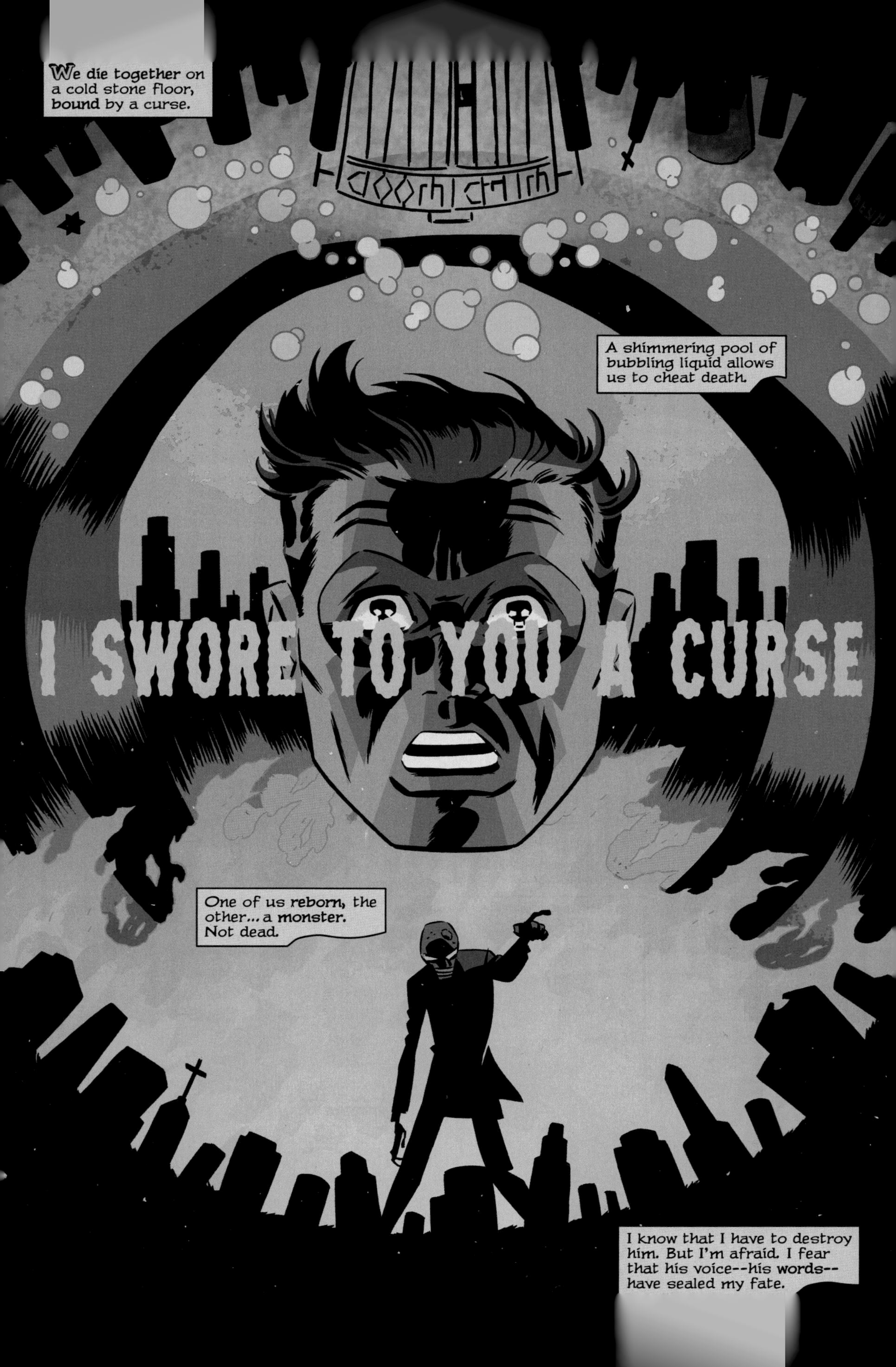
We die together on a cold stone floor, bound by a curse.
A shimmering pool of bubbling liquid allows us to cheat death.
I SWORE TO YOU A CURSE
One of us reborn, the other... a monster. Not dead.
I know that I have to destroy him. But I'm afraid. I fear that his voice--his words--have sealed my fate.

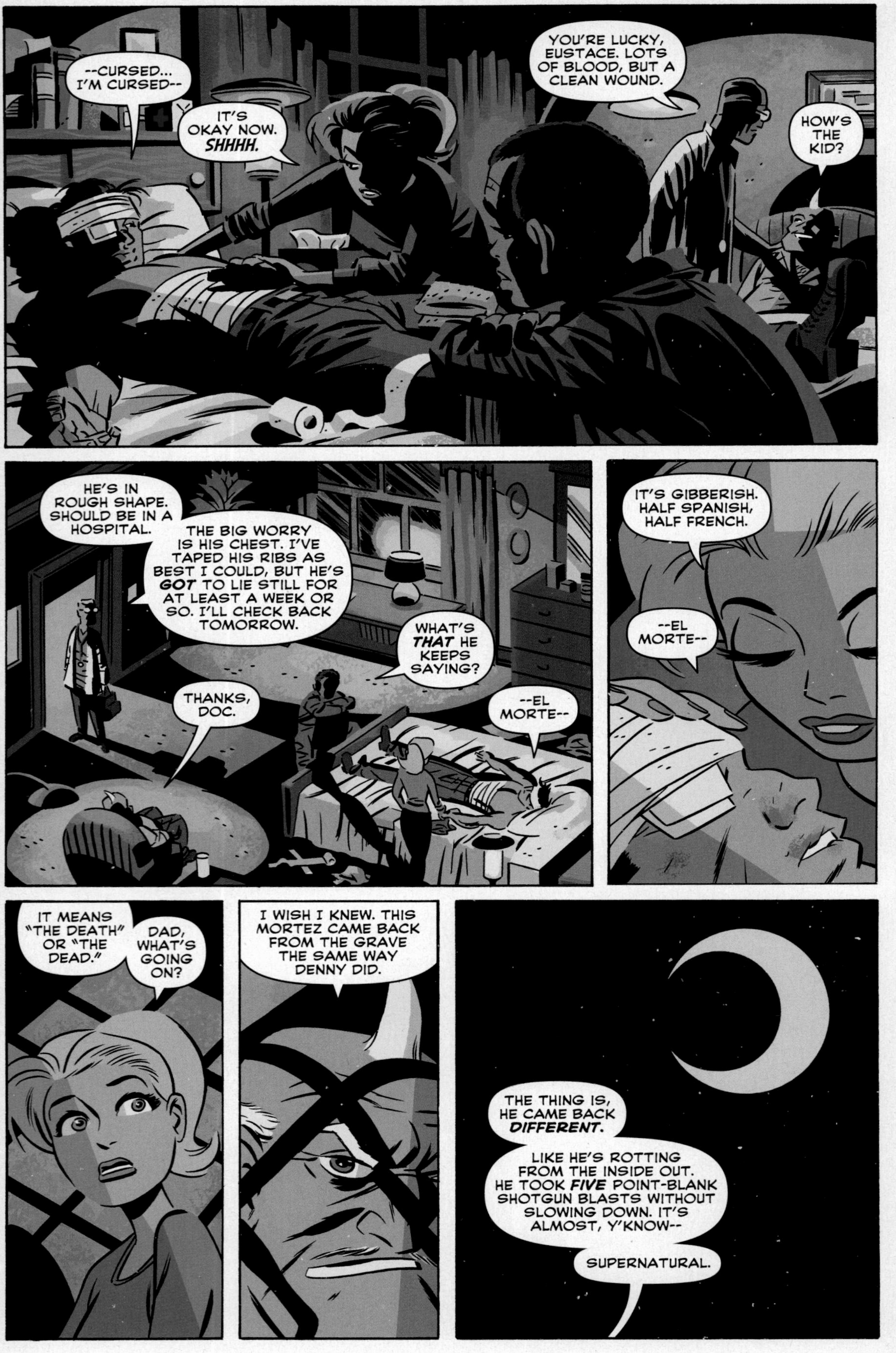
--CURSED... I'M CURSED--
IT'S OKAY NOW. SHHHH.
YOU'RE LUCKY, EUSTACE. LOTS OF BLOOD, BUT A CLEAN WOUND.
HOW'S THE KID?
HE'S IN ROUGH SHAPE. SHOULD BE IN A HOSPITAL.
THE BIG WORRY IS HIS CHEST. I'VE TAPED HIS RIBS AS BEST I COULD, BUT HE'S GOT TO LIE STILL FOR AT LEAST A WEEK OR SO. I'LL CHECK BACK TOMORROW.
THANKS, DOC.
WHAT'S THAT HE KEEPS SAYING?
--EL MORTE--
IT'S GIBBERISH. HALF SPANISH, HALF FRENCH.
--EL MORTE--
IT MEANS "THE DEATH" OR "THE DEAD."
DAD, WHAT'S GOING ON?
I WISH I KNEW. THIS MORTEZ CAME BACK FROM THE GRAVE THE SAME WAY DENNY DID.
THE THING IS, HE CAME BACK DIFFERENT.
LIKE HE'S ROTTING FROM THE INSIDE OUT. HE TOOK FIVE POINT-BLANK SHOTGUN BLASTS WITHOUT SLOWING DOWN. IT'S ALMOST, Y'KNOW--
SUPERNATURAL.

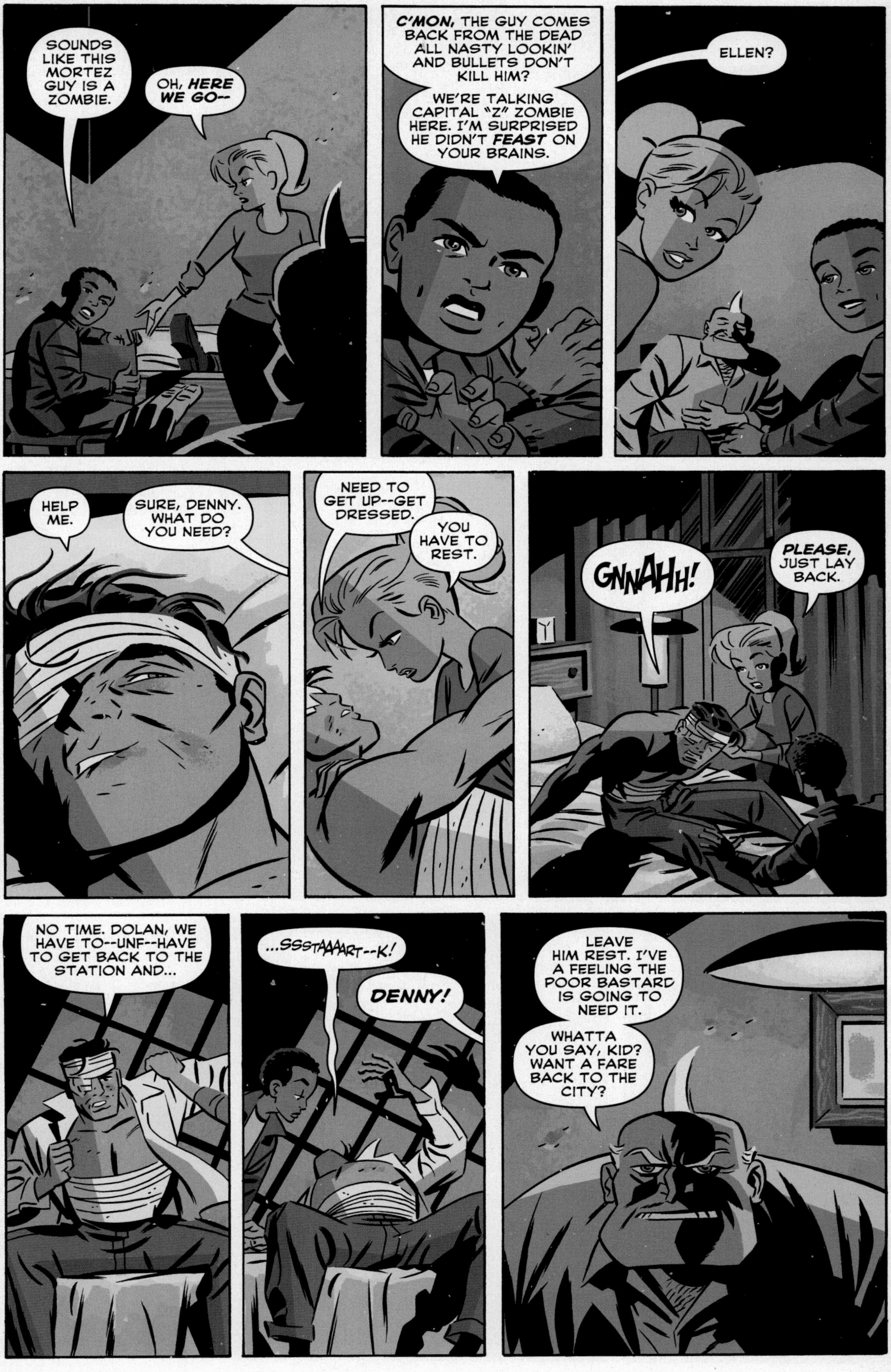
SOUNDS LIKE THIS MORTEZ GUY IS A ZOMBIE.
OH, **HERE WE GO--**
C'MON, THE GUY COMES BACK FROM THE DEAD ALL NASTY LOOKIN' AND BULLETS DON'T KILL HIM?
WE'RE TALKING CAPITAL "Z" ZOMBIE HERE. I'M SURPRISED HE DIDN'T **FEAST** ON YOUR BRAINS.
ELLEN?
HELP ME.
SURE, DENNY. WHAT DO YOU NEED?
NEED TO GET UP--GET DRESSED.
YOU HAVE TO REST.
GNNAHH!
PLEASE, JUST LAY BACK.
NO TIME. DOLAN, WE HAVE TO--UNF--HAVE TO GET BACK TO THE STATION AND...
...SSSTAAAART--K!
DENNY!
LEAVE HIM REST. I'VE A FEELING THE POOR BASTARD IS GOING TO NEED IT.
WHATTA YOU SAY, KID? WANT A FARE BACK TO THE CITY?

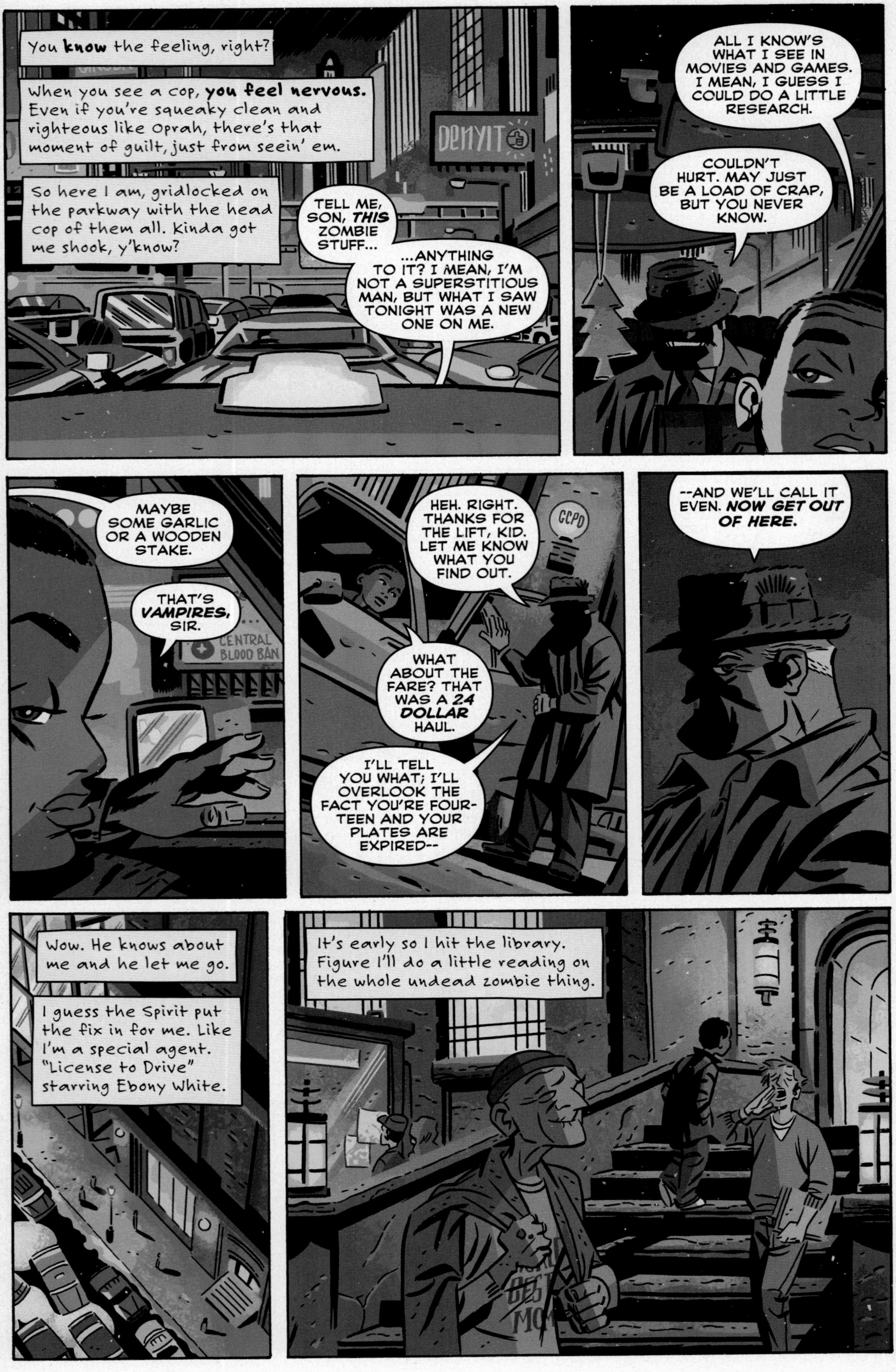
You **know** the feeling, right?
When you see a cop, **you feel nervous.** Even if you're squeaky clean and righteous like Oprah, there's that moment of guilt, just from seein' em.
So here I am, gridlocked on the parkway with the head cop of them all. Kinda got me shook, y'know?
DENYIT
TELL ME, SON, ***THIS*** ZOMBIE STUFF...
...ANYTHING TO IT? I MEAN, I'M NOT A SUPERSTITIOUS MAN, BUT WHAT I SAW TONIGHT WAS A NEW ONE ON ME.
ALL I KNOW'S WHAT I SEE IN MOVIES AND GAMES. I MEAN, I GUESS I COULD DO A LITTLE RESEARCH.
COULDN'T HURT. MAY JUST BE A LOAD OF CRAP, BUT YOU NEVER KNOW.
MAYBE SOME GARLIC OR A WOODEN STAKE.
THAT'S ***VAMPIRES,*** SIR.
CENTRAL BLOOD BAN
HEH. RIGHT. THANKS FOR THE LIFT, KID. LET ME KNOW WHAT YOU FIND OUT.
CCPD
WHAT ABOUT THE FARE? THAT WAS A ***24 DOLLAR*** HAUL.
I'LL TELL YOU WHAT; I'LL OVERLOOK THE FACT YOU'RE FOURTEEN AND YOUR PLATES ARE EXPIRED--
--AND WE'LL CALL IT EVEN. ***NOW GET OUT OF HERE.***
Wow. He knows about me and he let me go.
I guess the Spirit put the fix in for me. Like I'm a special agent. "License to Drive" starring Ebony White.
It's early so I hit the library. Figure I'll do a little reading on the whole undead zombie thing.

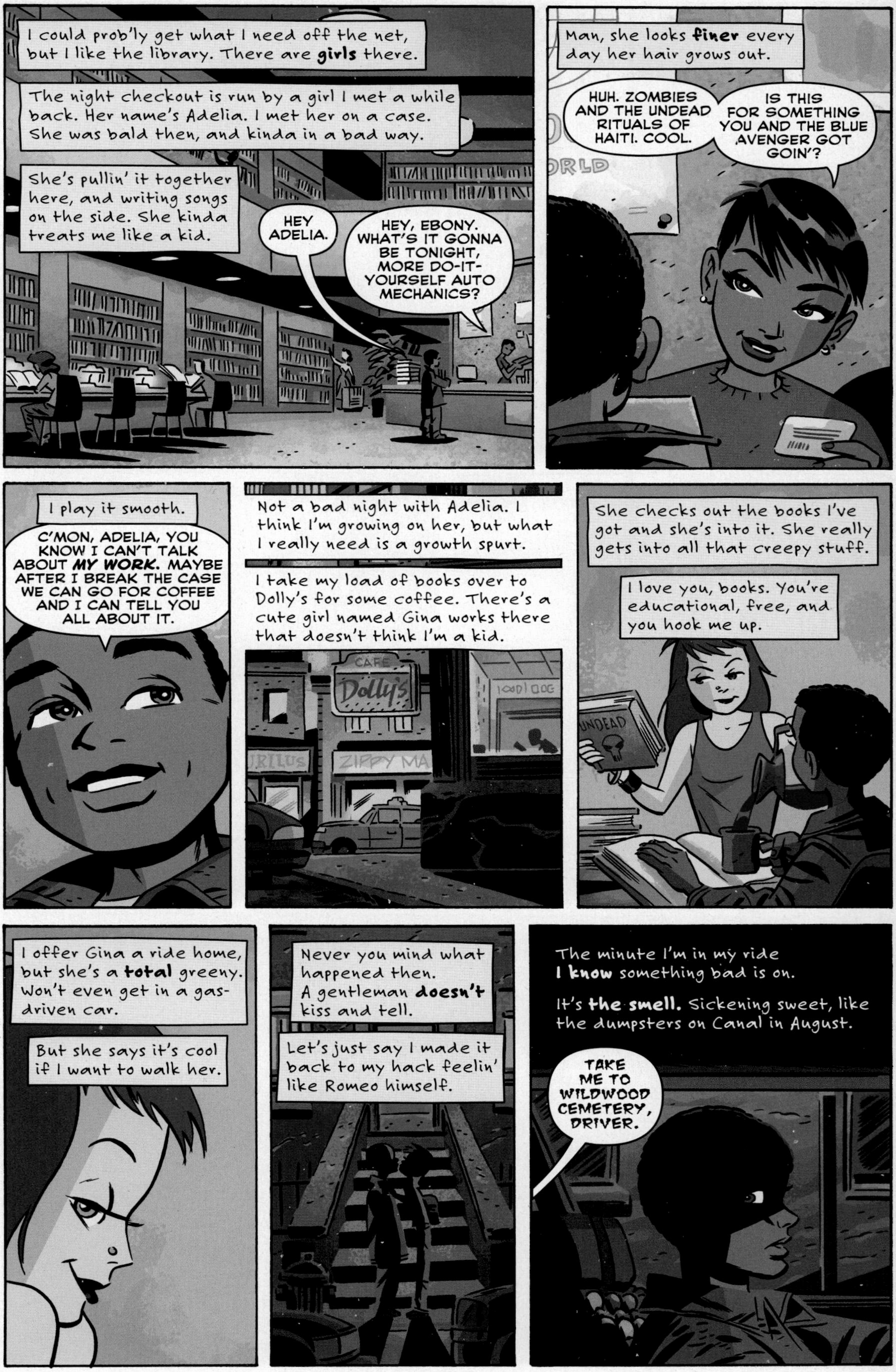
I could prob'ly get what I need off the net, but I like the library. There are **girls** there.
The night checkout is run by a girl I met a while back. Her name's Adelia. I met her on a case. She was bald then, and kinda in a bad way.
She's pullin' it together here, and writing songs on the side. She kinda treats me like a kid.
HEY ADELIA.
HEY, EBONY. WHAT'S IT GONNA BE TONIGHT, MORE DO-IT-YOURSELF AUTO MECHANICS?
Man, she looks **finer** every day her hair grows out.
HUH. ZOMBIES AND THE UNDEAD RITUALS OF HAITI. COOL.
IS THIS FOR SOMETHING YOU AND THE BLUE AVENGER GOT GOIN'?
I play it smooth.
C'MON, ADELIA, YOU KNOW I CAN'T TALK ABOUT ***MY WORK.*** MAYBE AFTER I BREAK THE CASE WE CAN GO FOR COFFEE AND I CAN TELL YOU ALL ABOUT IT.
Not a bad night with Adelia. I think I'm growing on her, but what I really need is a growth spurt.
I take my load of books over to Dolly's for some coffee. There's a cute girl named Gina works there that doesn't think I'm a kid.
CAFE
Dolly's
She checks out the books I've got and she's into it. She really gets into all that creepy stuff.
I love you, books. You're educational, free, and you hook me up.
UNDEAD
I offer Gina a ride home, but she's a **total** greeny. Won't even get in a gas-driven car.
But she says it's cool if I want to walk her.
Never you mind what happened then. A gentleman **doesn't** kiss and tell.
Let's just say I made it back to my hack feelin' like Romeo himself.
The minute I'm in my ride **I know** something bad is on.
It's **the smell.** Sickening sweet, like the dumpsters on Canal in August.
TAKE ME TO WILDWOOD CEMETERY, DRIVER.

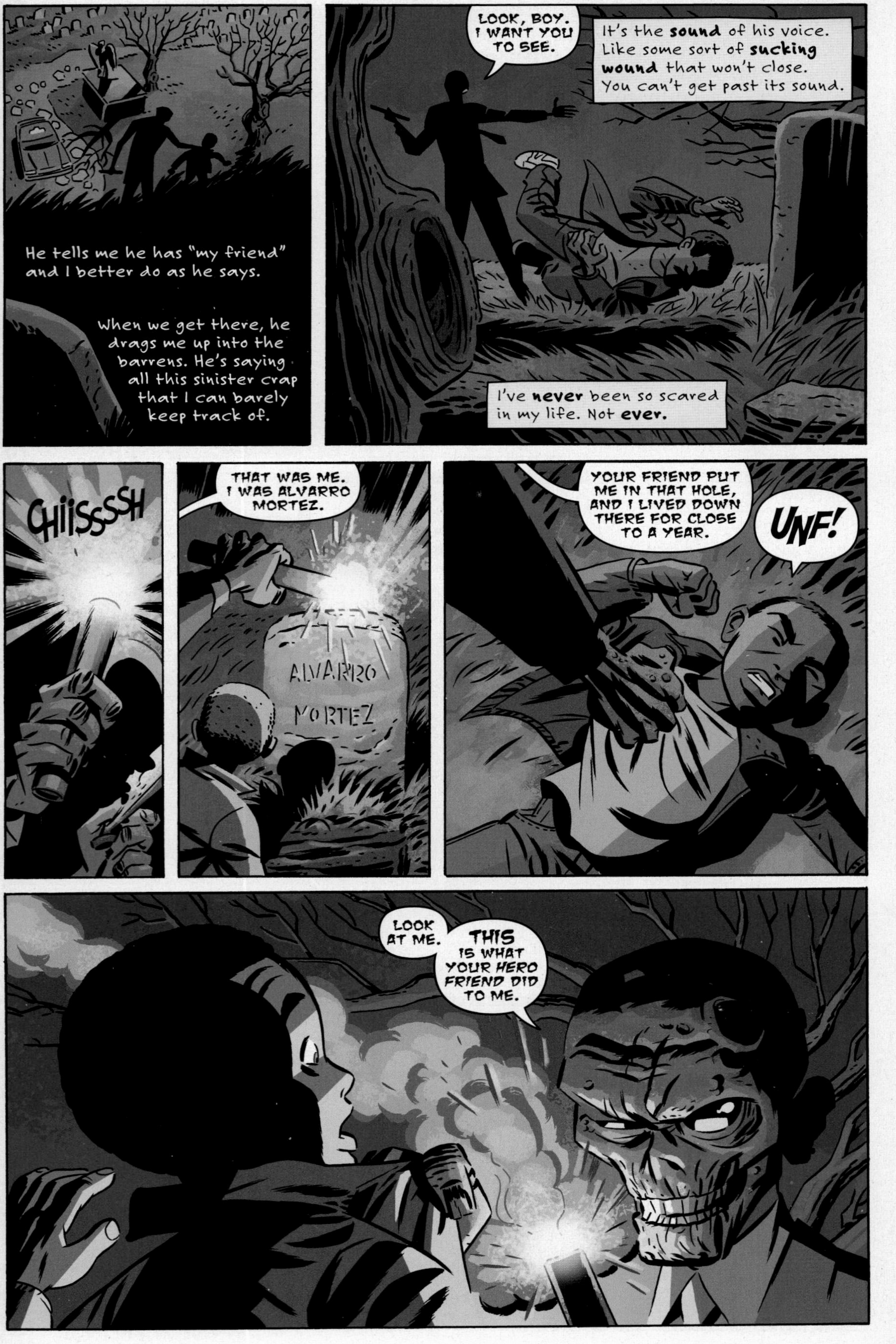
He tells me he has "my friend" and I better do as he says.
When we get there, he drags me up into the barrens. He's saying all this sinister crap that I can barely keep track of.
LOOK, BOY. I WANT YOU TO SEE.
It's the **sound** of his voice. Like some sort of **sucking wound** that won't close. You can't get past its sound.
I've **never** been so scared in my life. Not **ever**.
CHIISSSSH
THAT WAS ME. I WAS ALVARRO MORTEZ.
ALVARRO
MORTEZ
YOUR FRIEND PUT ME IN THAT HOLE, AND I LIVED DOWN THERE FOR CLOSE TO A YEAR.
UNF!
LOOK AT ME.
THIS IS WHAT YOUR HERO FRIEND DID TO ME.

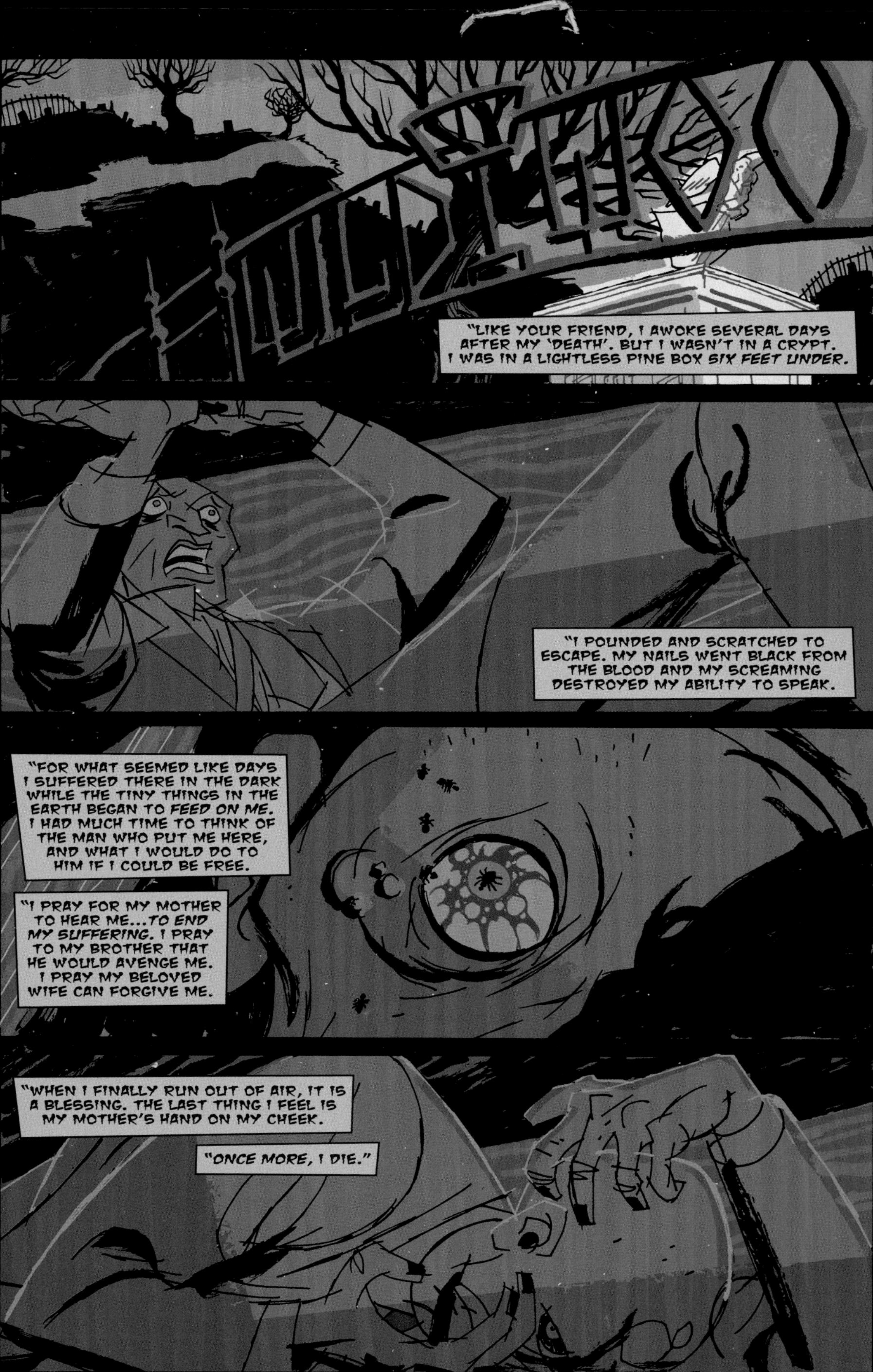
"LIKE YOUR FRIEND, I AWOKE SEVERAL DAYS AFTER MY 'DEATH'. BUT I WASN'T IN A CRYPT. I WAS IN A LIGHTLESS PINE BOX SIX FEET UNDER.
"I POUNDED AND SCRATCHED TO ESCAPE. MY NAILS WENT BLACK FROM THE BLOOD AND MY SCREAMING DESTROYED MY ABILITY TO SPEAK.
"FOR WHAT SEEMED LIKE DAYS I SUFFERED THERE IN THE DARK WHILE THE TINY THINGS IN THE EARTH BEGAN TO FEED ON ME. I HAD MUCH TIME TO THINK OF THE MAN WHO PUT ME HERE, AND WHAT I WOULD DO TO HIM IF I COULD BE FREE.
"I PRAY FOR MY MOTHER TO HEAR ME...TO END MY SUFFERING. I PRAY TO MY BROTHER THAT HE WOULD AVENGE ME. I PRAY MY BELOVED WIFE CAN FORGIVE ME.
"WHEN I FINALLY RUN OUT OF AIR, IT IS A BLESSING. THE LAST THING I FEEL IS MY MOTHER'S HAND ON MY CHEEK.
"ONCE MORE, I DIE."

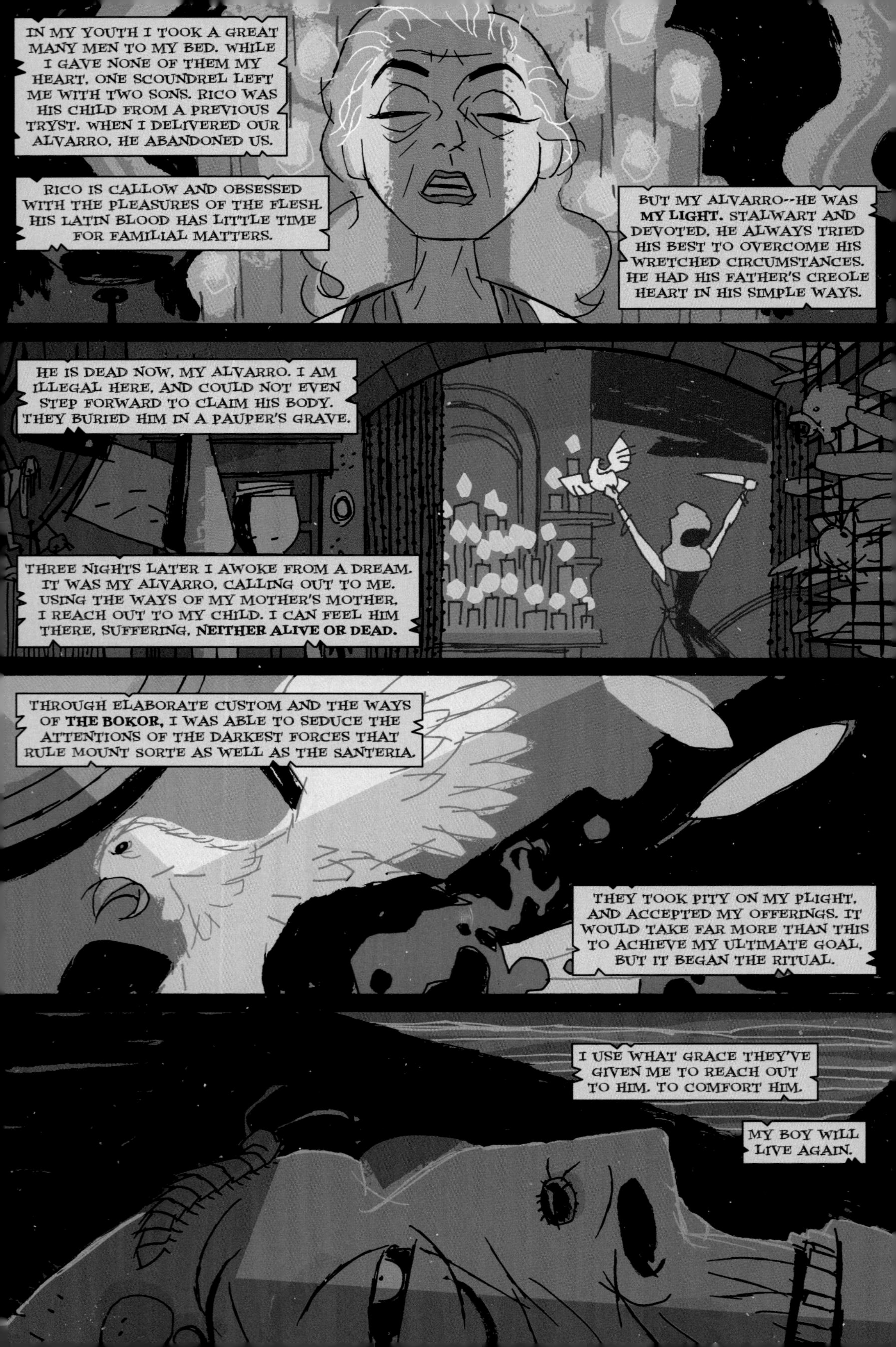
IN MY YOUTH I TOOK A GREAT MANY MEN TO MY BED. WHILE I GAVE NONE OF THEM MY HEART, ONE SCOUNDREL LEFT ME WITH TWO SONS. RICO WAS HIS CHILD FROM A PREVIOUS TRYST. WHEN I DELIVERED OUR ALVARRO, HE ABANDONED US.
RICO IS CALLOW AND OBSESSED WITH THE PLEASURES OF THE FLESH. HIS LATIN BLOOD HAS LITTLE TIME FOR FAMILIAL MATTERS.
BUT MY ALVARRO--HE WAS **MY LIGHT.** STALWART AND DEVOTED, HE ALWAYS TRIED HIS BEST TO OVERCOME HIS WRETCHED CIRCUMSTANCES. HE HAD HIS FATHER'S CREOLE HEART IN HIS SIMPLE WAYS.
HE IS DEAD NOW, MY ALVARRO. I AM ILLEGAL HERE, AND COULD NOT EVEN STEP FORWARD TO CLAIM HIS BODY. THEY BURIED HIM IN A PAUPER'S GRAVE.
THREE NIGHTS LATER I AWOKE FROM A DREAM. IT WAS MY ALVARRO, CALLING OUT TO ME. USING THE WAYS OF MY MOTHER'S MOTHER, I REACH OUT TO MY CHILD. I CAN FEEL HIM THERE, SUFFERING, **NEITHER ALIVE OR DEAD.**
THROUGH ELABORATE CUSTOM AND THE WAYS OF **THE BOKOR,** I WAS ABLE TO SEDUCE THE ATTENTIONS OF THE DARKEST FORCES THAT RULE MOUNT SORTE AS WELL AS THE SANTERIA.
THEY TOOK PITY ON MY PLIGHT, AND ACCEPTED MY OFFERINGS. IT WOULD TAKE FAR MORE THAN THIS TO ACHIEVE MY ULTIMATE GOAL, BUT IT BEGAN THE RITUAL.
I USE WHAT GRACE THEY'VE GIVEN ME TO REACH OUT TO HIM. TO COMFORT HIM.
MY BOY WILL LIVE AGAIN.

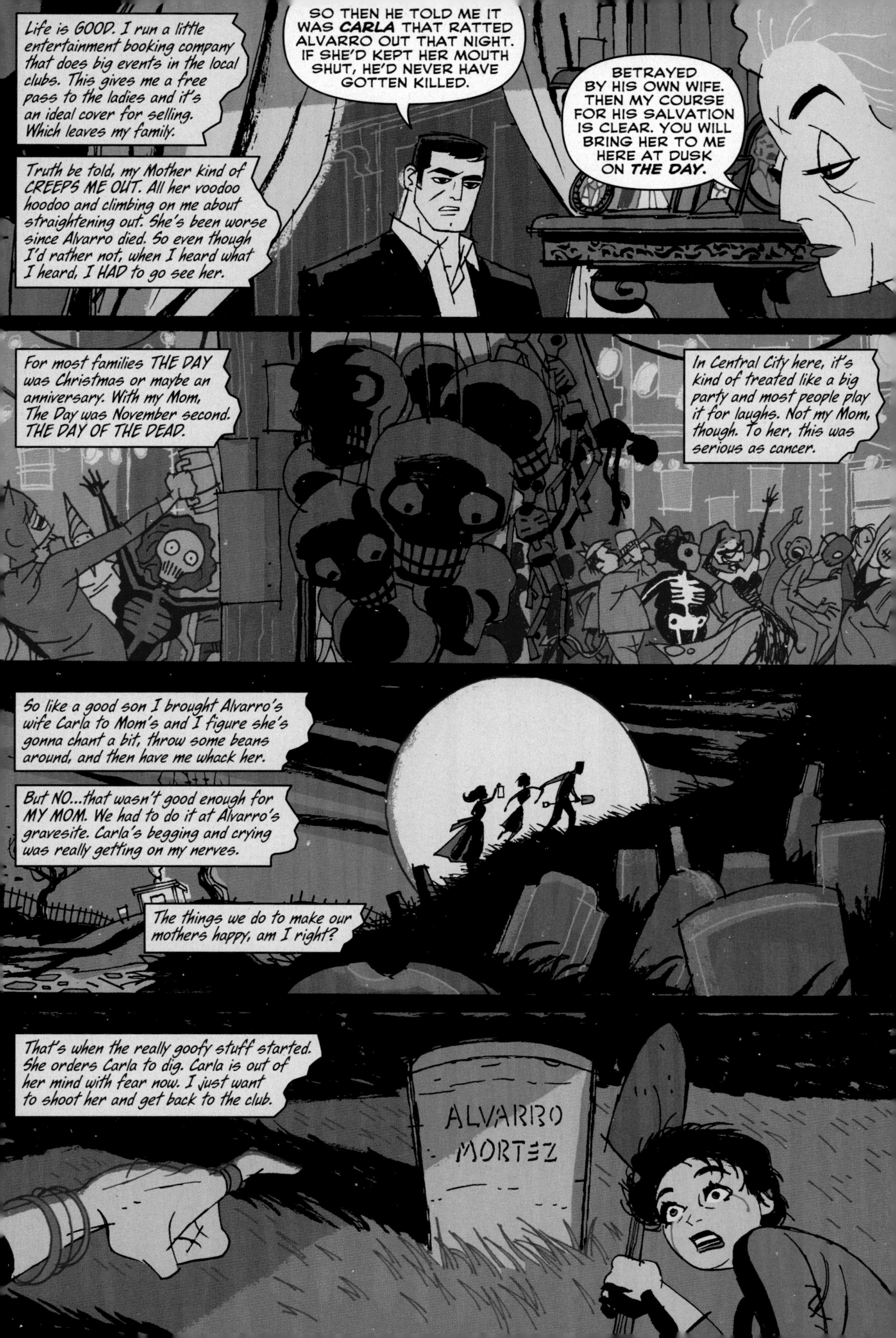
Life is GOOD. I run a little entertainment booking company that does big events in the local clubs. This gives me a free pass to the ladies and it's an ideal cover for selling. Which leaves my family.
Truth be told, my Mother kind of CREEPS ME OUT. All her voodoo hoodoo and climbing on me about straightening out. She's been worse since Alvarro died. So even though I'd rather not, when I heard what I heard, I HAD to go see her.
SO THEN HE TOLD ME IT WAS CARLA THAT RATTED ALVARRO OUT THAT NIGHT. IF SHE'D KEPT HER MOUTH SHUT, HE'D NEVER HAVE GOTTEN KILLED.
BETRAYED BY HIS OWN WIFE. THEN MY COURSE FOR HIS SALVATION IS CLEAR. YOU WILL BRING HER TO ME HERE AT DUSK ON THE DAY.
For most families THE DAY was Christmas or maybe an anniversary. With my Mom, The Day was November second. THE DAY OF THE DEAD.
In Central City here, it's kind of treated like a big party and most people play it for laughs. Not my Mom, though. To her, this was serious as cancer.
So like a good son I brought Alvarro's wife Carla to Mom's and I figure she's gonna chant a bit, throw some beans around, and then have me whack her.
But NO...that wasn't good enough for MY MOM. We had to do it at Alvarro's gravesite. Carla's begging and crying was really getting on my nerves.
The things we do to make our mothers happy, am I right?
That's when the really goofy stuff started. She orders Carla to dig. Carla is out of her mind with fear now. I just want to shoot her and get back to the club.
ALVARRO MORTEZ

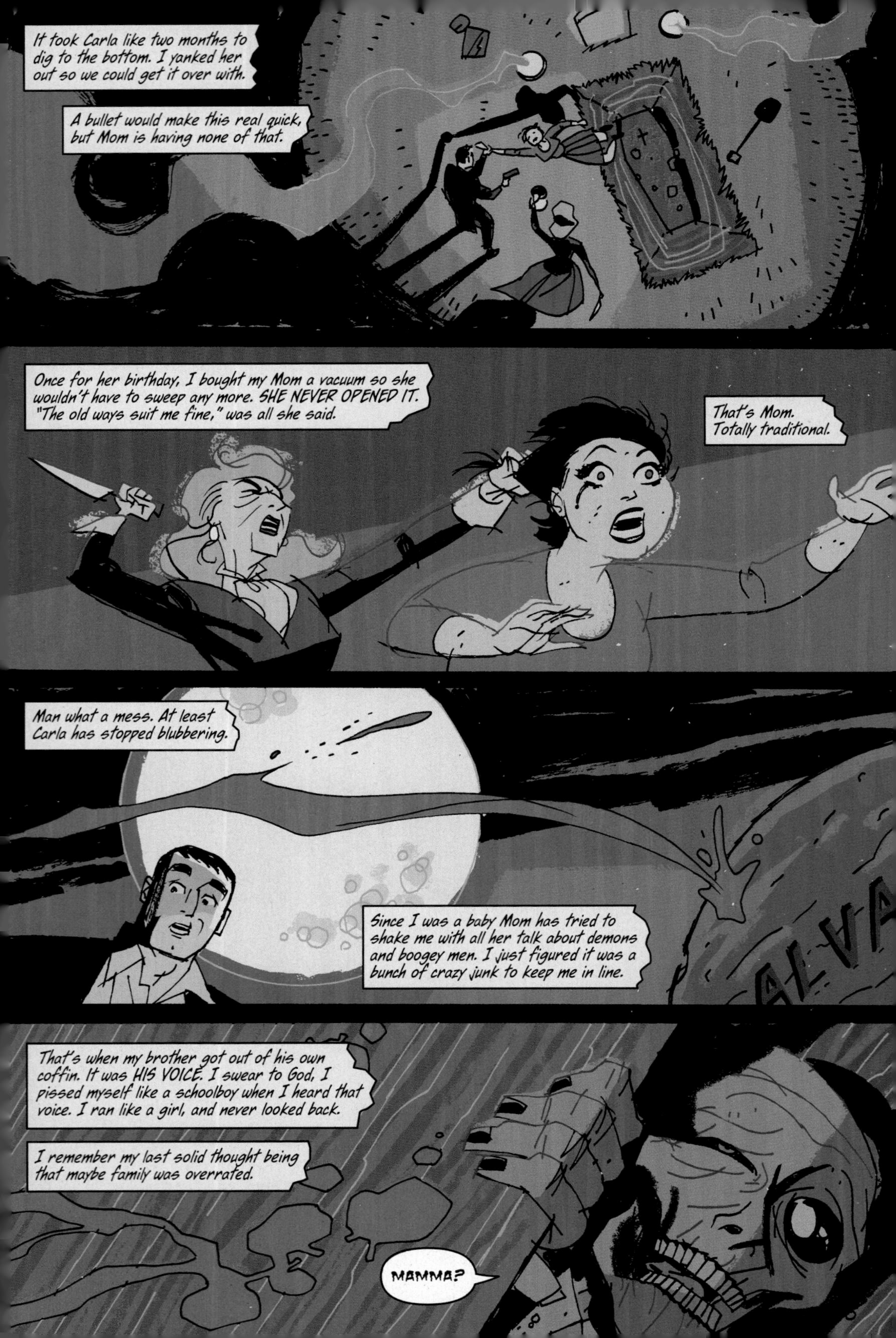

It took Carla like two months to dig to the bottom. I yanked her out so we could get it over with.
A bullet would make this real quick, but Mom is having none of that.
Once for her birthday, I bought my Mom a vacuum so she wouldn't have to sweep any more. SHE NEVER OPENED IT. "The old ways suit me fine," was all she said.
That's Mom. Totally traditional.
Man what a mess. At least Carla has stopped blubbering.
Since I was a baby Mom has tried to shake me with all her talk about demons and boogey men. I just figured it was a bunch of crazy junk to keep me in line.
That's when my brother got out of his own coffin. It was HIS VOICE. I swear to God, I pissed myself like a schoolboy when I heard that voice. I ran like a girl, and never looked back.
I remember my last solid thought being that maybe family was overrated.
MAMMA?

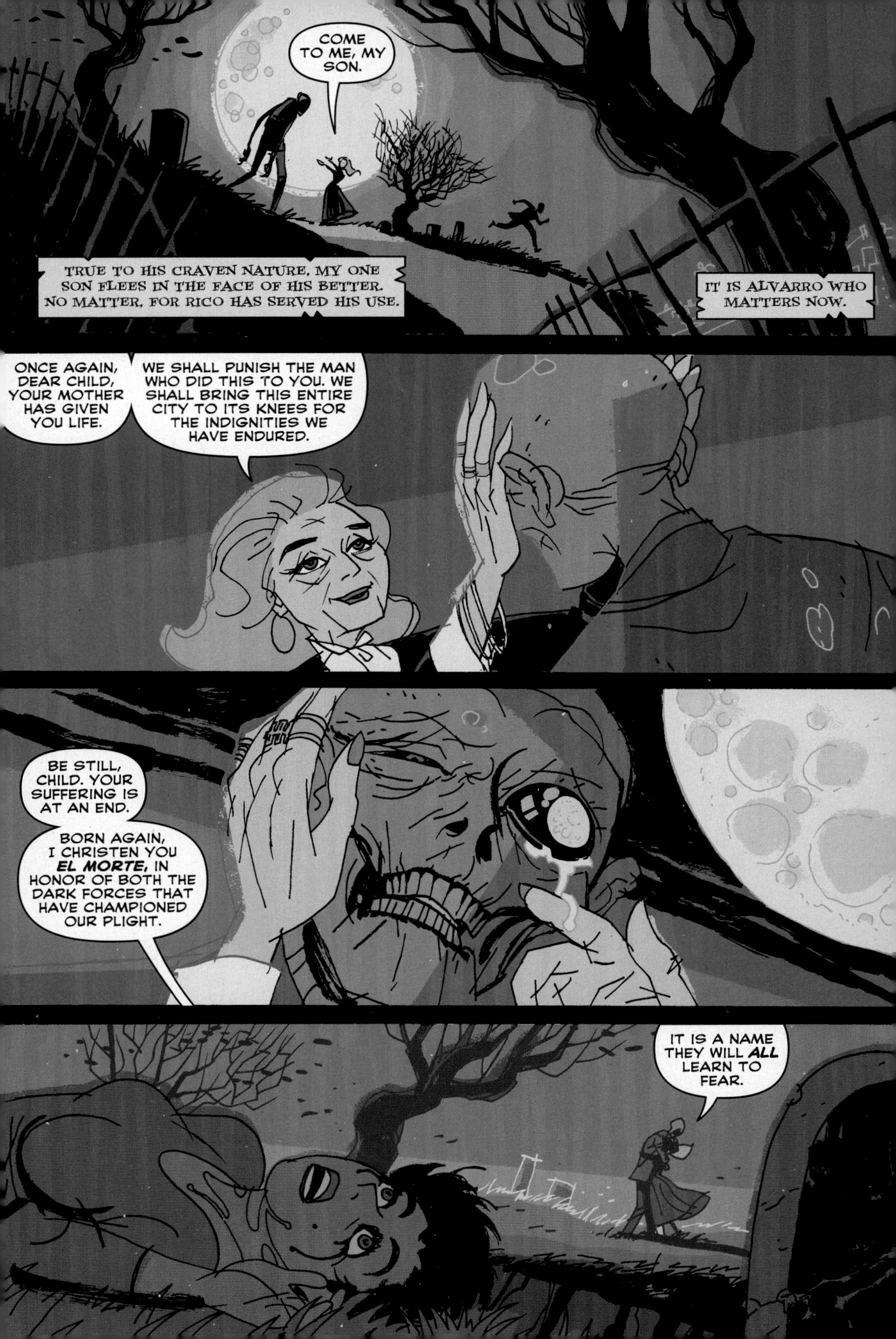
COME TO ME, MY SON.
TRUE TO HIS CRAVEN NATURE, MY ONE SON FLEES IN THE FACE OF HIS BETTER. NO MATTER, FOR RICO HAS SERVED HIS USE.
IT IS ALVARRO WHO MATTERS NOW.
ONCE AGAIN, DEAR CHILD, YOUR MOTHER HAS GIVEN YOU LIFE.
WE SHALL PUNISH THE MAN WHO DID THIS TO YOU. WE SHALL BRING THIS ENTIRE CITY TO ITS KNEES FOR THE INDIGNITIES WE HAVE ENDURED.
BE STILL, CHILD. YOUR SUFFERING IS AT AN END.
BORN AGAIN, I CHRISTEN YOU EL MORTE, IN HONOR OF BOTH THE DARK FORCES THAT HAVE CHAMPIONED OUR PLIGHT.
IT IS A NAME THEY WILL ALL LEARN TO FEAR.

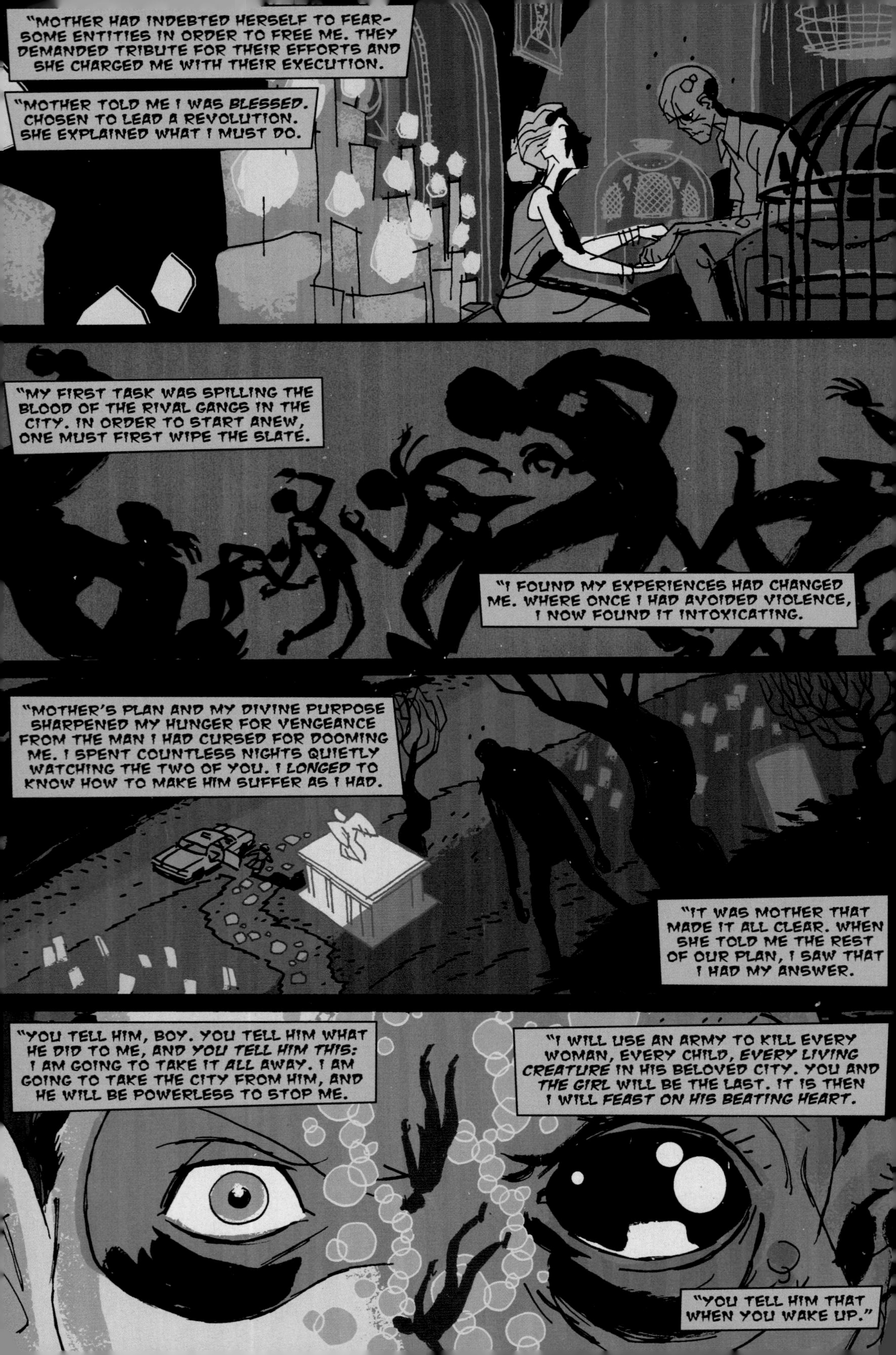
"MOTHER HAD INDEBTED HERSELF TO FEARSOME ENTITIES IN ORDER TO FREE ME. THEY DEMANDED TRIBUTE FOR THEIR EFFORTS AND SHE CHARGED ME WITH THEIR EXECUTION.
"MOTHER TOLD ME I WAS BLESSED. CHOSEN TO LEAD A REVOLUTION. SHE EXPLAINED WHAT I MUST DO.
"MY FIRST TASK WAS SPILLING THE BLOOD OF THE RIVAL GANGS IN THE CITY. IN ORDER TO START ANEW, ONE MUST FIRST WIPE THE SLATE.
"I FOUND MY EXPERIENCES HAD CHANGED ME. WHERE ONCE I HAD AVOIDED VIOLENCE, I NOW FOUND IT INTOXICATING.
"MOTHER'S PLAN AND MY DIVINE PURPOSE SHARPENED MY HUNGER FOR VENGEANCE FROM THE MAN I HAD CURSED FOR DOOMING ME. I SPENT COUNTLESS NIGHTS QUIETLY WATCHING THE TWO OF YOU. I LONGED TO KNOW HOW TO MAKE HIM SUFFER AS I HAD.
"IT WAS MOTHER THAT MADE IT ALL CLEAR. WHEN SHE TOLD ME THE REST OF OUR PLAN, I SAW THAT I HAD MY ANSWER.
"YOU TELL HIM, BOY. YOU TELL HIM WHAT HE DID TO ME, AND YOU TELL HIM THIS: I AM GOING TO TAKE IT ALL AWAY. I AM GOING TO TAKE THE CITY FROM HIM, AND HE WILL BE POWERLESS TO STOP ME.
"I WILL USE AN ARMY TO KILL EVERY WOMAN, EVERY CHILD, EVERY LIVING CREATURE IN HIS BELOVED CITY. YOU AND THE GIRL WILL BE THE LAST. IT IS THEN I WILL FEAST ON HIS BEATING HEART.
"YOU TELL HIM THAT WHEN YOU WAKE UP."

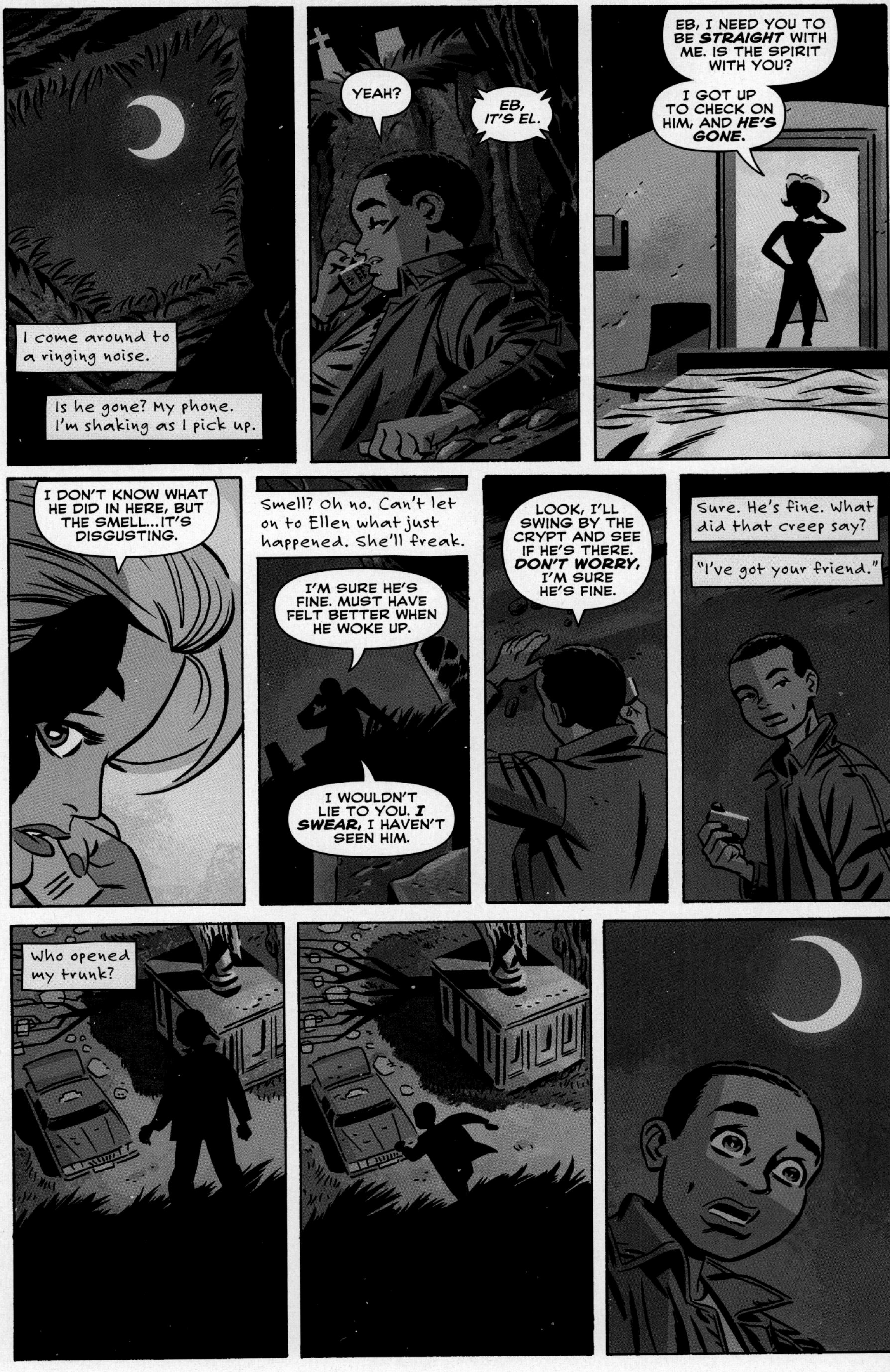
I come around to a ringing noise.
Is he gone? My phone. I'm shaking as I pick up.
YEAH?
EB, IT'S EL.
EB, I NEED YOU TO BE STRAIGHT WITH ME. IS THE SPIRIT WITH YOU?
I GOT UP TO CHECK ON HIM, AND HE'S GONE.
I DON'T KNOW WHAT HE DID IN HERE, BUT THE SMELL...IT'S DISGUSTING.
Smell? Oh no. Can't let on to Ellen what just happened. She'll freak.
I'M SURE HE'S FINE. MUST HAVE FELT BETTER WHEN HE WOKE UP.
I WOULDN'T LIE TO YOU. I SWEAR, I HAVEN'T SEEN HIM.
LOOK, I'LL SWING BY THE CRYPT AND SEE IF HE'S THERE. DON'T WORRY, I'M SURE HE'S FINE.
Sure. He's fine. What did that creep say?
"I've got your friend."
Who opened my trunk?

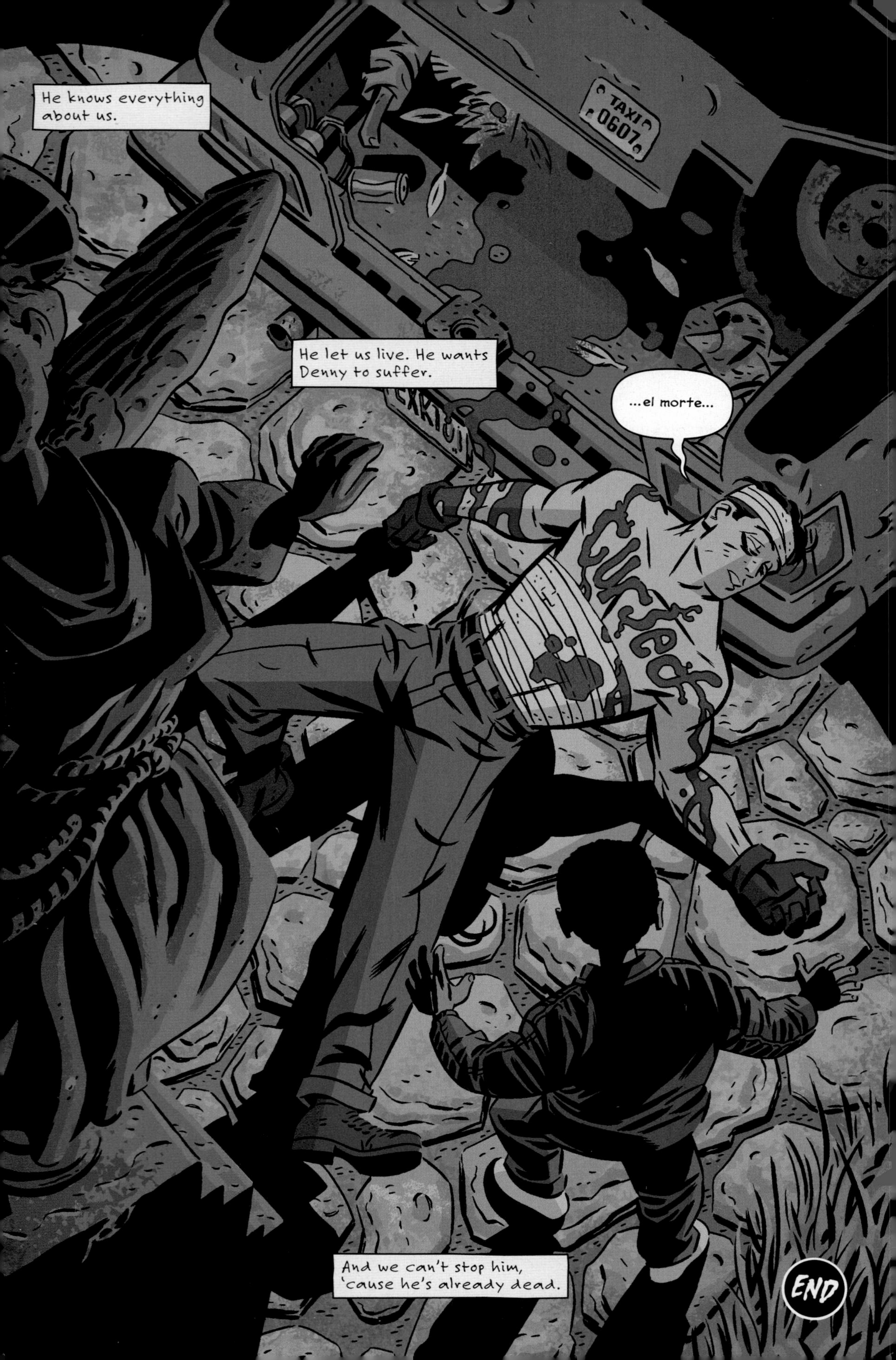
He knows everything about us.
TAXI 0607
He let us live. He wants Denny to suffer.
...el morte...
And we can't stop him, 'cause he's already dead.
END

4

ACTION • Mystery • ADVENTURE

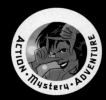

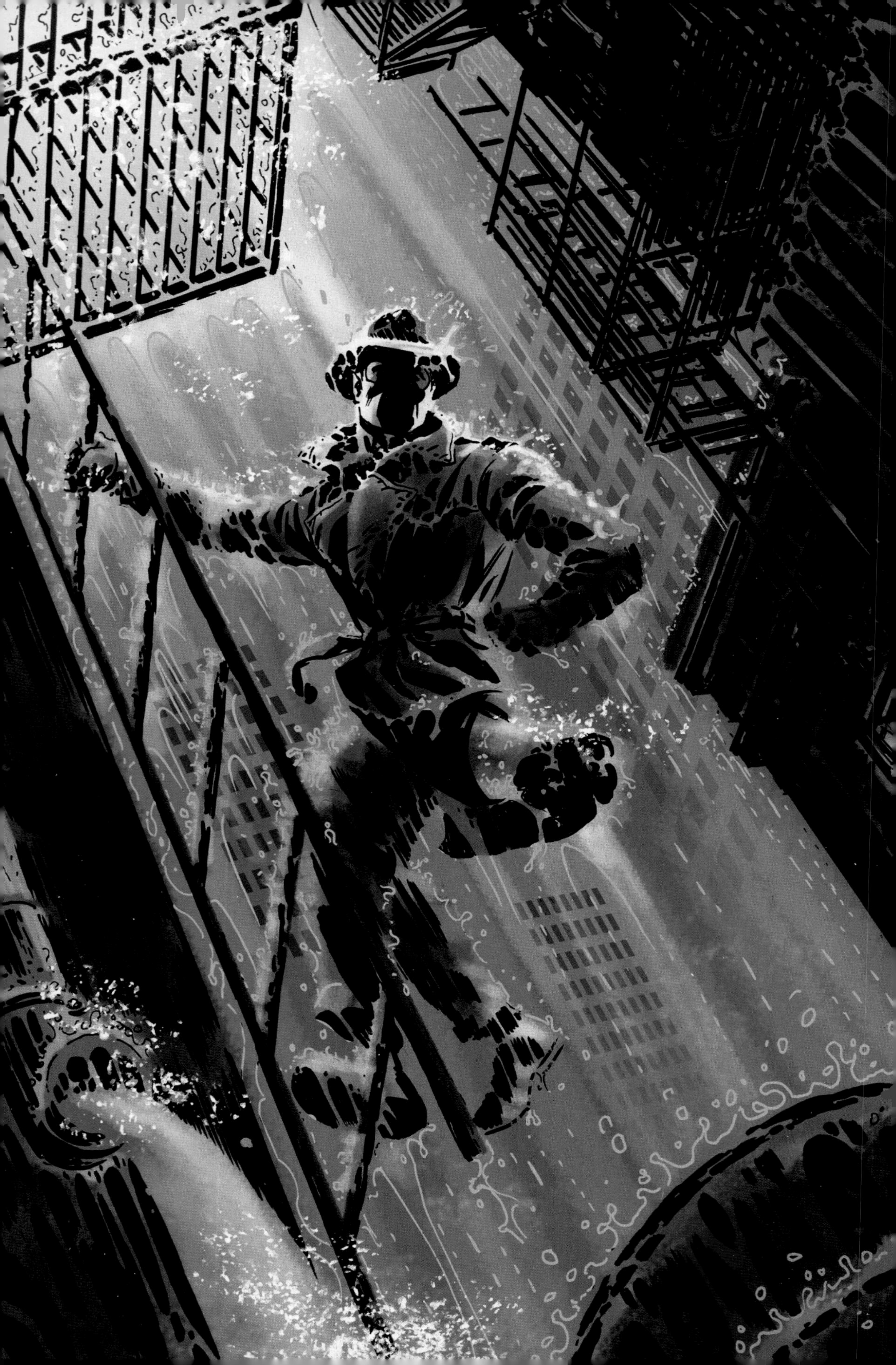

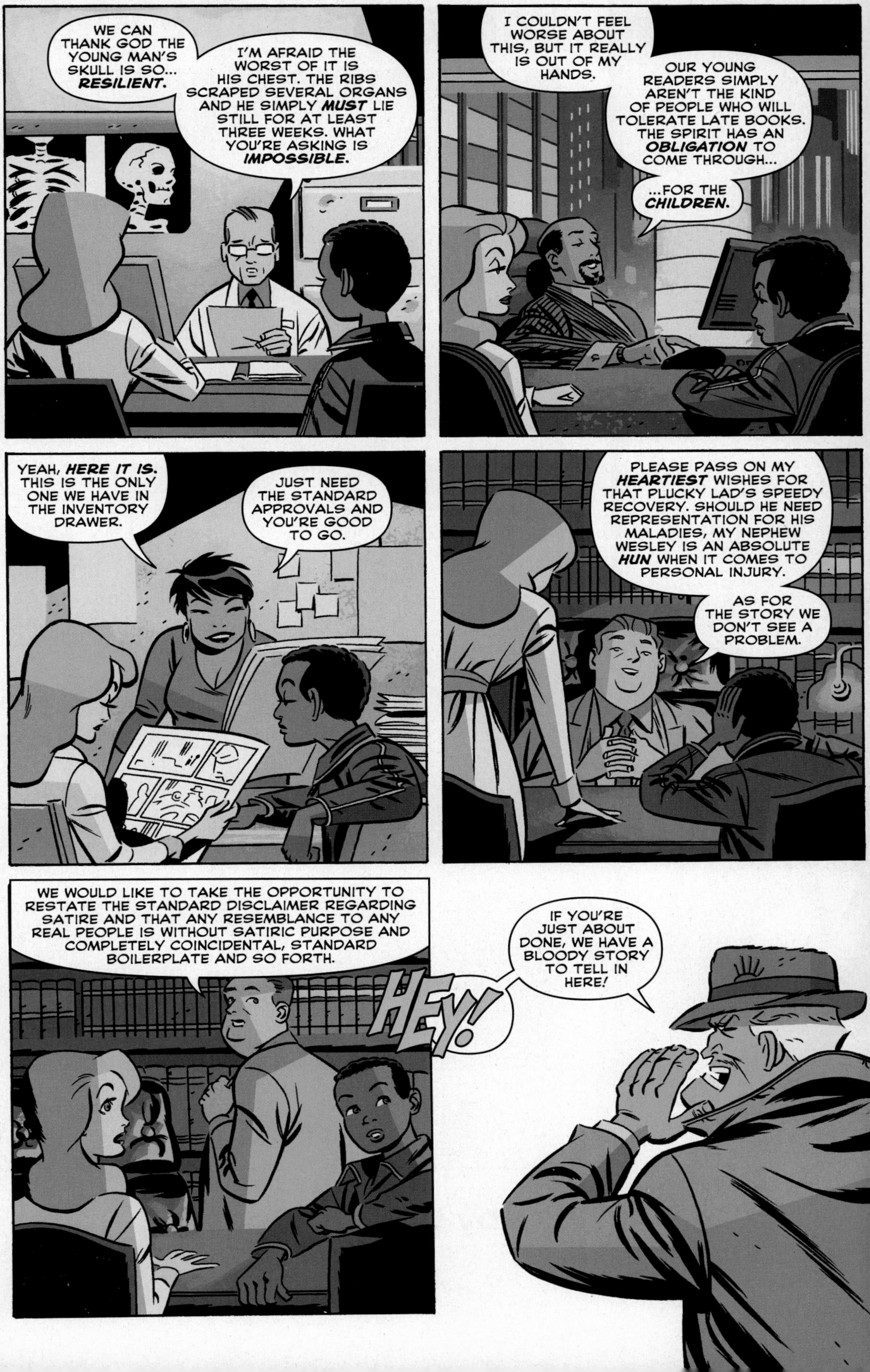
WE CAN THANK GOD THE YOUNG MAN'S SKULL IS SO... *RESILIENT*.
I'M AFRAID THE WORST OF IT IS HIS CHEST. THE RIBS SCRAPED SEVERAL ORGANS AND HE SIMPLY *MUST* LIE STILL FOR AT LEAST THREE WEEKS. WHAT YOU'RE ASKING IS *IMPOSSIBLE*.
I COULDN'T FEEL WORSE ABOUT THIS, BUT IT REALLY IS OUT OF MY HANDS.
OUR YOUNG READERS SIMPLY AREN'T THE KIND OF PEOPLE WHO WILL TOLERATE LATE BOOKS. THE SPIRIT HAS AN *OBLIGATION* TO COME THROUGH...
...FOR THE *CHILDREN*.
YEAH, *HERE IT IS*. THIS IS THE ONLY ONE WE HAVE IN THE INVENTORY DRAWER.
JUST NEED THE STANDARD APPROVALS AND YOU'RE GOOD TO GO.
PLEASE PASS ON MY *HEARTIEST* WISHES FOR THAT PLUCKY LAD'S SPEEDY RECOVERY. SHOULD HE NEED REPRESENTATION FOR HIS MALADIES, MY NEPHEW WESLEY IS AN ABSOLUTE *HUN* WHEN IT COMES TO PERSONAL INJURY.
AS FOR THE STORY WE DON'T SEE A PROBLEM.
WE WOULD LIKE TO TAKE THE OPPORTUNITY TO RESTATE THE STANDARD DISCLAIMER REGARDING SATIRE AND THAT ANY RESEMBLANCE TO ANY REAL PEOPLE IS WITHOUT SATIRIC PURPOSE AND COMPLETELY COINCIDENTAL, STANDARD BOILERPLATE AND SO FORTH.
HEY!
IF YOU'RE JUST ABOUT DONE, WE HAVE A BLOODY STORY TO TELL IN HERE!

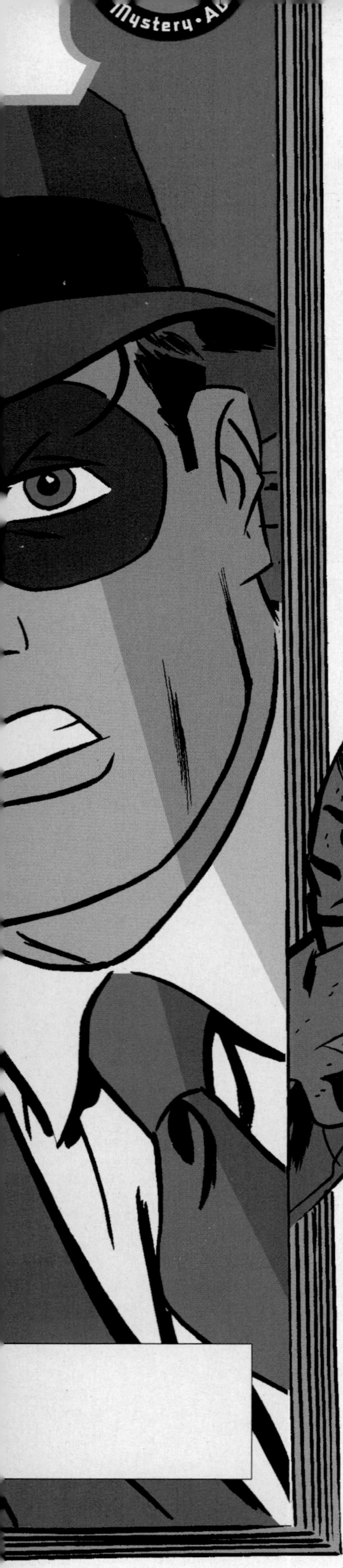

Will Eisner's THE SPIRIT:

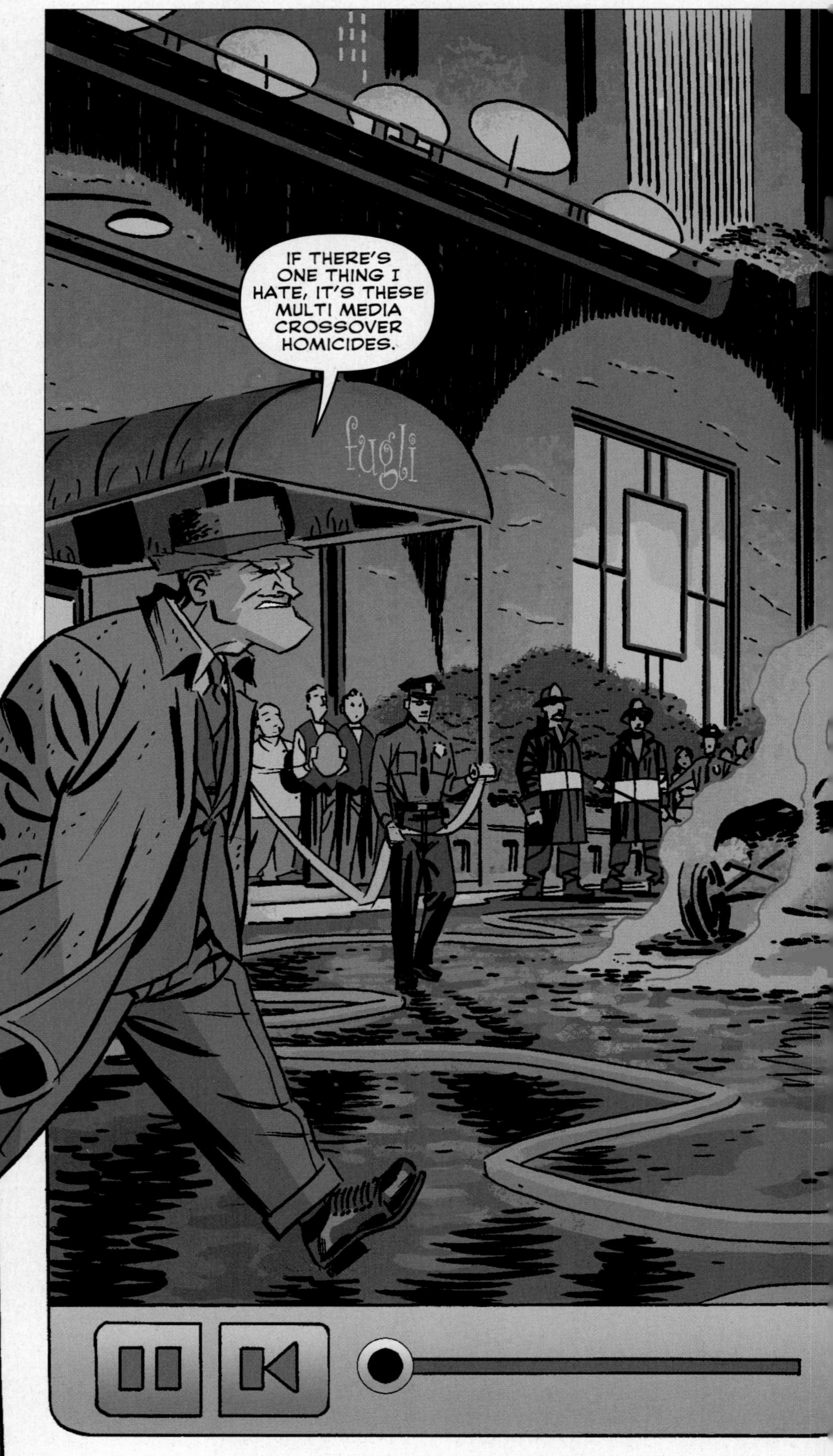

IF THERE'S ONE THING I HATE, IT'S THESE MULTI MEDIA CROSSOVER HOMICIDES.
fugli

by Darwyn Cooke

The Spirit created by Will Eisner

Death by Television

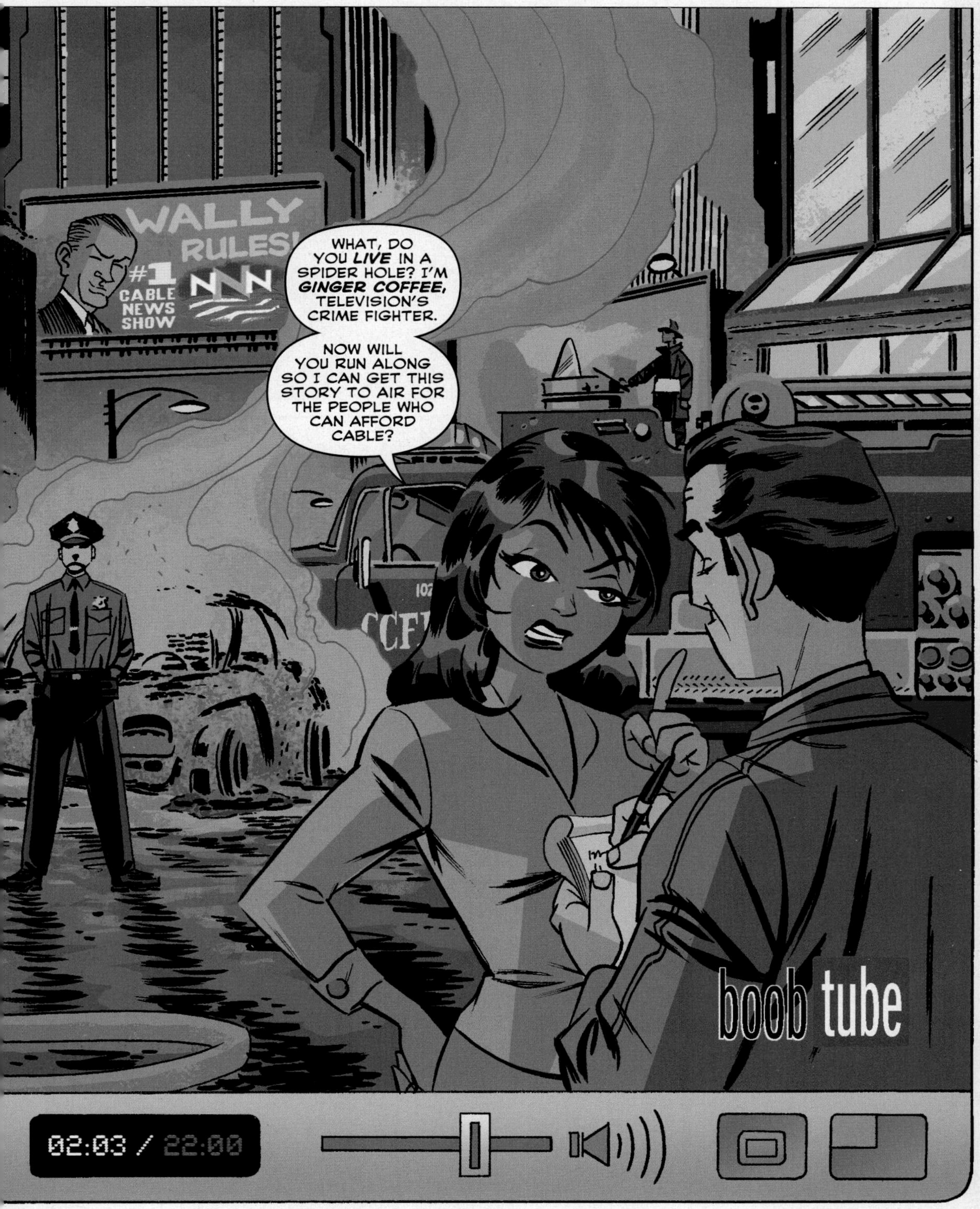
WALLY RULES!
#1 CABLE NEWS SHOW
NNN
WHAT, DO YOU *LIVE* IN A SPIDER HOLE? I'M ***GINGER COFFEE,*** TELEVISION'S CRIME FIGHTER.
NOW WILL YOU RUN ALONG SO I CAN GET THIS STORY TO AIR FOR THE PEOPLE WHO CAN AFFORD CABLE?
CCF
boob tube
02:03 / 22:00

J.Bone/Finishes

Jared Fletcher/Letters

Ben Abernathy Editor

Dave Stewart/Colors

Kristy Quinn/Ass't. Editor

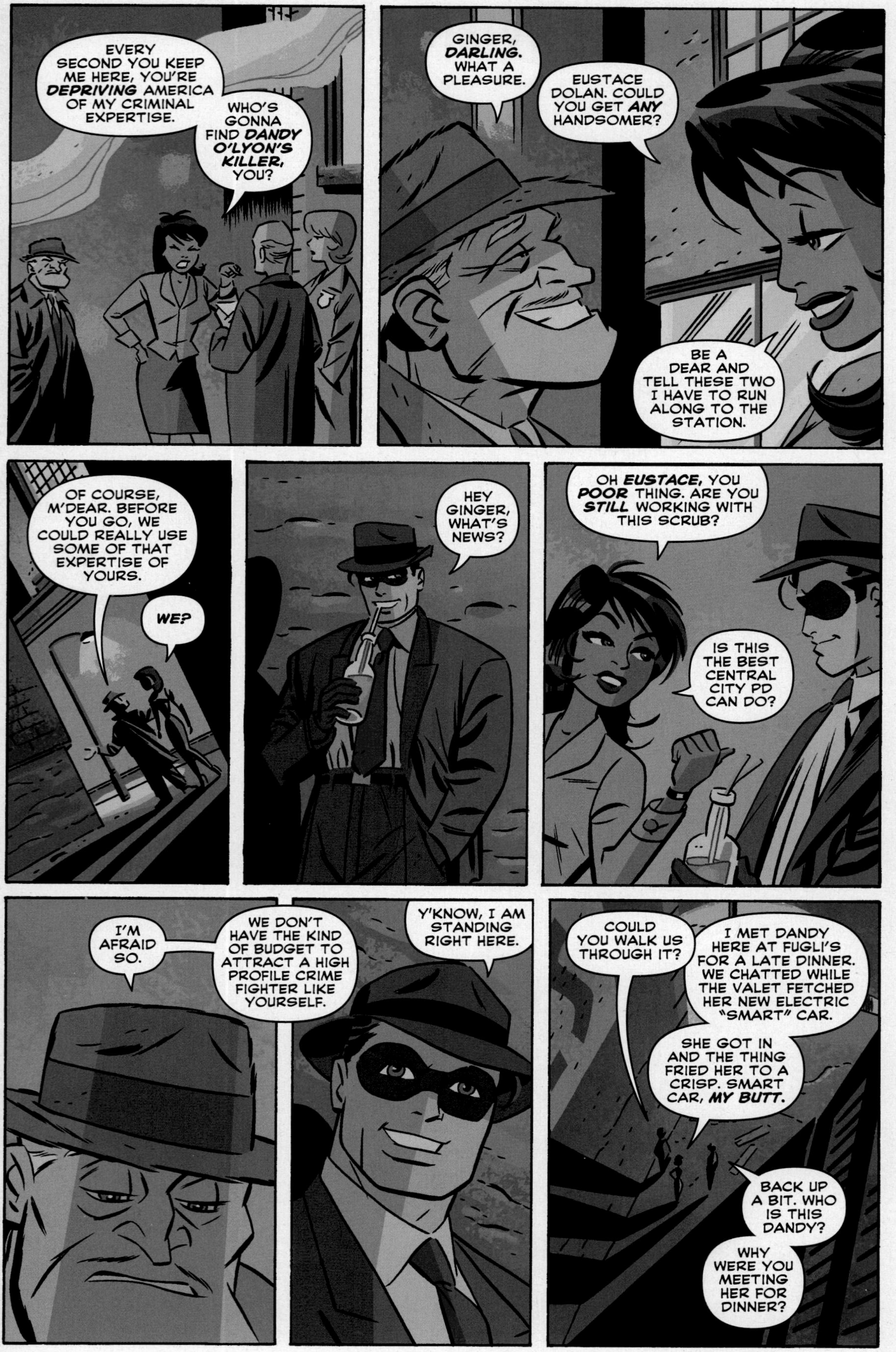
EVERY SECOND YOU KEEP ME HERE, YOU'RE DEPRIVING AMERICA OF MY CRIMINAL EXPERTISE.
WHO'S GONNA FIND DANDY O'LYON'S KILLER, YOU?
GINGER, DARLING. WHAT A PLEASURE.
EUSTACE DOLAN. COULD YOU GET ANY HANDSOMER?
BE A DEAR AND TELL THESE TWO I HAVE TO RUN ALONG TO THE STATION.
OF COURSE, M'DEAR. BEFORE YOU GO, WE COULD REALLY USE SOME OF THAT EXPERTISE OF YOURS.
WE?
HEY GINGER, WHAT'S NEWS?
OH EUSTACE, YOU POOR THING. ARE YOU STILL WORKING WITH THIS SCRUB?
IS THIS THE BEST CENTRAL CITY PD CAN DO?
I'M AFRAID SO.
WE DON'T HAVE THE KIND OF BUDGET TO ATTRACT A HIGH PROFILE CRIME FIGHTER LIKE YOURSELF.
Y'KNOW, I AM STANDING RIGHT HERE.
COULD YOU WALK US THROUGH IT?
I MET DANDY HERE AT FUGLI'S FOR A LATE DINNER. WE CHATTED WHILE THE VALET FETCHED HER NEW ELECTRIC "SMART" CAR.
SHE GOT IN AND THE THING FRIED HER TO A CRISP. SMART CAR, MY BUTT.
BACK UP A BIT. WHO IS THIS DANDY?
WHY WERE YOU MEETING HER FOR DINNER?

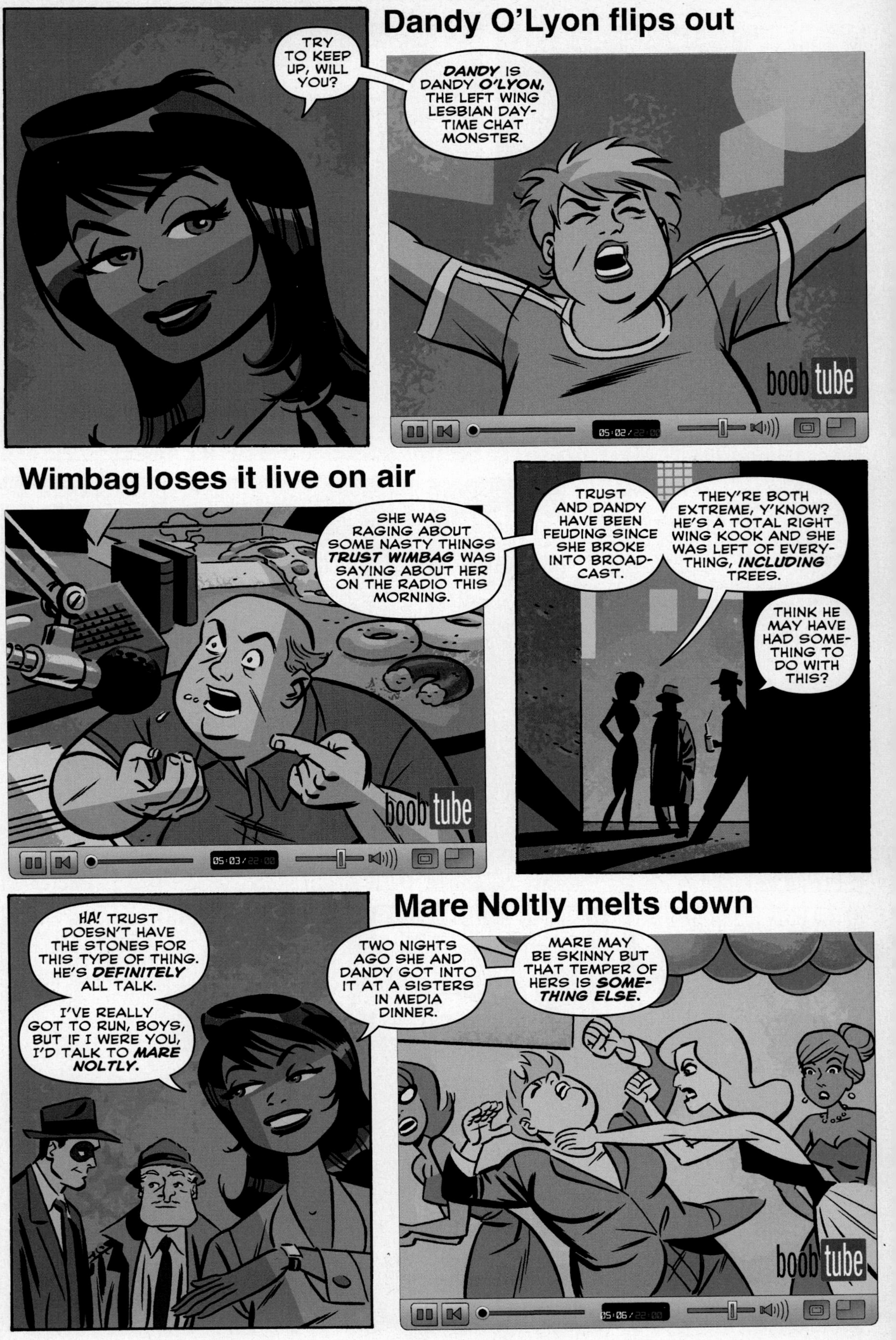
Dandy O'Lyon flips out
TRY TO KEEP UP, WILL YOU?
DANDY IS DANDY O'LYON, THE LEFT WING LESBIAN DAY-TIME CHAT MONSTER.
boob tube
05:02/22:00
Wimbag loses it live on air
SHE WAS RAGING ABOUT SOME NASTY THINGS TRUST WIMBAG WAS SAYING ABOUT HER ON THE RADIO THIS MORNING.
boob tube
05:03/22:00
TRUST AND DANDY HAVE BEEN FEUDING SINCE SHE BROKE INTO BROAD-CAST.
THEY'RE BOTH EXTREME, Y'KNOW? HE'S A TOTAL RIGHT WING KOOK AND SHE WAS LEFT OF EVERY-THING, INCLUDING TREES.
THINK HE MAY HAVE HAD SOME-THING TO DO WITH THIS?
HA! TRUST DOESN'T HAVE THE STONES FOR THIS TYPE OF THING. HE'S DEFINITELY ALL TALK.
I'VE REALLY GOT TO RUN, BOYS, BUT IF I WERE YOU, I'D TALK TO MARE NOLTLY.
Mare Noltly melts down
TWO NIGHTS AGO SHE AND DANDY GOT INTO IT AT A SISTERS IN MEDIA DINNER.
MARE MAY BE SKINNY BUT THAT TEMPER OF HERS IS SOME-THING ELSE.
boob tube
05:06/22:00

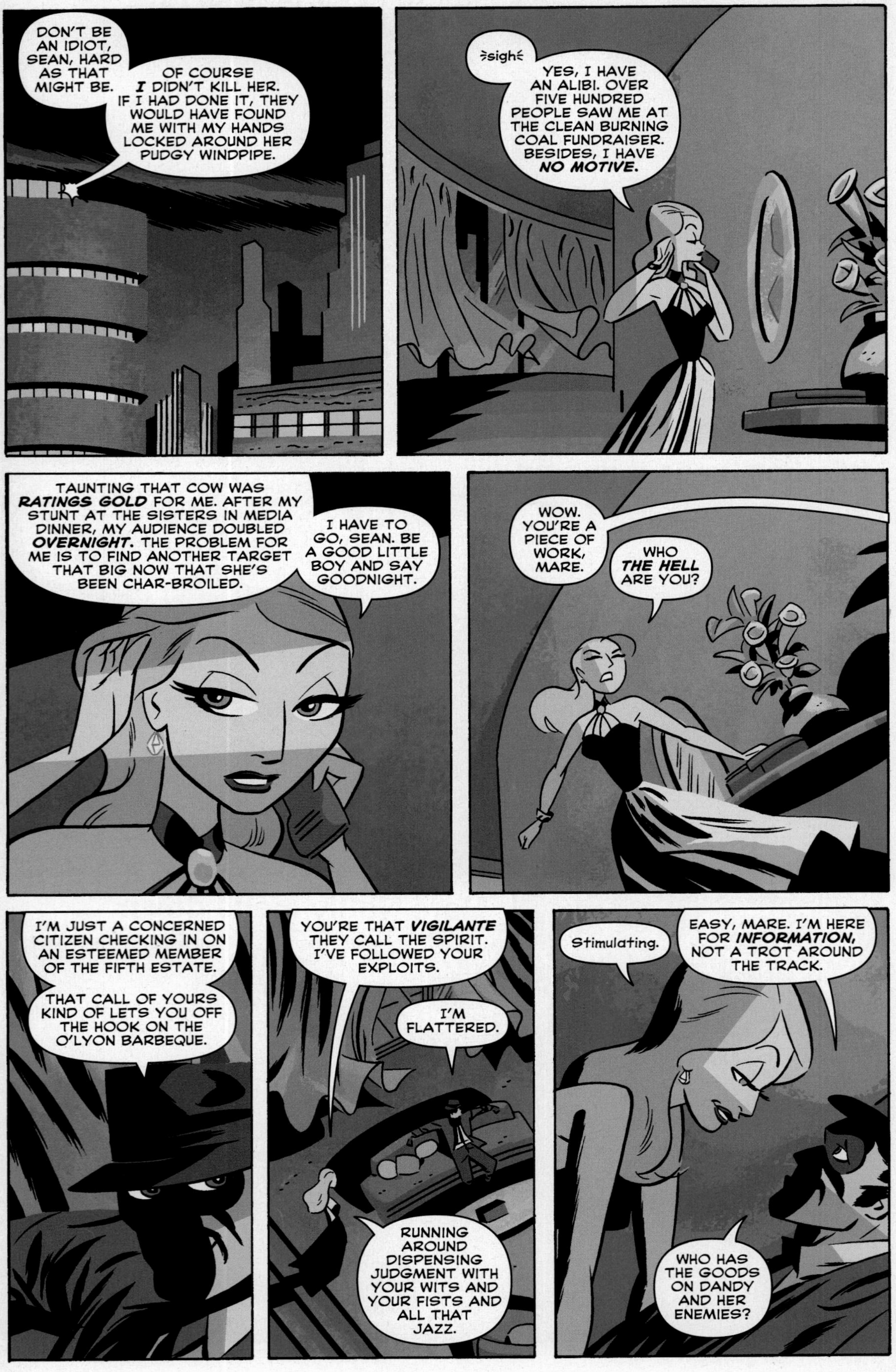
DON'T BE AN IDIOT, SEAN, HARD AS THAT MIGHT BE.
OF COURSE *I* DIDN'T KILL HER. IF I HAD DONE IT, THEY WOULD HAVE FOUND ME WITH MY HANDS LOCKED AROUND HER PUDGY WINDPIPE.
sigh
YES, I HAVE AN ALIBI. OVER FIVE HUNDRED PEOPLE SAW ME AT THE CLEAN BURNING COAL FUNDRAISER. BESIDES, I HAVE ***NO MOTIVE.***
TAUNTING THAT COW WAS ***RATINGS GOLD*** FOR ME. AFTER MY STUNT AT THE SISTERS IN MEDIA DINNER, MY AUDIENCE DOUBLED ***OVERNIGHT.*** THE PROBLEM FOR ME IS TO FIND ANOTHER TARGET THAT BIG NOW THAT SHE'S BEEN CHAR-BROILED.
I HAVE TO GO, SEAN. BE A GOOD LITTLE BOY AND SAY GOODNIGHT.
WOW. YOU'RE A PIECE OF WORK, MARE.
WHO ***THE HELL*** ARE YOU?
I'M JUST A CONCERNED CITIZEN CHECKING IN ON AN ESTEEMED MEMBER OF THE FIFTH ESTATE.
THAT CALL OF YOURS KIND OF LETS YOU OFF THE HOOK ON THE O'LYON BARBEQUE.
YOU'RE THAT ***VIGILANTE*** THEY CALL THE SPIRIT. I'VE FOLLOWED YOUR EXPLOITS.
I'M FLATTERED.
RUNNING AROUND DISPENSING JUDGMENT WITH YOUR WITS AND YOUR FISTS AND ALL THAT JAZZ.
Stimulating.
EASY, MARE. I'M HERE FOR ***INFORMATION,*** NOT A TROT AROUND THE TRACK.
WHO HAS THE GOODS ON DANDY AND HER ENEMIES?

Wally on a rampage

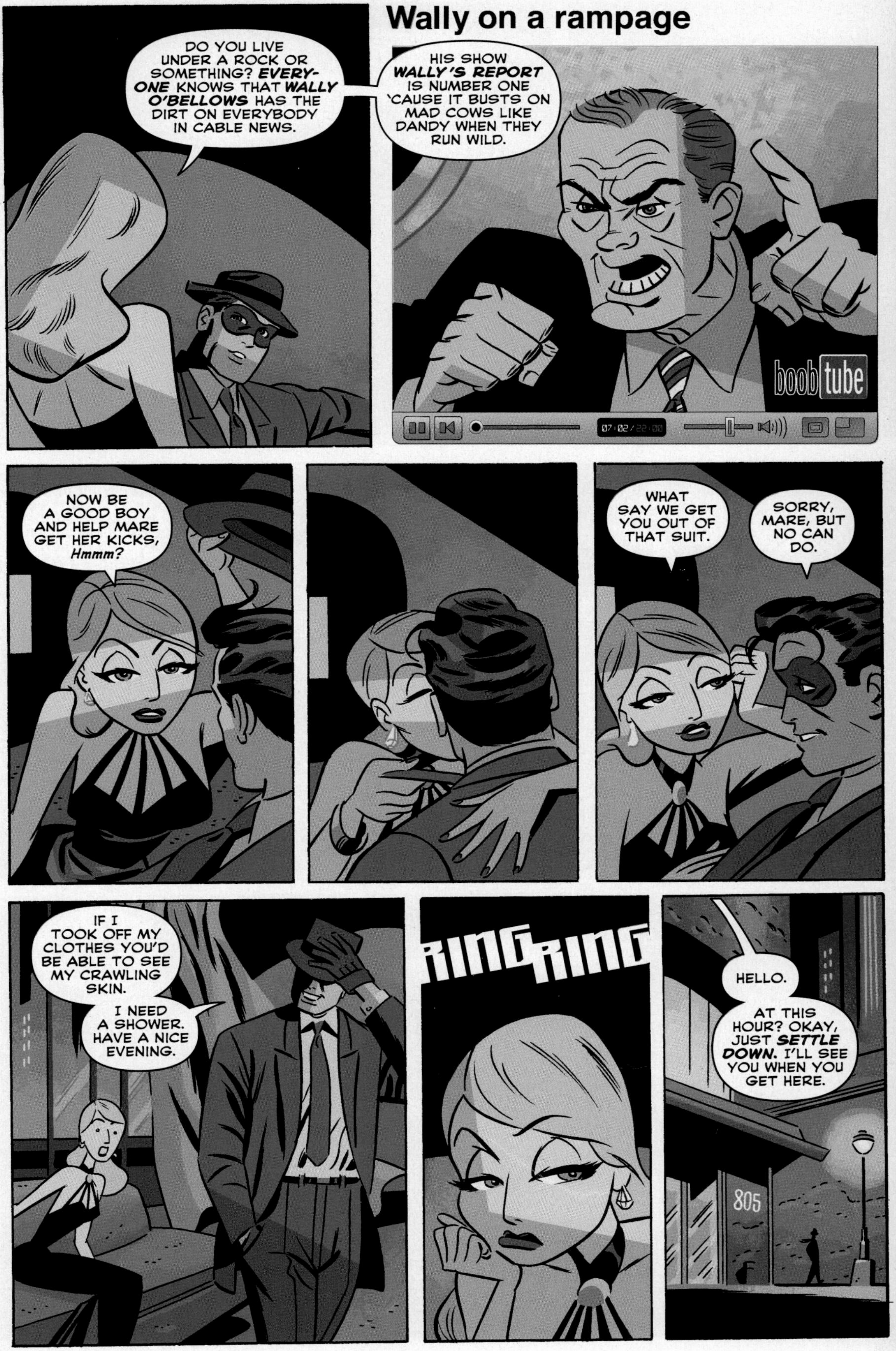

DO YOU LIVE UNDER A ROCK OR SOMETHING? EVERY-ONE KNOWS THAT WALLY O'BELLOWS HAS THE DIRT ON EVERYBODY IN CABLE NEWS.
HIS SHOW WALLY'S REPORT IS NUMBER ONE 'CAUSE IT BUSTS ON MAD COWS LIKE DANDY WHEN THEY RUN WILD.
boob tube
07:02/22:00
NOW BE A GOOD BOY AND HELP MARE GET HER KICKS, Hmmm?
WHAT SAY WE GET YOU OUT OF THAT SUIT.
SORRY, MARE, BUT NO CAN DO.
IF I TOOK OFF MY CLOTHES YOU'D BE ABLE TO SEE MY CRAWLING SKIN.
I NEED A SHOWER. HAVE A NICE EVENING.
RING RING
HELLO.
AT THIS HOUR? OKAY, JUST SETTLE DOWN. I'LL SEE YOU WHEN YOU GET HERE.
805

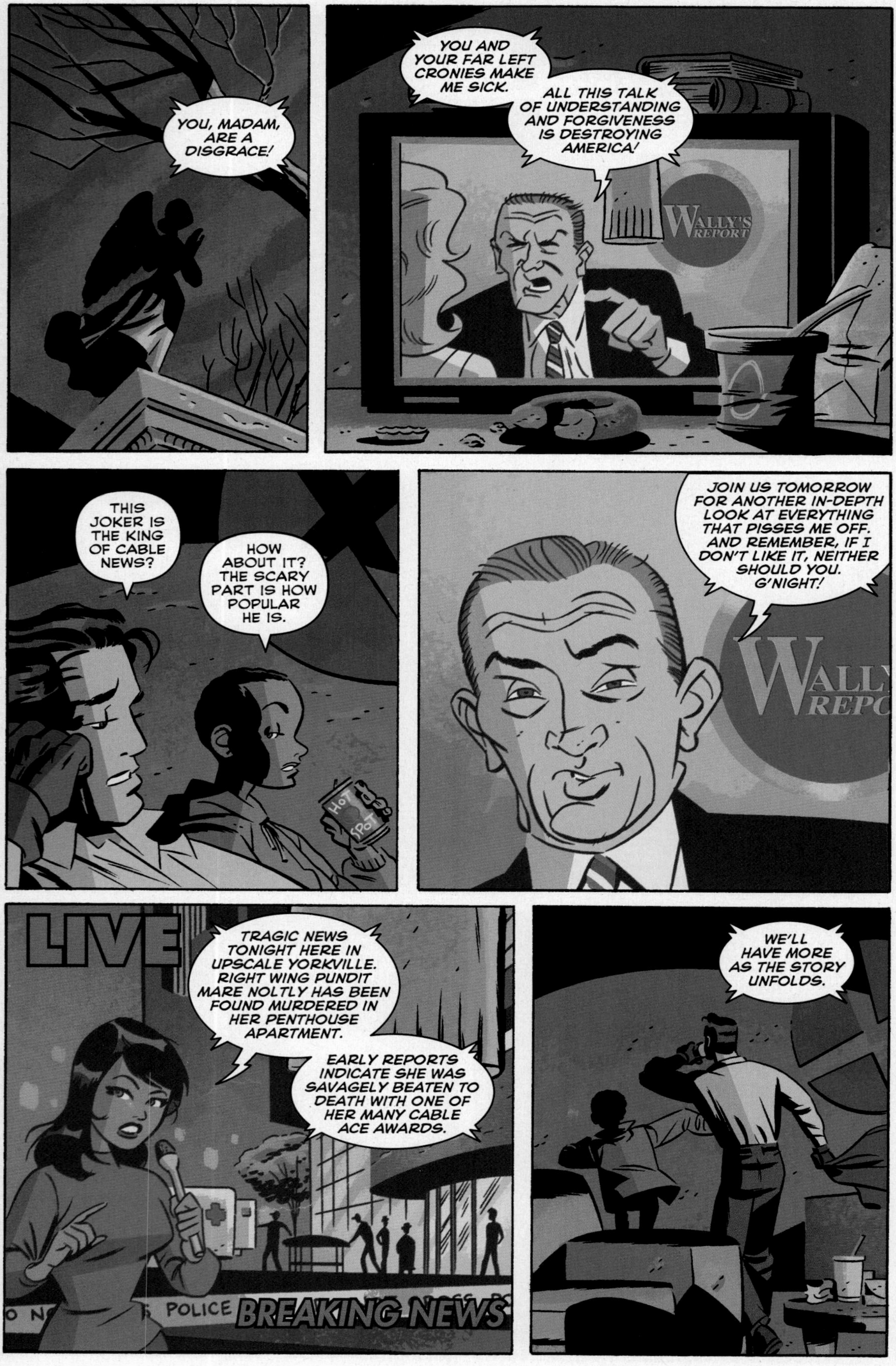
YOU, MADAM, ARE A DISGRACE!
YOU AND YOUR FAR LEFT CRONIES MAKE ME SICK.
ALL THIS TALK OF UNDERSTANDING AND FORGIVENESS IS DESTROYING AMERICA!
WALLY'S REPORT
THIS JOKER IS THE KING OF CABLE NEWS?
HOW ABOUT IT? THE SCARY PART IS HOW POPULAR HE IS.
HOT SPOT
JOIN US TOMORROW FOR ANOTHER IN-DEPTH LOOK AT EVERYTHING THAT PISSES ME OFF. AND REMEMBER, IF I DON'T LIKE IT, NEITHER SHOULD YOU. G'NIGHT!
LIVE
TRAGIC NEWS TONIGHT HERE IN UPSCALE YORKVILLE. RIGHT WING PUNDIT MARE NOLTLY HAS BEEN FOUND MURDERED IN HER PENTHOUSE APARTMENT.
EARLY REPORTS INDICATE SHE WAS SAVAGELY BEATEN TO DEATH WITH ONE OF HER MANY CABLE ACE AWARDS.
POLICE
BREAKING NEWS
WE'LL HAVE MORE AS THE STORY UNFOLDS.

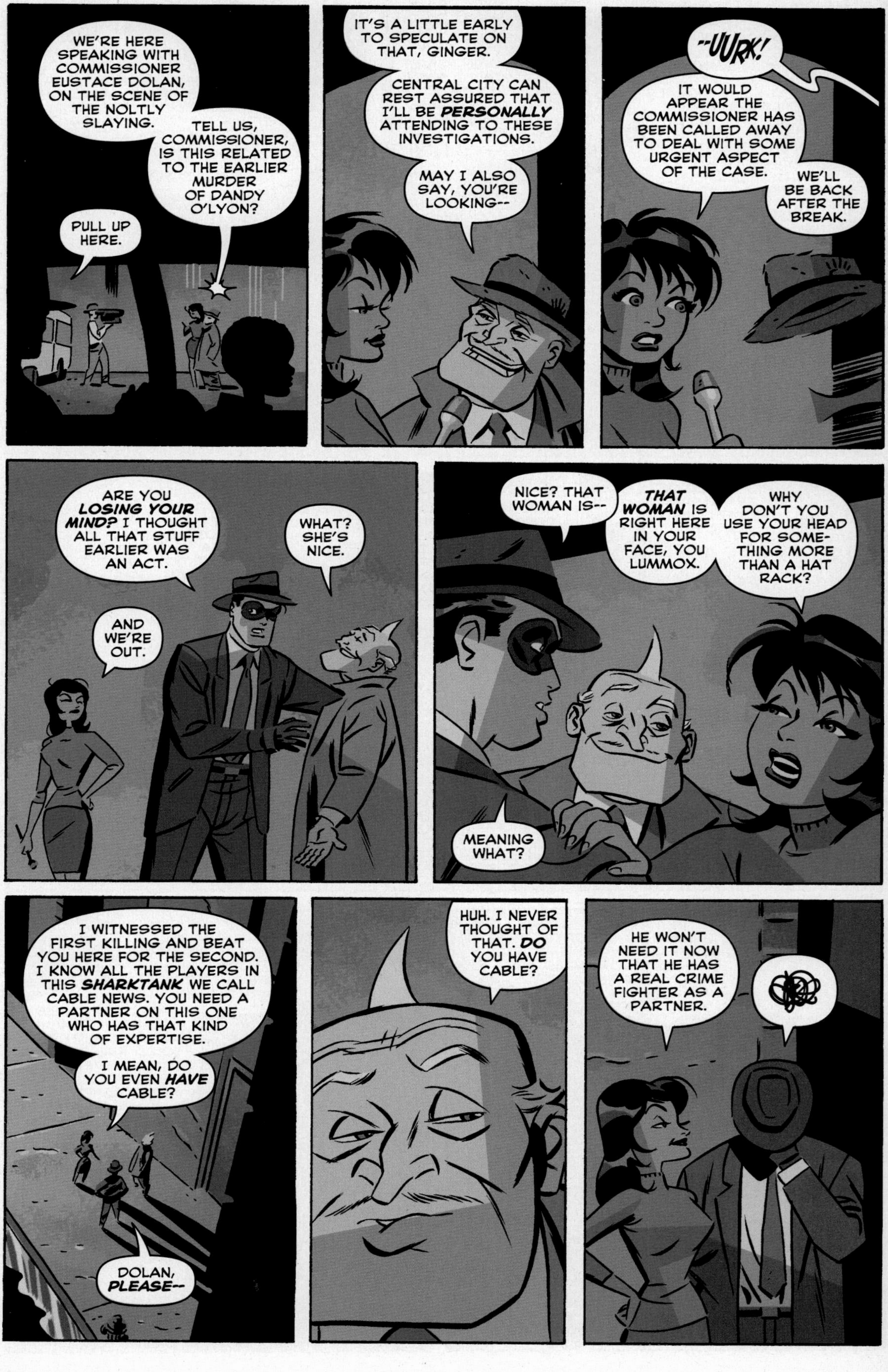
WE'RE HERE SPEAKING WITH COMMISSIONER EUSTACE DOLAN, ON THE SCENE OF THE NOLTLY SLAYING.
TELL US, COMMISSIONER, IS THIS RELATED TO THE EARLIER MURDER OF DANDY O'LYON?
PULL UP HERE.
IT'S A LITTLE EARLY TO SPECULATE ON THAT, GINGER.
CENTRAL CITY CAN REST ASSURED THAT I'LL BE PERSONALLY ATTENDING TO THESE INVESTIGATIONS.
MAY I ALSO SAY, YOU'RE LOOKING--
--UURK!
IT WOULD APPEAR THE COMMISSIONER HAS BEEN CALLED AWAY TO DEAL WITH SOME URGENT ASPECT OF THE CASE.
WE'LL BE BACK AFTER THE BREAK.
ARE YOU LOSING YOUR MIND? I THOUGHT ALL THAT STUFF EARLIER WAS AN ACT.
WHAT? SHE'S NICE.
AND WE'RE OUT.
NICE? THAT WOMAN IS--
THAT WOMAN IS RIGHT HERE IN YOUR FACE, YOU LUMMOX.
WHY DON'T YOU USE YOUR HEAD FOR SOMETHING MORE THAN A HAT RACK?
MEANING WHAT?
I WITNESSED THE FIRST KILLING AND BEAT YOU HERE FOR THE SECOND. I KNOW ALL THE PLAYERS IN THIS SHARKTANK WE CALL CABLE NEWS. YOU NEED A PARTNER ON THIS ONE WHO HAS THAT KIND OF EXPERTISE.
I MEAN, DO YOU EVEN HAVE CABLE?
DOLAN, PLEASE--
HUH. I NEVER THOUGHT OF THAT. DO YOU HAVE CABLE?
HE WON'T NEED IT NOW THAT HE HAS A REAL CRIME FIGHTER AS A PARTNER.

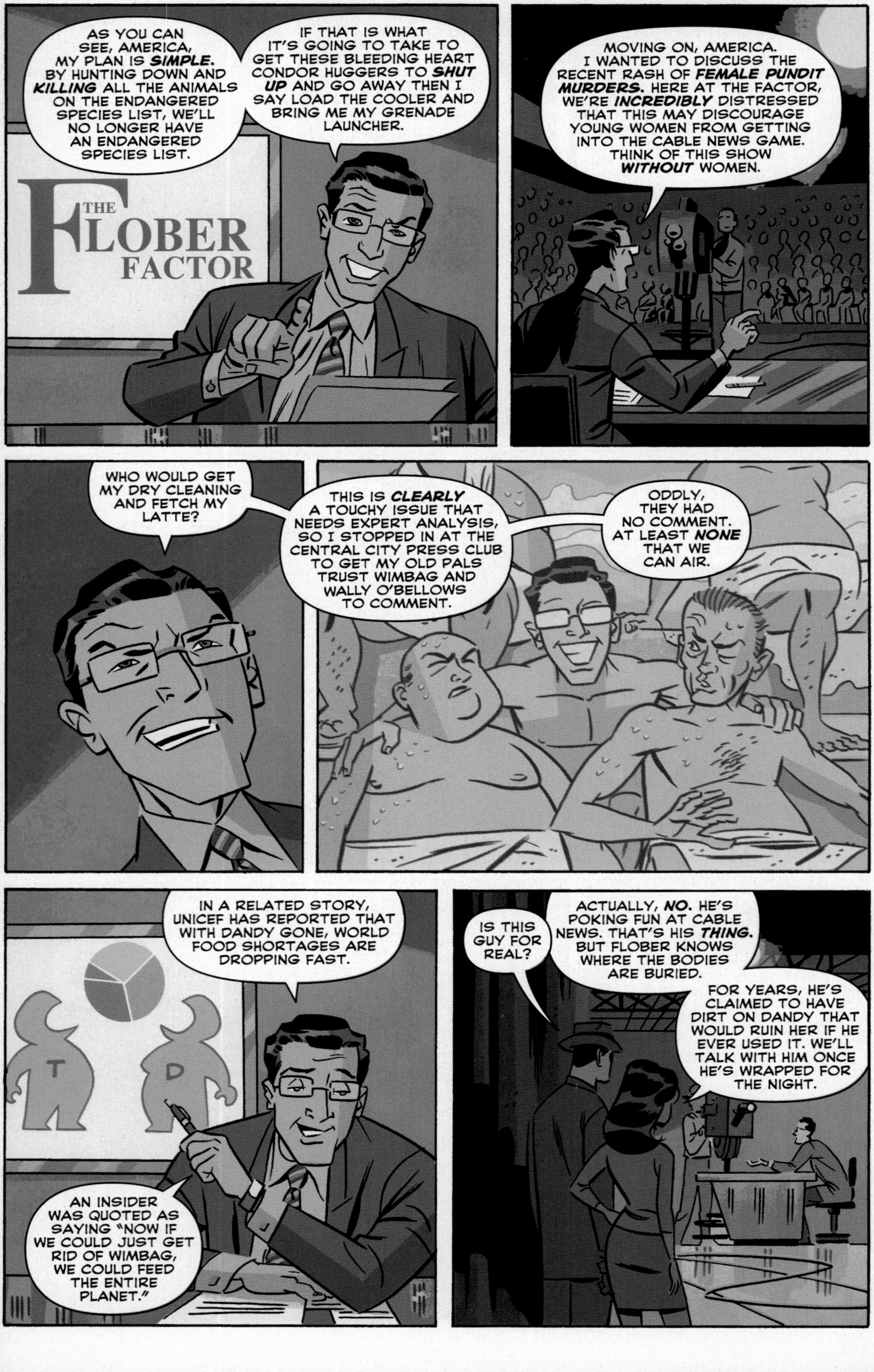
AS YOU CAN SEE, AMERICA, MY PLAN IS SIMPLE. BY HUNTING DOWN AND KILLING ALL THE ANIMALS ON THE ENDANGERED SPECIES LIST, WE'LL NO LONGER HAVE AN ENDANGERED SPECIES LIST.
IF THAT IS WHAT IT'S GOING TO TAKE TO GET THESE BLEEDING HEART CONDOR HUGGERS TO SHUT UP AND GO AWAY THEN I SAY LOAD THE COOLER AND BRING ME MY GRENADE LAUNCHER.
THE FLOBER FACTOR
MOVING ON, AMERICA. I WANTED TO DISCUSS THE RECENT RASH OF FEMALE PUNDIT MURDERS. HERE AT THE FACTOR, WE'RE INCREDIBLY DISTRESSED THAT THIS MAY DISCOURAGE YOUNG WOMEN FROM GETTING INTO THE CABLE NEWS GAME. THINK OF THIS SHOW WITHOUT WOMEN.
WHO WOULD GET MY DRY CLEANING AND FETCH MY LATTE?
THIS IS CLEARLY A TOUCHY ISSUE THAT NEEDS EXPERT ANALYSIS, SO I STOPPED IN AT THE CENTRAL CITY PRESS CLUB TO GET MY OLD PALS TRUST WIMBAG AND WALLY O'BELLOWS TO COMMENT.
ODDLY, THEY HAD NO COMMENT. AT LEAST NONE THAT WE CAN AIR.
IN A RELATED STORY, UNICEF HAS REPORTED THAT WITH DANDY GONE, WORLD FOOD SHORTAGES ARE DROPPING FAST.
T
D
AN INSIDER WAS QUOTED AS SAYING "NOW IF WE COULD JUST GET RID OF WIMBAG, WE COULD FEED THE ENTIRE PLANET."
IS THIS GUY FOR REAL?
ACTUALLY, NO. HE'S POKING FUN AT CABLE NEWS. THAT'S HIS THING. BUT FLOBER KNOWS WHERE THE BODIES ARE BURIED.
FOR YEARS, HE'S CLAIMED TO HAVE DIRT ON DANDY THAT WOULD RUIN HER IF HE EVER USED IT. WE'LL TALK WITH HIM ONCE HE'S WRAPPED FOR THE NIGHT.

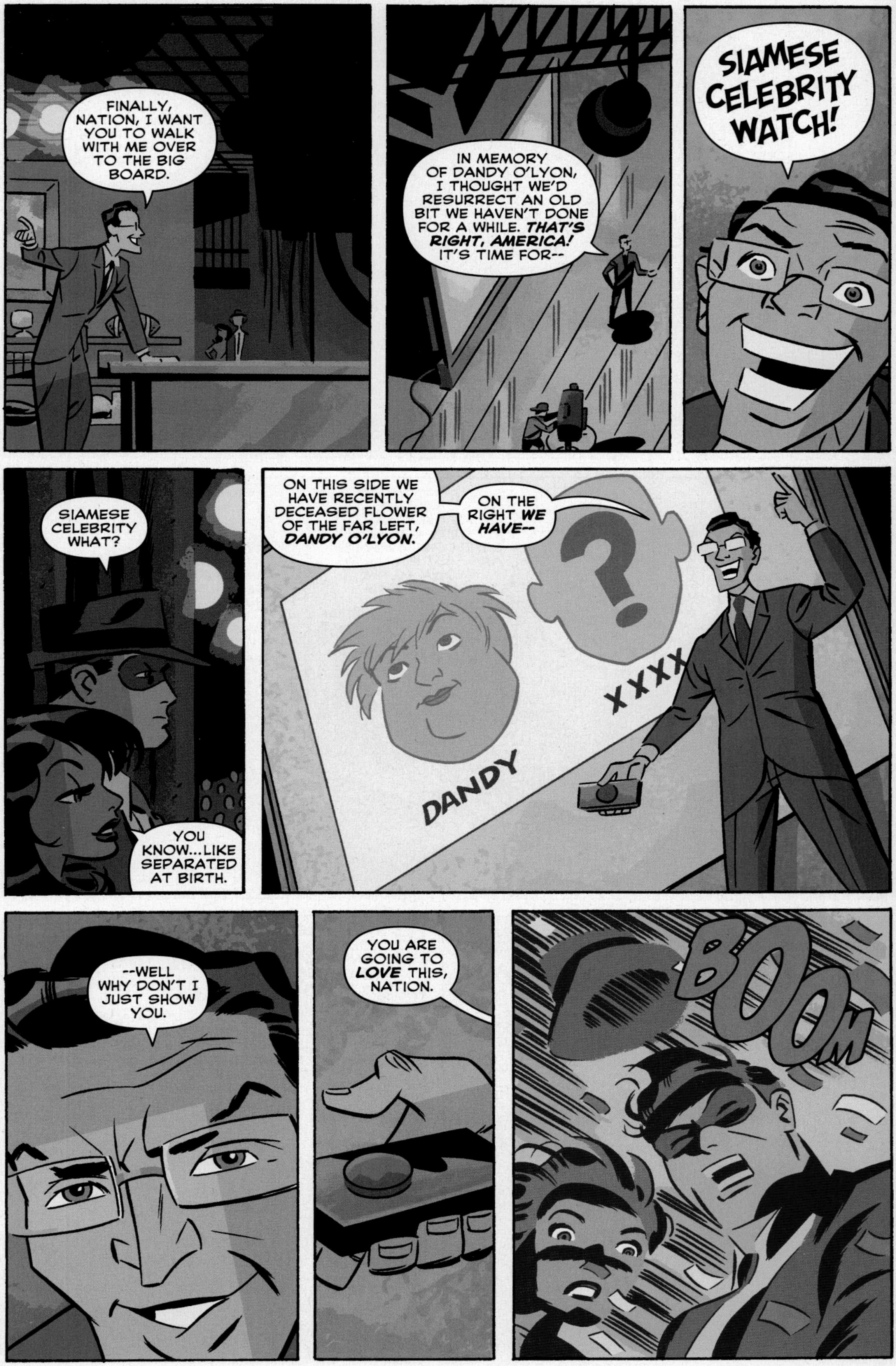
FINALLY, NATION, I WANT YOU TO WALK WITH ME OVER TO THE BIG BOARD.
IN MEMORY OF DANDY O'LYON, I THOUGHT WE'D RESURRECT AN OLD BIT WE HAVEN'T DONE FOR A WHILE. ***THAT'S RIGHT, AMERICA!*** IT'S TIME FOR--
SIAMESE CELEBRITY WATCH!
SIAMESE CELEBRITY WHAT?
YOU KNOW...LIKE SEPARATED AT BIRTH.
ON THIS SIDE WE HAVE RECENTLY DECEASED FLOWER OF THE FAR LEFT, ***DANDY O'LYON.***
ON THE RIGHT ***WE HAVE***--
XXXX
DANDY
--WELL WHY DON'T I JUST SHOW YOU.
YOU ARE GOING TO ***LOVE*** THIS, NATION.
BOOOM

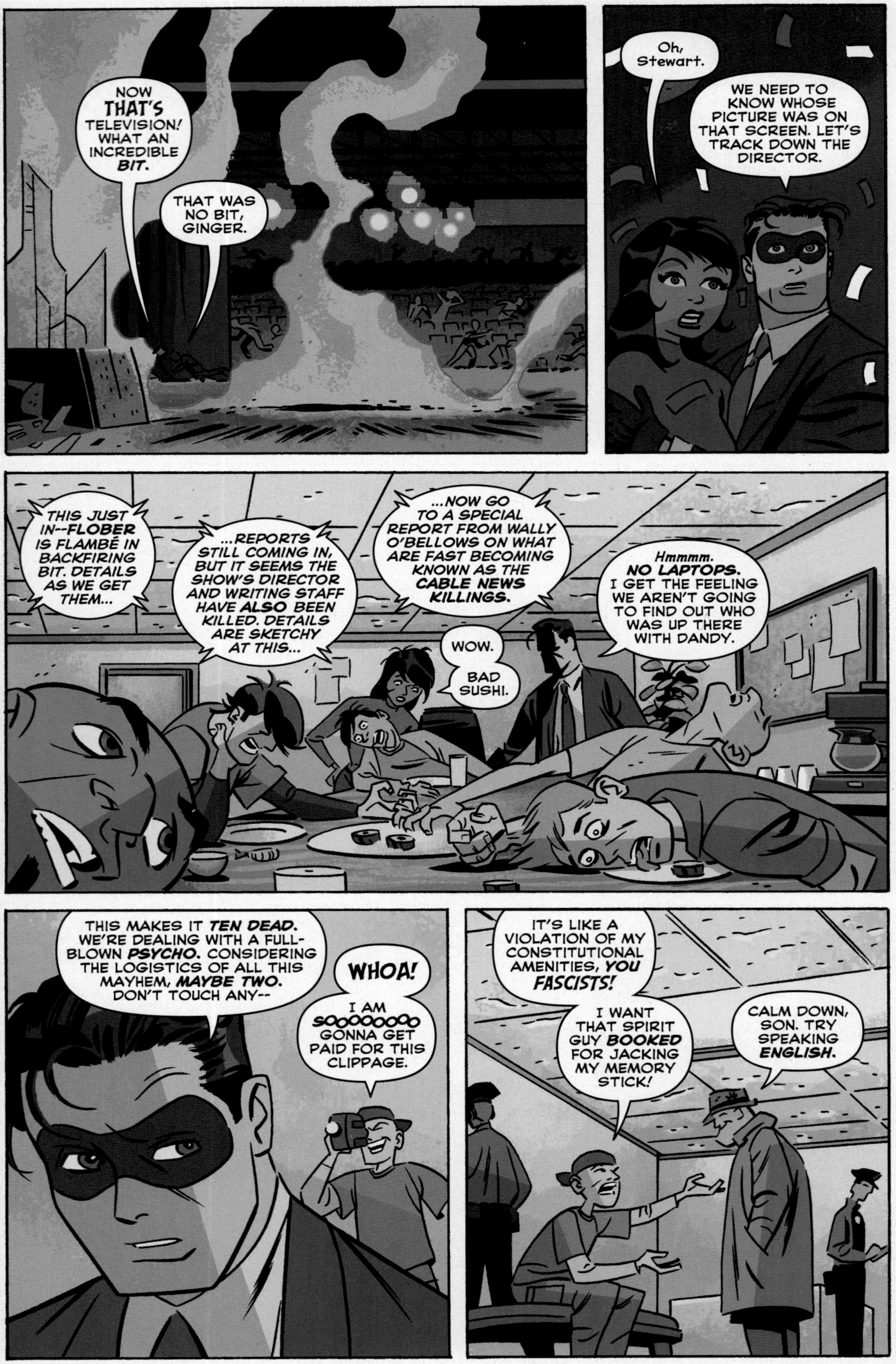
NOW THAT'S TELEVISION! WHAT AN INCREDIBLE BIT.
THAT WAS NO BIT, GINGER.
Oh, Stewart.
WE NEED TO KNOW WHOSE PICTURE WAS ON THAT SCREEN. LET'S TRACK DOWN THE DIRECTOR.
THIS JUST IN--FLOBER IS FLAMBÉ IN BACKFIRING BIT. DETAILS AS WE GET THEM...
...REPORTS STILL COMING IN, BUT IT SEEMS THE SHOW'S DIRECTOR AND WRITING STAFF HAVE ALSO BEEN KILLED. DETAILS ARE SKETCHY AT THIS...
...NOW GO TO A SPECIAL REPORT FROM WALLY O'BELLOWS ON WHAT ARE FAST BECOMING KNOWN AS THE CABLE NEWS KILLINGS.
WOW.
BAD SUSHI.
Hmmmm. NO LAPTOPS. I GET THE FEELING WE AREN'T GOING TO FIND OUT WHO WAS UP THERE WITH DANDY.
THIS MAKES IT TEN DEAD. WE'RE DEALING WITH A FULL-BLOWN PSYCHO. CONSIDERING THE LOGISTICS OF ALL THIS MAYHEM, MAYBE TWO. DON'T TOUCH ANY--
WHOA!
I AM SOOOOOOOO GONNA GET PAID FOR THIS CLIPPAGE.
IT'S LIKE A VIOLATION OF MY CONSTITUTIONAL AMENITIES, YOU FASCISTS!
I WANT THAT SPIRIT GUY BOOKED FOR JACKING MY MEMORY STICK!
CALM DOWN, SON. TRY SPEAKING ENGLISH.

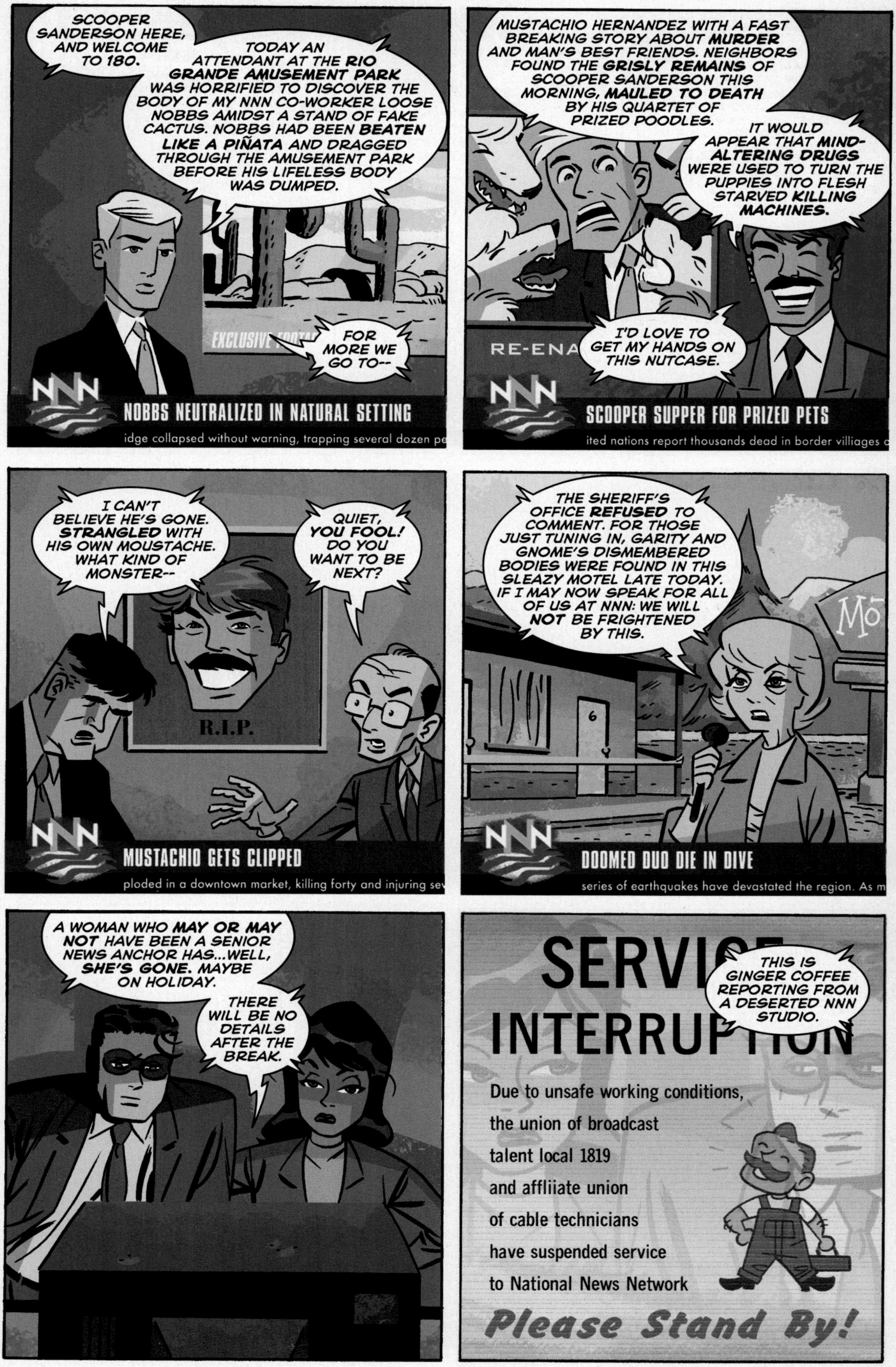
SCOOPER SANDERSON HERE, AND WELCOME TO 180.
TODAY AN ATTENDANT AT THE RIO GRANDE AMUSEMENT PARK WAS HORRIFIED TO DISCOVER THE BODY OF MY NNN CO-WORKER LOOSE NOBBS AMIDST A STAND OF FAKE CACTUS. NOBBS HAD BEEN BEATEN LIKE A PIÑATA AND DRAGGED THROUGH THE AMUSEMENT PARK BEFORE HIS LIFELESS BODY WAS DUMPED.
FOR MORE WE GO TO--
NNN
NOBBS NEUTRALIZED IN NATURAL SETTING
idge collapsed without warning, trapping several dozen pe
MUSTACHIO HERNANDEZ WITH A FAST BREAKING STORY ABOUT MURDER AND MAN'S BEST FRIENDS. NEIGHBORS FOUND THE GRISLY REMAINS OF SCOOPER SANDERSON THIS MORNING, MAULED TO DEATH BY HIS QUARTET OF PRIZED POODLES.
IT WOULD APPEAR THAT MIND-ALTERING DRUGS WERE USED TO TURN THE PUPPIES INTO FLESH STARVED KILLING MACHINES.
I'D LOVE TO GET MY HANDS ON THIS NUTCASE.
RE-ENA
NNN
SCOOPER SUPPER FOR PRIZED PETS
ited nations report thousands dead in border villiages a
I CAN'T BELIEVE HE'S GONE. STRANGLED WITH HIS OWN MOUSTACHE. WHAT KIND OF MONSTER--
QUIET, YOU FOOL! DO YOU WANT TO BE NEXT?
R.I.P.
NNN
MUSTACHIO GETS CLIPPED
ploded in a downtown market, killing forty and injuring sev
THE SHERIFF'S OFFICE REFUSED TO COMMENT. FOR THOSE JUST TUNING IN, GARITY AND GNOME'S DISMEMBERED BODIES WERE FOUND IN THIS SLEAZY MOTEL LATE TODAY. IF I MAY NOW SPEAK FOR ALL OF US AT NNN: WE WILL NOT BE FRIGHTENED BY THIS.
6
NNN
DOOMED DUO DIE IN DIVE
series of earthquakes have devastated the region. As m
A WOMAN WHO MAY OR MAY NOT HAVE BEEN A SENIOR NEWS ANCHOR HAS...WELL, SHE'S GONE. MAYBE ON HOLIDAY.
THERE WILL BE NO DETAILS AFTER THE BREAK.
SERVICE INTERRUPTION
THIS IS GINGER COFFEE REPORTING FROM A DESERTED NNN STUDIO.
Due to unsafe working conditions, the union of broadcast talent local 1819 and affliiate union of cable technicians have suspended service to National News Network
Please Stand By!

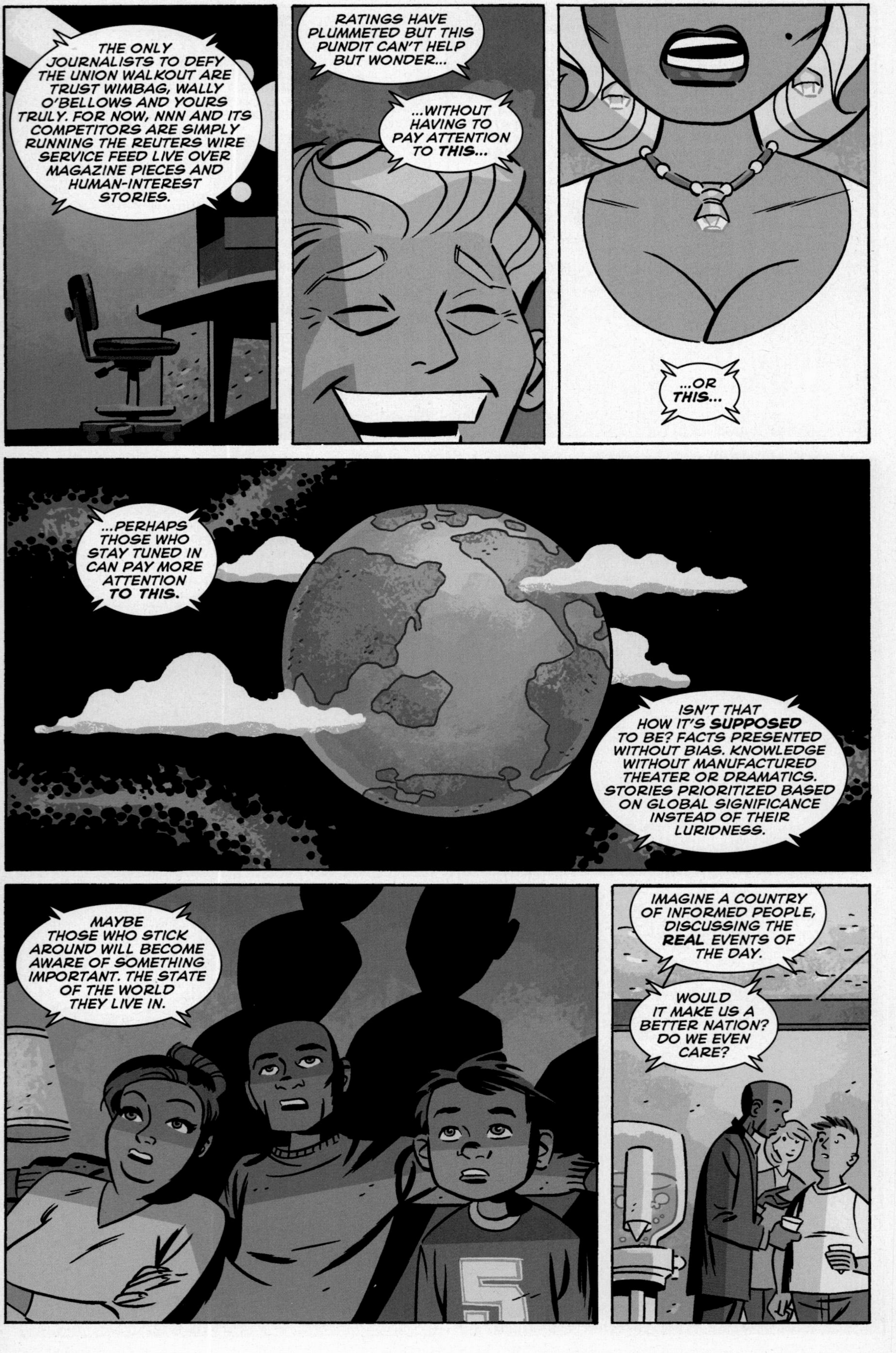
THE ONLY JOURNALISTS TO DEFY THE UNION WALKOUT ARE TRUST WIMBAG, WALLY O'BELLOWS AND YOURS TRULY. FOR NOW, NNN AND ITS COMPETITORS ARE SIMPLY RUNNING THE REUTERS WIRE SERVICE FEED LIVE OVER MAGAZINE PIECES AND HUMAN-INTEREST STORIES.
RATINGS HAVE PLUMMETED BUT THIS PUNDIT CAN'T HELP BUT WONDER...
...WITHOUT HAVING TO PAY ATTENTION TO THIS...
...OR THIS...
...PERHAPS THOSE WHO STAY TUNED IN CAN PAY MORE ATTENTION TO THIS.
ISN'T THAT HOW IT'S SUPPOSED TO BE? FACTS PRESENTED WITHOUT BIAS. KNOWLEDGE WITHOUT MANUFACTURED THEATER OR DRAMATICS. STORIES PRIORITIZED BASED ON GLOBAL SIGNIFICANCE INSTEAD OF THEIR LURIDNESS.
MAYBE THOSE WHO STICK AROUND WILL BECOME AWARE OF SOMETHING IMPORTANT. THE STATE OF THE WORLD THEY LIVE IN.
IMAGINE A COUNTRY OF INFORMED PEOPLE, DISCUSSING THE REAL EVENTS OF THE DAY.
WOULD IT MAKE US A BETTER NATION? DO WE EVEN CARE?
5

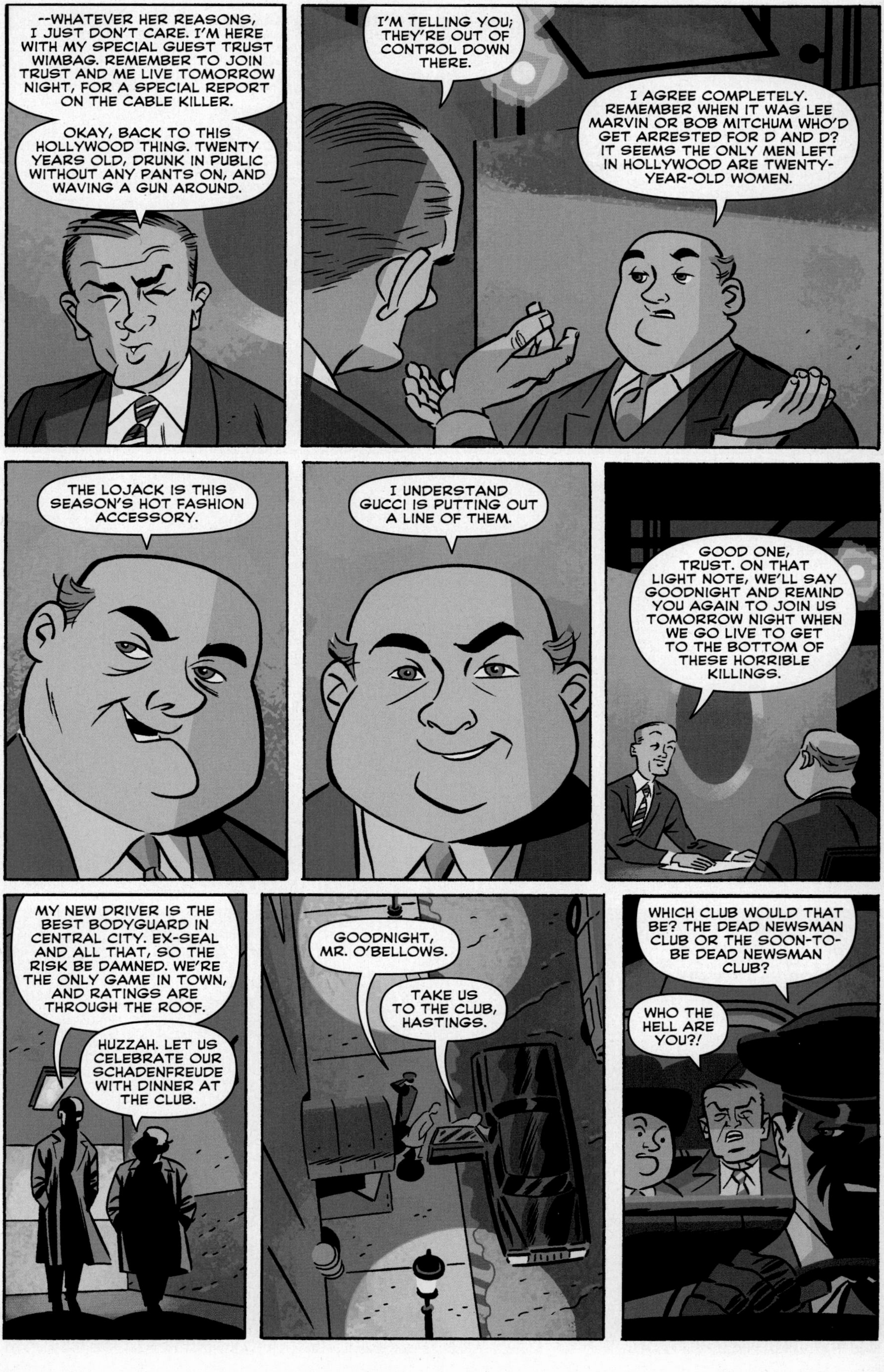
--WHATEVER HER REASONS, I JUST DON'T CARE. I'M HERE WITH MY SPECIAL GUEST TRUST WIMBAG. REMEMBER TO JOIN TRUST AND ME LIVE TOMORROW NIGHT, FOR A SPECIAL REPORT ON THE CABLE KILLER.
OKAY, BACK TO THIS HOLLYWOOD THING. TWENTY YEARS OLD, DRUNK IN PUBLIC WITHOUT ANY PANTS ON, AND WAVING A GUN AROUND.
I'M TELLING YOU; THEY'RE OUT OF CONTROL DOWN THERE.
I AGREE COMPLETELY. REMEMBER WHEN IT WAS LEE MARVIN OR BOB MITCHUM WHO'D GET ARRESTED FOR D AND D? IT SEEMS THE ONLY MEN LEFT IN HOLLYWOOD ARE TWENTY-YEAR-OLD WOMEN.
THE LOJACK IS THIS SEASON'S HOT FASHION ACCESSORY.
I UNDERSTAND GUCCI IS PUTTING OUT A LINE OF THEM.
GOOD ONE, TRUST. ON THAT LIGHT NOTE, WE'LL SAY GOODNIGHT AND REMIND YOU AGAIN TO JOIN US TOMORROW NIGHT WHEN WE GO LIVE TO GET TO THE BOTTOM OF THESE HORRIBLE KILLINGS.
MY NEW DRIVER IS THE BEST BODYGUARD IN CENTRAL CITY. EX-SEAL AND ALL THAT, SO THE RISK BE DAMNED. WE'RE THE ONLY GAME IN TOWN, AND RATINGS ARE THROUGH THE ROOF.
HUZZAH. LET US CELEBRATE OUR SCHADENFREUDE WITH DINNER AT THE CLUB.
GOODNIGHT, MR. O'BELLOWS.
TAKE US TO THE CLUB, HASTINGS.
WHICH CLUB WOULD THAT BE? THE DEAD NEWSMAN CLUB OR THE SOON-TO-BE DEAD NEWSMAN CLUB?
WHO THE HELL ARE YOU?!

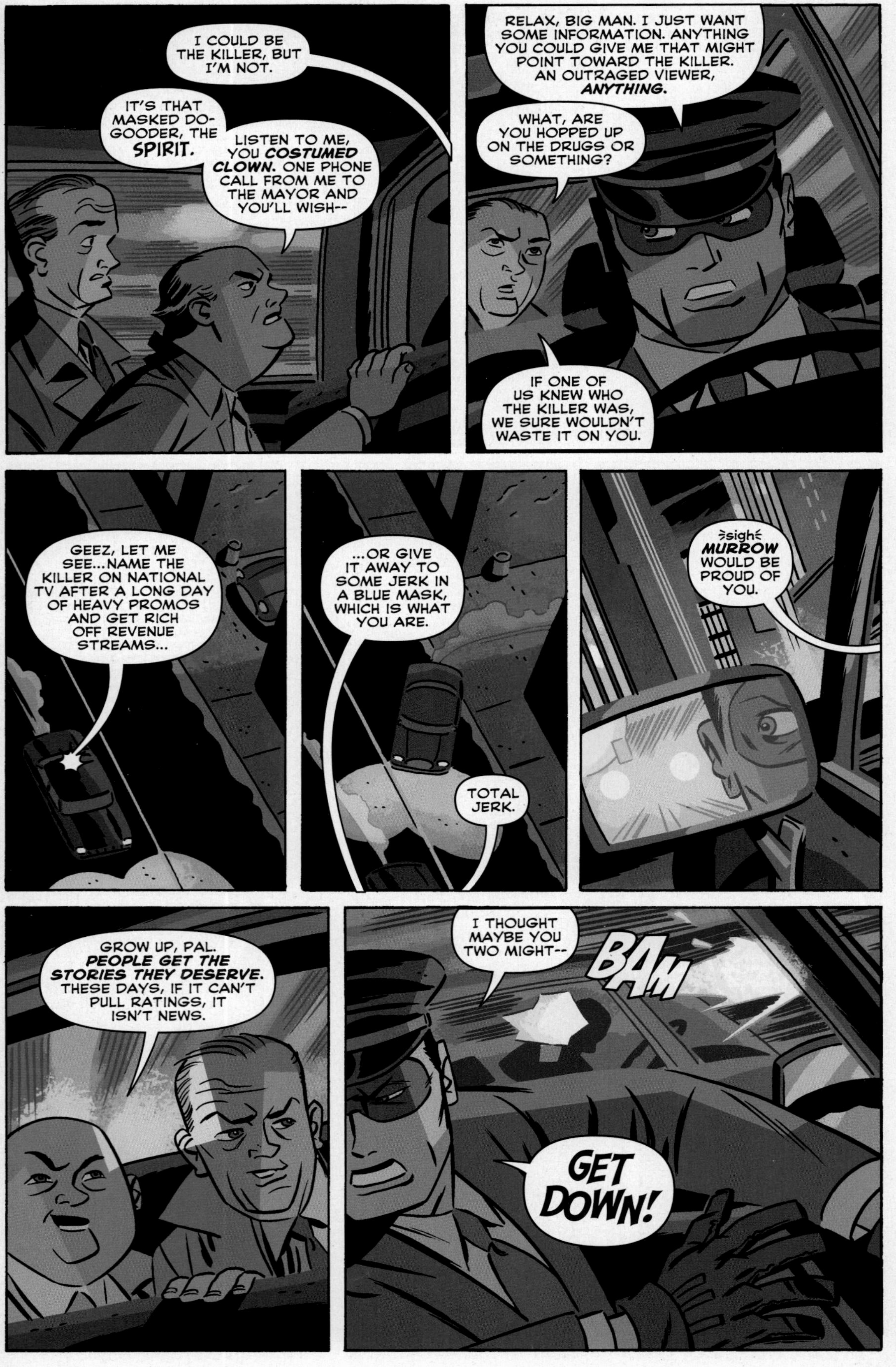
I COULD BE THE KILLER, BUT I'M NOT.
IT'S THAT MASKED DO-GOODER, THE SPIRIT.
LISTEN TO ME, YOU COSTUMED CLOWN. ONE PHONE CALL FROM ME TO THE MAYOR AND YOU'LL WISH--
RELAX, BIG MAN. I JUST WANT SOME INFORMATION. ANYTHING YOU COULD GIVE ME THAT MIGHT POINT TOWARD THE KILLER. AN OUTRAGED VIEWER, ANYTHING.
WHAT, ARE YOU HOPPED UP ON THE DRUGS OR SOMETHING?
IF ONE OF US KNEW WHO THE KILLER WAS, WE SURE WOULDN'T WASTE IT ON YOU.
GEEZ, LET ME SEE...NAME THE KILLER ON NATIONAL TV AFTER A LONG DAY OF HEAVY PROMOS AND GET RICH OFF REVENUE STREAMS...
...OR GIVE IT AWAY TO SOME JERK IN A BLUE MASK, WHICH IS WHAT YOU ARE.
TOTAL JERK.
sigh MURROW WOULD BE PROUD OF YOU.
GROW UP, PAL. PEOPLE GET THE STORIES THEY DESERVE. THESE DAYS, IF IT CAN'T PULL RATINGS, IT ISN'T NEWS.
I THOUGHT MAYBE YOU TWO MIGHT--
BAM
GET DOWN!

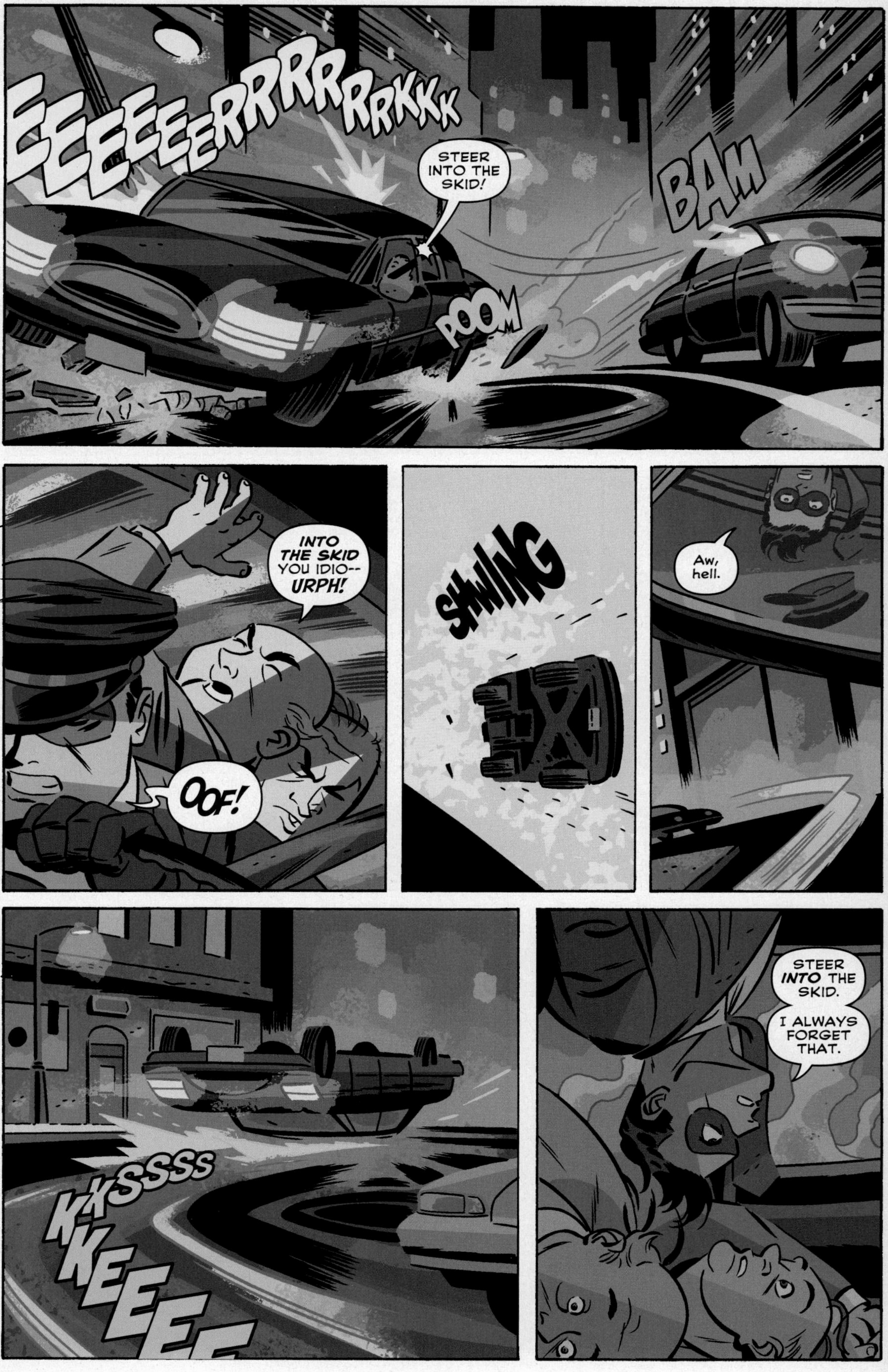
EEEEEERRRRRRRKKK
STEER INTO THE SKID!
BAM
POOM
INTO THE SKID YOU IDIO-- URPH!
OOF!
SHWING
Aw, hell.
KKSSSS
KKEEEEE
STEER INTO THE SKID.
I ALWAYS FORGET THAT.

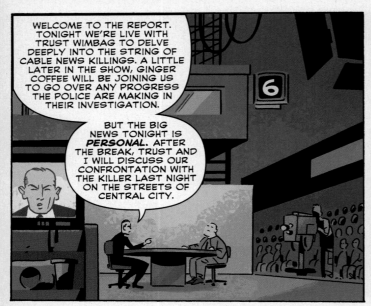

WELCOME TO THE REPORT. TONIGHT WE'RE LIVE WITH TRUST WIMBAG TO DELVE DEEPLY INTO THE STRING OF CABLE NEWS KILLINGS. A LITTLE LATER IN THE SHOW, GINGER COFFEE WILL BE JOINING US TO GO OVER ANY PROGRESS THE POLICE ARE MAKING IN THEIR INVESTIGATION.

BUT THE BIG NEWS TONIGHT IS *PERSONAL*. AFTER THE BREAK, TRUST AND I WILL DISCUSS OUR CONFRONTATION WITH THE KILLER LAST NIGHT ON THE STREETS OF CENTRAL CITY.

DON'T GO AWAY, 'CAUSE YOU'RE NOT GOING TO WANNA MISS THIS REPORT.

SO YOU'RE BIG TIME NOW?

HEY. WELL, WALLY'S REPORT IS THE NUMBER ONE SHOW. ACTUALLY RIGHT NOW, IT'S THE *ONLY* SHOW.

IT'S A GREAT CHANCE FOR ME TO BREAK THROUGH TO A BIGGER MARKET.

HOW 'BOUT YOU? ANY NEW LEADS WITH THE KILLINGS?

THAT'S *ENOUGH*, GINGER.

WHY'D YOU DO IT?

WHAT ARE YOU TALKING ABOUT?

I DROPPED BY YOUR PLACE LAST NIGHT TO TELL YOU ABOUT THE ATTACK.

FROM DOWN THE WAY I SAW YOU DUMPING *THIS* IN YOUR NEIGHBOR'S TRASH.

FOR GOD'S SAKE, WHY HAVE YOU KILLED ALL THESE PEOPLE?

Y-YOU'RE CRAZY. I'M NO KILLER!

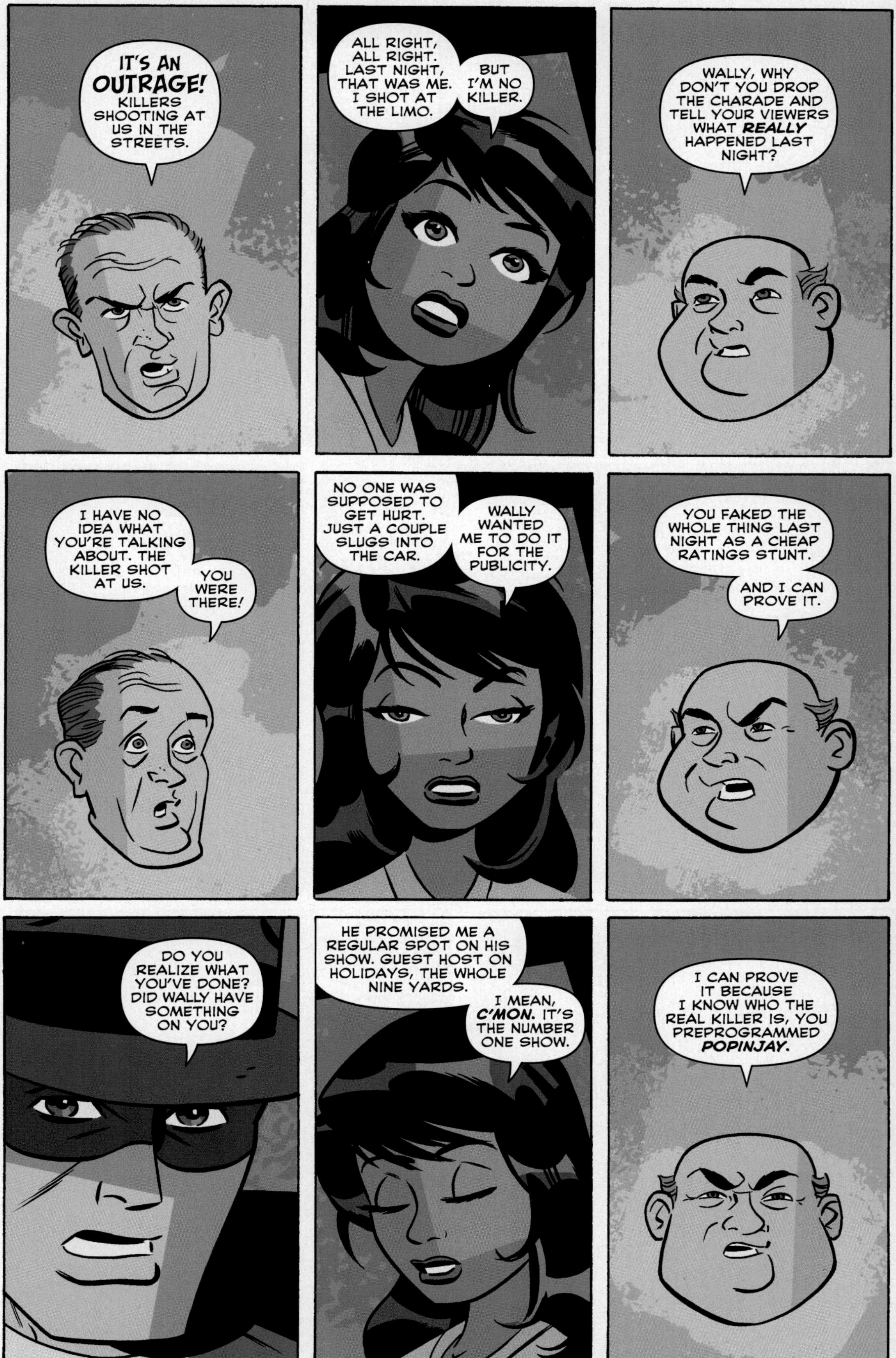
IT'S AN OUTRAGE! KILLERS SHOOTING AT US IN THE STREETS.
ALL RIGHT, ALL RIGHT. LAST NIGHT, THAT WAS ME. I SHOT AT THE LIMO.
BUT I'M NO KILLER.
WALLY, WHY DON'T YOU DROP THE CHARADE AND TELL YOUR VIEWERS WHAT REALLY HAPPENED LAST NIGHT?
I HAVE NO IDEA WHAT YOU'RE TALKING ABOUT. THE KILLER SHOT AT US.
YOU WERE THERE!
NO ONE WAS SUPPOSED TO GET HURT. JUST A COUPLE SLUGS INTO THE CAR.
WALLY WANTED ME TO DO IT FOR THE PUBLICITY.
YOU FAKED THE WHOLE THING LAST NIGHT AS A CHEAP RATINGS STUNT.
AND I CAN PROVE IT.
DO YOU REALIZE WHAT YOU'VE DONE? DID WALLY HAVE SOMETHING ON YOU?
HE PROMISED ME A REGULAR SPOT ON HIS SHOW. GUEST HOST ON HOLIDAYS, THE WHOLE NINE YARDS.
I MEAN, C'MON. IT'S THE NUMBER ONE SHOW.
I CAN PROVE IT BECAUSE I KNOW WHO THE REAL KILLER IS, YOU PREPROGRAMMED POPINJAY.

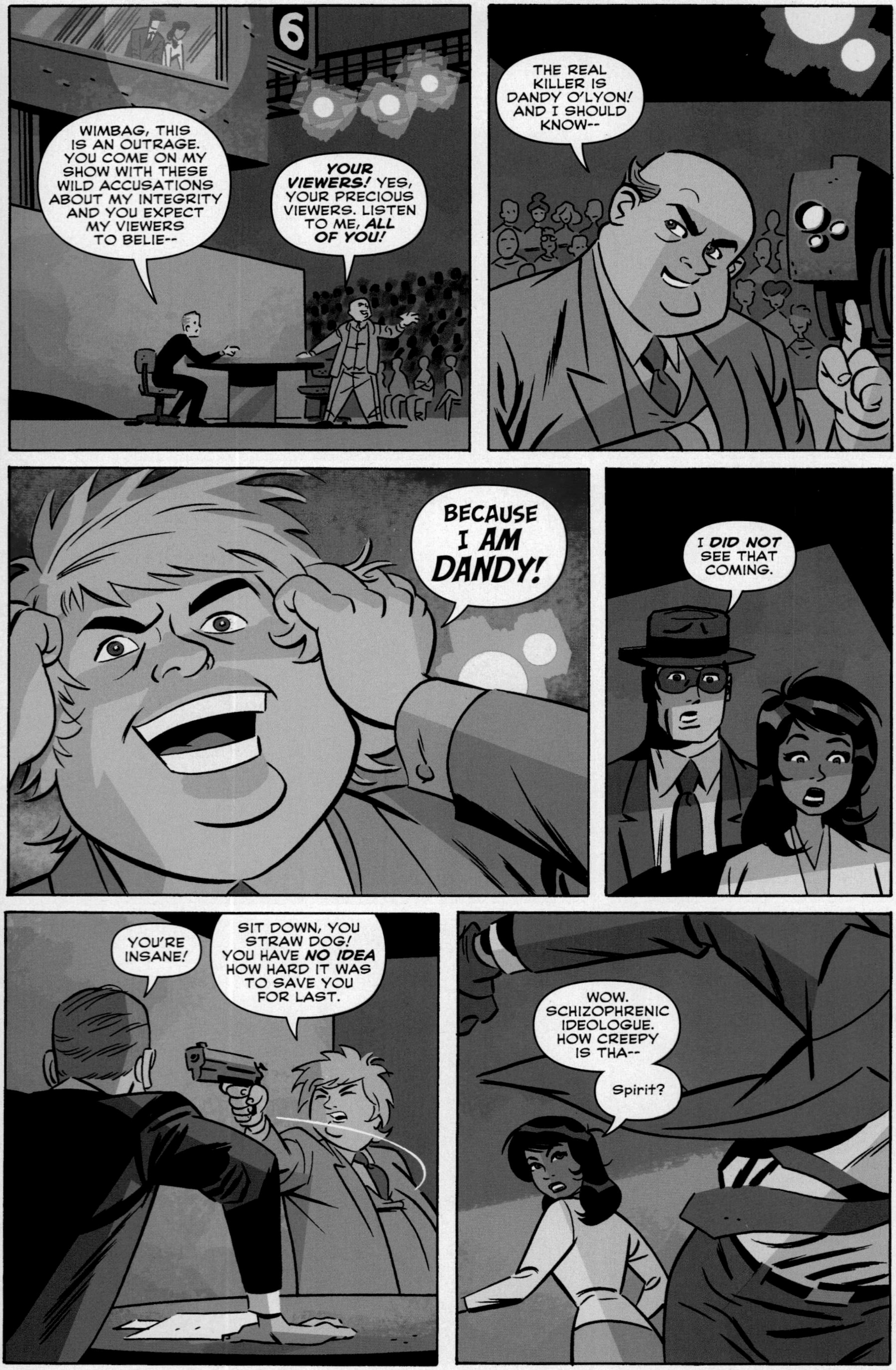

6
WIMBAG, THIS IS AN OUTRAGE. YOU COME ON MY SHOW WITH THESE WILD ACCUSATIONS ABOUT MY INTEGRITY AND YOU EXPECT MY VIEWERS TO BELIE--
YOUR VIEWERS! YES, YOUR PRECIOUS VIEWERS. LISTEN TO ME, *ALL OF YOU!*
THE REAL KILLER IS DANDY O'LYON! AND I SHOULD KNOW--
BECAUSE I *AM* DANDY!
I *DID NOT* SEE THAT COMING.
YOU'RE INSANE!
SIT DOWN, YOU STRAW DOG! YOU HAVE *NO IDEA* HOW HARD IT WAS TO SAVE YOU FOR LAST.
WOW. SCHIZOPHRENIC IDEOLOGUE. HOW CREEPY IS THA--
Spirit?

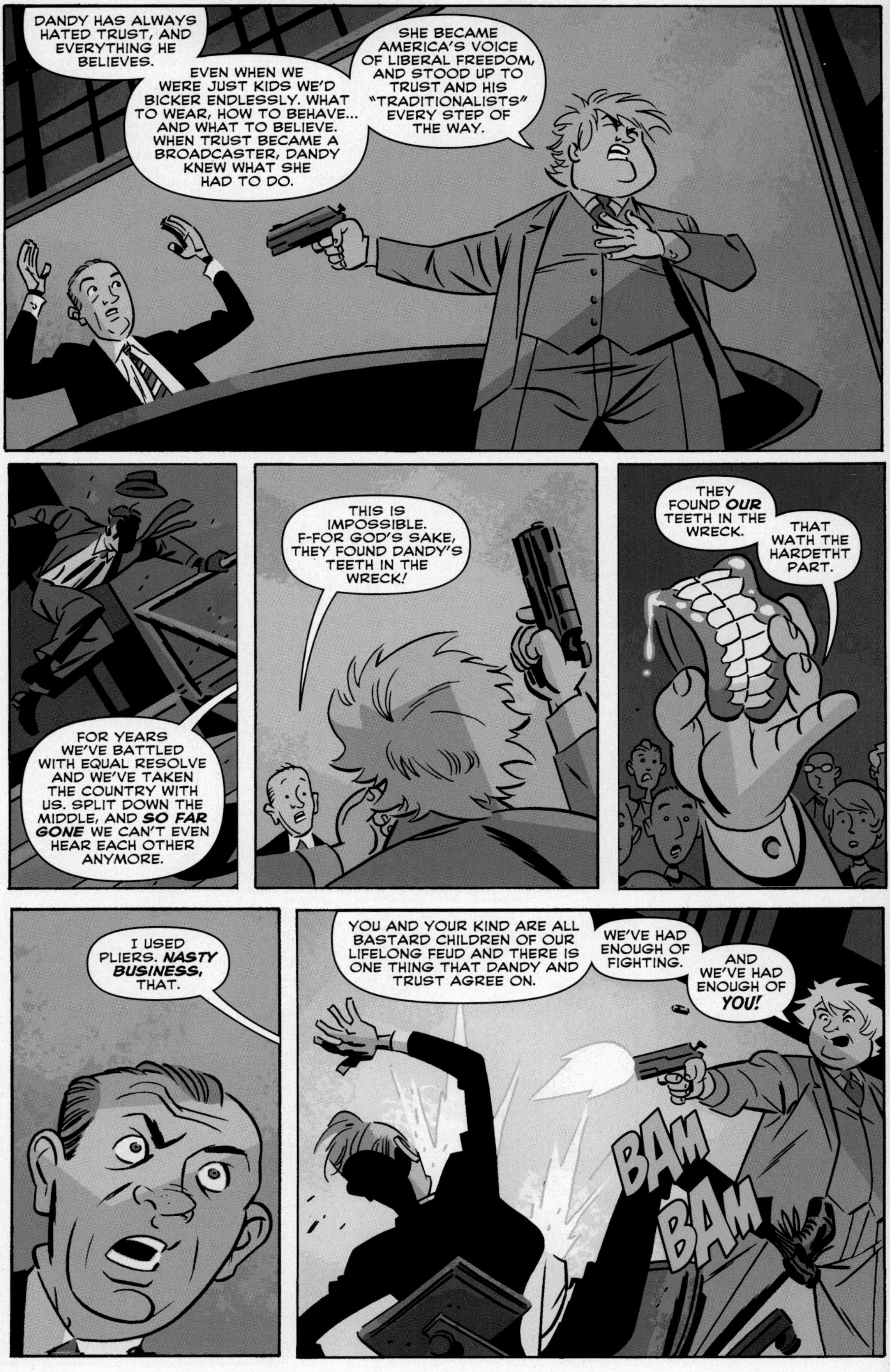

DANDY HAS ALWAYS HATED TRUST, AND EVERYTHING HE BELIEVES.
EVEN WHEN WE WERE JUST KIDS WE'D BICKER ENDLESSLY. WHAT TO WEAR, HOW TO BEHAVE... AND WHAT TO BELIEVE. WHEN TRUST BECAME A BROADCASTER, DANDY KNEW WHAT SHE HAD TO DO.
SHE BECAME AMERICA'S VOICE OF LIBERAL FREEDOM, AND STOOD UP TO TRUST AND HIS "TRADITIONALISTS" EVERY STEP OF THE WAY.
FOR YEARS WE'VE BATTLED WITH EQUAL RESOLVE AND WE'VE TAKEN THE COUNTRY WITH US. SPLIT DOWN THE MIDDLE, AND ***SO FAR GONE*** WE CAN'T EVEN HEAR EACH OTHER ANYMORE.
THIS IS IMPOSSIBLE. F-FOR GOD'S SAKE, THEY FOUND DANDY'S TEETH IN THE WRECK!
THEY FOUND ***OUR*** TEETH IN THE WRECK.
THAT WATH THE HARDETHT PART.
I USED PLIERS. ***NASTY BUSINESS,*** THAT.
YOU AND YOUR KIND ARE ALL BASTARD CHILDREN OF OUR LIFELONG FEUD AND THERE IS ONE THING THAT DANDY AND TRUST AGREE ON.
WE'VE HAD ENOUGH OF FIGHTING.
AND WE'VE HAD ENOUGH OF ***YOU!***
BAM
BAM

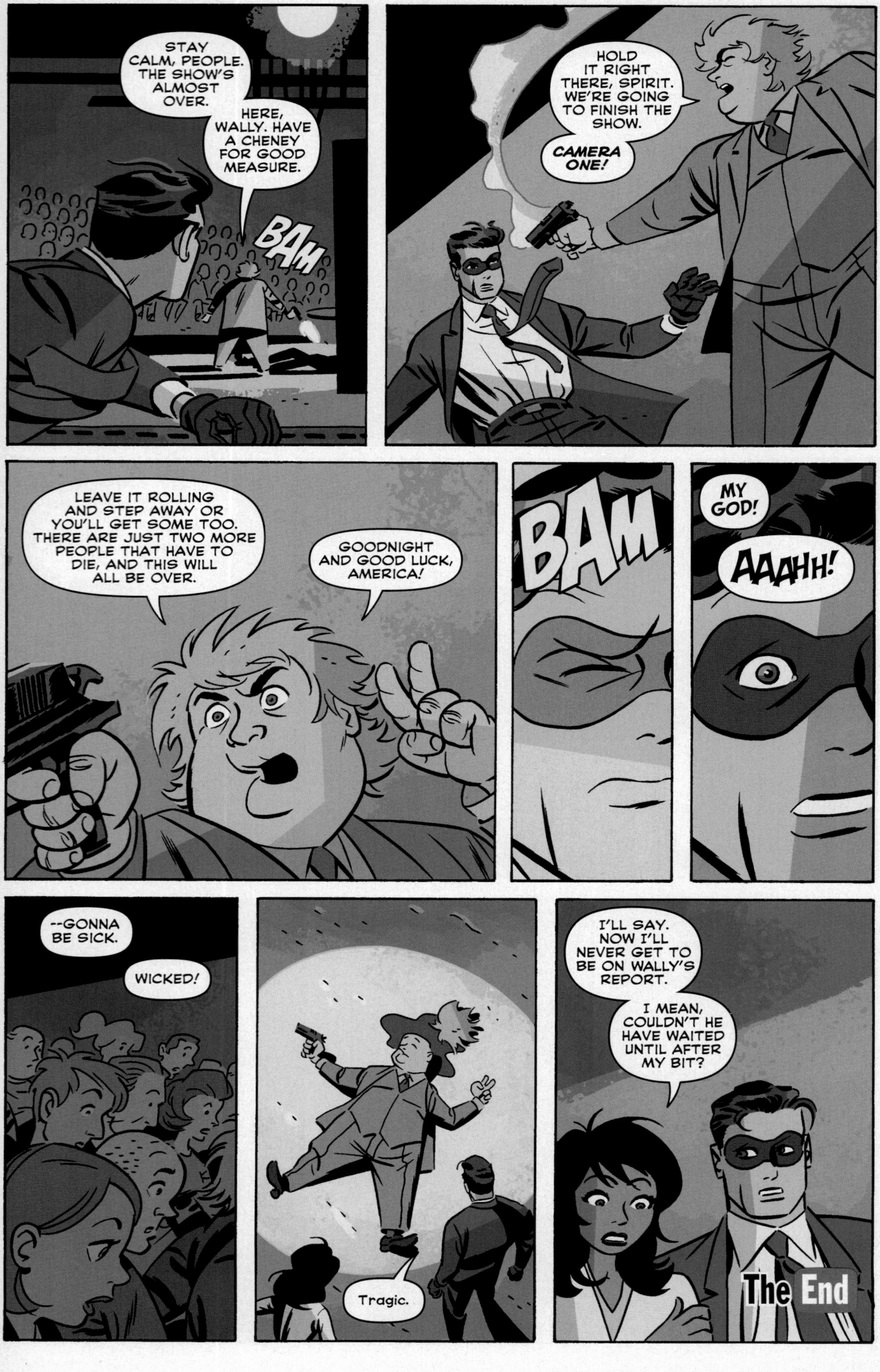
STAY CALM, PEOPLE. THE SHOW'S ALMOST OVER.
HERE, WALLY. HAVE A CHENEY FOR GOOD MEASURE.
BAM
HOLD IT RIGHT THERE, SPIRIT. WE'RE GOING TO FINISH THE SHOW.
CAMERA ONE!
LEAVE IT ROLLING AND STEP AWAY OR YOU'LL GET SOME TOO. THERE ARE JUST TWO MORE PEOPLE THAT HAVE TO DIE, AND THIS WILL ALL BE OVER.
GOODNIGHT AND GOOD LUCK, AMERICA!
BAM
MY GOD!
AAAHH!
--GONNA BE SICK.
WICKED!
Tragic.
I'LL SAY. NOW I'LL NEVER GET TO BE ON WALLY'S REPORT.
I MEAN, COULDN'T HE HAVE WAITED UNTIL AFTER MY BIT?
The End

5

ACTION • Mystery • ADVENTURE

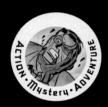

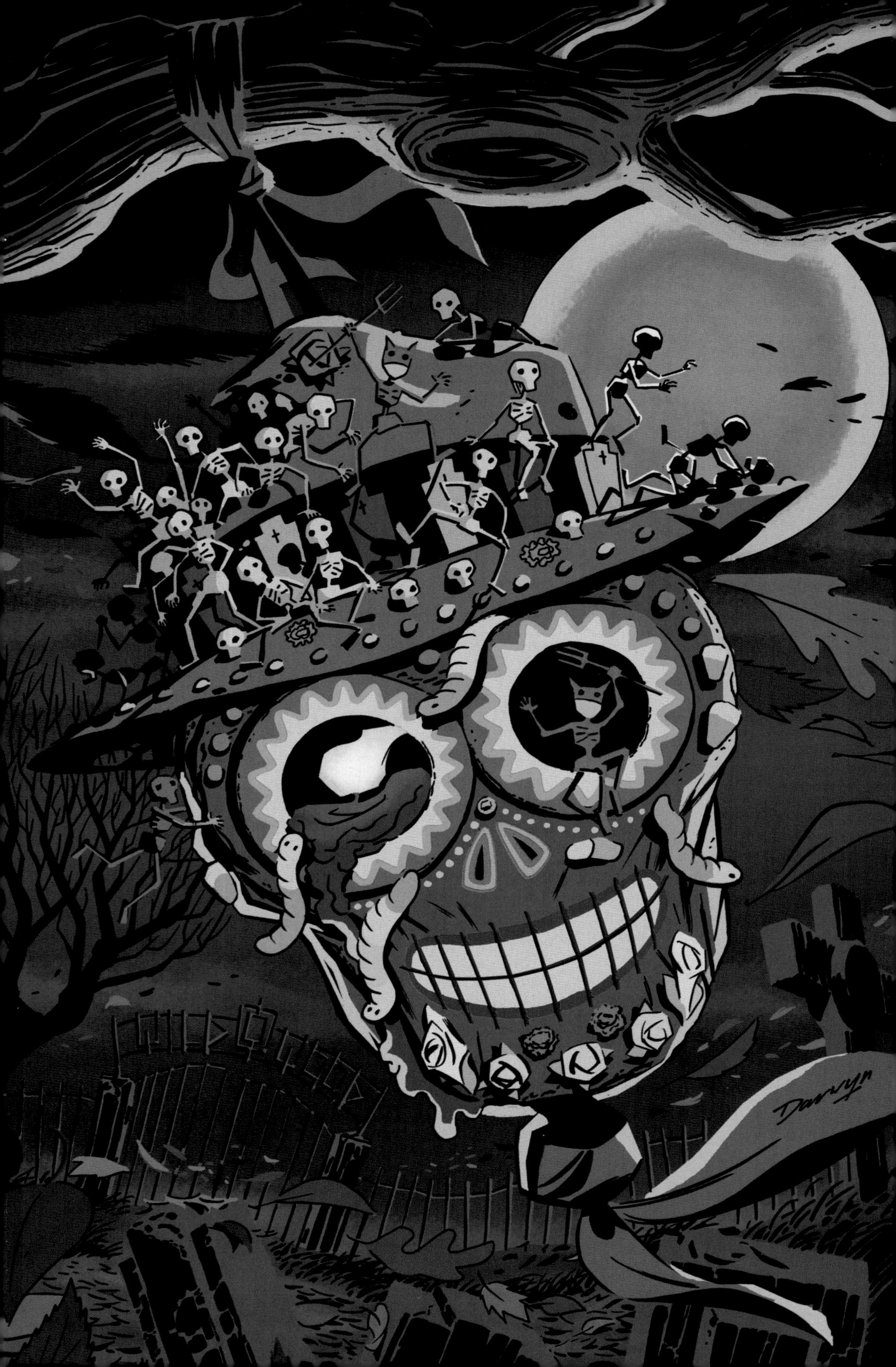
Darwyn

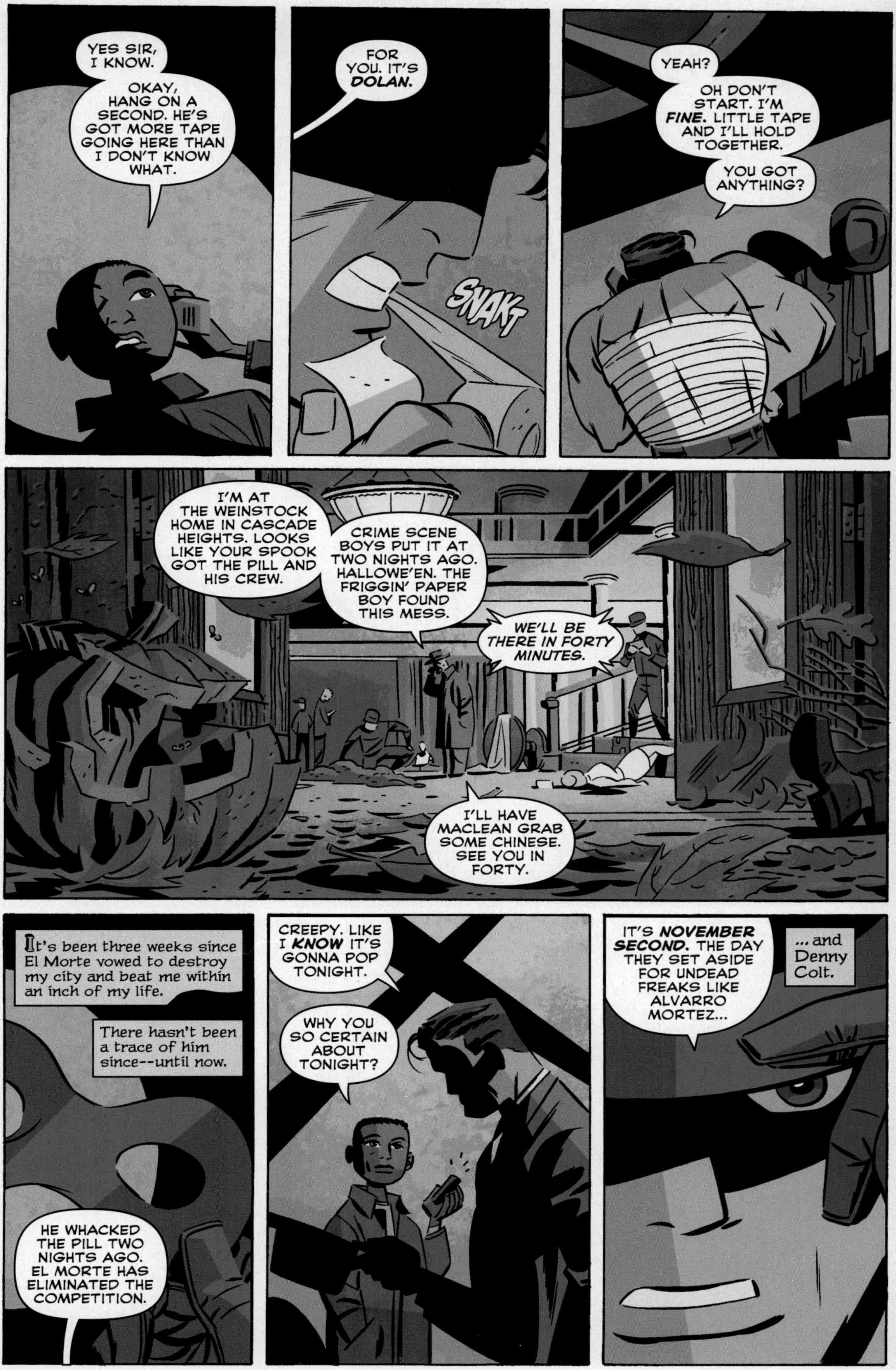
YES SIR, I KNOW.
OKAY, HANG ON A SECOND. HE'S GOT MORE TAPE GOING HERE THAN I DON'T KNOW WHAT.
FOR YOU. IT'S DOLAN.
SNAKT
YEAH?
OH DON'T START. I'M FINE. LITTLE TAPE AND I'LL HOLD TOGETHER.
YOU GOT ANYTHING?
I'M AT THE WEINSTOCK HOME IN CASCADE HEIGHTS. LOOKS LIKE YOUR SPOOK GOT THE PILL AND HIS CREW.
CRIME SCENE BOYS PUT IT AT TWO NIGHTS AGO. HALLOWE'EN. THE FRIGGIN' PAPER BOY FOUND THIS MESS.
WE'LL BE THERE IN FORTY MINUTES.
I'LL HAVE MACLEAN GRAB SOME CHINESE. SEE YOU IN FORTY.
It's been three weeks since El Morte vowed to destroy my city and beat me within an inch of my life.
There hasn't been a trace of him since--until now.
HE WHACKED THE PILL TWO NIGHTS AGO. EL MORTE HAS ELIMINATED THE COMPETITION.
CREEPY. LIKE I KNOW IT'S GONNA POP TONIGHT.
WHY YOU SO CERTAIN ABOUT TONIGHT?
IT'S NOVEMBER SECOND. THE DAY THEY SET ASIDE FOR UNDEAD FREAKS LIKE ALVARRO MORTEZ...
...and Denny Colt.

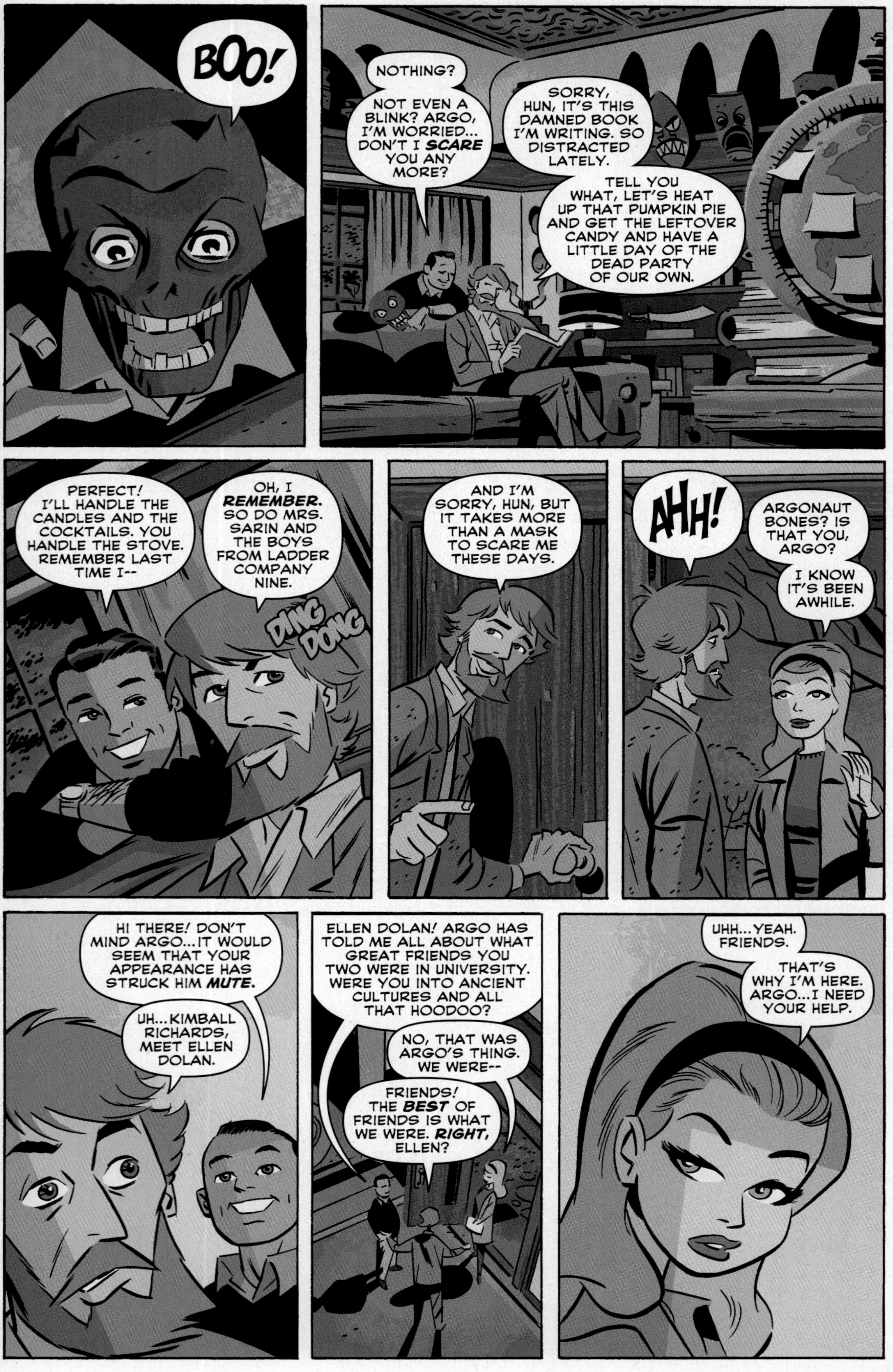
BOO!
NOTHING?
NOT EVEN A BLINK? ARGO, I'M WORRIED... DON'T I SCARE YOU ANY MORE?
SORRY, HUN, IT'S THIS DAMNED BOOK I'M WRITING. SO DISTRACTED LATELY.
TELL YOU WHAT, LET'S HEAT UP THAT PUMPKIN PIE AND GET THE LEFTOVER CANDY AND HAVE A LITTLE DAY OF THE DEAD PARTY OF OUR OWN.
PERFECT! I'LL HANDLE THE CANDLES AND THE COCKTAILS. YOU HANDLE THE STOVE. REMEMBER LAST TIME I--
OH, I REMEMBER. SO DO MRS. SARIN AND THE BOYS FROM LADDER COMPANY NINE.
DING DONG
AND I'M SORRY, HUN, BUT IT TAKES MORE THAN A MASK TO SCARE ME THESE DAYS.
AHH!
ARGONAUT BONES? IS THAT YOU, ARGO?
I KNOW IT'S BEEN AWHILE.
HI THERE! DON'T MIND ARGO...IT WOULD SEEM THAT YOUR APPEARANCE HAS STRUCK HIM MUTE.
UH...KIMBALL RICHARDS, MEET ELLEN DOLAN.
ELLEN DOLAN! ARGO HAS TOLD ME ALL ABOUT WHAT GREAT FRIENDS YOU TWO WERE IN UNIVERSITY. WERE YOU INTO ANCIENT CULTURES AND ALL THAT HOODOO?
NO, THAT WAS ARGO'S THING. WE WERE--
FRIENDS! THE BEST OF FRIENDS IS WHAT WE WERE. RIGHT, ELLEN?
UHH...YEAH. FRIENDS.
THAT'S WHY I'M HERE. ARGO...I NEED YOUR HELP.

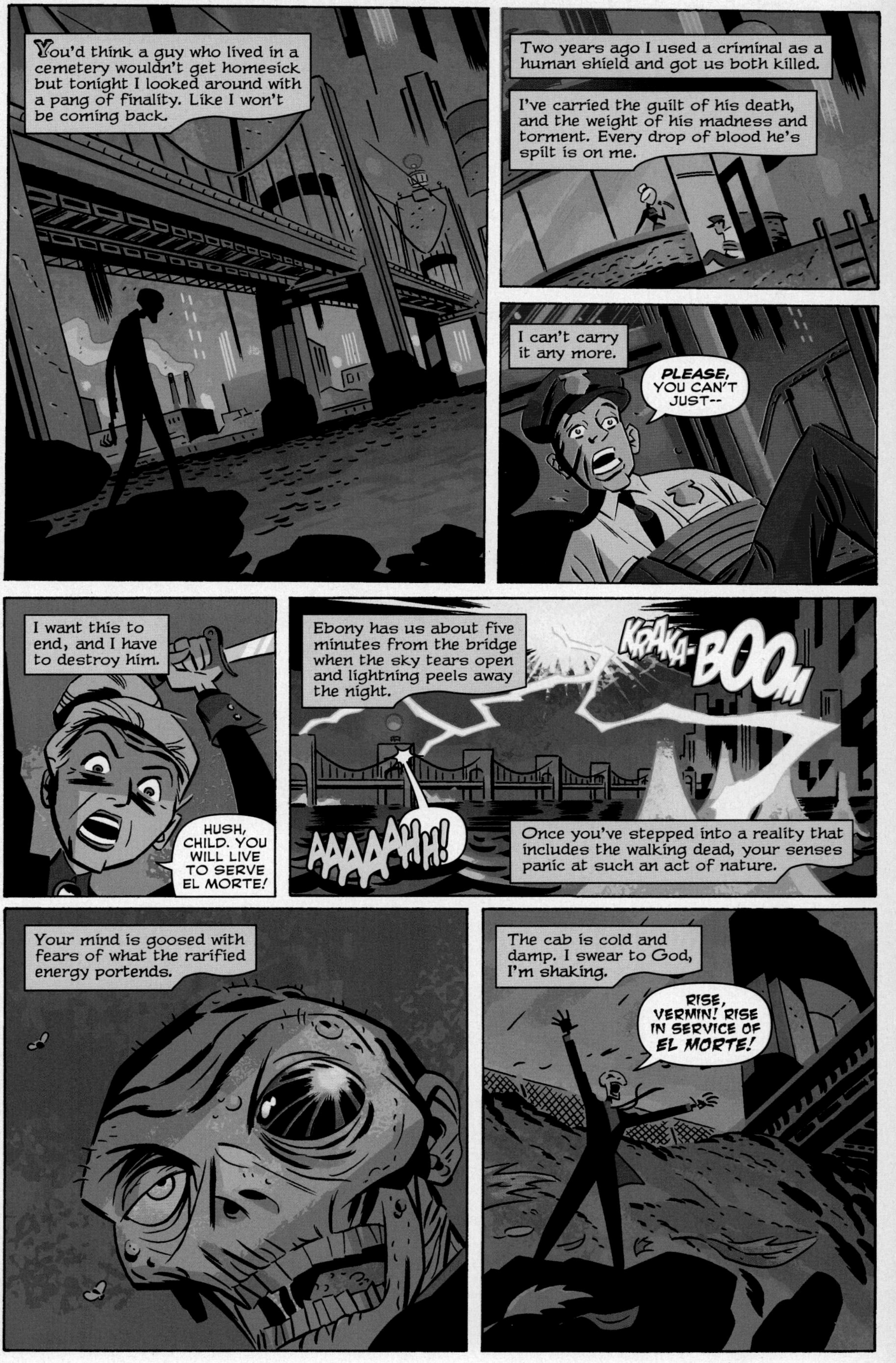
You'd think a guy who lived in a cemetery wouldn't get homesick but tonight I looked around with a pang of finality. Like I won't be coming back.
Two years ago I used a criminal as a human shield and got us both killed.
I've carried the guilt of his death, and the weight of his madness and torment. Every drop of blood he's spilt is on me.
I can't carry it any more.
PLEASE, YOU CAN'T JUST--
I want this to end, and I have to destroy him.
HUSH, CHILD. YOU WILL LIVE TO SERVE EL MORTE!
Ebony has us about five minutes from the bridge when the sky tears open and lightning peels away the night.
KRAKA-BOOM
AAAAAHH!
Once you've stepped into a reality that includes the walking dead, your senses panic at such an act of nature.
Your mind is goosed with fears of what the rarified energy portends.
The cab is cold and damp. I swear to God, I'm shaking.
RISE, VERMIN! RISE IN SERVICE OF EL MORTE!

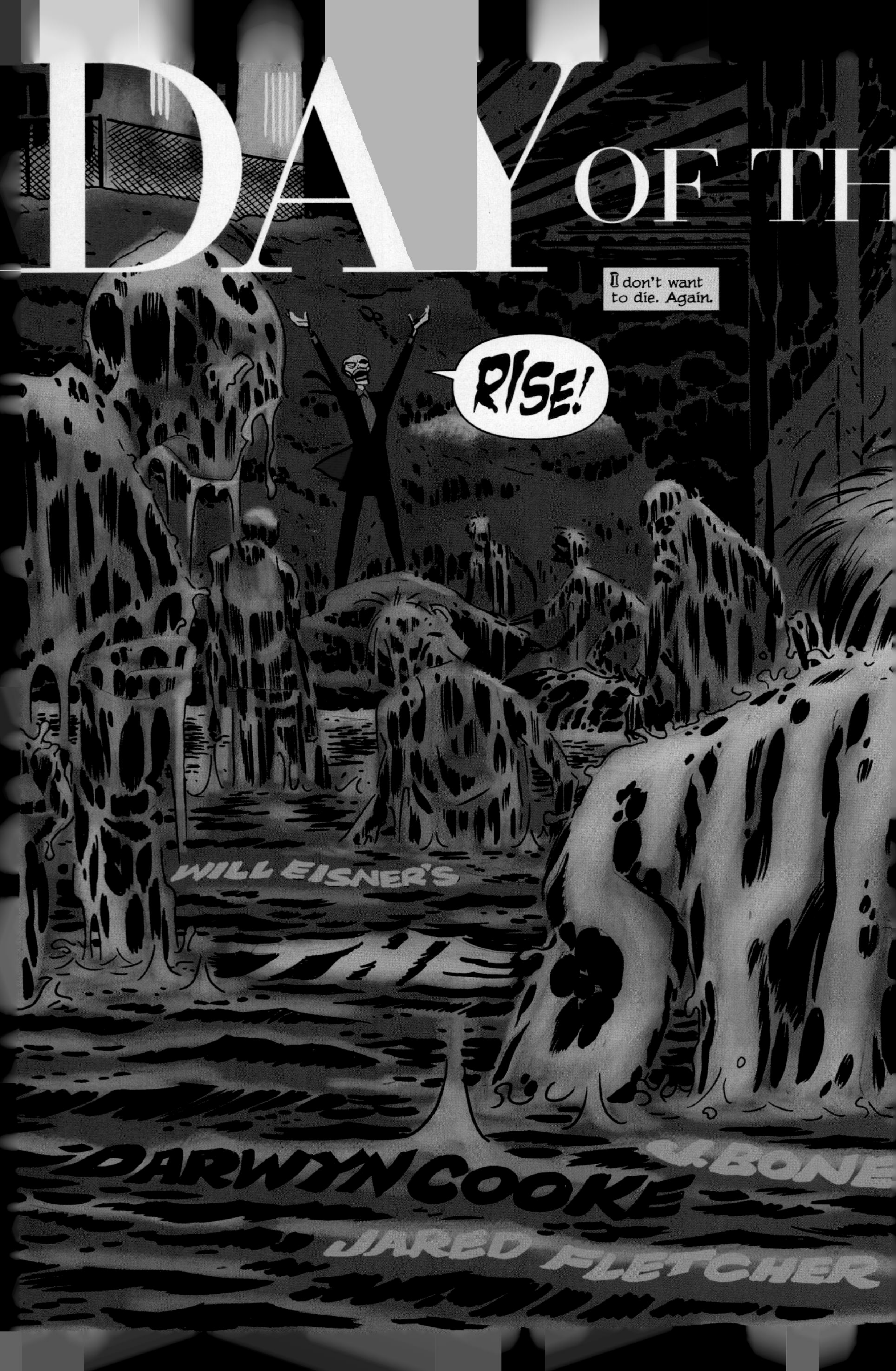
DAY OF TH
I don't want to die. Again.
RISE!
WILL EISNER'S
DARWYN COOKE
J. BONE
JARED FLETCHER

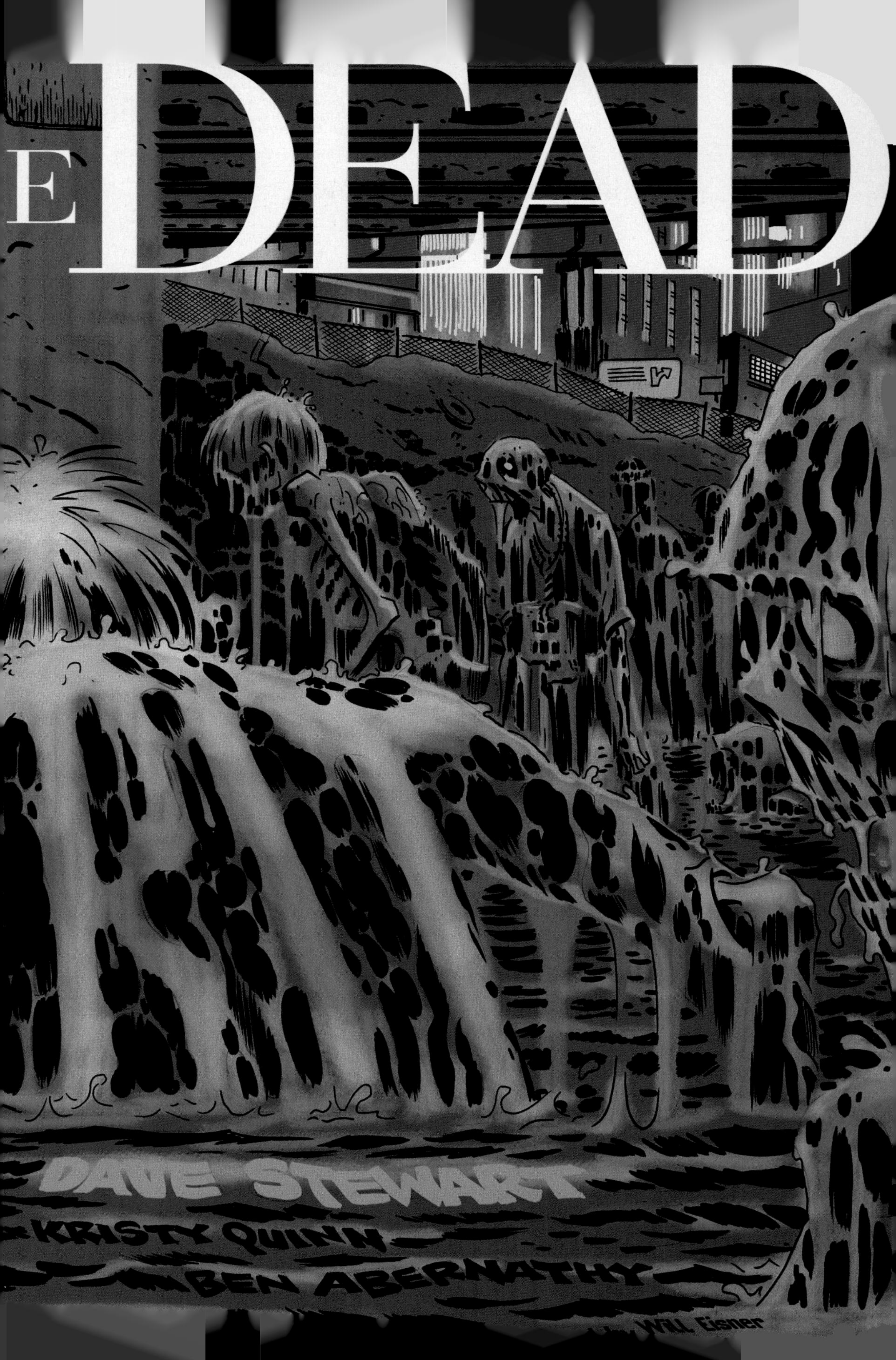
E DEAD
DAVE STEWART
KRISTY QUINN
BEN ABERNATHY
Will Eisner

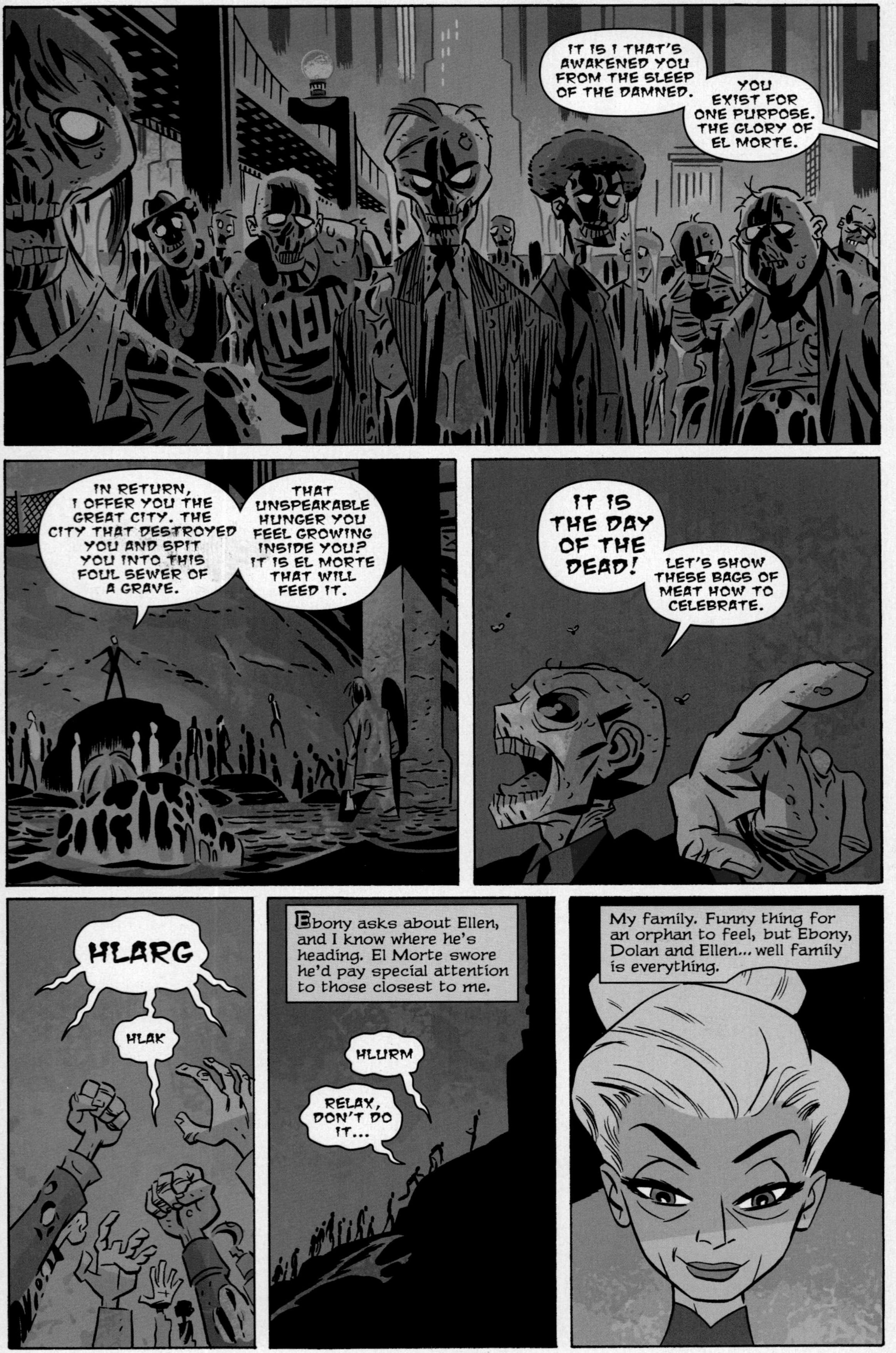
IT IS I THAT'S AWAKENED YOU FROM THE SLEEP OF THE DAMNED.
YOU EXIST FOR ONE PURPOSE. THE GLORY OF EL MORTE.
IN RETURN, I OFFER YOU THE GREAT CITY. THE CITY THAT DESTROYED YOU AND SPIT YOU INTO THIS FOUL SEWER OF A GRAVE.
THAT UNSPEAKABLE HUNGER YOU FEEL GROWING INSIDE YOU? IT IS EL MORTE THAT WILL FEED IT.
IT IS THE DAY OF THE DEAD!
LET'S SHOW THESE BAGS OF MEAT HOW TO CELEBRATE.
HLARG
HLAK
Ebony asks about Ellen, and I know where he's heading. El Morte swore he'd pay special attention to those closest to me.
HLURM
RELAX, DON'T DO IT...
My family. Funny thing for an orphan to feel, but Ebony, Dolan and Ellen... well family is everything.

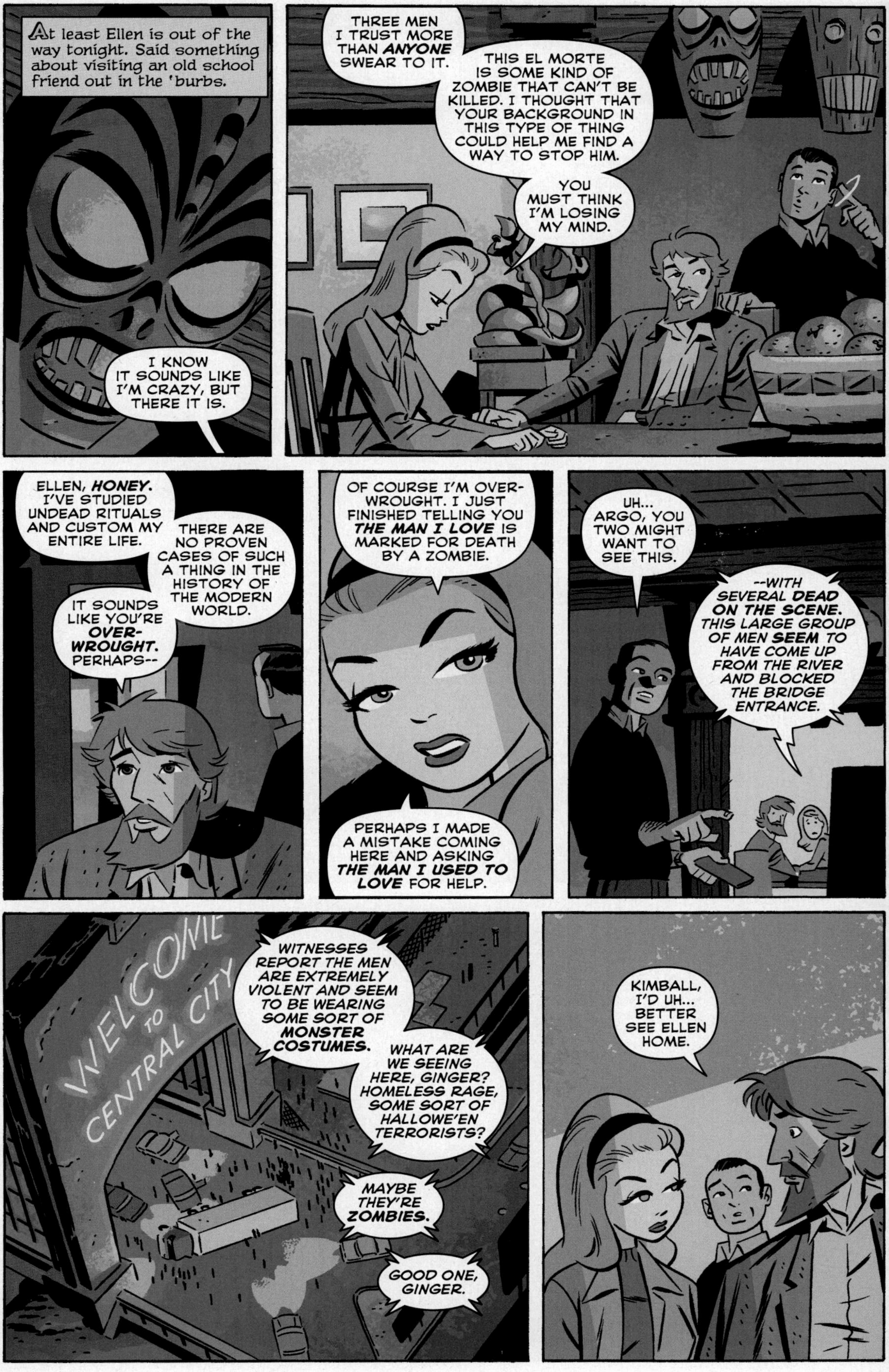
At least Ellen is out of the way tonight. Said something about visiting an old school friend out in the 'burbs.
I KNOW IT SOUNDS LIKE I'M CRAZY, BUT THERE IT IS.
THREE MEN I TRUST MORE THAN ANYONE SWEAR TO IT.
THIS EL MORTE IS SOME KIND OF ZOMBIE THAT CAN'T BE KILLED. I THOUGHT THAT YOUR BACKGROUND IN THIS TYPE OF THING COULD HELP ME FIND A WAY TO STOP HIM.
YOU MUST THINK I'M LOSING MY MIND.
ELLEN, HONEY. I'VE STUDIED UNDEAD RITUALS AND CUSTOM MY ENTIRE LIFE.
THERE ARE NO PROVEN CASES OF SUCH A THING IN THE HISTORY OF THE MODERN WORLD.
IT SOUNDS LIKE YOU'RE OVER-WROUGHT. PERHAPS--
OF COURSE I'M OVER-WROUGHT. I JUST FINISHED TELLING YOU THE MAN I LOVE IS MARKED FOR DEATH BY A ZOMBIE.
PERHAPS I MADE A MISTAKE COMING HERE AND ASKING THE MAN I USED TO LOVE FOR HELP.
UH... ARGO, YOU TWO MIGHT WANT TO SEE THIS.
--WITH SEVERAL DEAD ON THE SCENE. THIS LARGE GROUP OF MEN SEEM TO HAVE COME UP FROM THE RIVER AND BLOCKED THE BRIDGE ENTRANCE.
WELCOME TO CENTRAL CITY
WITNESSES REPORT THE MEN ARE EXTREMELY VIOLENT AND SEEM TO BE WEARING SOME SORT OF MONSTER COSTUMES.
WHAT ARE WE SEEING HERE, GINGER? HOMELESS RAGE, SOME SORT OF HALLOWE'EN TERRORISTS?
MAYBE THEY'RE ZOMBIES.
GOOD ONE, GINGER.
KIMBALL, I'D UH... BETTER SEE ELLEN HOME.

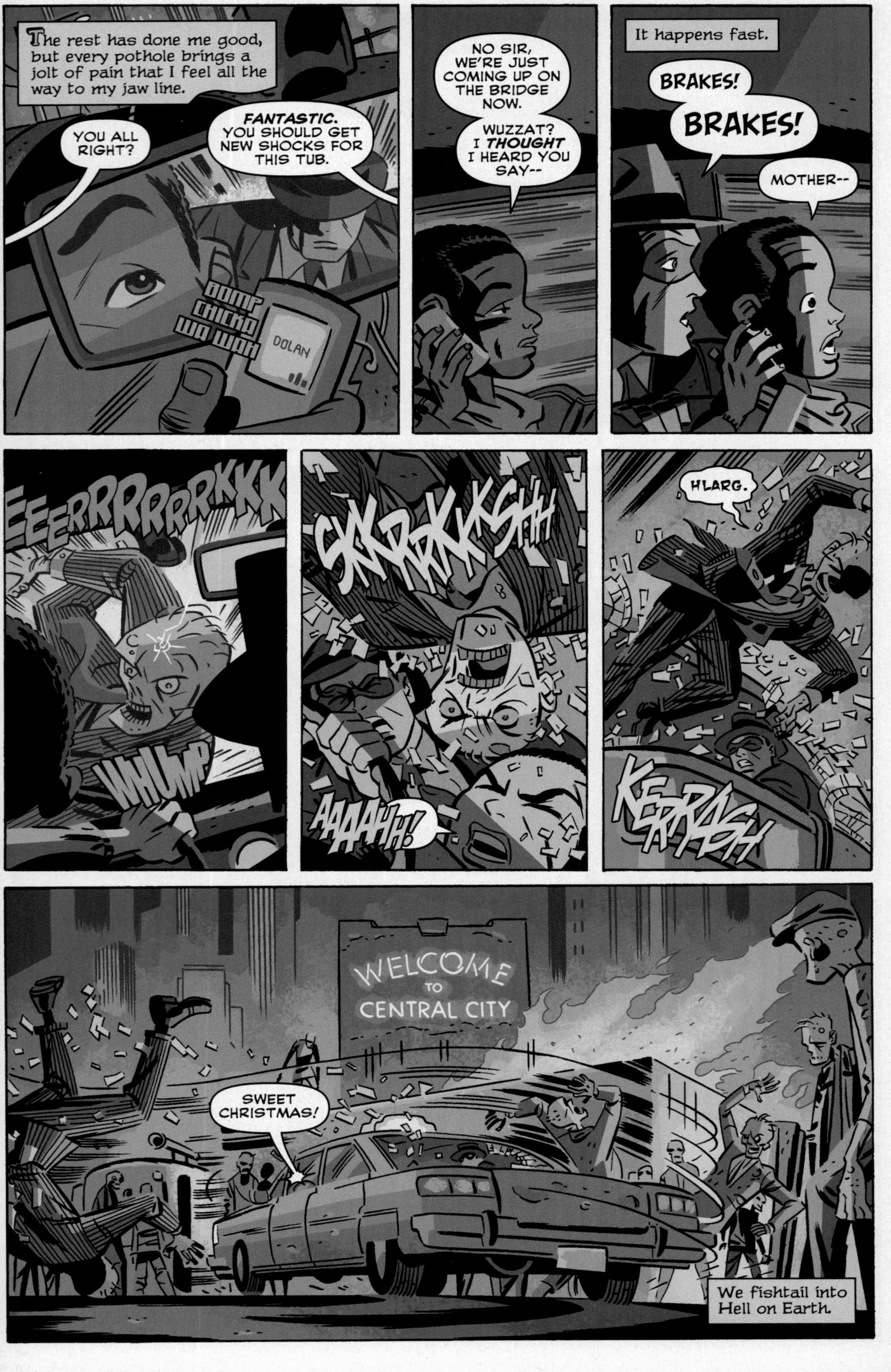
The rest has done me good, but every pothole brings a jolt of pain that I feel all the way to my jaw line.
YOU ALL RIGHT?
FANTASTIC. YOU SHOULD GET NEW SHOCKS FOR THIS TUB.
BOMP CHICKA WA WAH
DOLAN
NO SIR, WE'RE JUST COMING UP ON THE BRIDGE NOW.
WUZZAT? I THOUGHT I HEARD YOU SAY--
It happens fast.
BRAKES!
BRAKES!
MOTHER--
EEERRRRRRRKKK
WHUMP
SKKRRKKKSHH
AAAAHH!
HLARG.
KERRASH
WELCOME TO CENTRAL CITY
SWEET CHRISTMAS!
We fishtail into Hell on Earth.

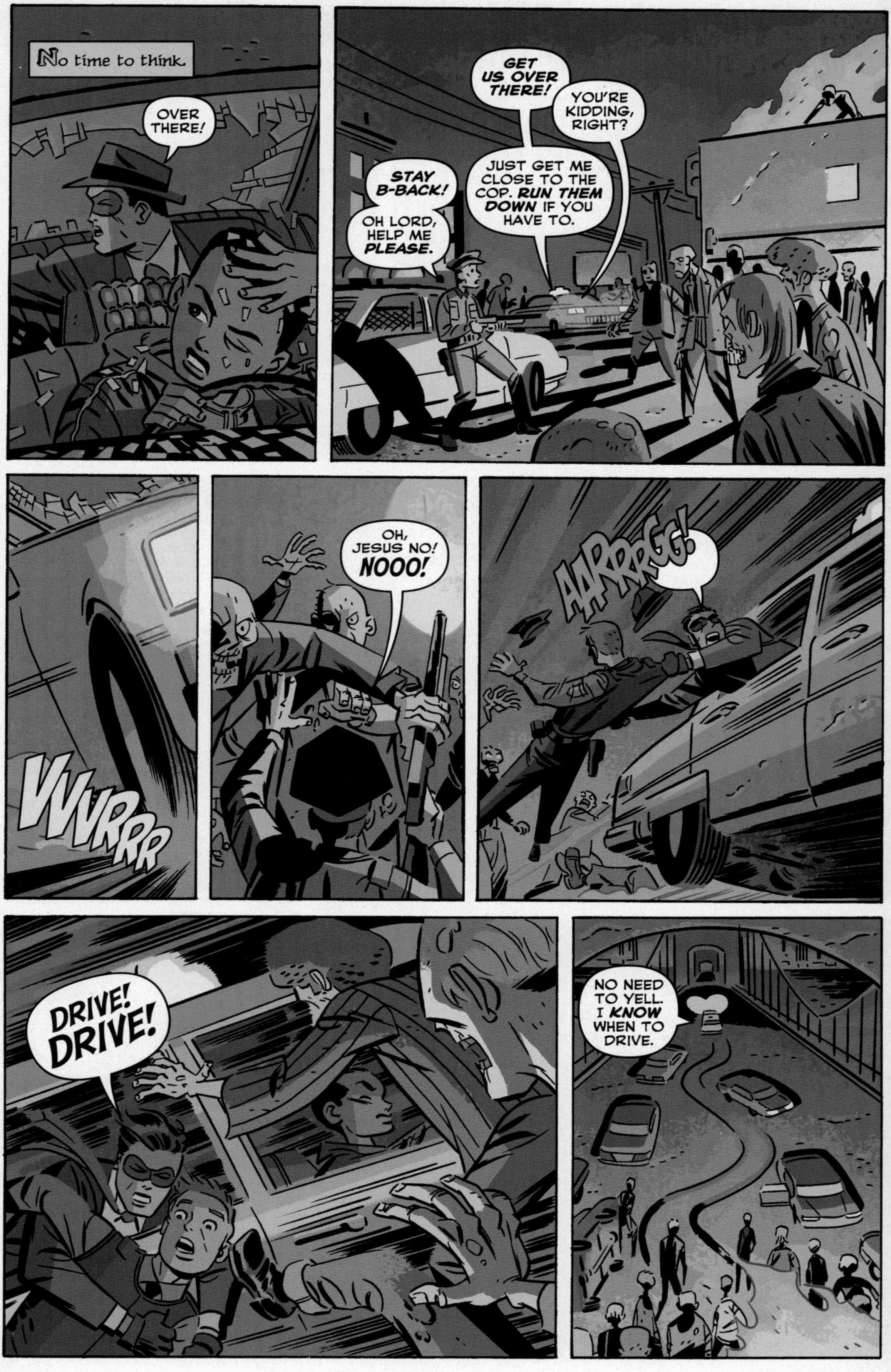
No time to think.
OVER THERE!
GET US OVER THERE!
YOU'RE KIDDING, RIGHT?
STAY B-BACK!
OH LORD, HELP ME PLEASE.
JUST GET ME CLOSE TO THE COP. RUN THEM DOWN IF YOU HAVE TO.
VVVRRR
OH, JESUS NO! NOOO!
AARRRGG!
DRIVE! DRIVE!
NO NEED TO YELL. I KNOW WHEN TO DRIVE.

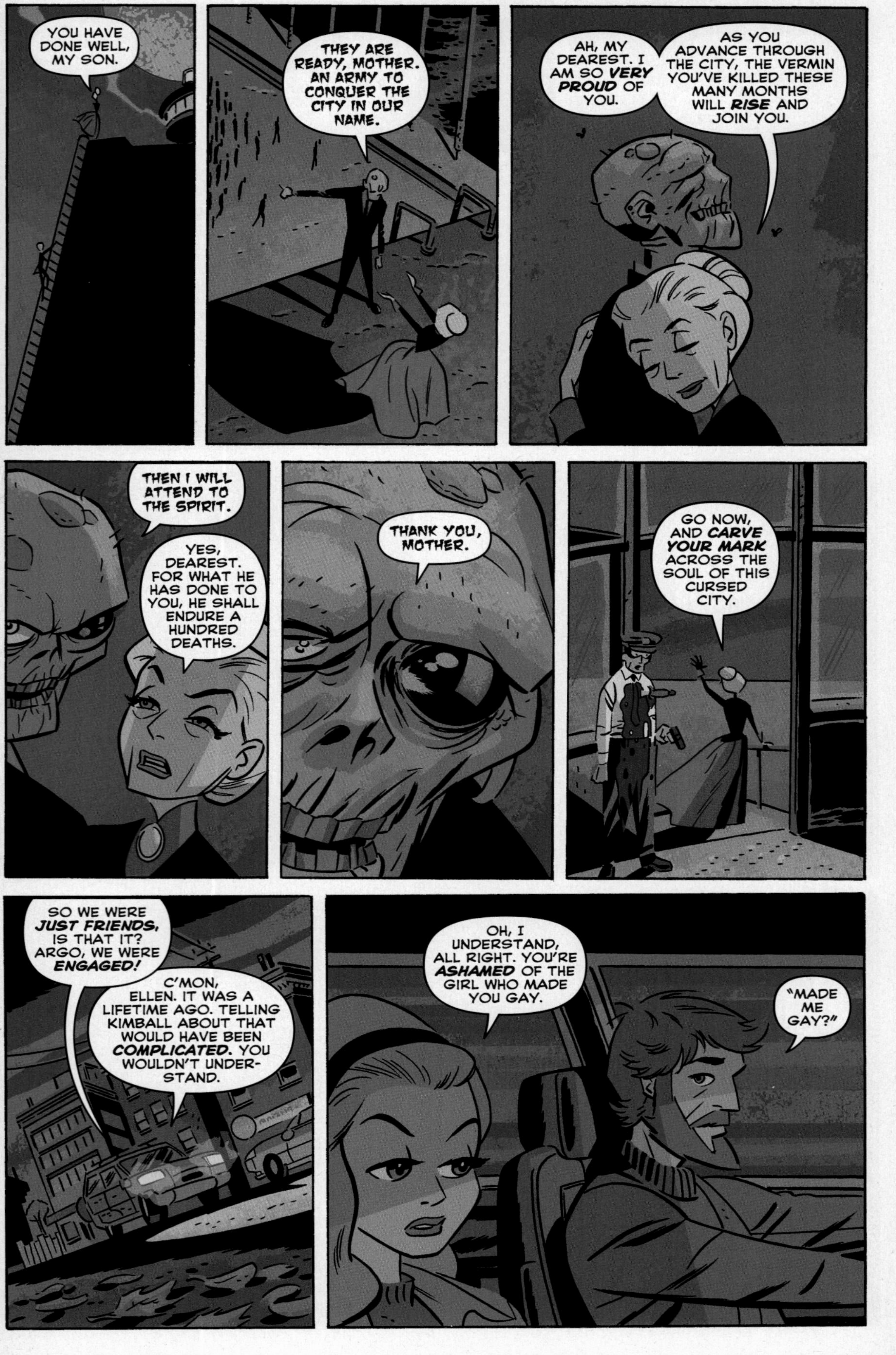
YOU HAVE DONE WELL, MY SON.
THEY ARE READY, MOTHER. AN ARMY TO CONQUER THE CITY IN OUR NAME.
AH, MY DEAREST. I AM SO *VERY PROUD* OF YOU.
AS YOU ADVANCE THROUGH THE CITY, THE VERMIN YOU'VE KILLED THESE MANY MONTHS WILL *RISE* AND JOIN YOU.
THEN I WILL ATTEND TO THE SPIRIT.
YES, DEAREST. FOR WHAT HE HAS DONE TO YOU, HE SHALL ENDURE A HUNDRED DEATHS.
THANK YOU, MOTHER.
GO NOW, AND *CARVE YOUR MARK* ACROSS THE SOUL OF THIS CURSED CITY.
SO WE WERE *JUST FRIENDS,* IS THAT IT? ARGO, WE WERE *ENGAGED!*
C'MON, ELLEN. IT WAS A LIFETIME AGO. TELLING KIMBALL ABOUT THAT WOULD HAVE BEEN *COMPLICATED.* YOU WOULDN'T UNDER-STAND.
OH, I UNDERSTAND, ALL RIGHT. YOU'RE *ASHAMED* OF THE GIRL WHO MADE YOU GAY.
"MADE ME GAY?"

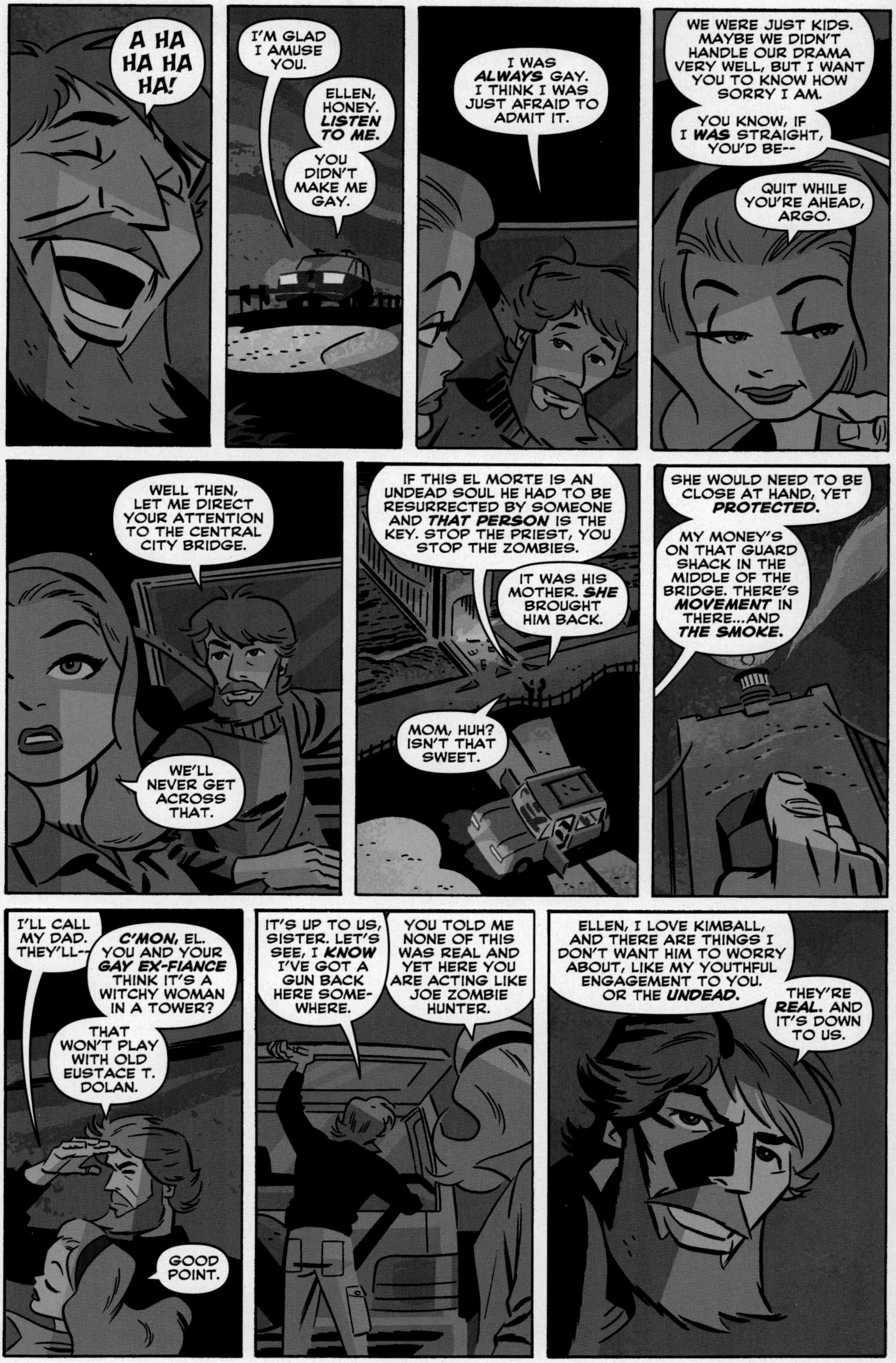

A HA HA HA HA!
I'M GLAD I AMUSE YOU.
ELLEN, HONEY. LISTEN TO ME.
YOU DIDN'T MAKE ME GAY.
I WAS ALWAYS GAY. I THINK I WAS JUST AFRAID TO ADMIT IT.
WE WERE JUST KIDS. MAYBE WE DIDN'T HANDLE OUR DRAMA VERY WELL, BUT I WANT YOU TO KNOW HOW SORRY I AM.
YOU KNOW, IF I WAS STRAIGHT, YOU'D BE--
QUIT WHILE YOU'RE AHEAD, ARGO.
WELL THEN, LET ME DIRECT YOUR ATTENTION TO THE CENTRAL CITY BRIDGE.
WE'LL NEVER GET ACROSS THAT.
IF THIS EL MORTE IS AN UNDEAD SOUL HE HAD TO BE RESURRECTED BY SOMEONE AND THAT PERSON IS THE KEY. STOP THE PRIEST, YOU STOP THE ZOMBIES.
IT WAS HIS MOTHER. SHE BROUGHT HIM BACK.
MOM, HUH? ISN'T THAT SWEET.
SHE WOULD NEED TO BE CLOSE AT HAND, YET PROTECTED.
MY MONEY'S ON THAT GUARD SHACK IN THE MIDDLE OF THE BRIDGE. THERE'S MOVEMENT IN THERE...AND THE SMOKE.
I'LL CALL MY DAD. THEY'LL--
C'MON, EL. YOU AND YOUR GAY EX-FIANCE THINK IT'S A WITCHY WOMAN IN A TOWER?
THAT WON'T PLAY WITH OLD EUSTACE T. DOLAN.
GOOD POINT.
IT'S UP TO US, SISTER. LET'S SEE, I KNOW I'VE GOT A GUN BACK HERE SOME-WHERE.
YOU TOLD ME NONE OF THIS WAS REAL AND YET HERE YOU ARE ACTING LIKE JOE ZOMBIE HUNTER.
ELLEN, I LOVE KIMBALL, AND THERE ARE THINGS I DON'T WANT HIM TO WORRY ABOUT, LIKE MY YOUTHFUL ENGAGEMENT TO YOU. OR THE UNDEAD.
THEY'RE REAL. AND IT'S DOWN TO US.

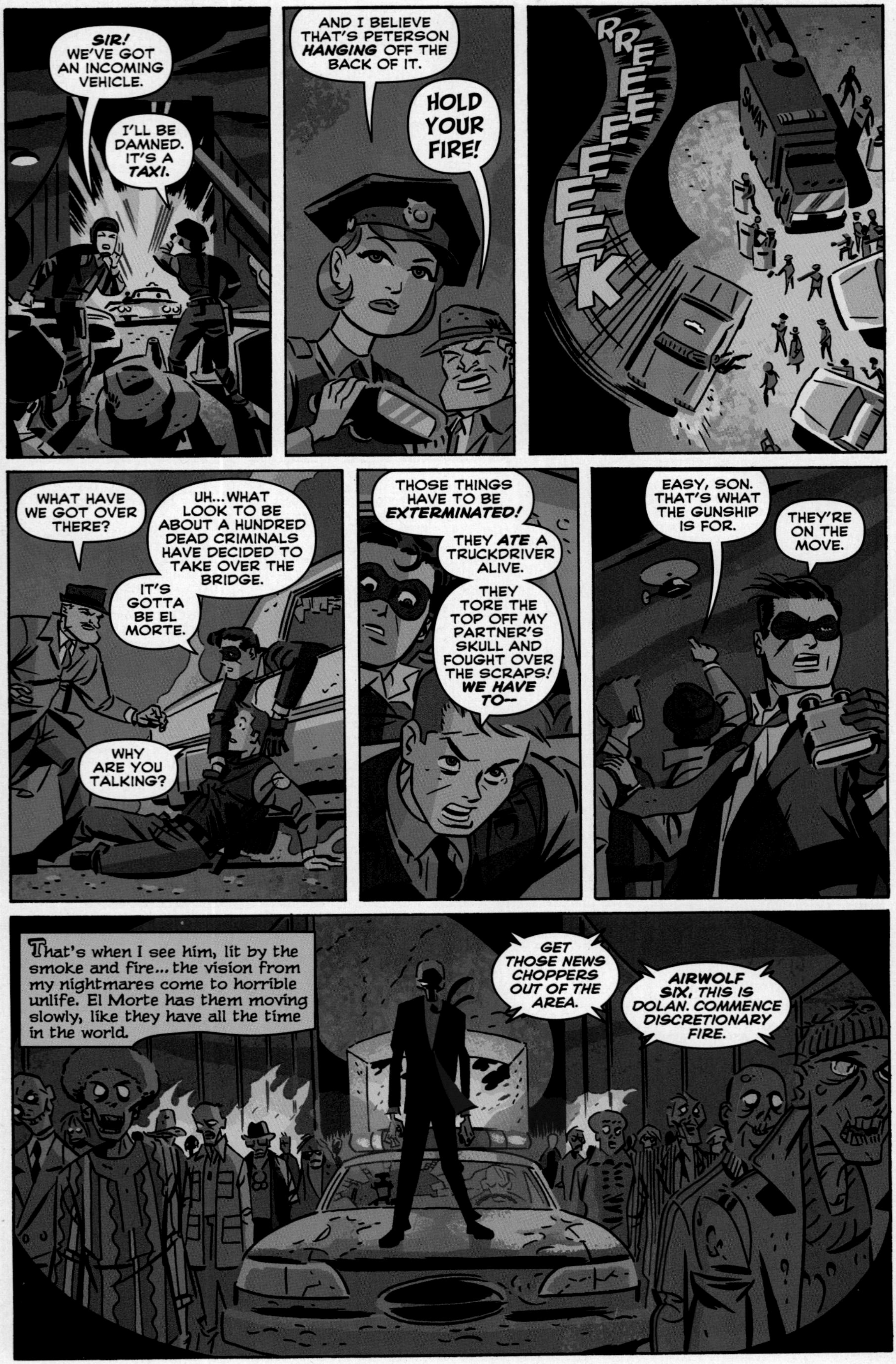

SIR! WE'VE GOT AN INCOMING VEHICLE.
I'LL BE DAMNED. IT'S A TAXI.
AND I BELIEVE THAT'S PETERSON HANGING OFF THE BACK OF IT.
HOLD YOUR FIRE!
RREEEEEEEK
WHAT HAVE WE GOT OVER THERE?
UH...WHAT LOOK TO BE ABOUT A HUNDRED DEAD CRIMINALS HAVE DECIDED TO TAKE OVER THE BRIDGE.
IT'S GOTTA BE EL MORTE.
WHY ARE YOU TALKING?
THOSE THINGS HAVE TO BE EXTERMINATED!
THEY ATE A TRUCKDRIVER ALIVE.
THEY TORE THE TOP OFF MY PARTNER'S SKULL AND FOUGHT OVER THE SCRAPS! WE HAVE TO--
EASY, SON. THAT'S WHAT THE GUNSHIP IS FOR.
THEY'RE ON THE MOVE.
That's when I see him, lit by the smoke and fire... the vision from my nightmares come to horrible unlife. El Morte has them moving slowly, like they have all the time in the world.
GET THOSE NEWS CHOPPERS OUT OF THE AREA.
AIRWOLF SIX, THIS IS DOLAN. COMMENCE DISCRETIONARY FIRE.

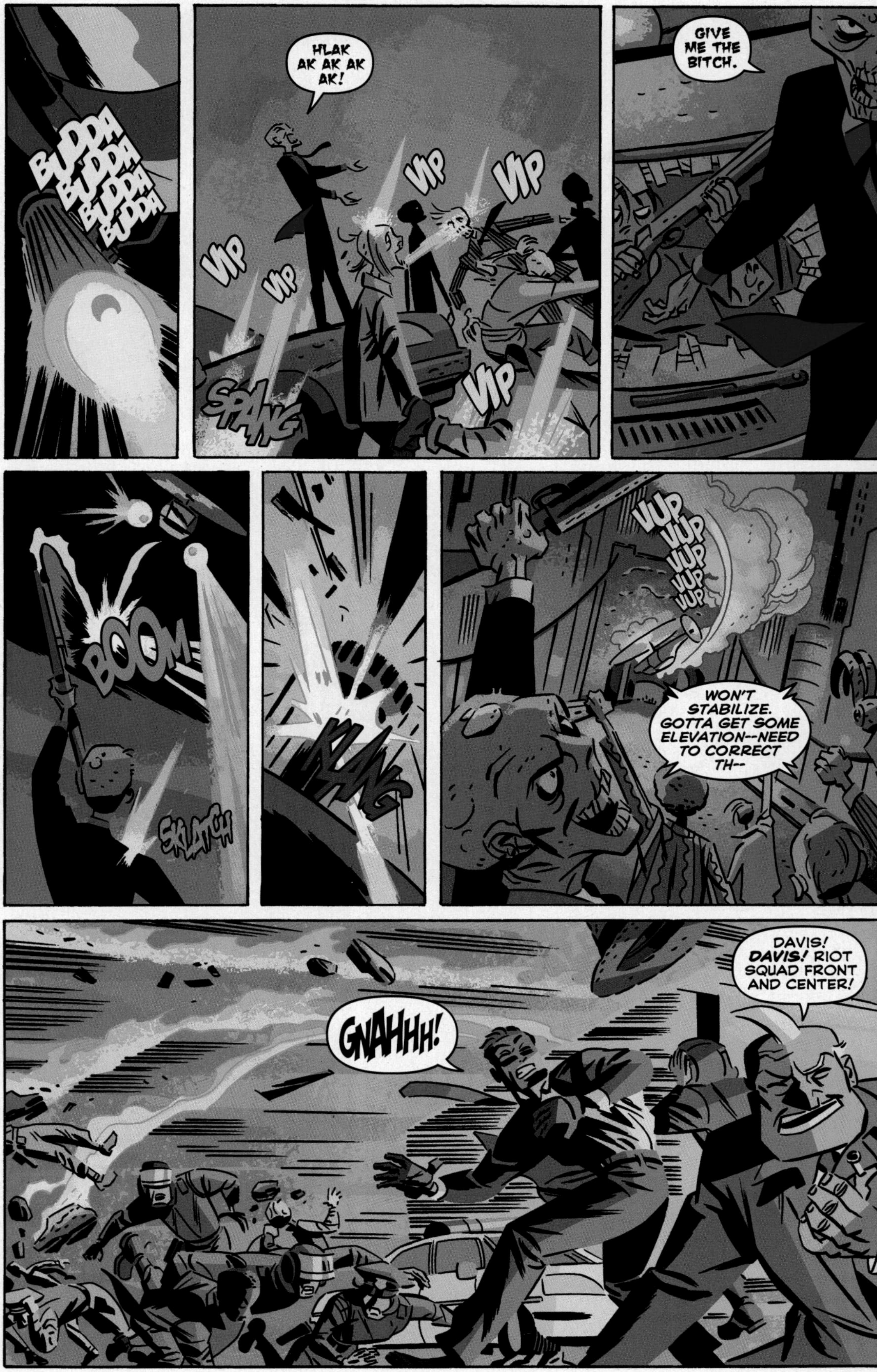
BUDDA BUDDA BUDDA BUDDA
H'LAK AK AK AK AK!
VIP
VIP
VIP
VIP
SPANG
VIP
GIVE ME THE BITCH.
BOOM
SKLATCH
KLANG
VUP VUP VUP VUP VUP
WON'T STABILIZE. GOTTA GET SOME ELEVATION--NEED TO CORRECT TH--
GNAHHH!
DAVIS! DAVIS! RIOT SQUAD FRONT AND CENTER!

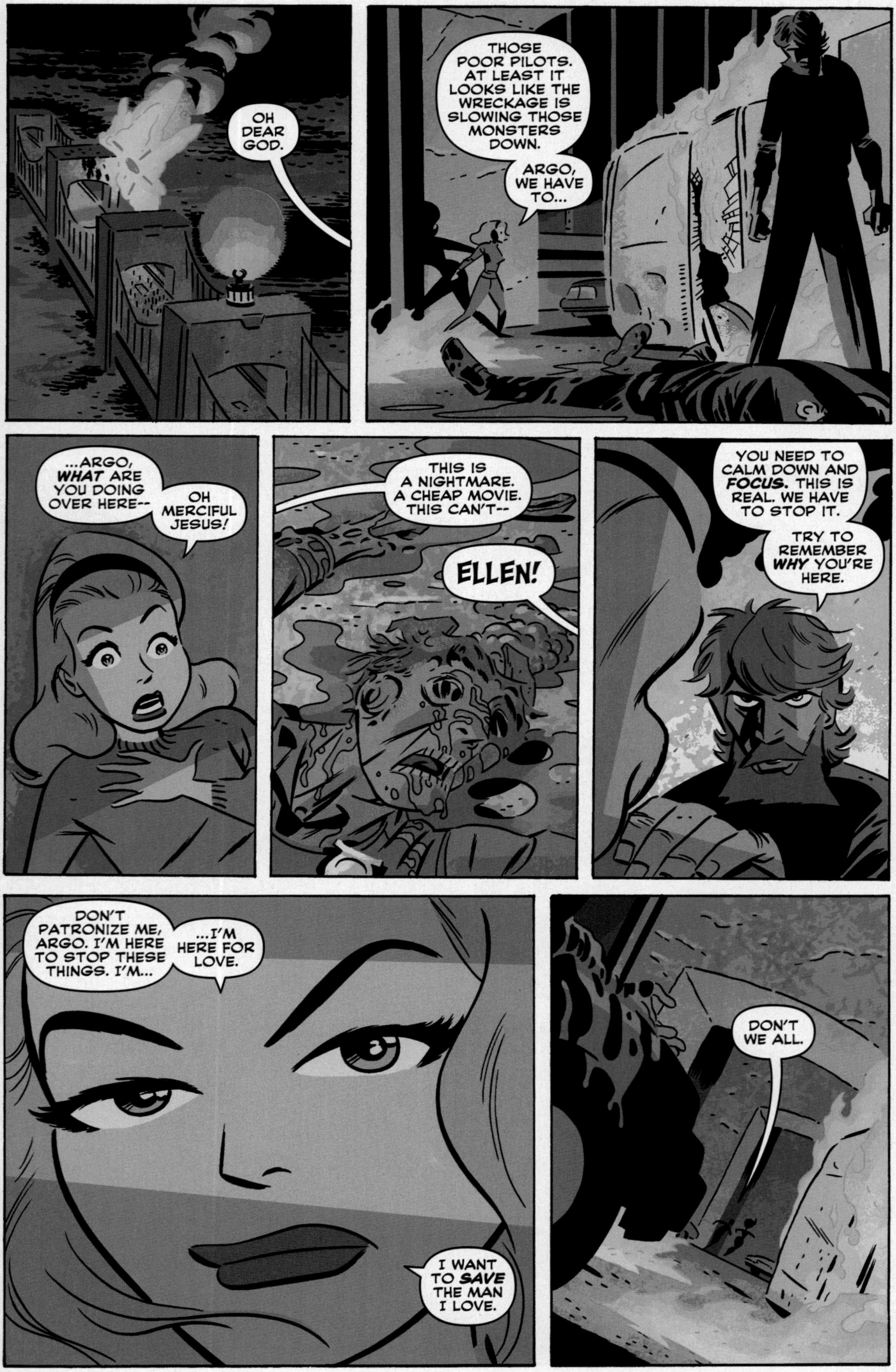
OH DEAR GOD.
THOSE POOR PILOTS. AT LEAST IT LOOKS LIKE THE WRECKAGE IS SLOWING THOSE MONSTERS DOWN.
ARGO, WE HAVE TO...
...ARGO, WHAT ARE YOU DOING OVER HERE--
OH MERCIFUL JESUS!
THIS IS A NIGHTMARE. A CHEAP MOVIE. THIS CAN'T--
ELLEN!
YOU NEED TO CALM DOWN AND FOCUS. THIS IS REAL. WE HAVE TO STOP IT.
TRY TO REMEMBER WHY YOU'RE HERE.
DON'T PATRONIZE ME, ARGO. I'M HERE TO STOP THESE THINGS. I'M...
...I'M HERE FOR LOVE.
I WANT TO SAVE THE MAN I LOVE.
DON'T WE ALL.

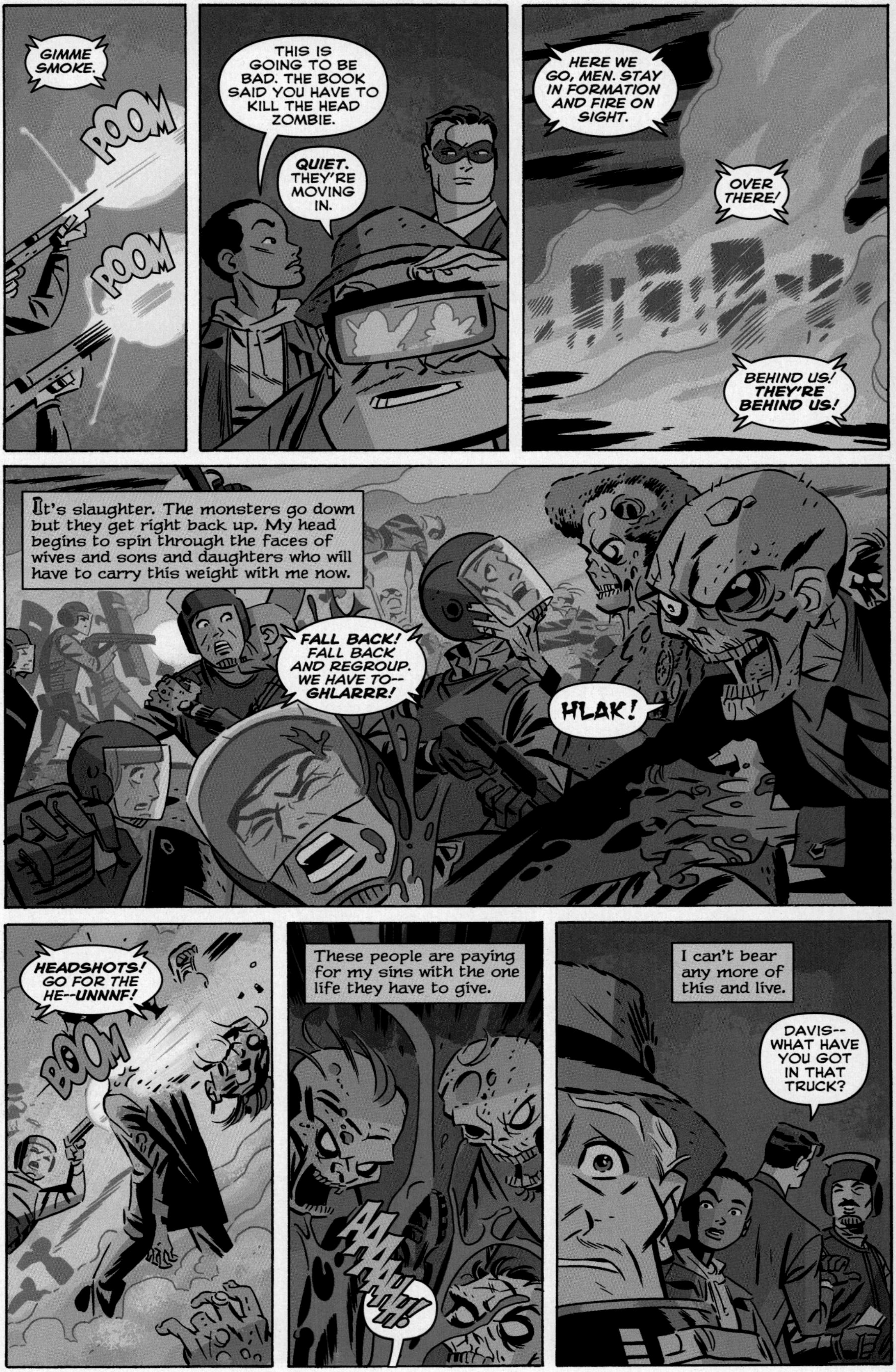
GIMME SMOKE.
POOM
POOM
THIS IS GOING TO BE BAD. THE BOOK SAID YOU HAVE TO KILL THE HEAD ZOMBIE.
QUIET. THEY'RE MOVING IN.
HERE WE GO, MEN. STAY IN FORMATION AND FIRE ON SIGHT.
OVER THERE!
BEHIND US! THEY'RE BEHIND US!
It's slaughter. The monsters go down but they get right back up. My head begins to spin through the faces of wives and sons and daughters who will have to carry this weight with me now.
FALL BACK! FALL BACK AND REGROUP. WE HAVE TO-- GHLARRR!
HLAK!
HEADSHOTS! GO FOR THE HE--UNNNF!
BOOM
These people are paying for my sins with the one life they have to give.
AAAHH!!
I can't bear any more of this and live.
DAVIS-- WHAT HAVE YOU GOT IN THAT TRUCK?

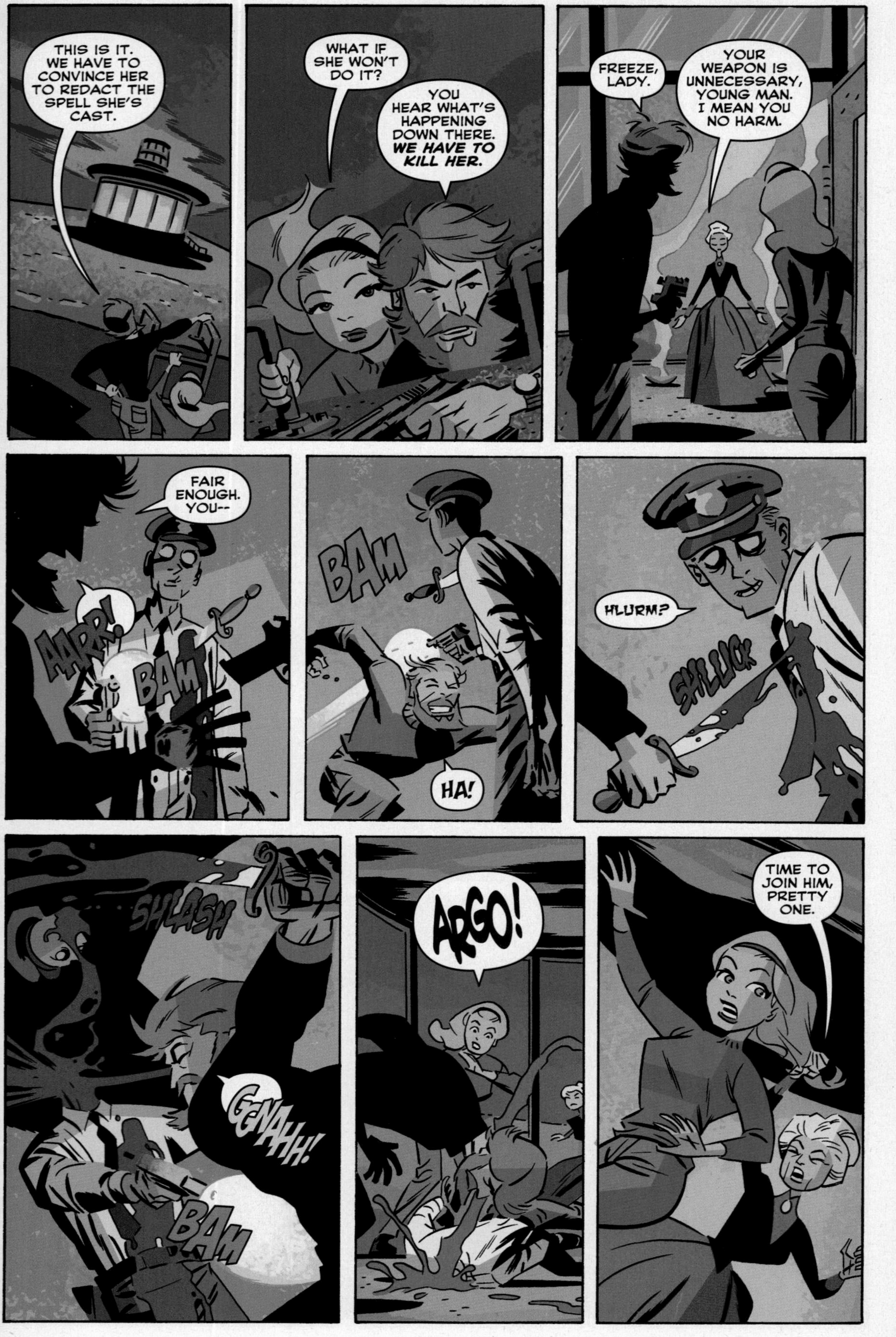
THIS IS IT. WE HAVE TO CONVINCE HER TO REDACT THE SPELL SHE'S CAST.
WHAT IF SHE WON'T DO IT?
YOU HEAR WHAT'S HAPPENING DOWN THERE. WE HAVE TO KILL HER.
FREEZE, LADY.
YOUR WEAPON IS UNNECESSARY, YOUNG MAN. I MEAN YOU NO HARM.
FAIR ENOUGH. YOU--
AARR!
BAM
BAM
HA!
HLURM?
SHLLICK
SHLASH
GGNAHH!
BAM
ARGO!
TIME TO JOIN HIM, PRETTY ONE.

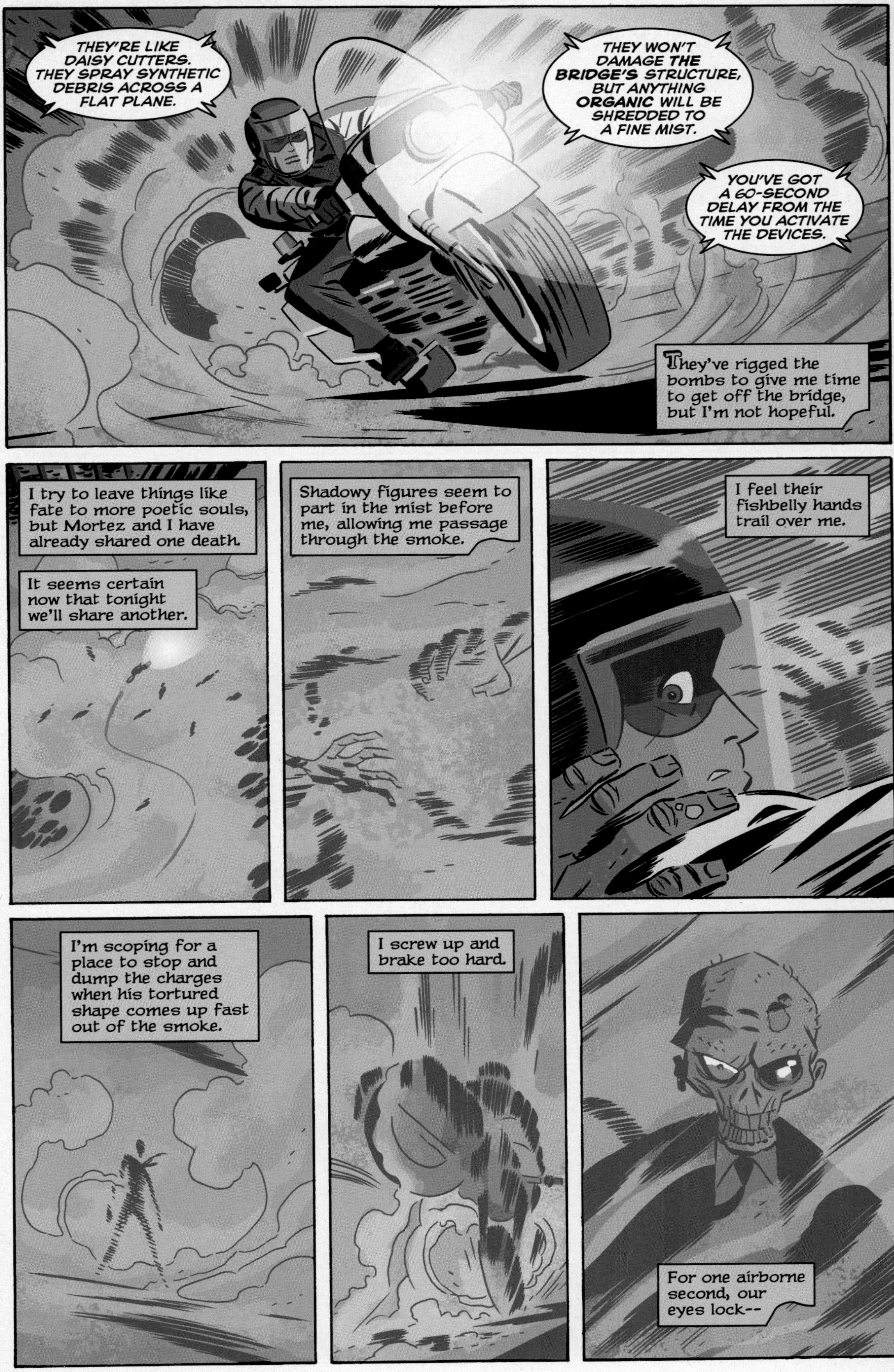
THEY'RE LIKE DAISY CUTTERS. THEY SPRAY SYNTHETIC DEBRIS ACROSS A FLAT PLANE.
THEY WON'T DAMAGE THE BRIDGE'S STRUCTURE, BUT ANYTHING ORGANIC WILL BE SHREDDED TO A FINE MIST.
YOU'VE GOT A 60-SECOND DELAY FROM THE TIME YOU ACTIVATE THE DEVICES.
They've rigged the bombs to give me time to get off the bridge, but I'm not hopeful.
I try to leave things like fate to more poetic souls, but Mortez and I have already shared one death.
It seems certain now that tonight we'll share another.
Shadowy figures seem to part in the mist before me, allowing me passage through the smoke.
I feel their fishbelly hands trail over me.
I'm scoping for a place to stop and dump the charges when his tortured shape comes up fast out of the smoke.
I screw up and brake too hard.
For one airborne second, our eyes lock--

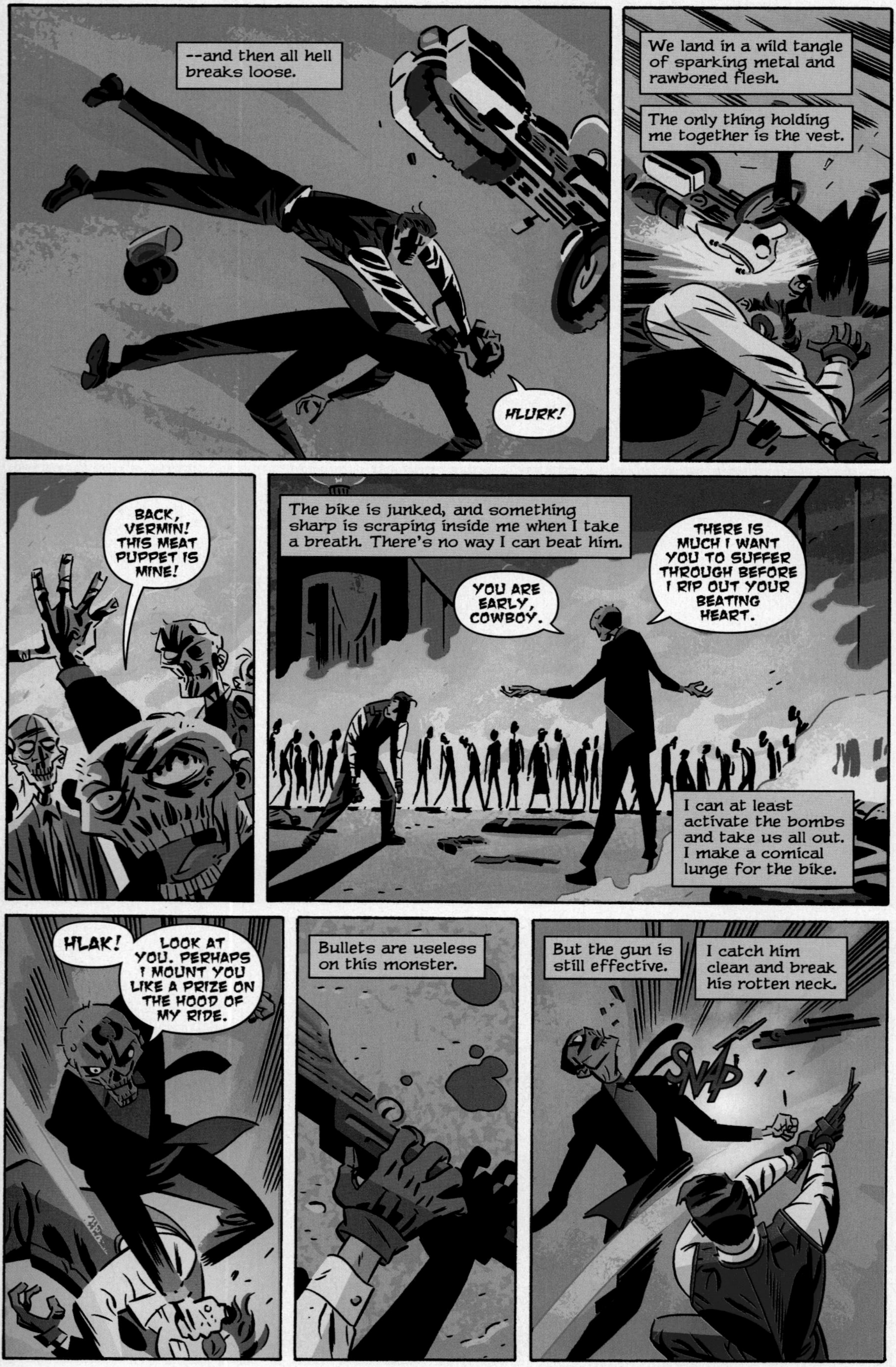
--and then all hell breaks loose.
HLURK!
We land in a wild tangle of sparking metal and rawboned flesh.
The only thing holding me together is the vest.
BACK, VERMIN! THIS MEAT PUPPET IS MINE!
The bike is junked, and something sharp is scraping inside me when I take a breath. There's no way I can beat him.
YOU ARE EARLY, COWBOY.
THERE IS MUCH I WANT YOU TO SUFFER THROUGH BEFORE I RIP OUT YOUR BEATING HEART.
I can at least activate the bombs and take us all out. I make a comical lunge for the bike.
HLAK!
LOOK AT YOU. PERHAPS I MOUNT YOU LIKE A PRIZE ON THE HOOD OF MY RIDE.
Bullets are useless on this monster.
But the gun is still effective.
I catch him clean and break his rotten neck.
SNAP

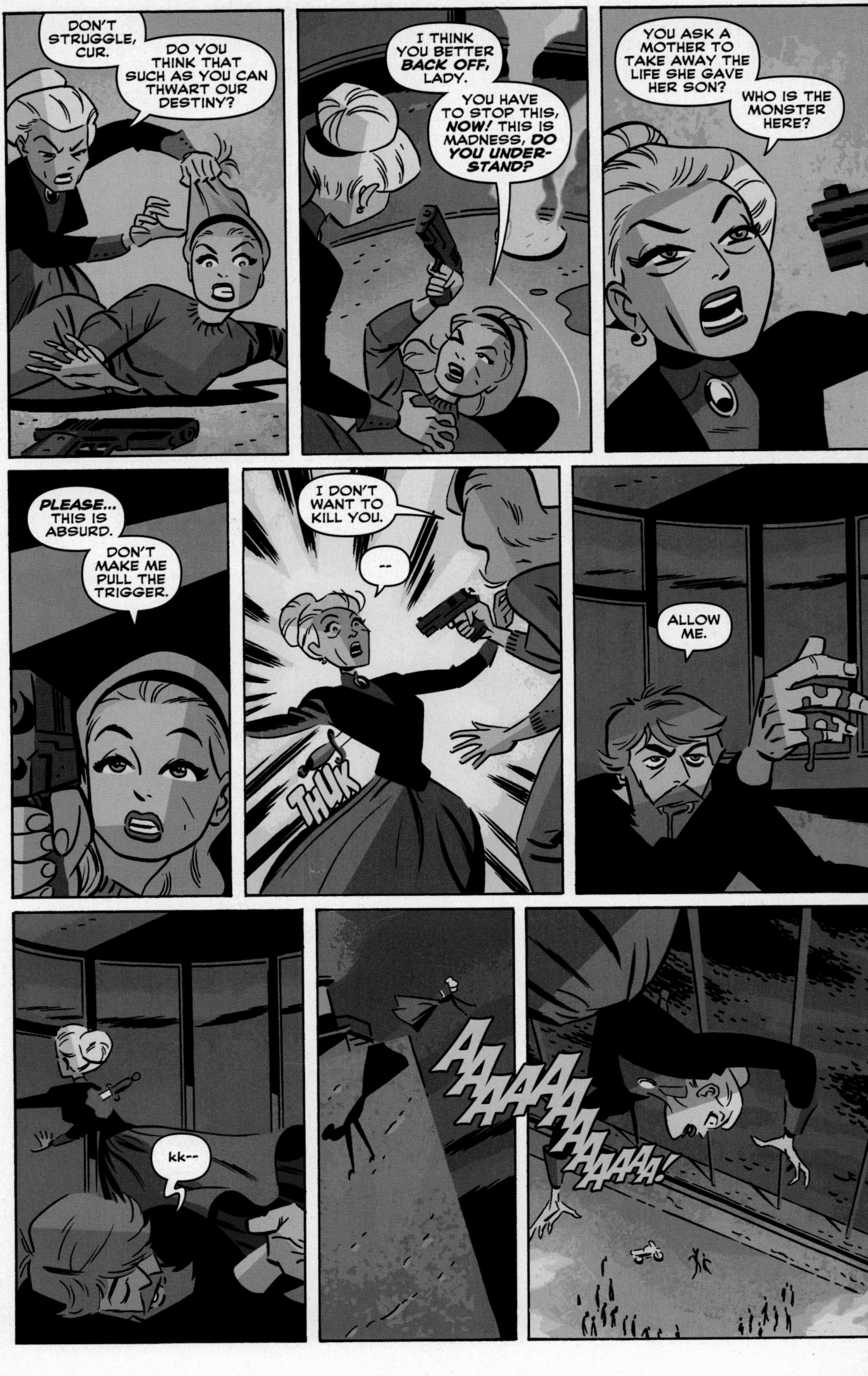
DON'T STRUGGLE, CUR.
DO YOU THINK THAT SUCH AS YOU CAN THWART OUR DESTINY?
I THINK YOU BETTER BACK OFF, LADY.
YOU HAVE TO STOP THIS, NOW! THIS IS MADNESS, DO YOU UNDER-STAND?
YOU ASK A MOTHER TO TAKE AWAY THE LIFE SHE GAVE HER SON?
WHO IS THE MONSTER HERE?
PLEASE... THIS IS ABSURD.
DON'T MAKE ME PULL THE TRIGGER.
I DON'T WANT TO KILL YOU.
--
THUK
ALLOW ME.
kk--
AAAAAAAAAAAAAAAA!

I drive the rush of adrenaline and splintered oak straight through that bag of puss it calls an eye.

His rotten vertebrae pop and saw at horrible angles.

He swings blind and catches me hard in the face. My legs are numb, but my ribs can tell I've landed on the bike.

I SUPPOSE IT'S TURTLE-NECKS FOR ME FROM NOW ON. HLAK!

I WANT YOU TO LIVE LONG ENOUGH TO SEE YOUR WOMAN SCREAM FOR ME.

MAYBE I'LL JUST TEAR OFF YOUR HANDS AND FEET.

Laugh it up, you ugly bastard.

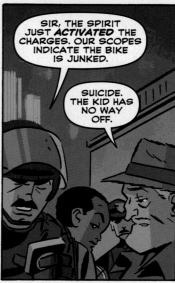

SIR, THE SPIRIT JUST *ACTIVATED* THE CHARGES. OUR SCOPES INDICATE THE BIKE IS JUNKED.

SUICIDE. THE KID HAS NO WAY OFF.

So this is it.

Two years ago I died trying to save the city.

My life since... El Morte's murderous existence... are crimes against the natural order. We belong together, in the earth beneath the Wildwood trees.

But I want to die as Me.

I peel the mask away for the last time and that's when I see the angel falling from the sky above.

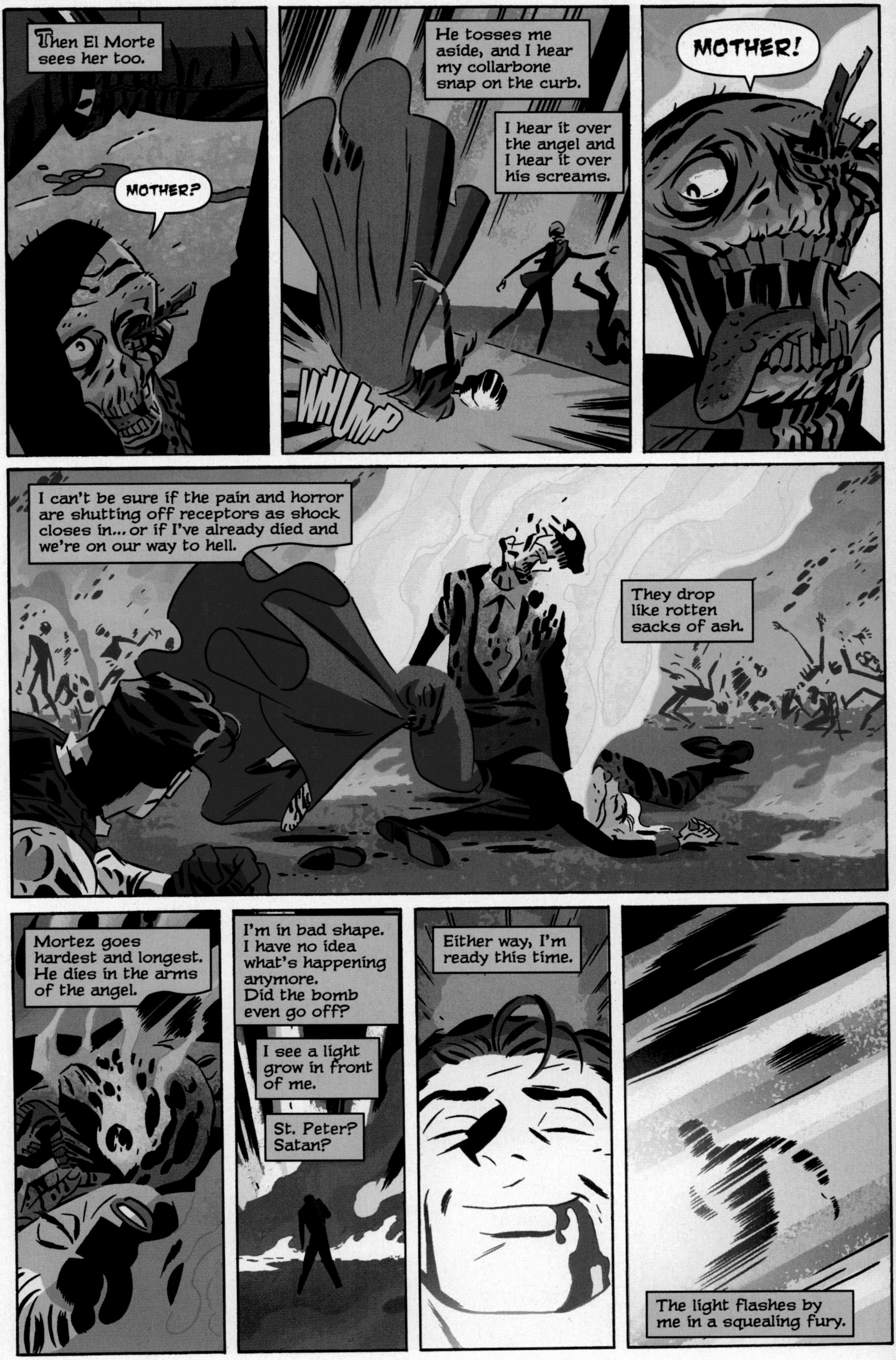
Then El Morte sees her too.
MOTHER?
He tosses me aside, and I hear my collarbone snap on the curb.
I hear it over the angel and I hear it over his screams.
WHUMP
MOTHER!
I can't be sure if the pain and horror are shutting off receptors as shock closes in... or if I've already died and we're on our way to hell.
They drop like rotten sacks of ash.
Mortez goes hardest and longest. He dies in the arms of the angel.
I'm in bad shape. I have no idea what's happening anymore. Did the bomb even go off?
I see a light grow in front of me.
St. Peter? Satan?
Either way, I'm ready this time.
The light flashes by me in a squealing fury.

There is the sound of more destruction, and the air below the bridge seems to erupt with hellfire.

I wonder if this is all my delusion.

You did it, Argo.

You saved us all.

Can anyone else feel this?

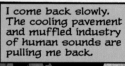

I come back slowly. The cooling pavement and muffled industry of human sounds are pulling me back.

Her touch comes first.

When I open my eyes it's her that I see.

Like being reborn.

WELCOME TO CENTRAL CITY

End

6

ACTION • Mystery • ADVENTURE

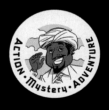

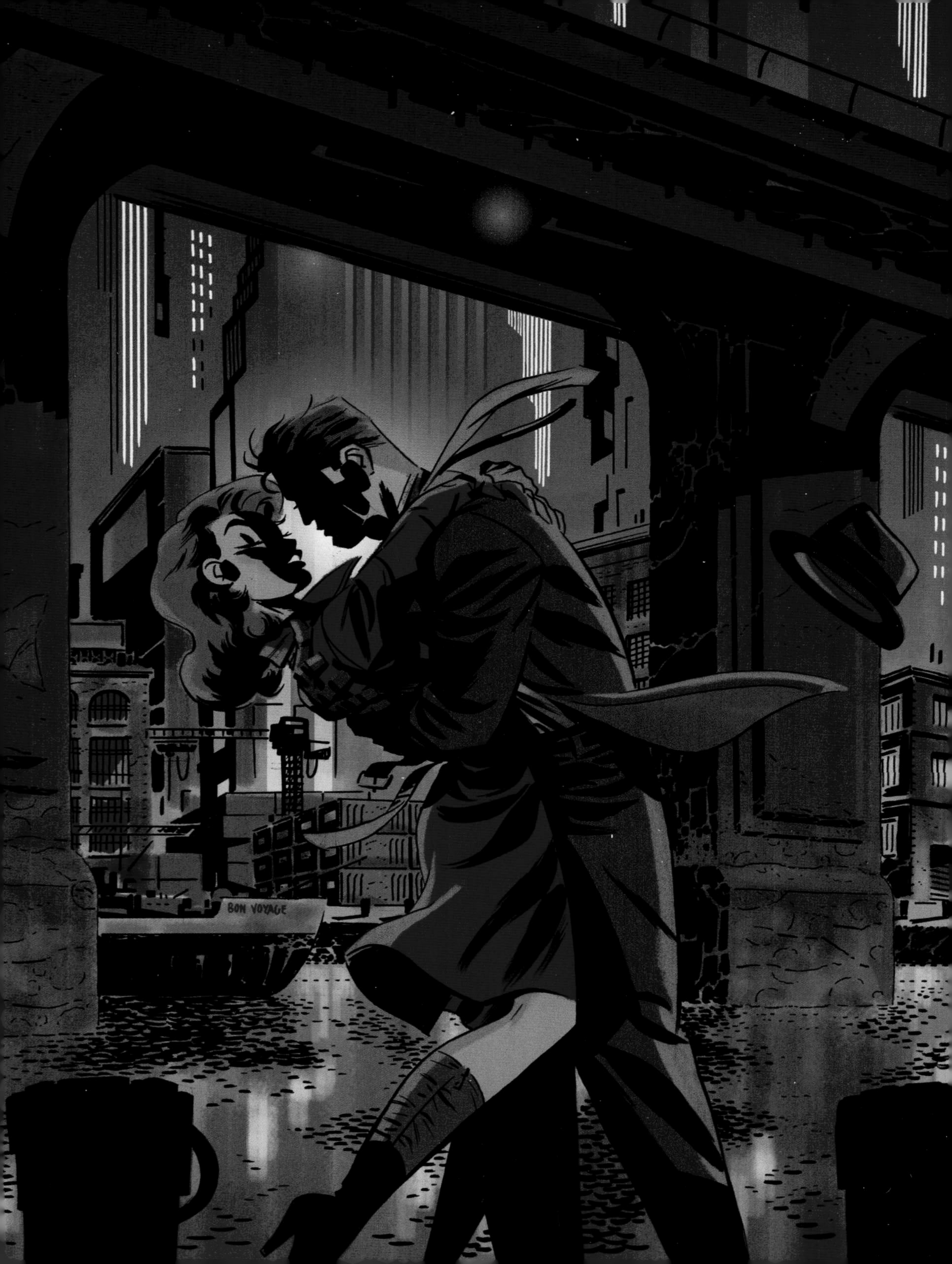
BON VOYAGE

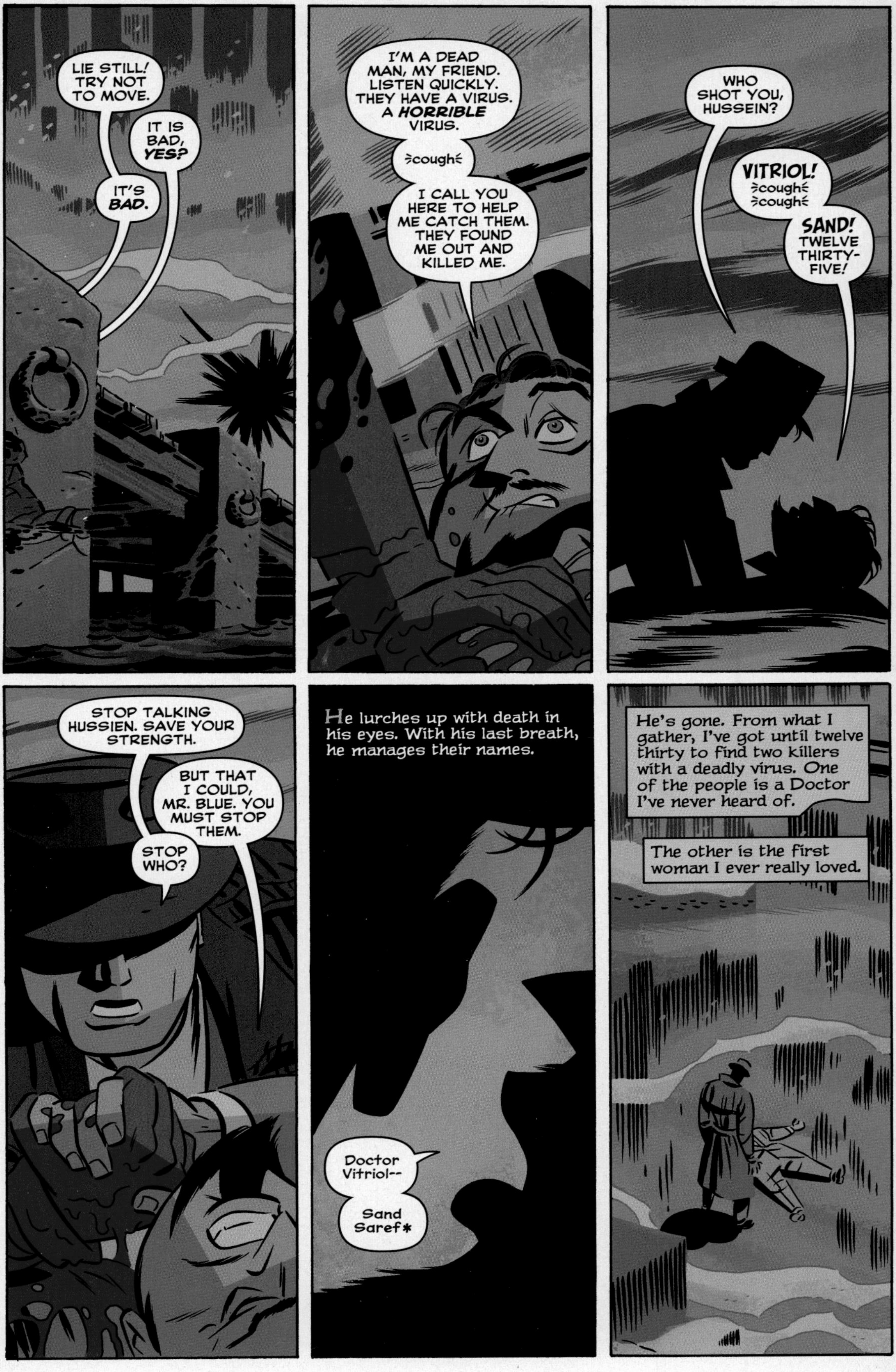

LIE STILL! TRY NOT TO MOVE.
IT IS BAD, YES?
IT'S BAD.
I'M A DEAD MAN, MY FRIEND. LISTEN QUICKLY. THEY HAVE A VIRUS. A HORRIBLE VIRUS.
cough
I CALL YOU HERE TO HELP ME CATCH THEM. THEY FOUND ME OUT AND KILLED ME.
WHO SHOT YOU, HUSSEIN?
VITRIOL! cough cough
SAND! TWELVE THIRTY-FIVE!
STOP TALKING HUSSIEN. SAVE YOUR STRENGTH.
BUT THAT I COULD, MR. BLUE. YOU MUST STOP THEM.
STOP WHO?
He lurches up with death in his eyes. With his last breath, he manages their names.
Doctor Vitriol--
Sand Saref*
He's gone. From what I gather, I've got until twelve thirty to find two killers with a deadly virus. One of the people is a Doctor I've never heard of.
The other is the first woman I ever really loved.

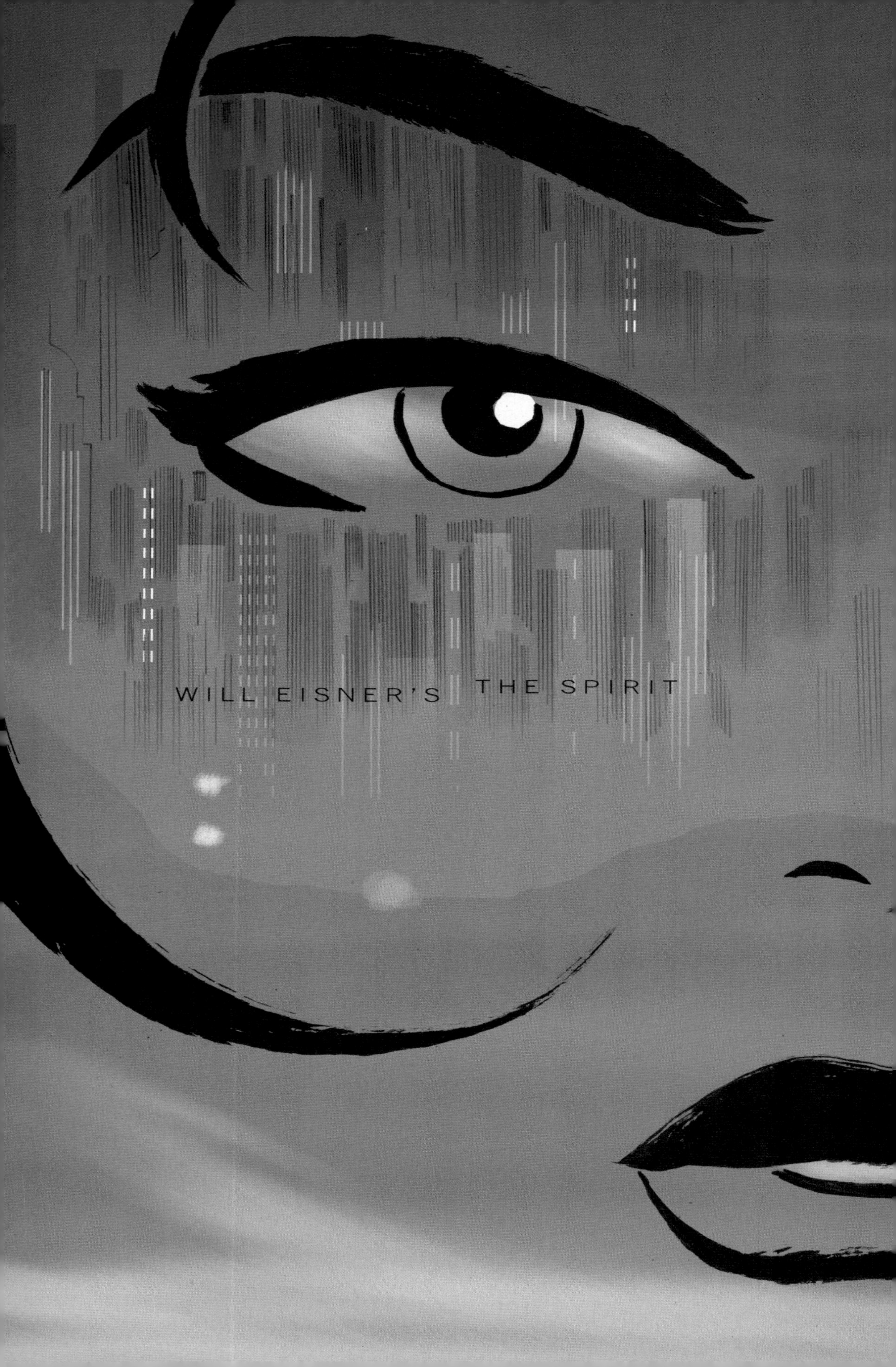
WILL EISNER'S THE SPIRIT

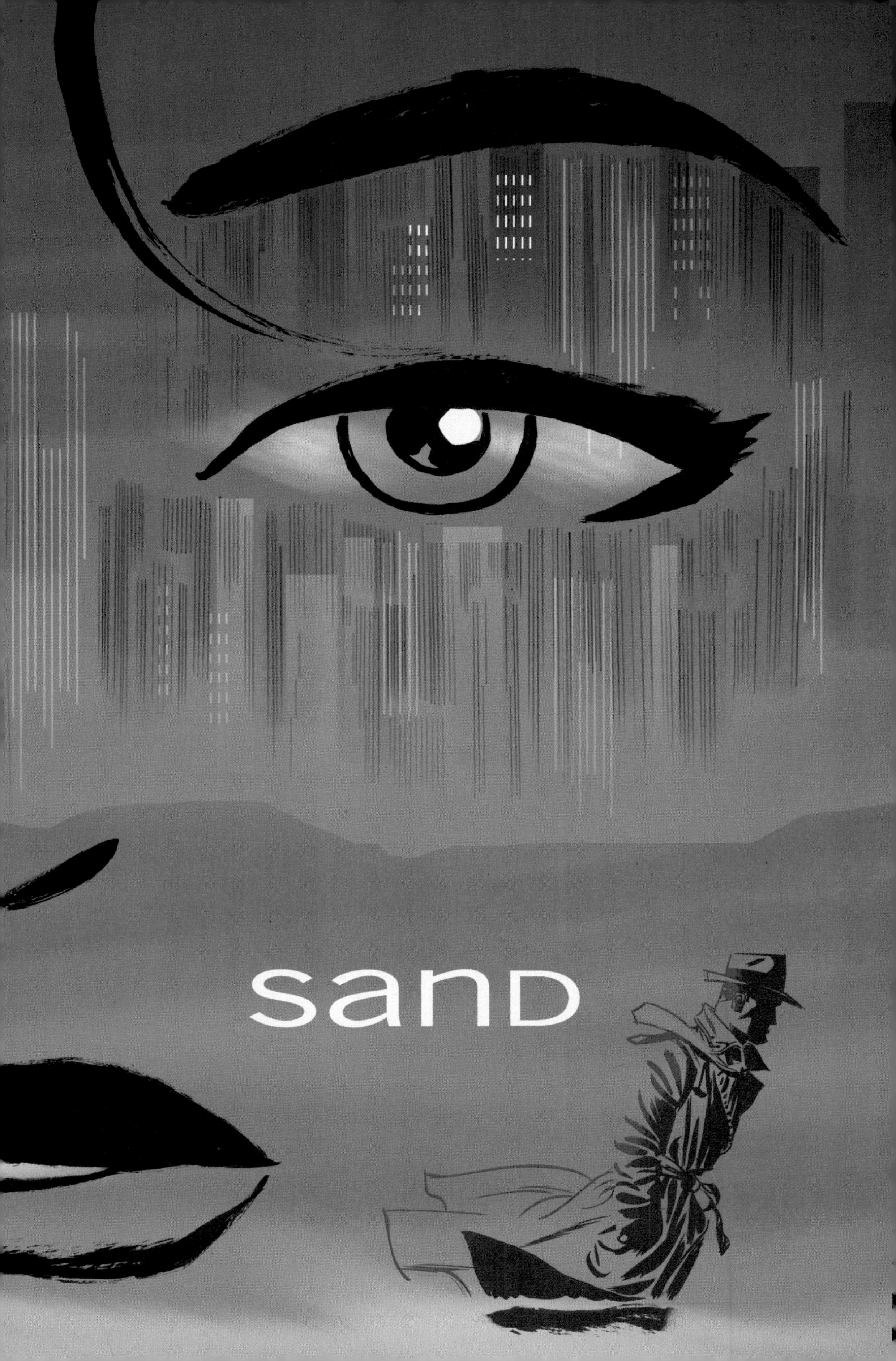
sand

I push back the racing nausea I feel when I hear her name. I struggle to keep the lid on memories I buried years ago.

I take a moment and say a prayer for my friend.

What a character. I wonder if I'll ever know who he really was.

I find three sets of ID. Two Israeli, one Saudi. Two knives, a tazer and about fourteen hundred in cash.

A hotel keycard.

Maybe twelve thirty-five isn't a time but a room number.

SOHO

The distant whine of sirens cut through the fog.

I can't deal with the cops tonight.

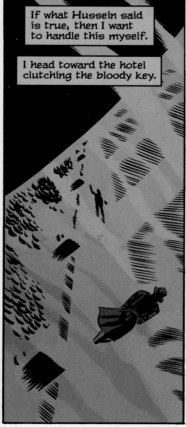

If what Hussein said is true, then I want to handle this myself.

I head toward the hotel clutching the bloody key.

You try to push the memories down, but sometime they push back.

They bob to the surface, deep and black as drums of pitch.

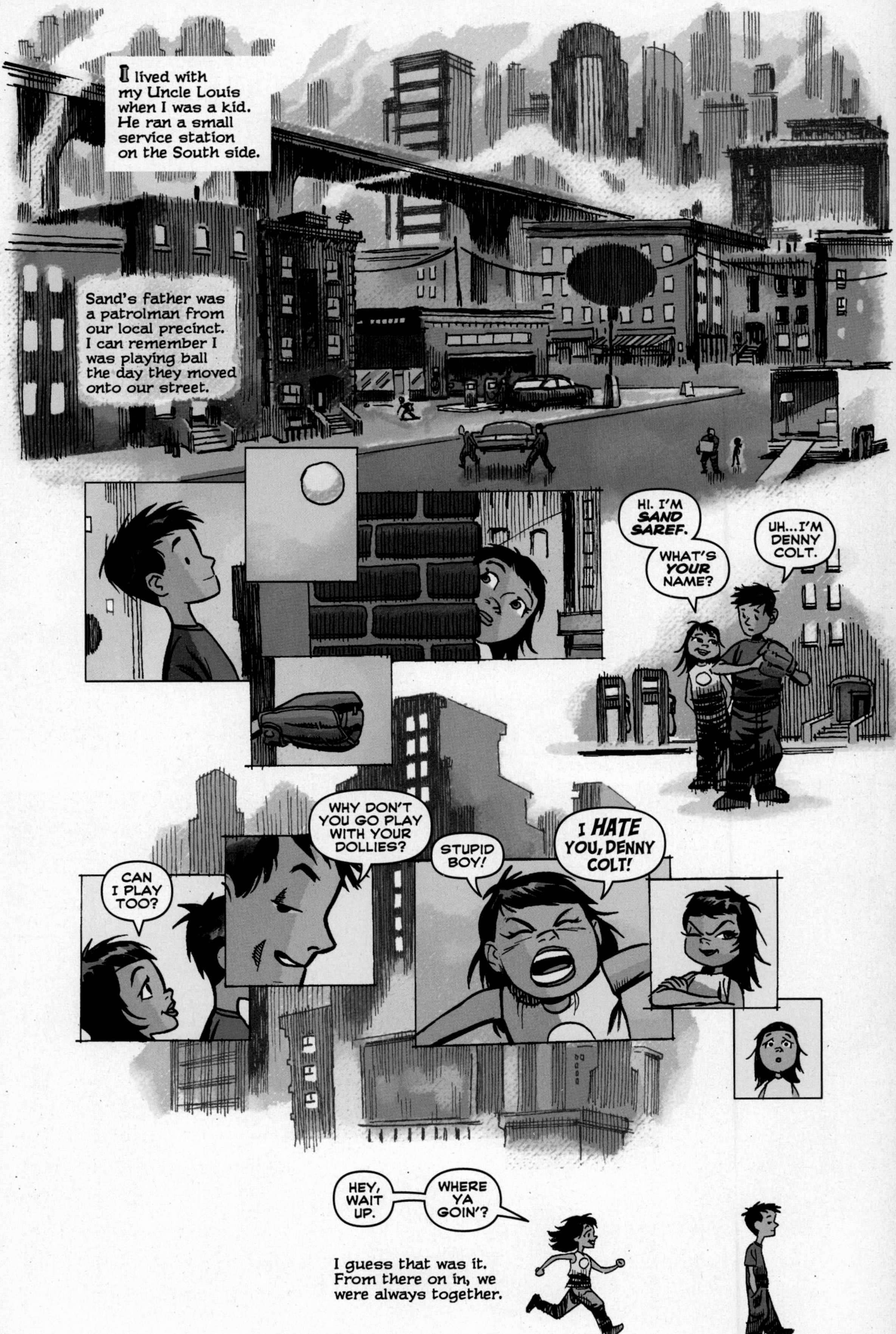
I lived with my Uncle Louis when I was a kid. He ran a small service station on the South side.
Sand's father was a patrolman from our local precinct. I can remember I was playing ball the day they moved onto our street.
HI. I'M SAND SAREF.
WHAT'S YOUR NAME?
UH...I'M DENNY COLT.
CAN I PLAY TOO?
WHY DON'T YOU GO PLAY WITH YOUR DOLLIES?
STUPID BOY!
I HATE YOU, DENNY COLT!
HEY, WAIT UP.
WHERE YA GOIN'?
I guess that was it. From there on in, we were always together.

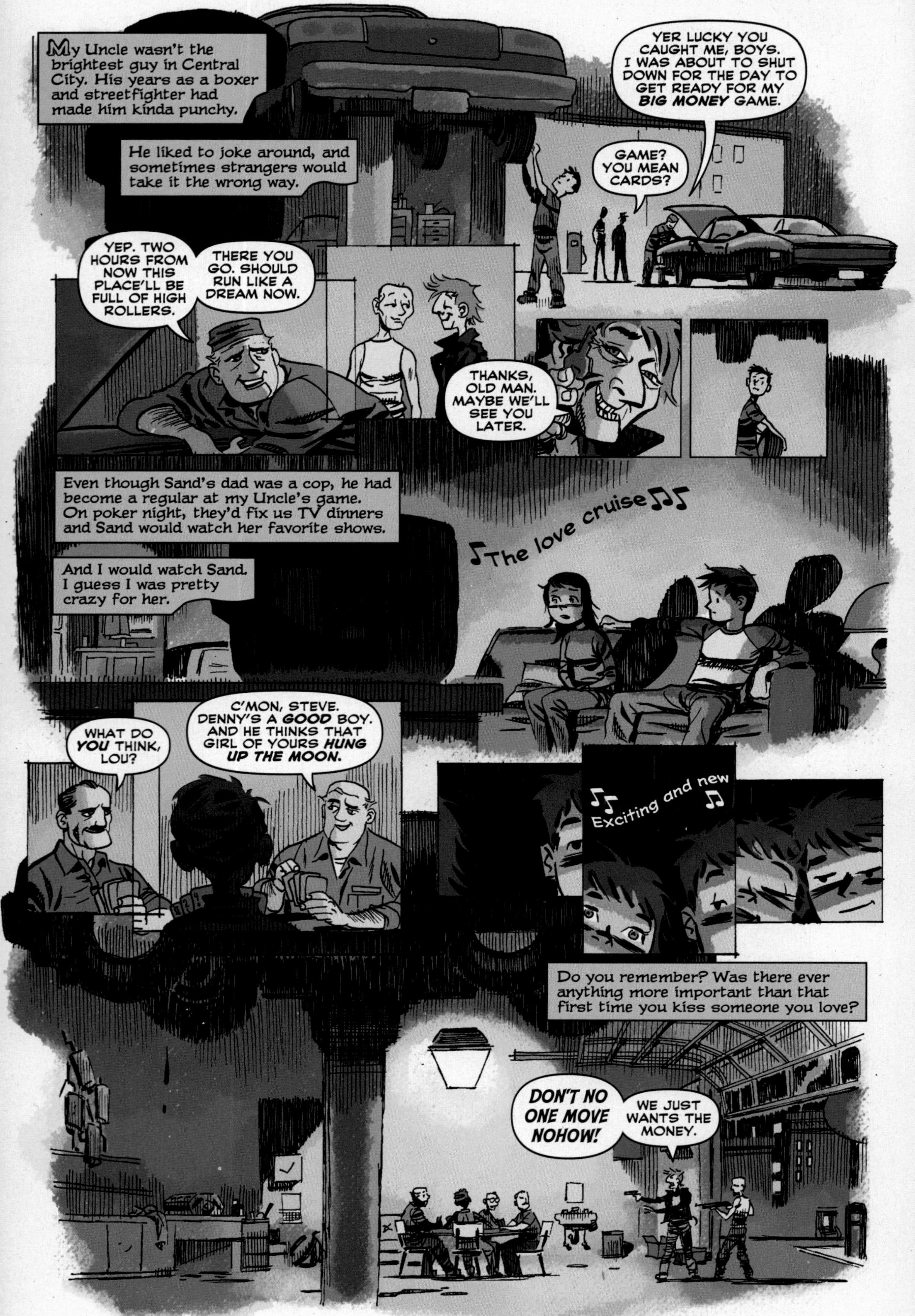
My Uncle wasn't the brightest guy in Central City. His years as a boxer and streetfighter had made him kinda punchy.
YER LUCKY YOU CAUGHT ME, BOYS. I WAS ABOUT TO SHUT DOWN FOR THE DAY TO GET READY FOR MY BIG MONEY GAME.
He liked to joke around, and sometimes strangers would take it the wrong way.
GAME? YOU MEAN CARDS?
YEP. TWO HOURS FROM NOW THIS PLACE'LL BE FULL OF HIGH ROLLERS.
THERE YOU GO. SHOULD RUN LIKE A DREAM NOW.
THANKS, OLD MAN. MAYBE WE'LL SEE YOU LATER.
Even though Sand's dad was a cop, he had become a regular at my Uncle's game. On poker night, they'd fix us TV dinners and Sand would watch her favorite shows.
The love cruise
And I would watch Sand. I guess I was pretty crazy for her.
WHAT DO YOU THINK, LOU?
C'MON, STEVE. DENNY'S A GOOD BOY. AND HE THINKS THAT GIRL OF YOURS HUNG UP THE MOON.
Exciting and new
Do you remember? Was there ever anything more important than that first time you kiss someone you love?
DON'T NO ONE MOVE NOHOW!
WE JUST WANTS THE MONEY.

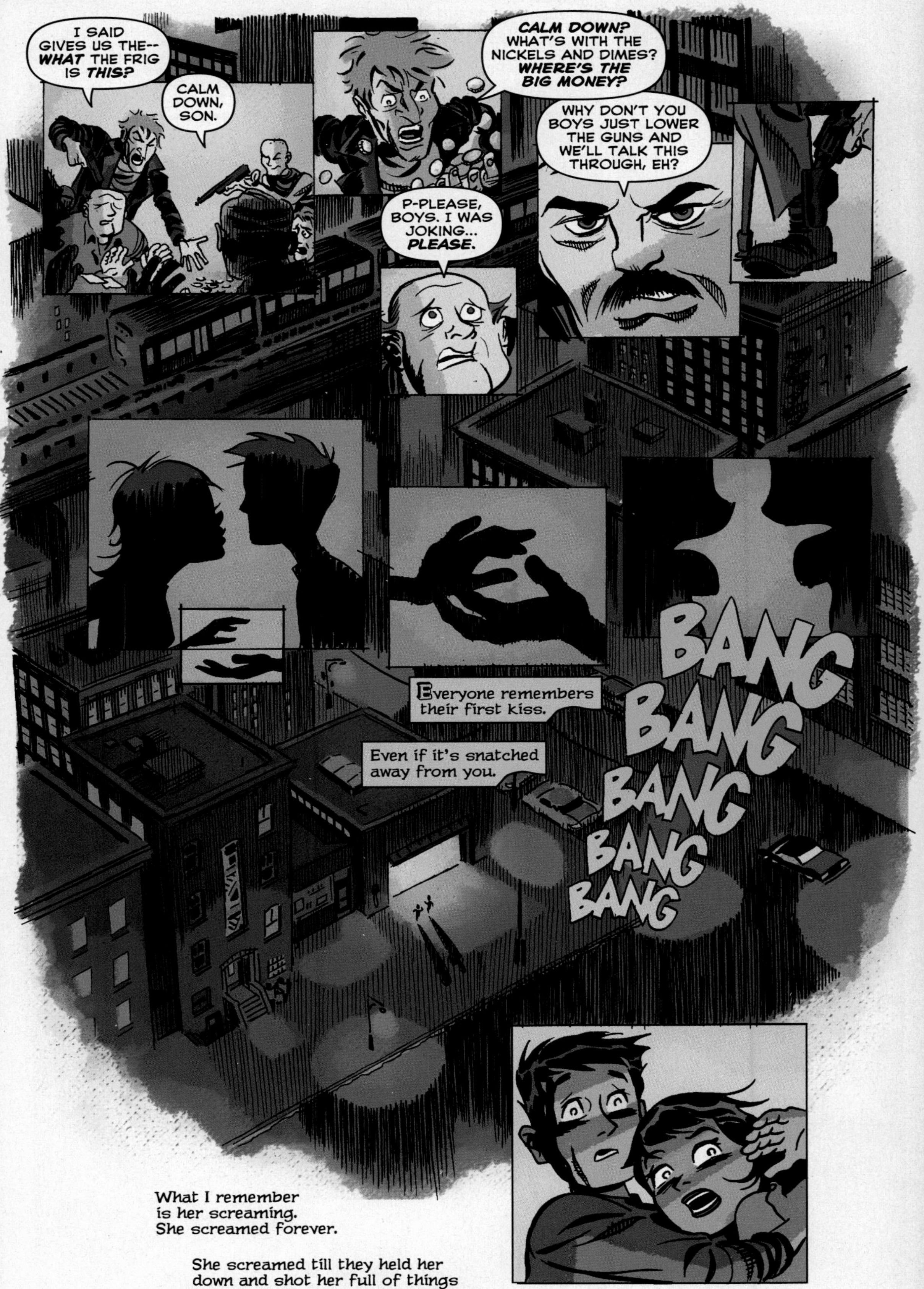

I SAID GIVES US THE-- *WHAT* THE FRIG IS *THIS?*
CALM DOWN, SON.
CALM DOWN? WHAT'S WITH THE NICKELS AND DIMES? *WHERE'S THE BIG MONEY?*
WHY DON'T YOU BOYS JUST LOWER THE GUNS AND WE'LL TALK THIS THROUGH, EH?
P-PLEASE, BOYS. I WAS JOKING... *PLEASE.*
BANG BANG BANG BANG BANG
Everyone remembers their first kiss.
Even if it's snatched away from you.
What I remember is her screaming. She screamed forever.
She screamed till they held her down and shot her full of things that made her scream in her sleep.

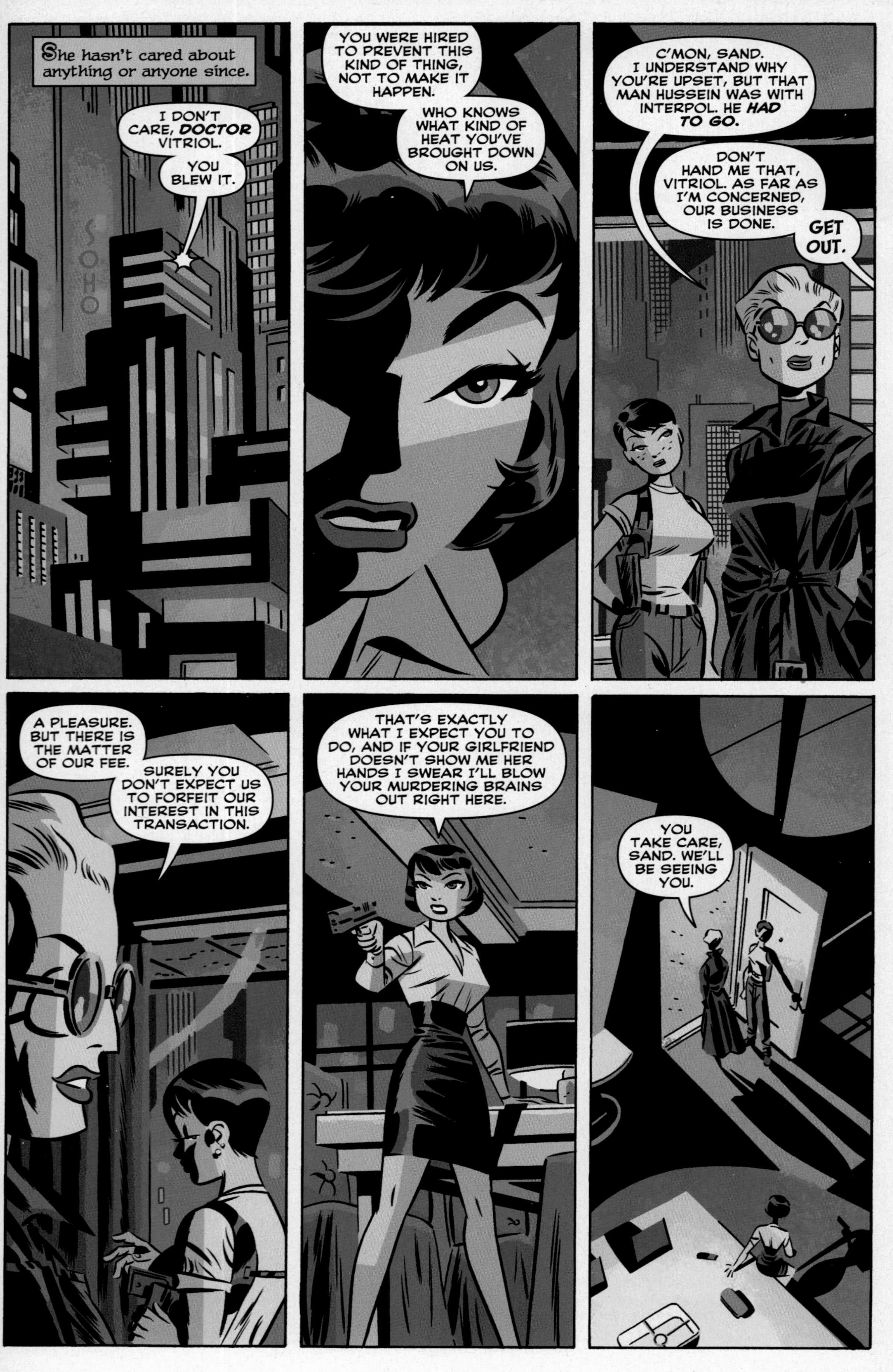
She hasn't cared about anything or anyone since.
I DON'T CARE, DOCTOR VITRIOL.
YOU BLEW IT.
SOHO
YOU WERE HIRED TO PREVENT THIS KIND OF THING, NOT TO MAKE IT HAPPEN.
WHO KNOWS WHAT KIND OF HEAT YOU'VE BROUGHT DOWN ON US.
C'MON, SAND. I UNDERSTAND WHY YOU'RE UPSET, BUT THAT MAN HUSSEIN WAS WITH INTERPOL. HE HAD TO GO.
DON'T HAND ME THAT, VITRIOL. AS FAR AS I'M CONCERNED, OUR BUSINESS IS DONE.
GET OUT.
A PLEASURE. BUT THERE IS THE MATTER OF OUR FEE.
SURELY YOU DON'T EXPECT US TO FORFEIT OUR INTEREST IN THIS TRANSACTION.
THAT'S EXACTLY WHAT I EXPECT YOU TO DO, AND IF YOUR GIRLFRIEND DOESN'T SHOW ME HER HANDS I SWEAR I'LL BLOW YOUR MURDERING BRAINS OUT RIGHT HERE.
YOU TAKE CARE, SAND. WE'LL BE SEEING YOU.

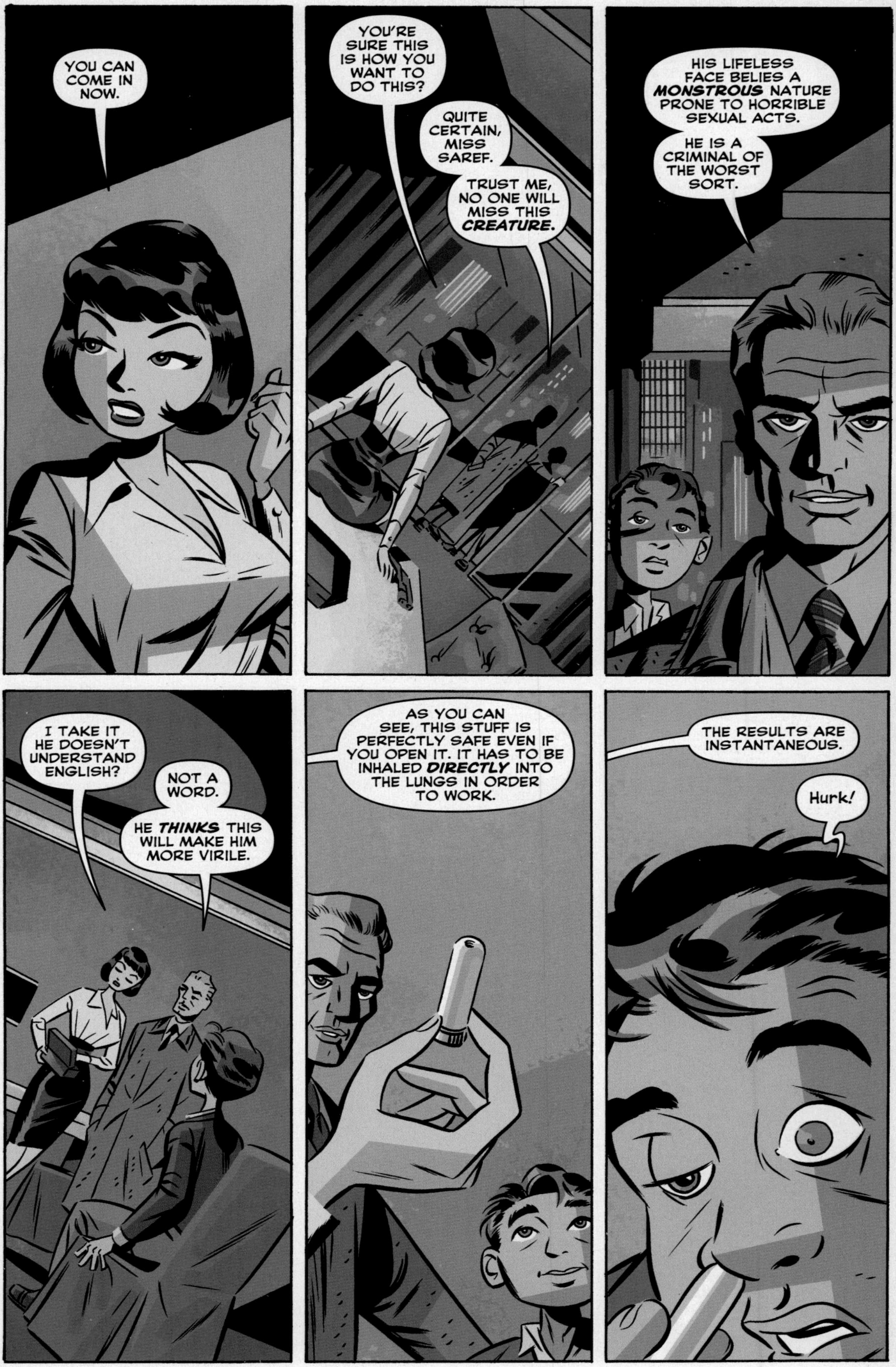
YOU CAN COME IN NOW.
YOU'RE SURE THIS IS HOW YOU WANT TO DO THIS?
QUITE CERTAIN, MISS SAREF.
TRUST ME, NO ONE WILL MISS THIS *CREATURE*.
HIS LIFELESS FACE BELIES A *MONSTROUS* NATURE PRONE TO HORRIBLE SEXUAL ACTS.
HE IS A CRIMINAL OF THE WORST SORT.
I TAKE IT HE DOESN'T UNDERSTAND ENGLISH?
NOT A WORD.
HE *THINKS* THIS WILL MAKE HIM MORE VIRILE.
AS YOU CAN SEE, THIS STUFF IS PERFECTLY SAFE EVEN IF YOU OPEN IT. IT HAS TO BE INHALED *DIRECTLY* INTO THE LUNGS IN ORDER TO WORK.
THE RESULTS ARE INSTANTANEOUS.
Hurk!

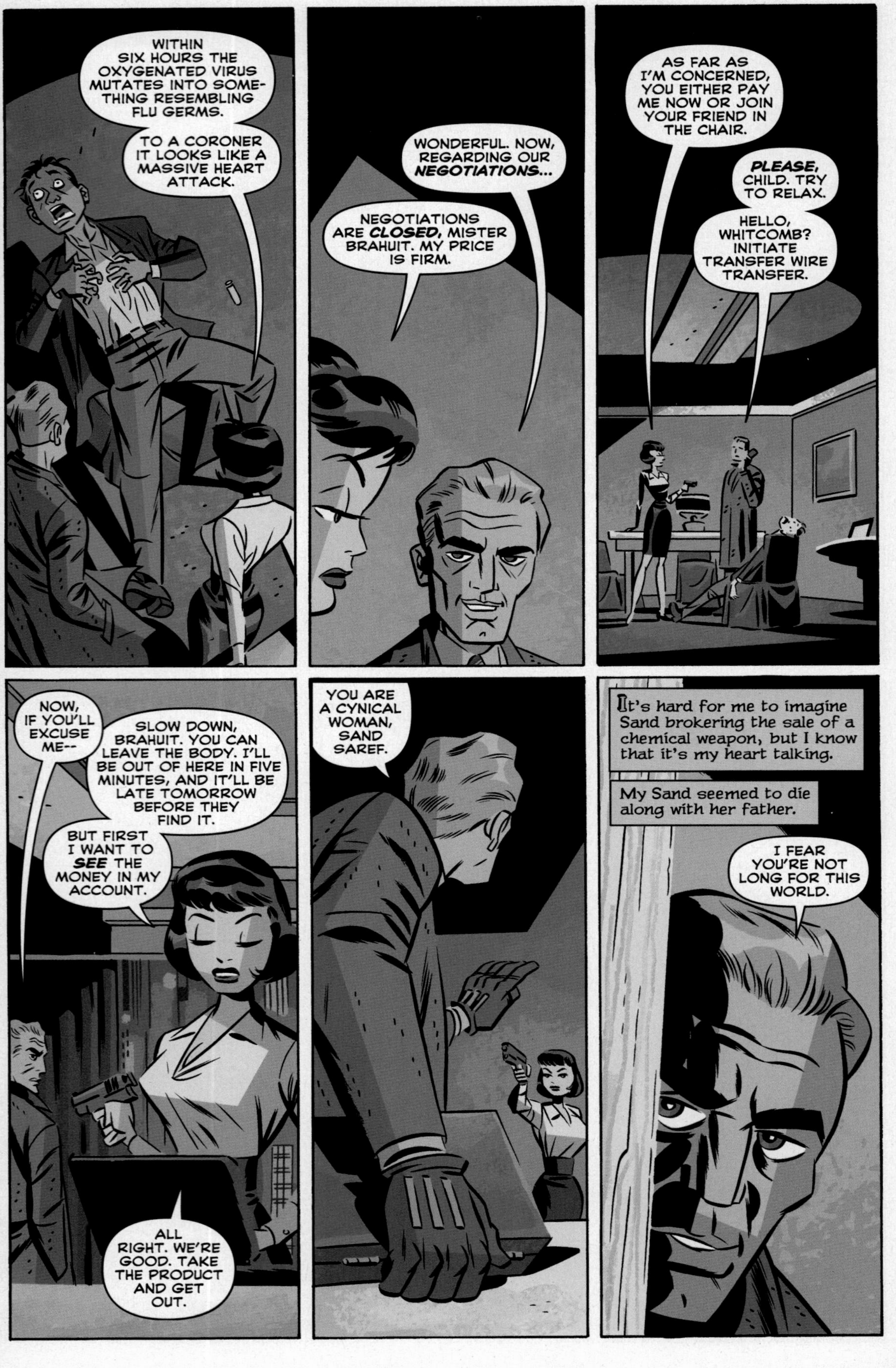
WITHIN SIX HOURS THE OXYGENATED VIRUS MUTATES INTO SOME-THING RESEMBLING FLU GERMS.
TO A CORONER IT LOOKS LIKE A MASSIVE HEART ATTACK.
WONDERFUL. NOW, REGARDING OUR *NEGOTIATIONS...*
NEGOTIATIONS ARE **CLOSED,** MISTER BRAHUIT. MY PRICE IS FIRM.
AS FAR AS I'M CONCERNED, YOU EITHER PAY ME NOW OR JOIN YOUR FRIEND IN THE CHAIR.
PLEASE, CHILD. TRY TO RELAX.
HELLO, WHITCOMB? INITIATE TRANSFER WIRE TRANSFER.
NOW, IF YOU'LL EXCUSE ME--
SLOW DOWN, BRAHUIT. YOU CAN LEAVE THE BODY. I'LL BE OUT OF HERE IN FIVE MINUTES, AND IT'LL BE LATE TOMORROW BEFORE THEY FIND IT.
BUT FIRST I WANT TO ***SEE*** THE MONEY IN MY ACCOUNT.
ALL RIGHT. WE'RE GOOD. TAKE THE PRODUCT AND GET OUT.
YOU ARE A CYNICAL WOMAN, SAND SAREF.
It's hard for me to imagine Sand brokering the sale of a chemical weapon, but I know that it's my heart talking.
My Sand seemed to die along with her father.
I FEAR YOU'RE NOT LONG FOR THIS WORLD.

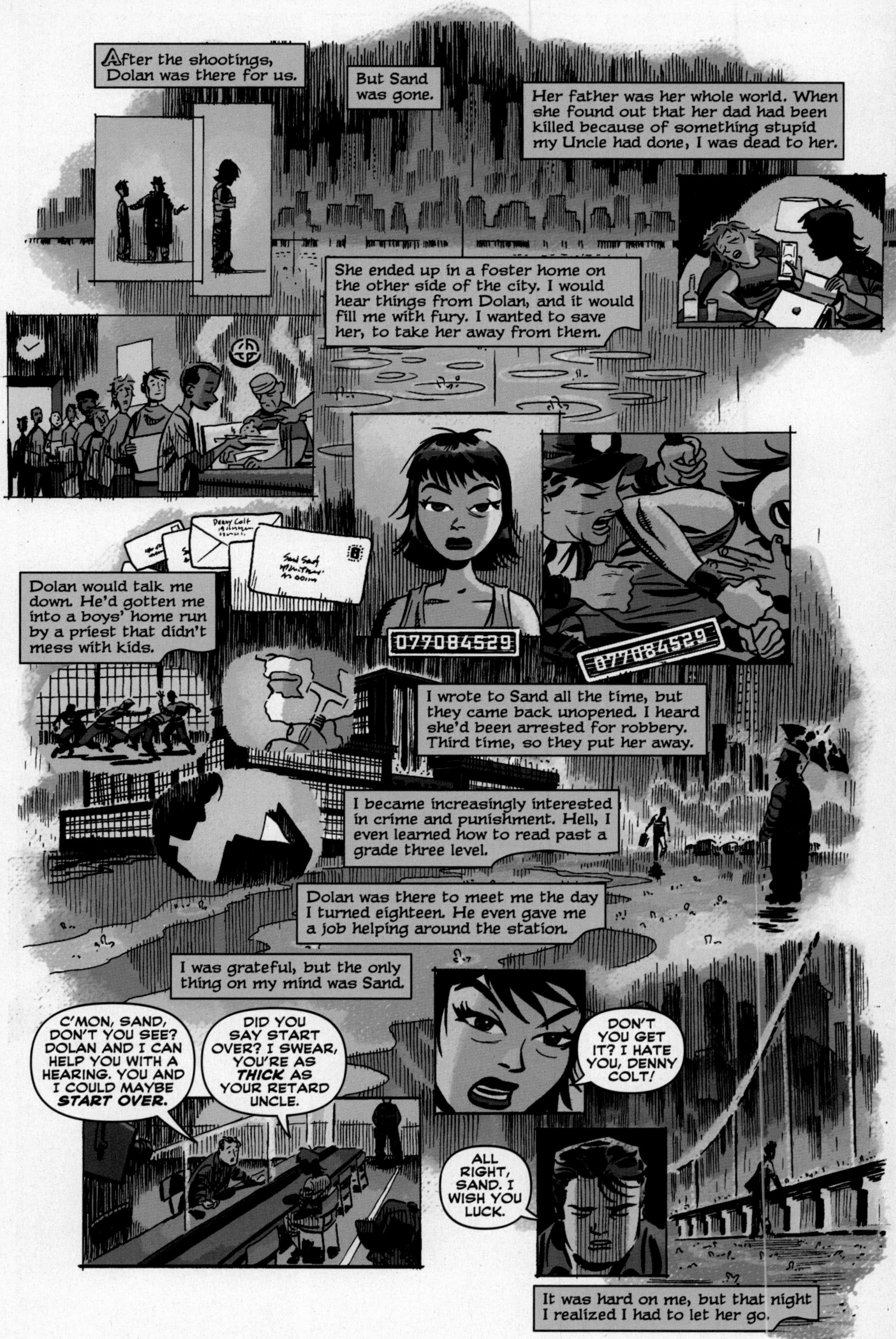
After the shootings, Dolan was there for us.
But Sand was gone.
Her father was her whole world. When she found out that her dad had been killed because of something stupid my Uncle had done, I was dead to her.
She ended up in a foster home on the other side of the city. I would hear things from Dolan, and it would fill me with fury. I wanted to save her, to take her away from them.
Denny Colt
Sand Saref
Dolan would talk me down. He'd gotten me into a boys' home run by a priest that didn't mess with kids.
077084529
077084529
I wrote to Sand all the time, but they came back unopened. I heard she'd been arrested for robbery. Third time, so they put her away.
I became increasingly interested in crime and punishment. Hell, I even learned how to read past a grade three level.
Dolan was there to meet me the day I turned eighteen. He even gave me a job helping around the station.
I was grateful, but the only thing on my mind was Sand.
C'MON, SAND, DON'T YOU SEE? DOLAN AND I CAN HELP YOU WITH A HEARING. YOU AND I COULD MAYBE *START OVER*.
DID YOU SAY START OVER? I SWEAR, YOU'RE AS *THICK* AS YOUR RETARD UNCLE.
DON'T YOU GET IT? I HATE YOU, DENNY COLT!
ALL RIGHT, SAND. I WISH YOU LUCK.
It was hard on me, but that night I realized I had to let her go.

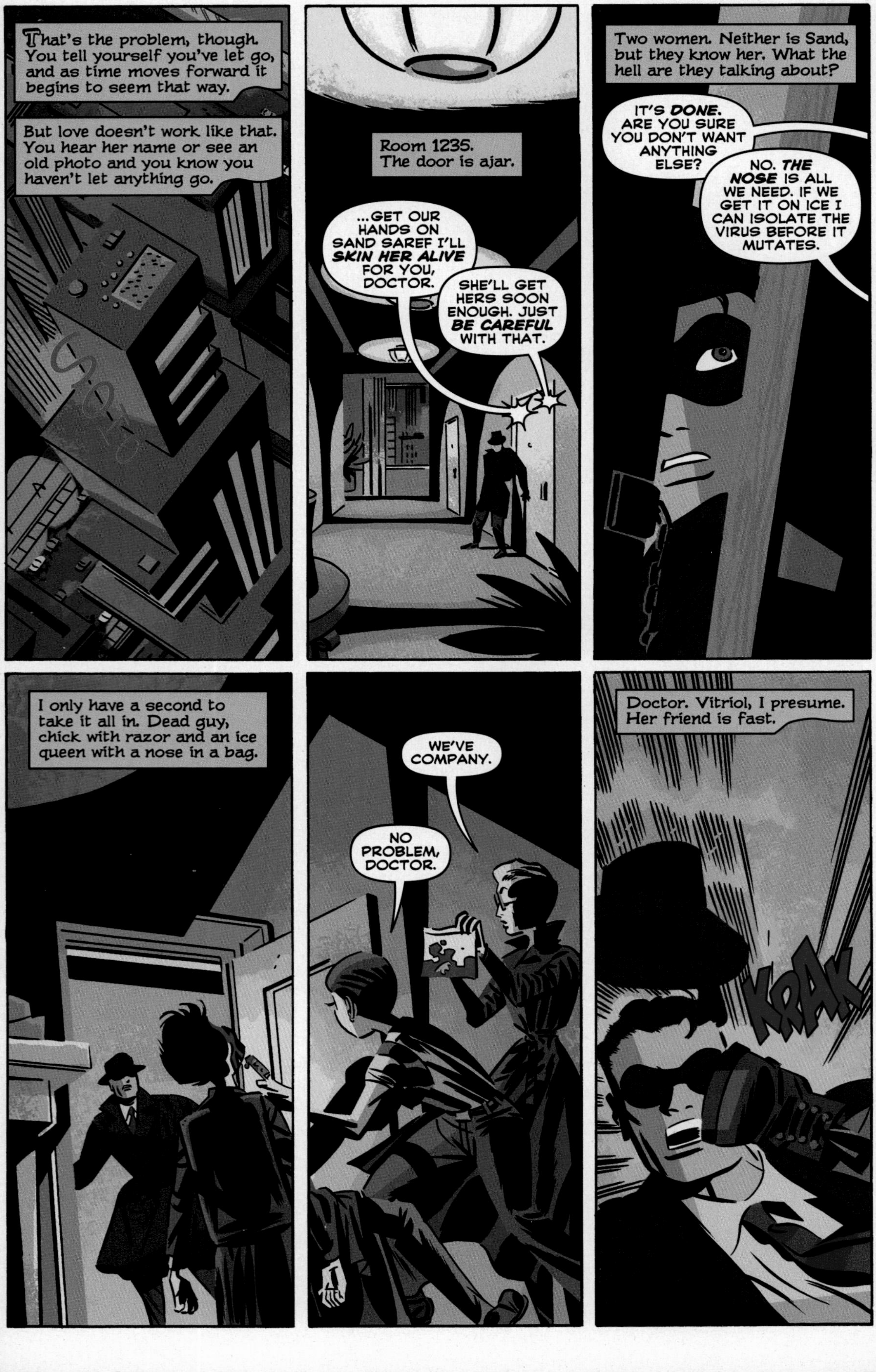
That's the problem, though. You tell yourself you've let go, and as time moves forward it begins to seem that way.
But love doesn't work like that. You hear her name or see an old photo and you know you haven't let anything go.
Room 1235. The door is ajar.
...GET OUR HANDS ON SAND SAREF I'LL SKIN HER ALIVE FOR YOU, DOCTOR.
SHE'LL GET HERS SOON ENOUGH. JUST BE CAREFUL WITH THAT.
Two women. Neither is Sand, but they know her. What the hell are they talking about?
IT'S DONE. ARE YOU SURE YOU DON'T WANT ANYTHING ELSE?
NO. THE NOSE IS ALL WE NEED. IF WE GET IT ON ICE I CAN ISOLATE THE VIRUS BEFORE IT MUTATES.
I only have a second to take it all in. Dead guy, chick with razor and an ice queen with a nose in a bag.
WE'VE COMPANY.
NO PROBLEM, DOCTOR.
Doctor. Vitriol, I presume. Her friend is fast.
KRAK

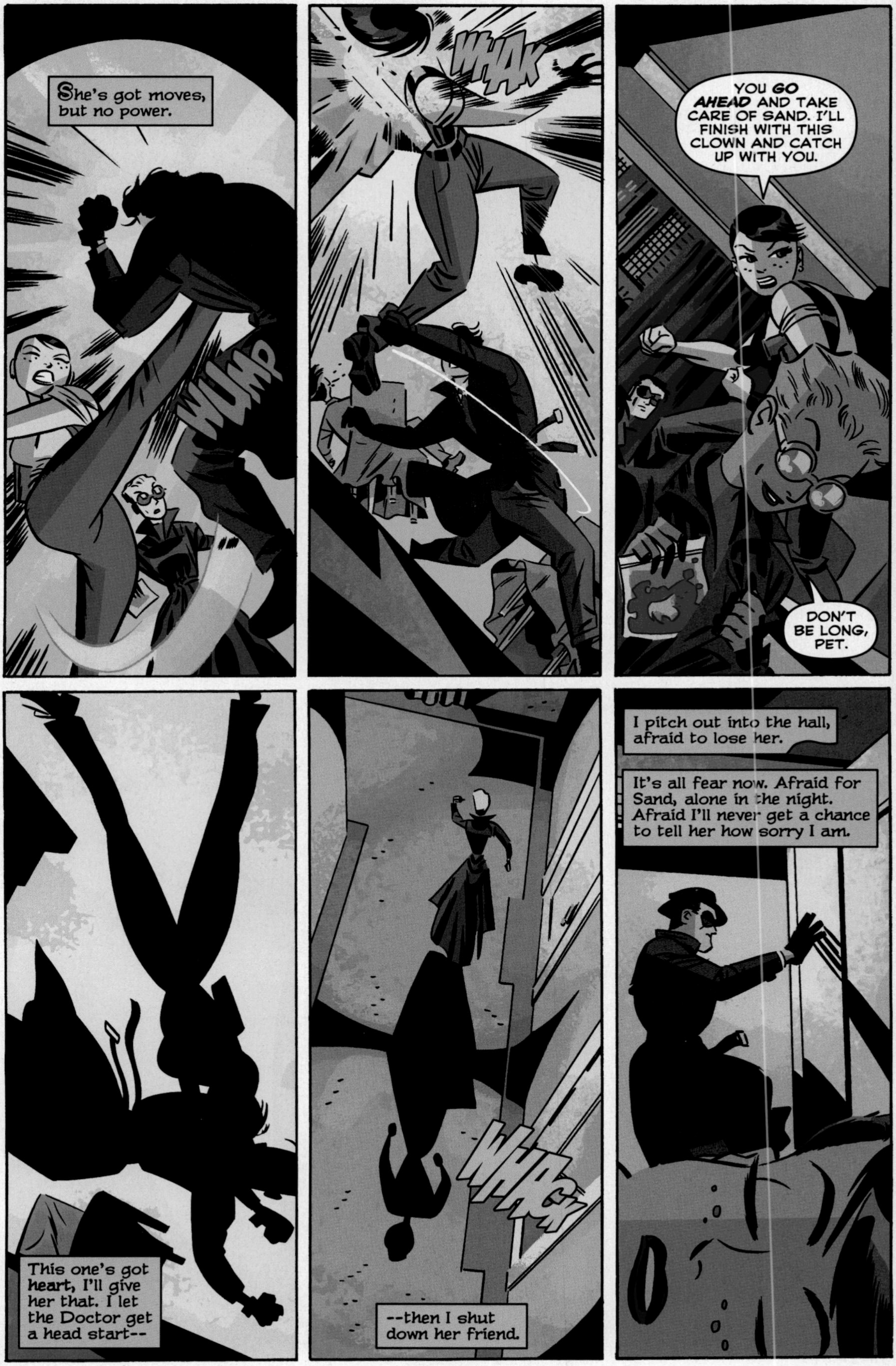
She's got moves, but no power.
WUMP
WHAK
YOU GO AHEAD AND TAKE CARE OF SAND. I'LL FINISH WITH THIS CLOWN AND CATCH UP WITH YOU.
DON'T BE LONG, PET.
This one's got heart, I'll give her that. I let the Doctor get a head start--
WHACK
--then I shut down her friend.
I pitch out into the hall, afraid to lose her.
It's all fear now. Afraid for Sand, alone in the night. Afraid I'll never get a chance to tell her how sorry I am.

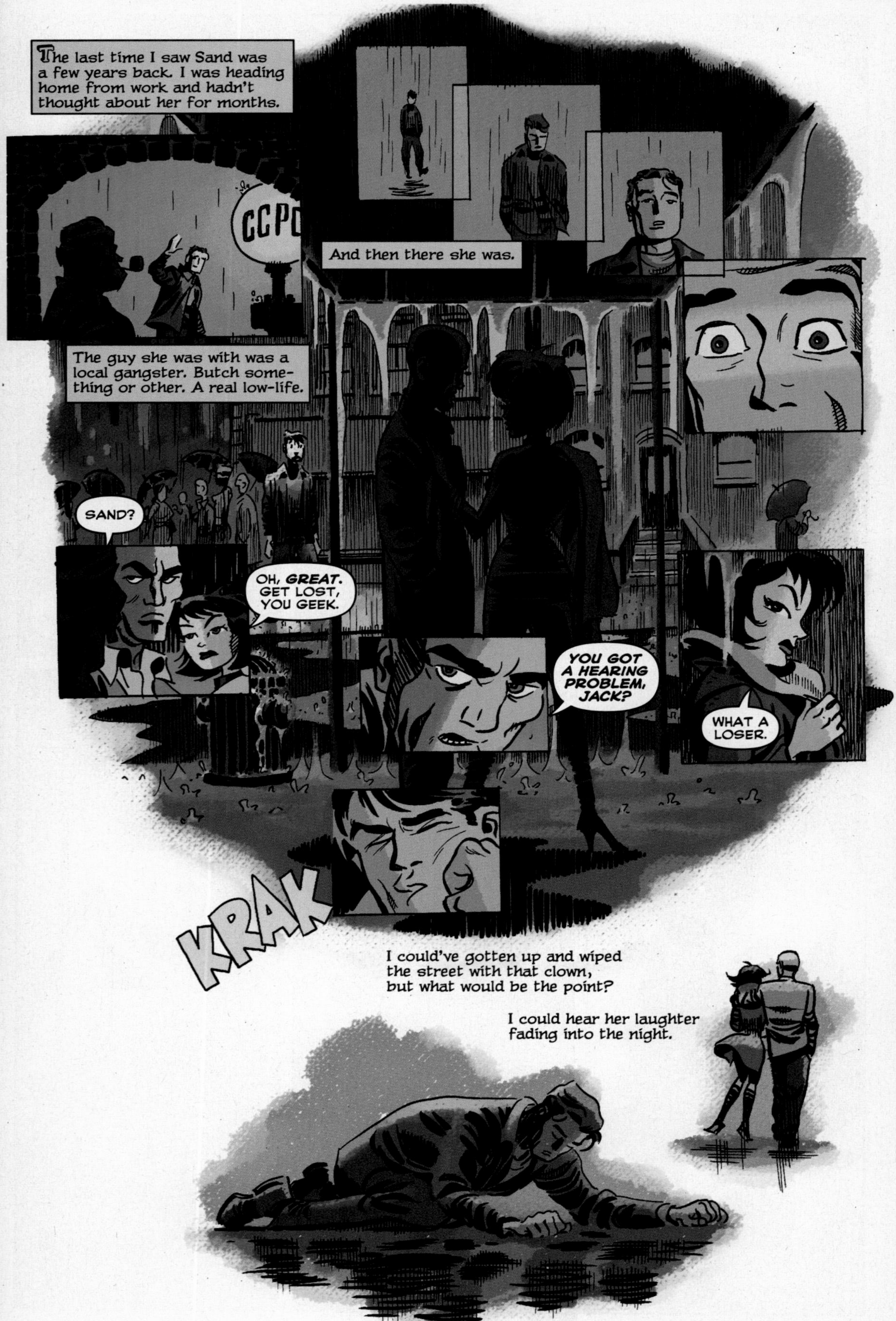
The last time I saw Sand was a few years back. I was heading home from work and hadn't thought about her for months.
CCPD
And then there she was.
The guy she was with was a local gangster. Butch something or other. A real low-life.
SAND?
OH, GREAT. GET LOST, YOU GEEK.
YOU GOT A HEARING PROBLEM, JACK?
WHAT A LOSER.
KRAK
I could've gotten up and wiped the street with that clown, but what would be the point?
I could hear her laughter fading into the night.

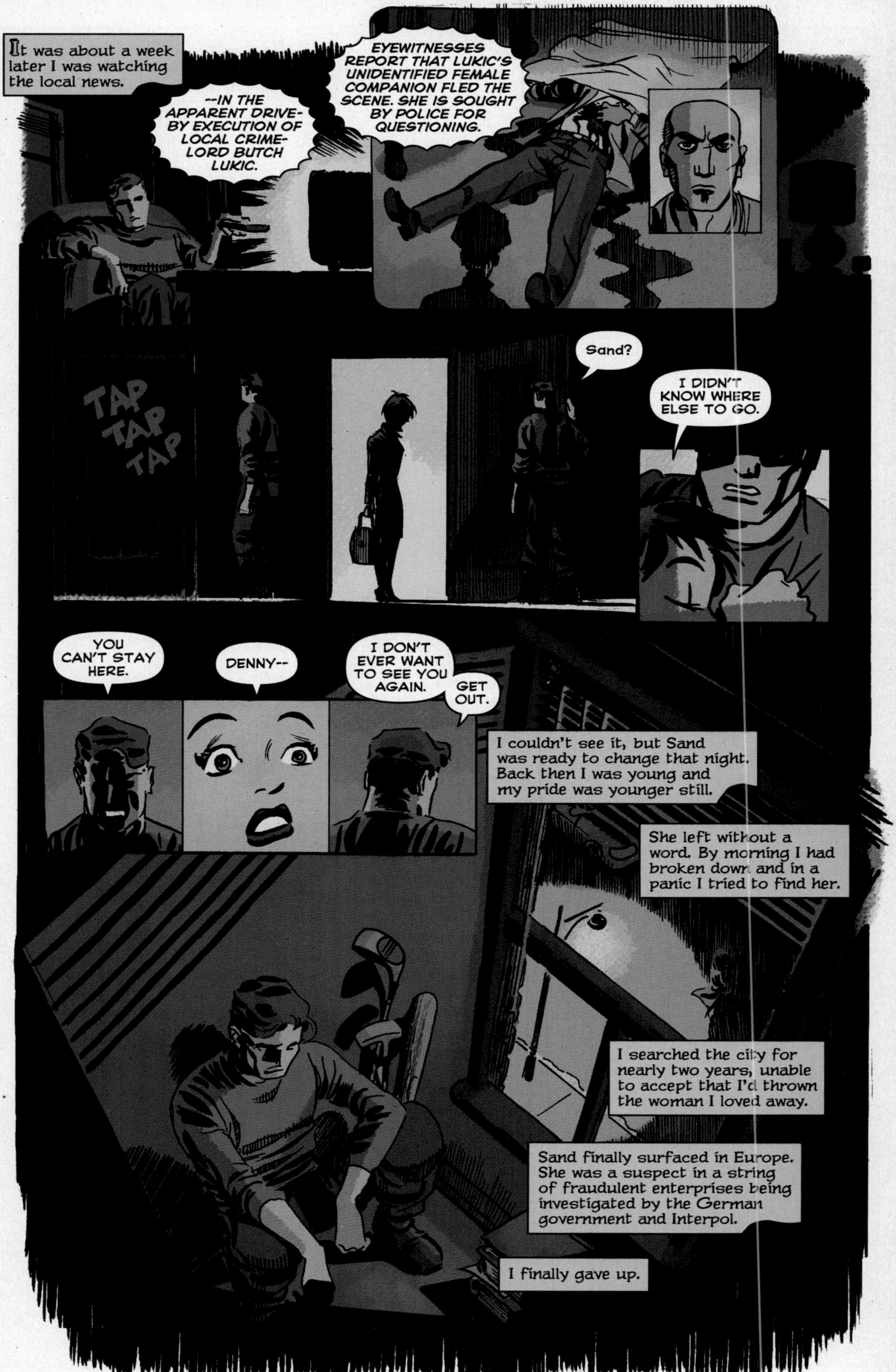
It was about a week later I was watching the local news.
--IN THE APPARENT DRIVE-BY EXECUTION OF LOCAL CRIME-LORD BUTCH LUKIC.
EYEWITNESSES REPORT THAT LUKIC'S UNIDENTIFIED FEMALE COMPANION FLED THE SCENE. SHE IS SOUGHT BY POLICE FOR QUESTIONING.
TAP TAP TAP
Sand?
I DIDN'T KNOW WHERE ELSE TO GO.
YOU CAN'T STAY HERE.
DENNY--
I DON'T EVER WANT TO SEE YOU AGAIN.
GET OUT.
I couldn't see it, but Sand was ready to change that night. Back then I was young and my pride was younger still.
She left without a word. By morning I had broken down and in a panic I tried to find her.
I searched the city for nearly two years, unable to accept that I'd thrown the woman I loved away.
Sand finally surfaced in Europe. She was a suspect in a string of fraudulent enterprises being investigated by the German government and Interpol.
I finally gave up.

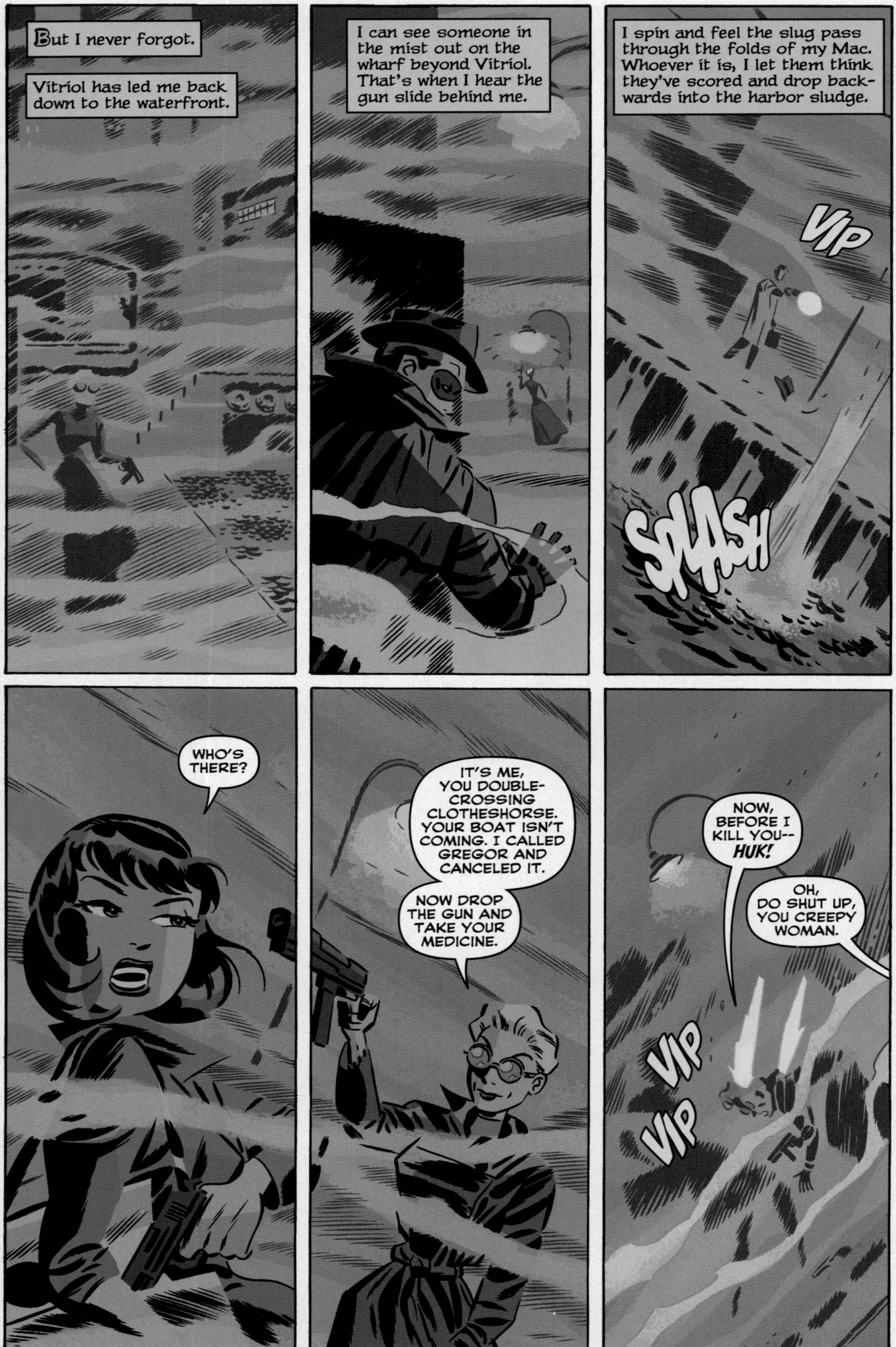
But I never forgot.
Vitriol has led me back down to the waterfront.
I can see someone in the mist out on the wharf beyond Vitriol. That's when I hear the gun slide behind me.
I spin and feel the slug pass through the folds of my Mac. Whoever it is, I let them think they've scored and drop backwards into the harbor sludge.
VIP
SPLASH
WHO'S THERE?
IT'S ME, YOU DOUBLE-CROSSING CLOTHESHORSE. YOUR BOAT ISN'T COMING. I CALLED GREGOR AND CANCELED IT.
NOW DROP THE GUN AND TAKE YOUR MEDICINE.
NOW, BEFORE I KILL YOU-- *HUK!*
OH, DO SHUT UP, YOU CREEPY WOMAN.
VIP
VIP

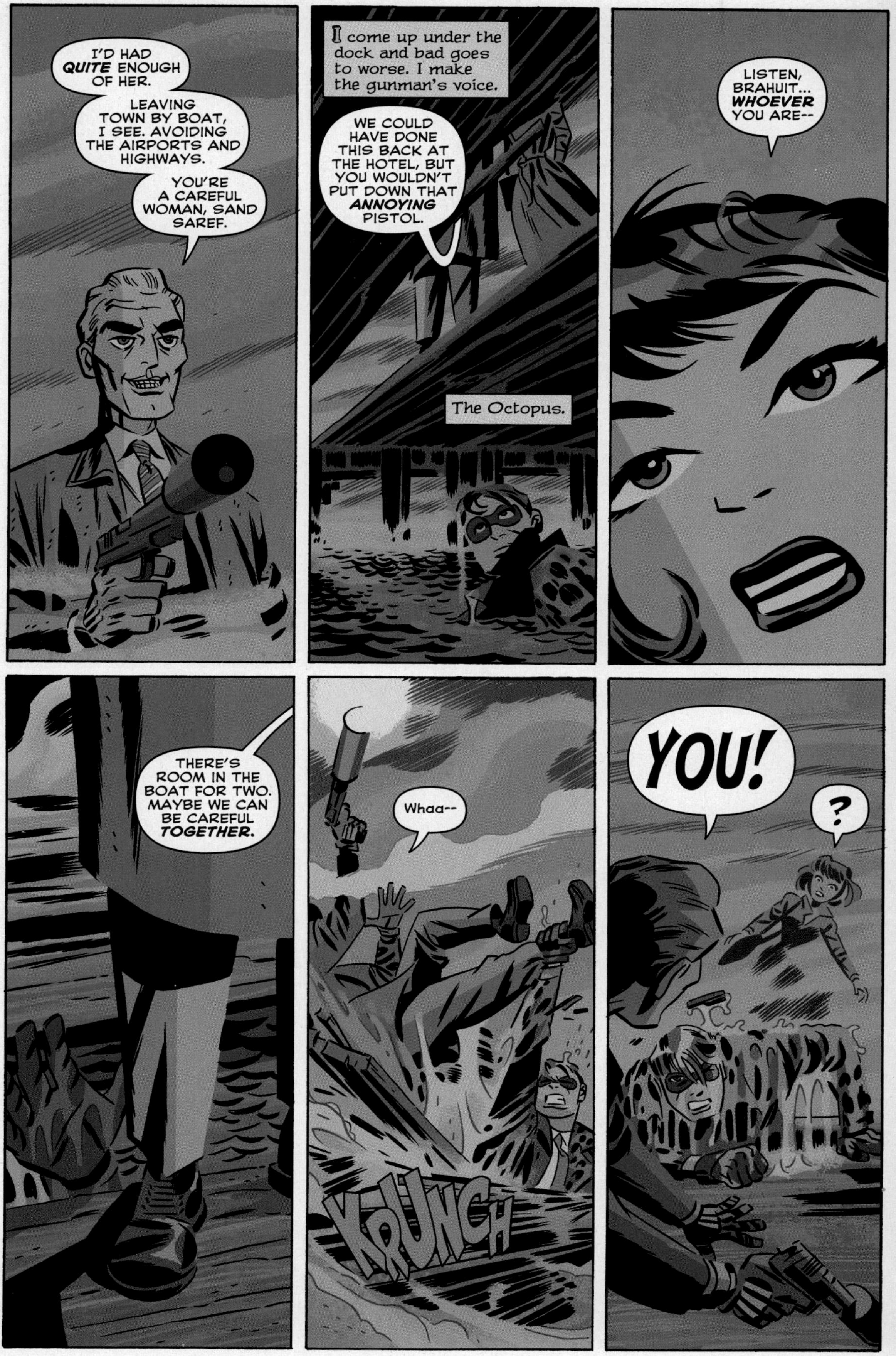
I'D HAD QUITE ENOUGH OF HER.
LEAVING TOWN BY BOAT, I SEE. AVOIDING THE AIRPORTS AND HIGHWAYS.
YOU'RE A CAREFUL WOMAN, SAND SAREF.
I come up under the dock and bad goes to worse. I make the gunman's voice.
WE COULD HAVE DONE THIS BACK AT THE HOTEL, BUT YOU WOULDN'T PUT DOWN THAT ANNOYING PISTOL.
The Octopus.
LISTEN, BRAHUIT... WHOEVER YOU ARE--
THERE'S ROOM IN THE BOAT FOR TWO. MAYBE WE CAN BE CAREFUL TOGETHER.
Whaa--
KRUNCH
YOU!
?

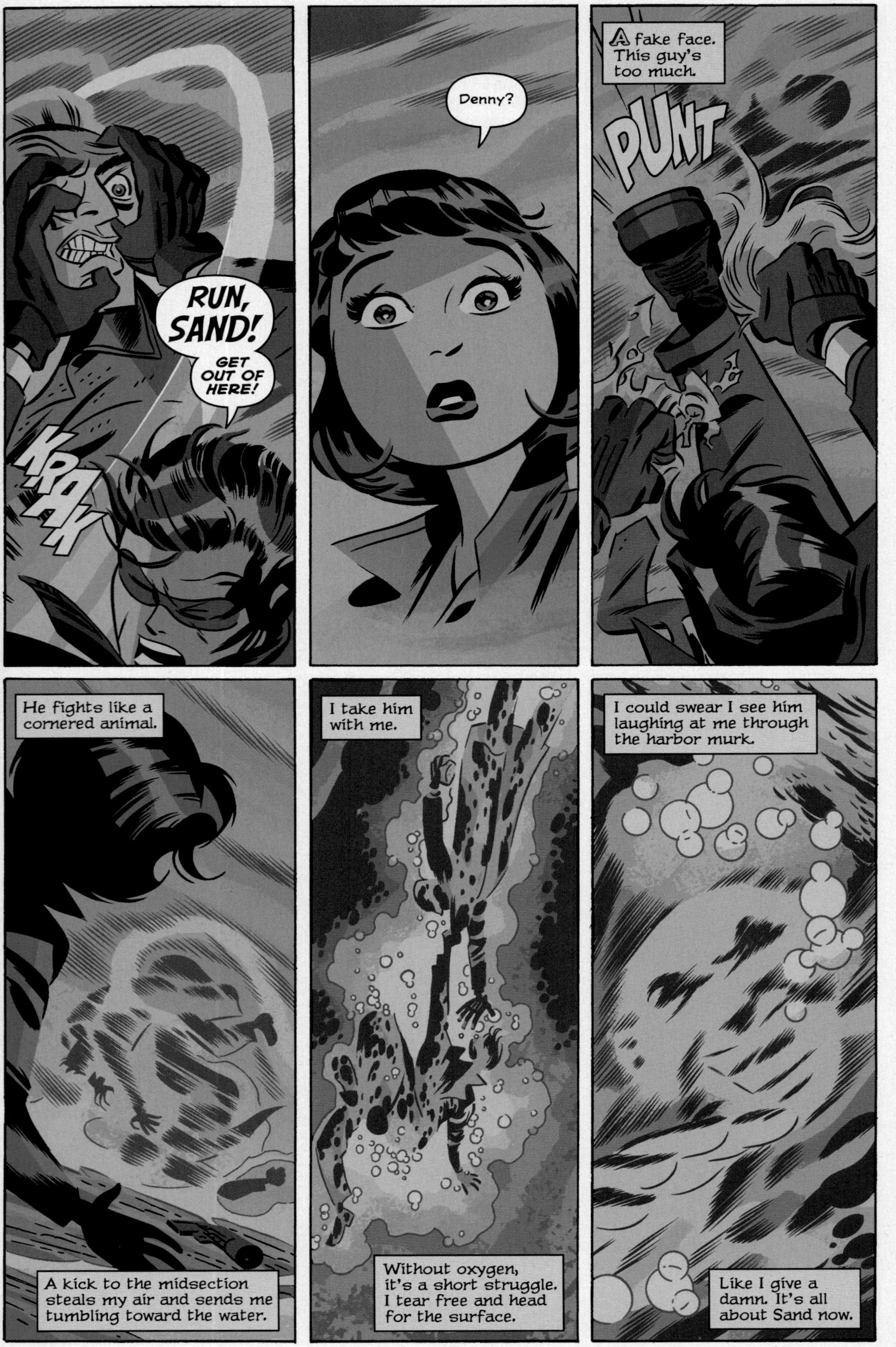
RUN, SAND!
GET OUT OF HERE!
KRAK
Denny?
A fake face. This guy's too much.
PUNT
He fights like a cornered animal.
A kick to the midsection steals my air and sends me tumbling toward the water.
I take him with me.
Without oxygen, it's a short struggle. I tear free and head for the surface.
I could swear I see him laughing at me through the harbor murk.
Like I give a damn. It's all about Sand now.

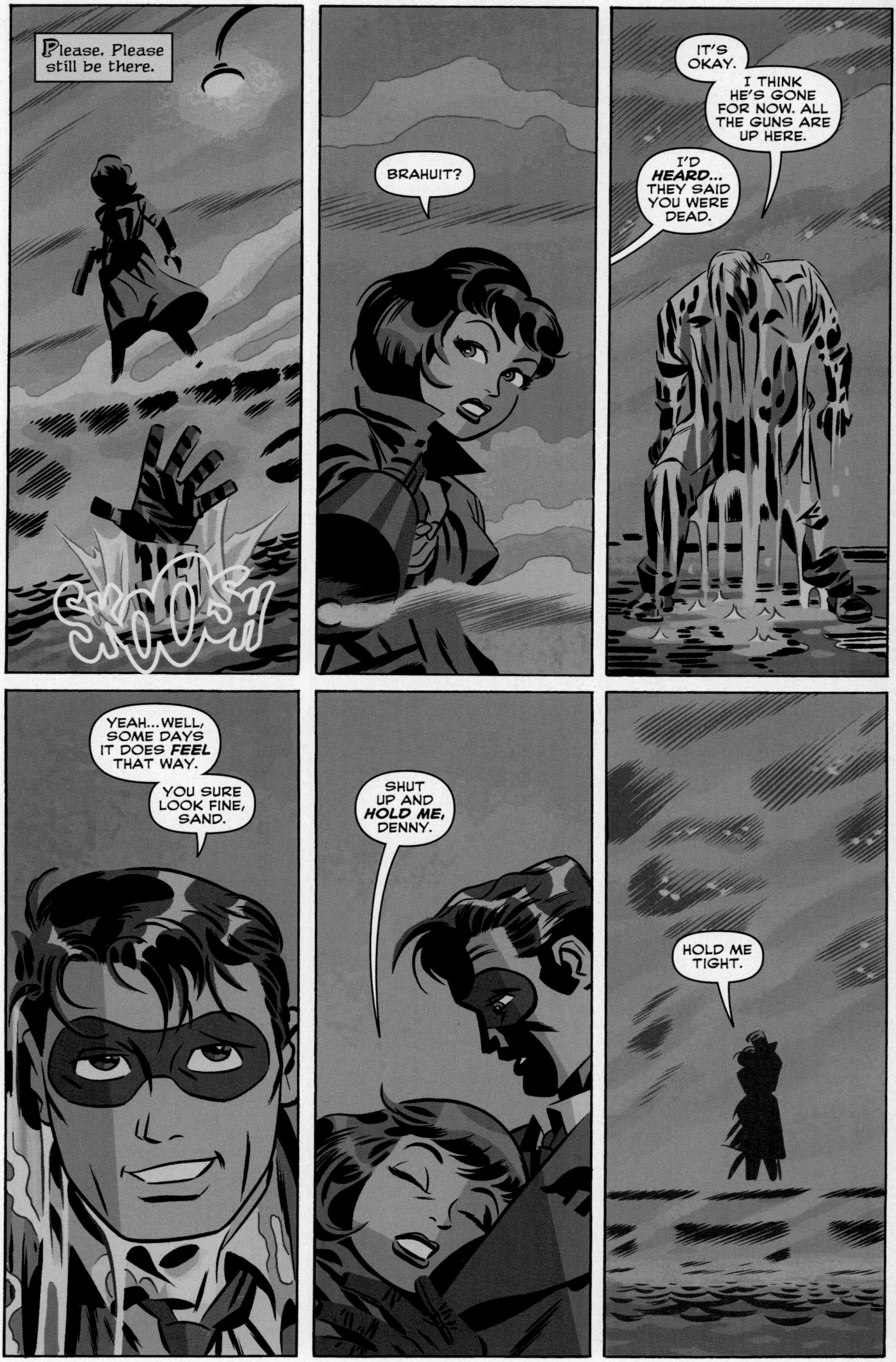
Please. Please still be there.
SKROOSH
BRAHUIT?
IT'S OKAY.
I THINK HE'S GONE FOR NOW. ALL THE GUNS ARE UP HERE.
I'D HEARD... THEY SAID YOU WERE DEAD.
YEAH...WELL, SOME DAYS IT DOES FEEL THAT WAY.
YOU SURE LOOK FINE, SAND.
SHUT UP AND HOLD ME, DENNY.
HOLD ME TIGHT.

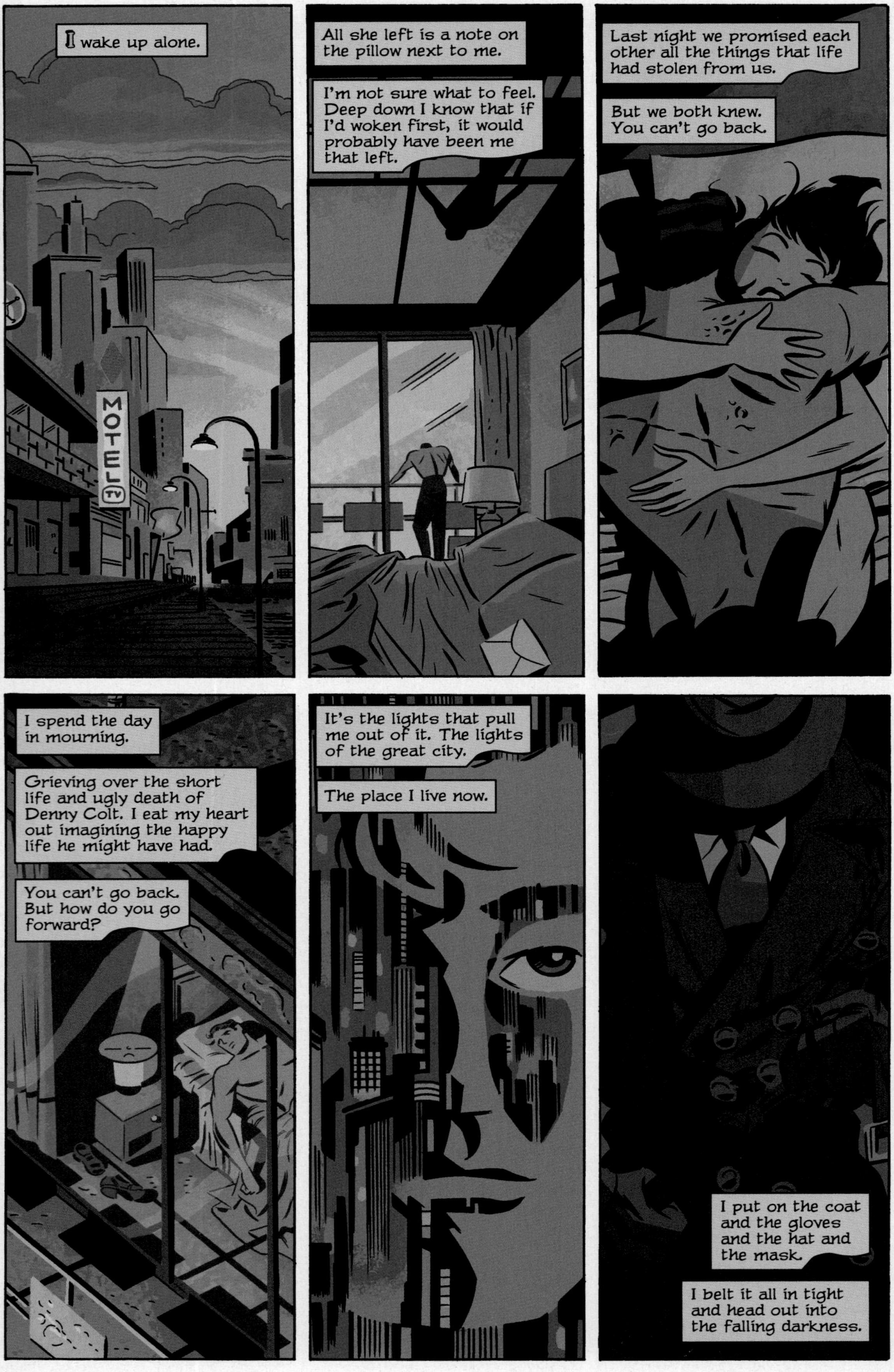
I wake up alone.
All she left is a note on the pillow next to me.
I'm not sure what to feel. Deep down I know that if I'd woken first, it would probably have been me that left.
Last night we promised each other all the things that life had stolen from us.
But we both knew. You can't go back.
MOTEL
TV
I spend the day in mourning.
Grieving over the short life and ugly death of Denny Colt. I eat my heart out imagining the happy life he might have had.
You can't go back. But how do you go forward?
It's the lights that pull me out of it. The lights of the great city.
The place I live now.
I put on the coat and the gloves and the hat and the mask.
I belt it all in tight and head out into the falling darkness.

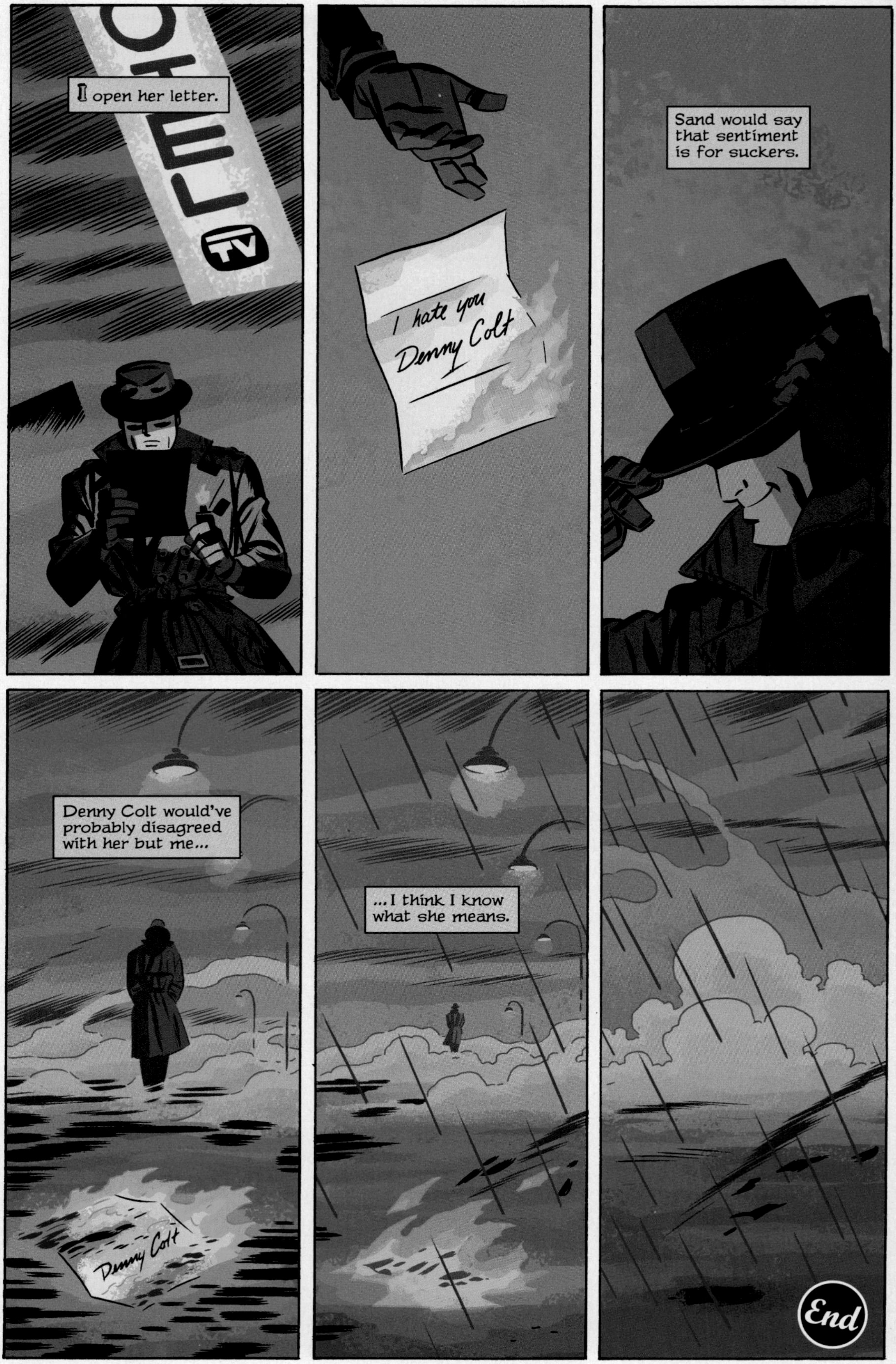
I open her letter.
TV
I hate you Denny Colt
Sand would say that sentiment is for suckers.
Denny Colt would've probably disagreed with her but me...
Denny Colt
...I think I know what she means.
End

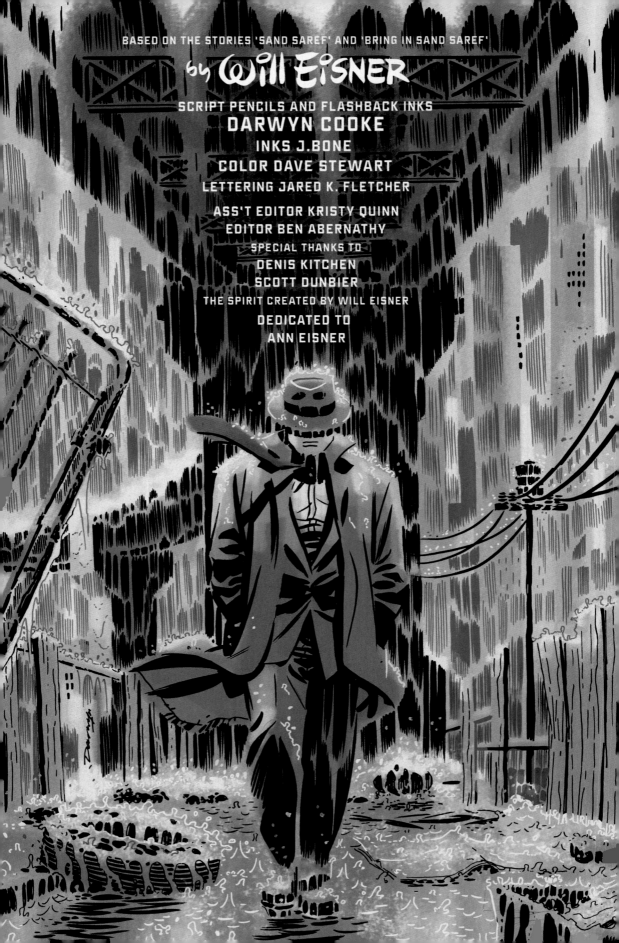

BASED ON THE STORIES 'SAND SAREF' AND 'BRING IN SAND SAREF'
by WILL EISNER

SCRIPT PENCILS AND FLASHBACK INKS
DARWYN COOKE

INKS J. BONE

COLOR DAVE STEWART

LETTERING JARED K. FLETCHER

ASS'T EDITOR KRISTY QUINN
EDITOR BEN ABERNATHY
SPECIAL THANKS TO
DENIS KITCHEN
SCOTT DUNBIER
THE SPIRIT CREATED BY WILL EISNER
DEDICATED TO
ANN EISNER

7

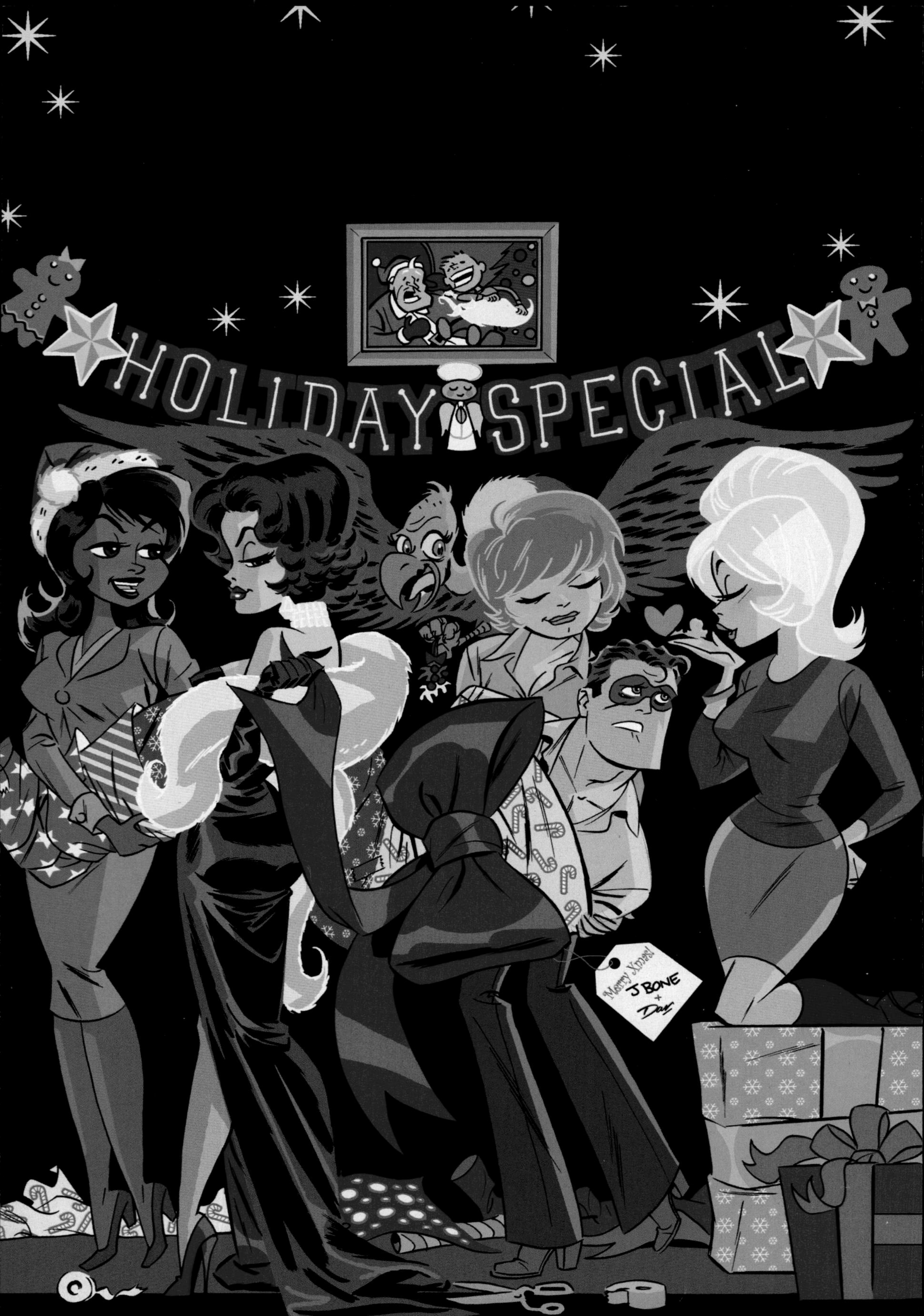
HOLIDAY SPECIAL
Merry Xmas!
J BONE
+
Dave

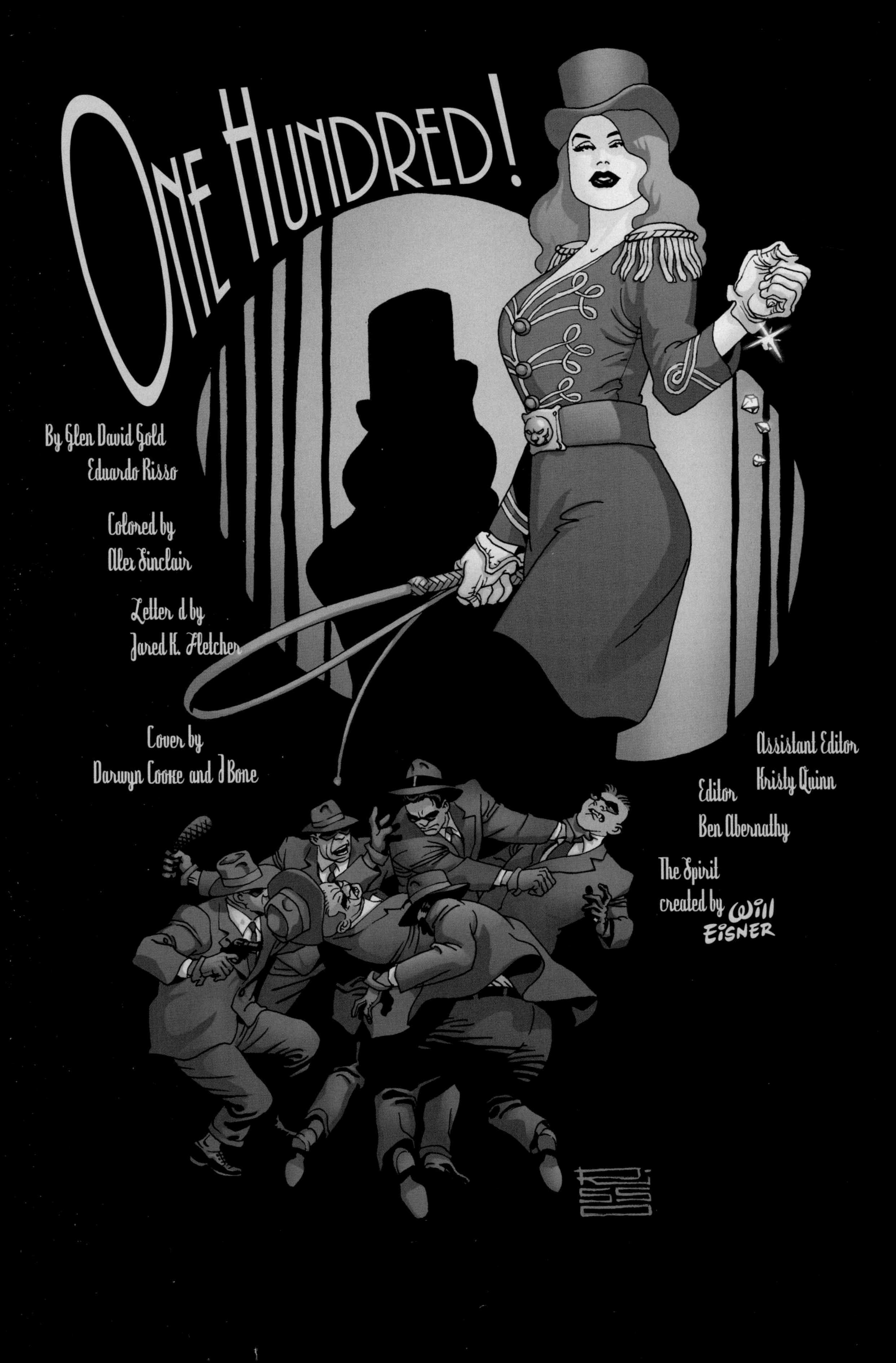
One Hundred!
By Glen David Gold
Eduardo Risso
Colored by
Alex Sinclair
Letter d by
Jared K. Fletcher
Cover by
Darwyn Cooke and J Bone
Assistant Editor
Kristy Quinn
Editor
Ben Abernathy
The Spirit
created by Will
Eisner

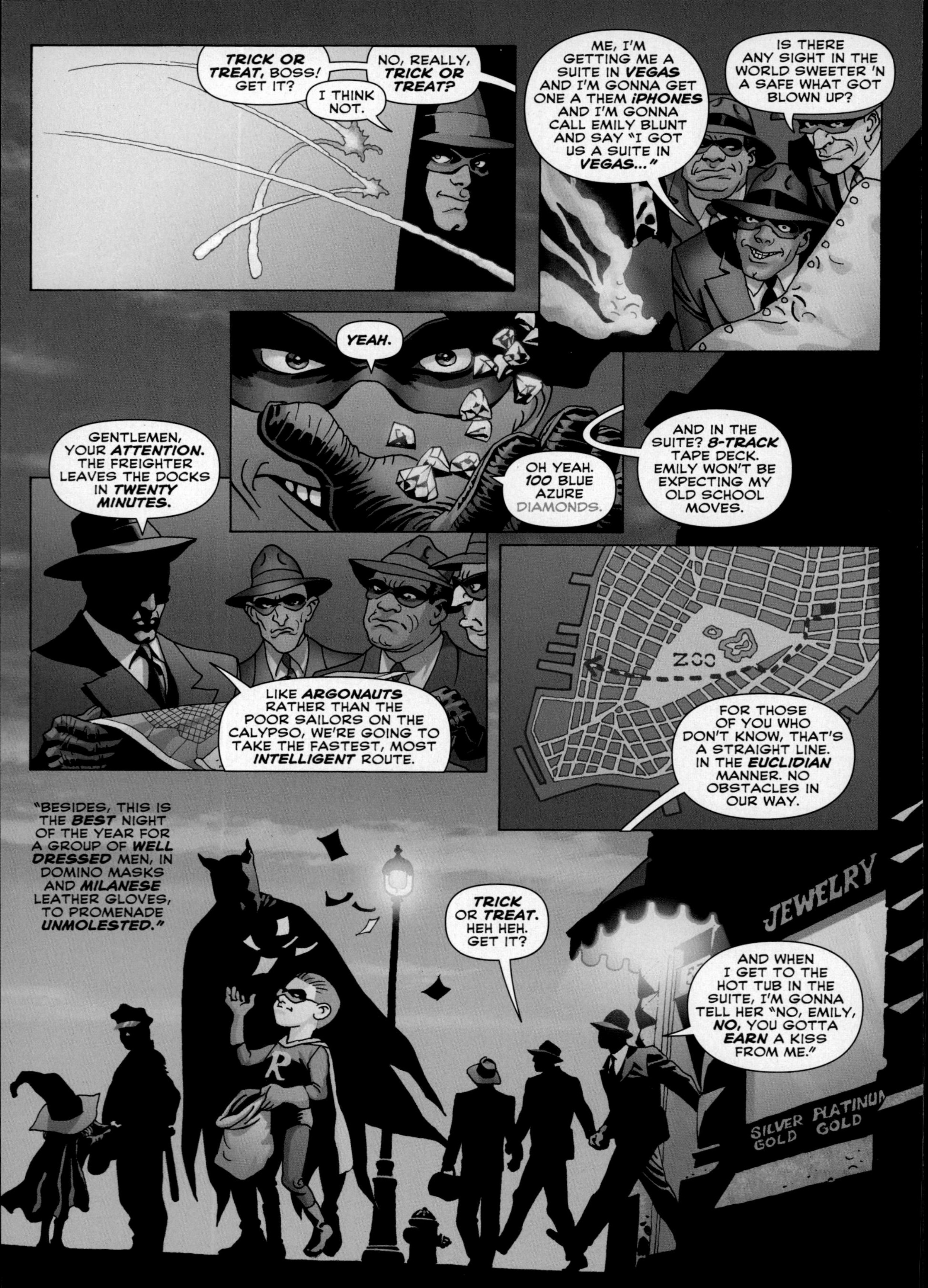

TRICK OR TREAT, BOSS! GET IT?
NO, REALLY, TRICK OR TREAT?
I THINK NOT.
ME, I'M GETTING ME A SUITE IN VEGAS AND I'M GONNA GET ONE A THEM iPHONES AND I'M GONNA CALL EMILY BLUNT AND SAY "I GOT US A SUITE IN VEGAS..."
IS THERE ANY SIGHT IN THE WORLD SWEETER 'N A SAFE WHAT GOT BLOWN UP?
YEAH.
OH YEAH. 100 BLUE AZURE DIAMONDS.
AND IN THE SUITE? 8-TRACK TAPE DECK. EMILY WON'T BE EXPECTING MY OLD SCHOOL MOVES.
GENTLEMEN, YOUR ATTENTION. THE FREIGHTER LEAVES THE DOCKS IN TWENTY MINUTES.
LIKE ARGONAUTS RATHER THAN THE POOR SAILORS ON THE CALYPSO, WE'RE GOING TO TAKE THE FASTEST, MOST INTELLIGENT ROUTE.
ZOO
FOR THOSE OF YOU WHO DON'T KNOW, THAT'S A STRAIGHT LINE. IN THE EUCLIDIAN MANNER. NO OBSTACLES IN OUR WAY.
"BESIDES, THIS IS THE BEST NIGHT OF THE YEAR FOR A GROUP OF WELL DRESSED MEN, IN DOMINO MASKS AND MILANESE LEATHER GLOVES, TO PROMENADE UNMOLESTED."
TRICK OR TREAT. HEH HEH. GET IT?
JEWELRY
AND WHEN I GET TO THE HOT TUB IN THE SUITE, I'M GONNA TELL HER "NO, EMILY, NO, YOU GOTTA EARN A KISS FROM ME."
SILVER PLATINUM GOLD GOLD

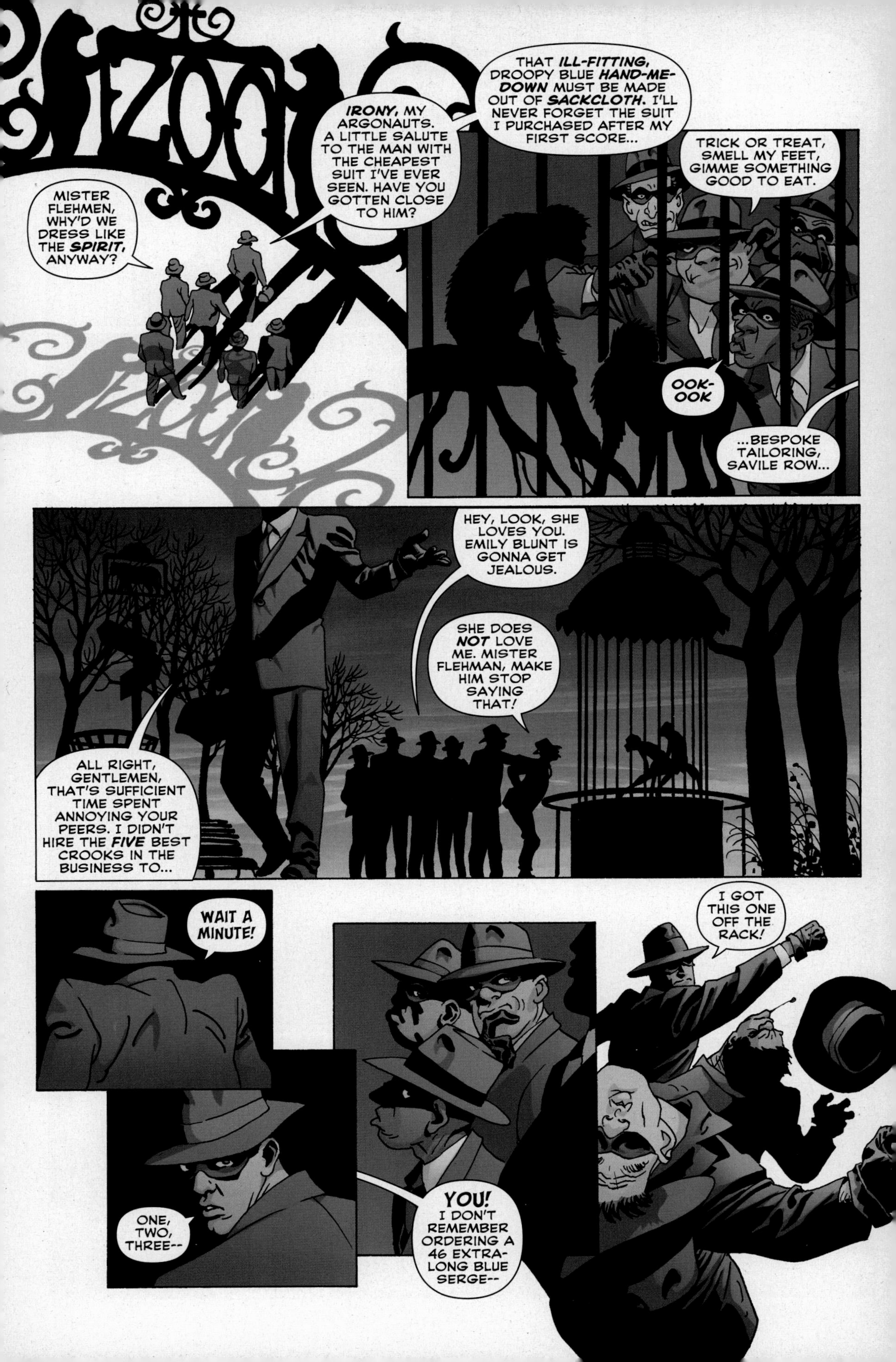
ZOO
MISTER FLEHMEN, WHY'D WE DRESS LIKE THE *SPIRIT*, ANYWAY?
IRONY, MY ARGONAUTS. A LITTLE SALUTE TO THE MAN WITH THE CHEAPEST SUIT I'VE EVER SEEN. HAVE YOU GOTTEN CLOSE TO HIM?
THAT *ILL-FITTING*, DROOPY BLUE *HAND-ME-DOWN* MUST BE MADE OUT OF *SACKCLOTH*. I'LL NEVER FORGET THE SUIT I PURCHASED AFTER MY FIRST SCORE...
TRICK OR TREAT, SMELL MY FEET, GIMME SOMETHING GOOD TO EAT.
OOK-OOK
...BESPOKE TAILORING, SAVILE ROW...
HEY, LOOK, SHE LOVES YOU. EMILY BLUNT IS GONNA GET JEALOUS.
SHE DOES *NOT* LOVE ME. MISTER FLEHMAN, MAKE HIM STOP SAYING THAT!
ALL RIGHT, GENTLEMEN, THAT'S SUFFICIENT TIME SPENT ANNOYING YOUR PEERS. I DIDN'T HIRE THE *FIVE* BEST CROOKS IN THE BUSINESS TO...
WAIT A MINUTE!
ONE, TWO, THREE--
YOU! I DON'T REMEMBER ORDERING A 46 EXTRA-LONG BLUE SERGE--
I GOT THIS ONE OFF THE RACK!

OH *PYRRHIC* VICTORY! THIS WAS THE *WORST* ESCAPE ROUTE *EVER*. NOW I CAN ONLY DIVIDE UP THE DIAMONDS FIVE-- FOUR--THREE-- SAY, I HAVE A NIFTY IDEA!

SLOW DOWN, FLEHMAN.

SORRY TO RUIN THE CREASE IN YOUR TROUSERS!

NOT IN THE *FACE*, NOT IN THE-- *OOF!*

FLEHMAN, YOU'LL DO THE *PERP* WALK, NOT THE...

"...CATWALK...

"OH, NO."

It's not gonna--

There's no way that--

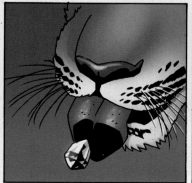

100 DIAMONDS LOST IN A TIGER CAGE. *HOLY SMOKES!*

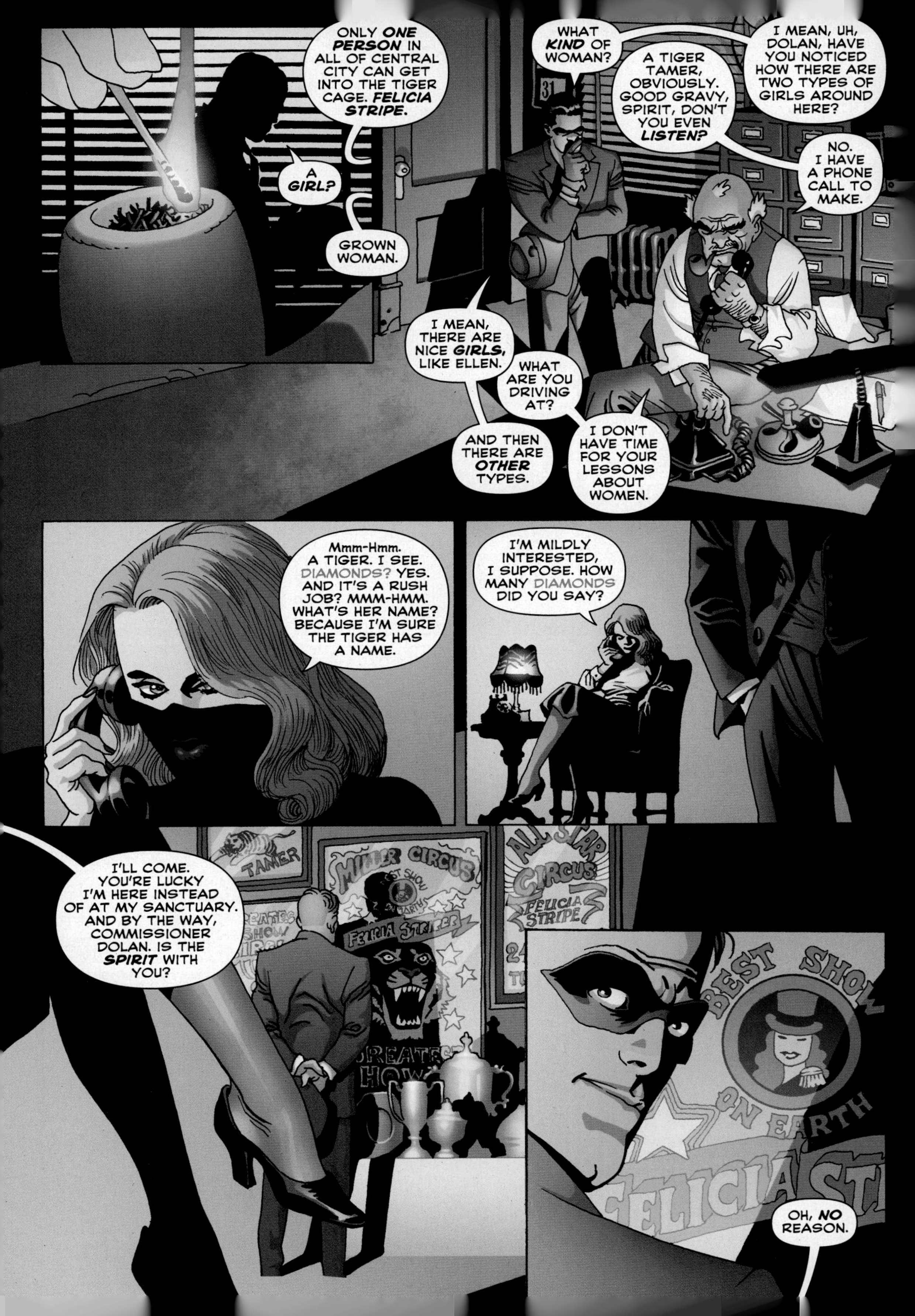

ONLY ONE PERSON IN ALL OF CENTRAL CITY CAN GET INTO THE TIGER CAGE. FELICIA STRIPE.
A GIRL?
GROWN WOMAN.
WHAT KIND OF WOMAN?
A TIGER TAMER, OBVIOUSLY. GOOD GRAVY, SPIRIT, DON'T YOU EVEN LISTEN?
I MEAN, UH, DOLAN, HAVE YOU NOTICED HOW THERE ARE TWO TYPES OF GIRLS AROUND HERE?
NO. I HAVE A PHONE CALL TO MAKE.
I MEAN, THERE ARE NICE GIRLS, LIKE ELLEN.
WHAT ARE YOU DRIVING AT?
AND THEN THERE ARE OTHER TYPES.
I DON'T HAVE TIME FOR YOUR LESSONS ABOUT WOMEN.
Mmm-Hmm. A TIGER. I SEE. DIAMONDS? YES. AND IT'S A RUSH JOB? MMM-HMM. WHAT'S HER NAME? BECAUSE I'M SURE THE TIGER HAS A NAME.
I'M MILDLY INTERESTED, I SUPPOSE. HOW MANY DIAMONDS DID YOU SAY?
I'LL COME. YOU'RE LUCKY I'M HERE INSTEAD OF AT MY SANCTUARY. AND BY THE WAY, COMMISSIONER DOLAN. IS THE SPIRIT WITH YOU?
TAMER
MILLER CIRCUS
ALL STAR CIRCUS
FELICIA STRIPE
BEST SHOW ON EARTH
OH, NO REASON.

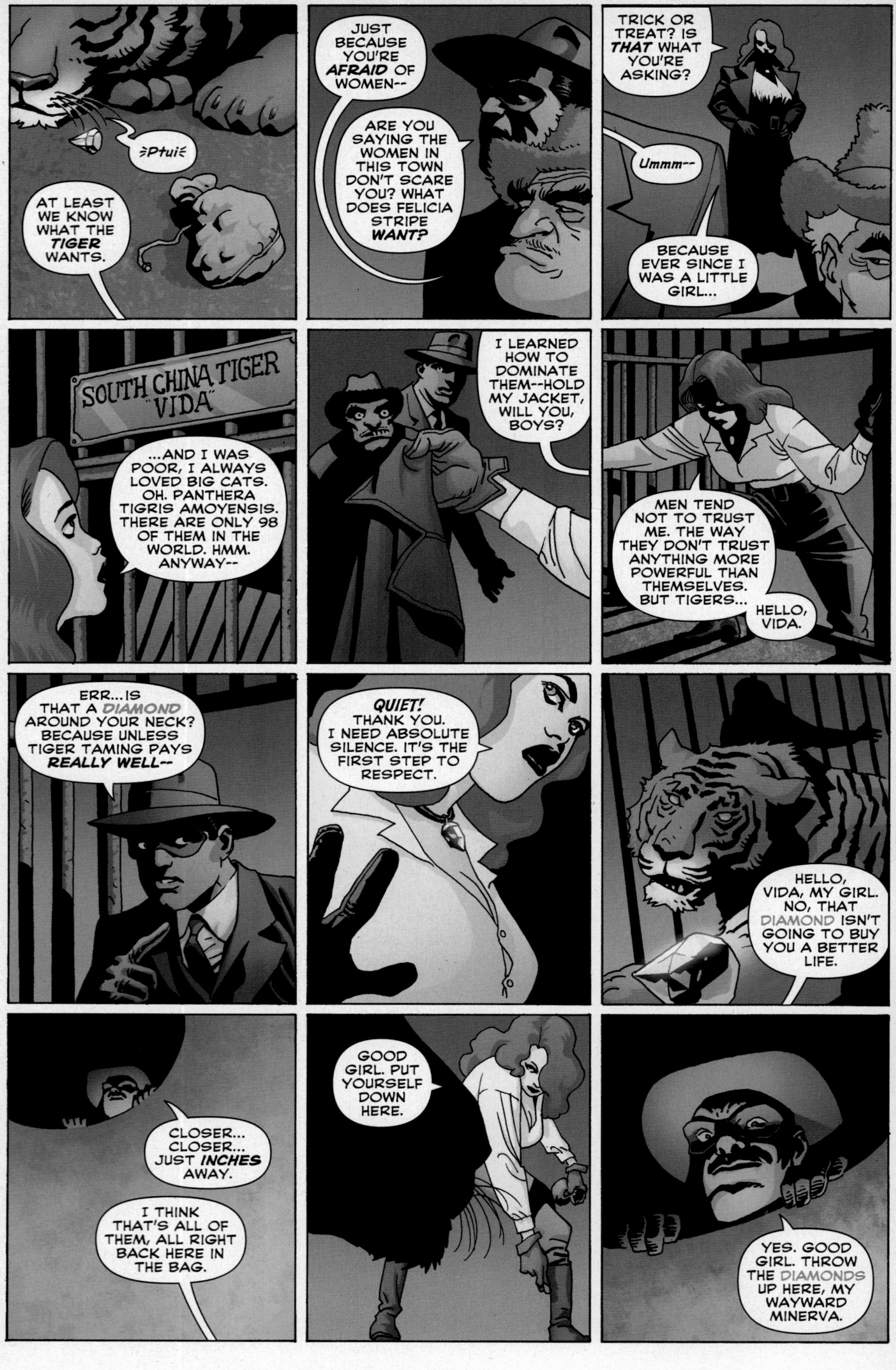

≥Ptui≤
AT LEAST WE KNOW WHAT THE TIGER WANTS.
JUST BECAUSE YOU'RE AFRAID OF WOMEN--
ARE YOU SAYING THE WOMEN IN THIS TOWN DON'T SCARE YOU? WHAT DOES FELICIA STRIPE WANT?
TRICK OR TREAT? IS THAT WHAT YOU'RE ASKING?
Ummm--
BECAUSE EVER SINCE I WAS A LITTLE GIRL...
SOUTH CHINA TIGER "VIDA"
...AND I WAS POOR, I ALWAYS LOVED BIG CATS. OH. PANTHERA TIGRIS AMOYENSIS. THERE ARE ONLY 98 OF THEM IN THE WORLD. HMM. ANYWAY--
I LEARNED HOW TO DOMINATE THEM--HOLD MY JACKET, WILL YOU, BOYS?
MEN TEND NOT TO TRUST ME. THE WAY THEY DON'T TRUST ANYTHING MORE POWERFUL THAN THEMSELVES. BUT TIGERS...
HELLO, VIDA.
ERR...IS THAT A DIAMOND AROUND YOUR NECK? BECAUSE UNLESS TIGER TAMING PAYS REALLY WELL--
QUIET! THANK YOU. I NEED ABSOLUTE SILENCE. IT'S THE FIRST STEP TO RESPECT.
HELLO, VIDA, MY GIRL. NO, THAT DIAMOND ISN'T GOING TO BUY YOU A BETTER LIFE.
CLOSER... CLOSER... JUST INCHES AWAY.
I THINK THAT'S ALL OF THEM, ALL RIGHT BACK HERE IN THE BAG.
GOOD GIRL. PUT YOURSELF DOWN HERE.
YES. GOOD GIRL. THROW THE DIAMONDS UP HERE, MY WAYWARD MINERVA.

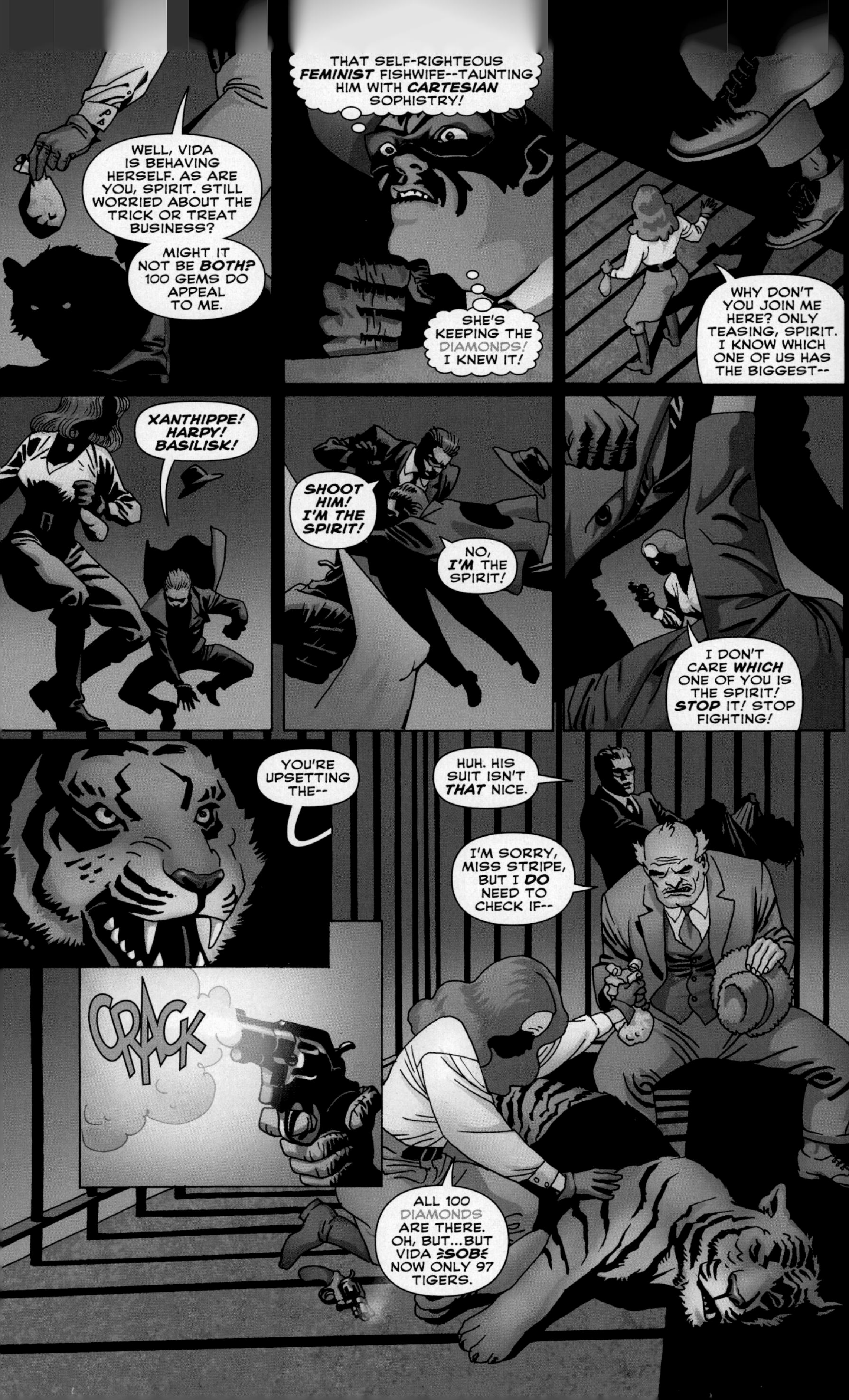

WELL, VIDA IS BEHAVING HERSELF. AS ARE YOU, SPIRIT. STILL WORRIED ABOUT THE TRICK OR TREAT BUSINESS?
MIGHT IT NOT BE BOTH? 100 GEMS DO APPEAL TO ME.
THAT SELF-RIGHTEOUS FEMINIST FISHWIFE--TAUNTING HIM WITH CARTESIAN SOPHISTRY!
SHE'S KEEPING THE DIAMONDS! I KNEW IT!
WHY DON'T YOU JOIN ME HERE? ONLY TEASING, SPIRIT. I KNOW WHICH ONE OF US HAS THE BIGGEST--
XANTHIPPE! HARPY! BASILISK!
SHOOT HIM! I'M THE SPIRIT!
NO, I'M THE SPIRIT!
I DON'T CARE WHICH ONE OF YOU IS THE SPIRIT! STOP IT! STOP FIGHTING!
YOU'RE UPSETTING THE--
HUH. HIS SUIT ISN'T THAT NICE.
I'M SORRY, MISS STRIPE, BUT I DO NEED TO CHECK IF--
CRACK
ALL 100 DIAMONDS ARE THERE. OH, BUT...BUT VIDA *SOB* NOW ONLY 97 TIGERS.

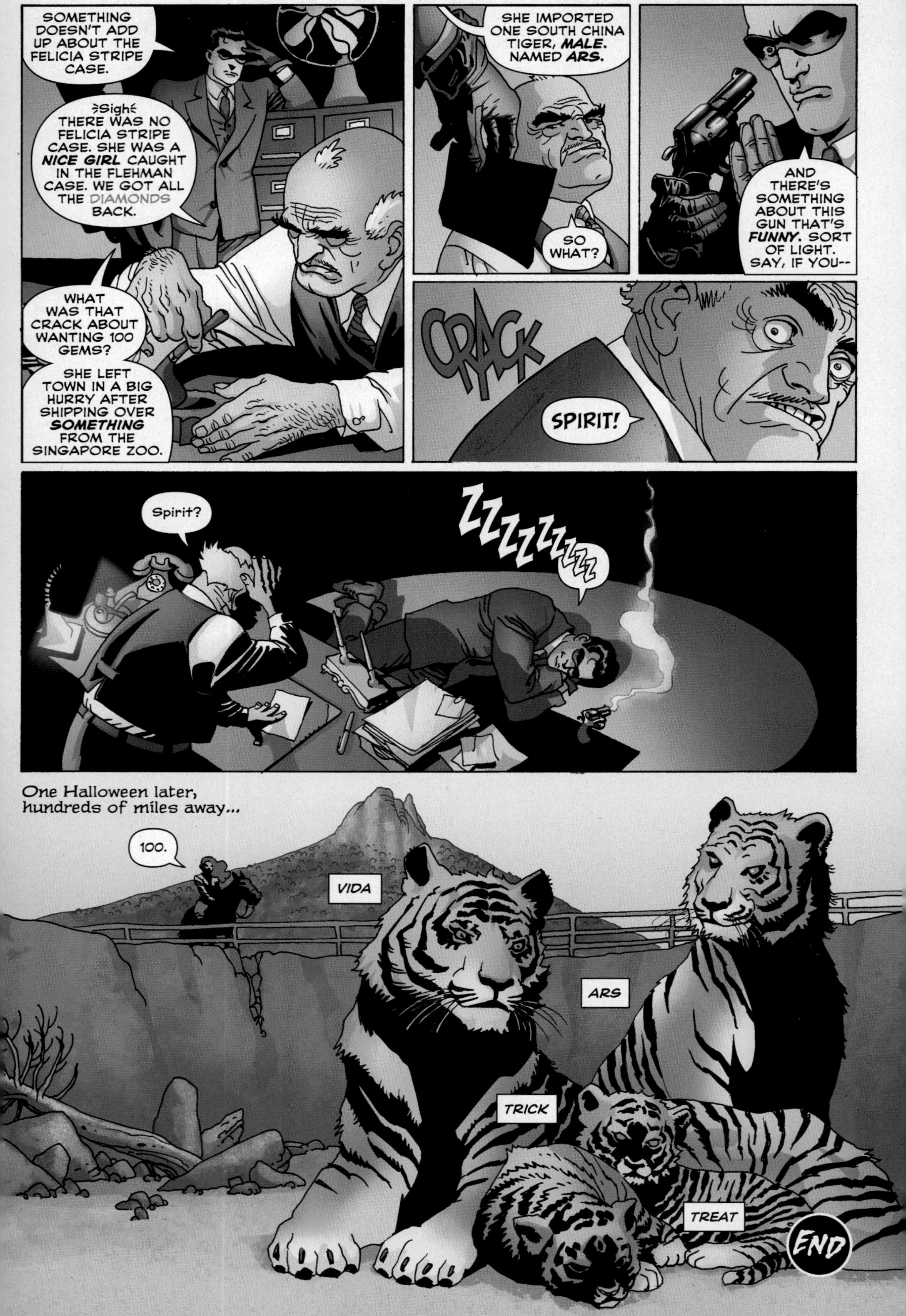
SOMETHING DOESN'T ADD UP ABOUT THE FELICIA STRIPE CASE.
≥Sigh≤ THERE WAS NO FELICIA STRIPE CASE. SHE WAS A **NICE GIRL** CAUGHT IN THE FLEHMAN CASE. WE GOT ALL THE DIAMONDS BACK.
WHAT WAS THAT CRACK ABOUT WANTING 100 GEMS?
SHE LEFT TOWN IN A BIG HURRY AFTER SHIPPING OVER **SOMETHING** FROM THE SINGAPORE ZOO.
SHE IMPORTED ONE SOUTH CHINA TIGER, **MALE**. NAMED **ARS**.
SO WHAT?
AND THERE'S SOMETHING ABOUT THIS GUN THAT'S **FUNNY**. SORT OF LIGHT. SAY, IF YOU--
CRACK
SPIRIT!
Spirit?
ZZZZZZZZZZ
One Halloween later, hundreds of miles away...
100.
VIDA
ARS
TRICK
TREAT
END

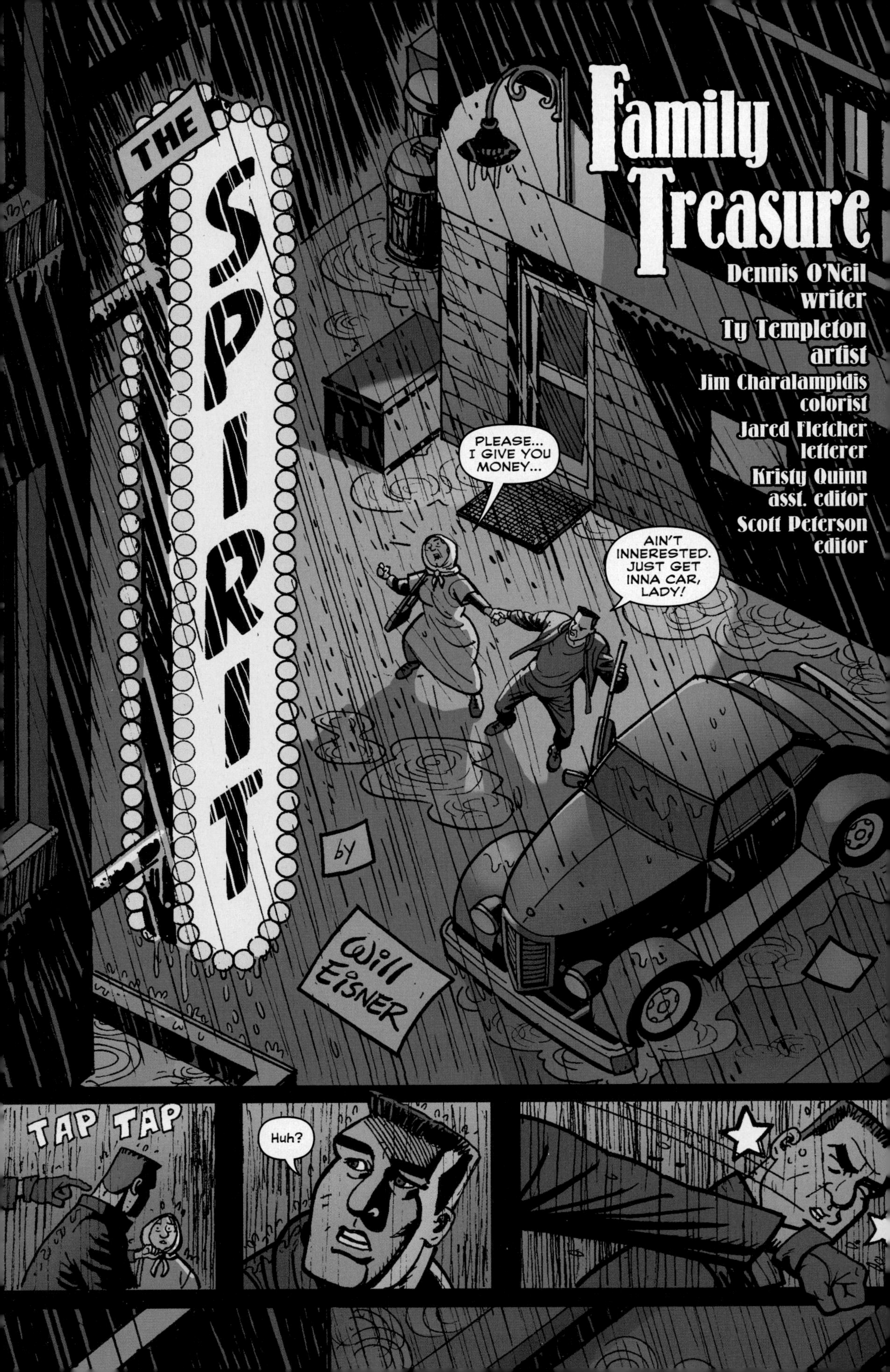
THE SPIRIT
by
Will Eisner
Family Treasure
Dennis O'Neil writer
Ty Templeton artist
Jim Charalampidis colorist
Jared Fletcher letterer
Kristy Quinn asst. editor
Scott Peterson editor
PLEASE... I GIVE YOU MONEY...
AIN'T INNERESTED. JUST GET INNA CAR, LADY!
TAP TAP
Huh?

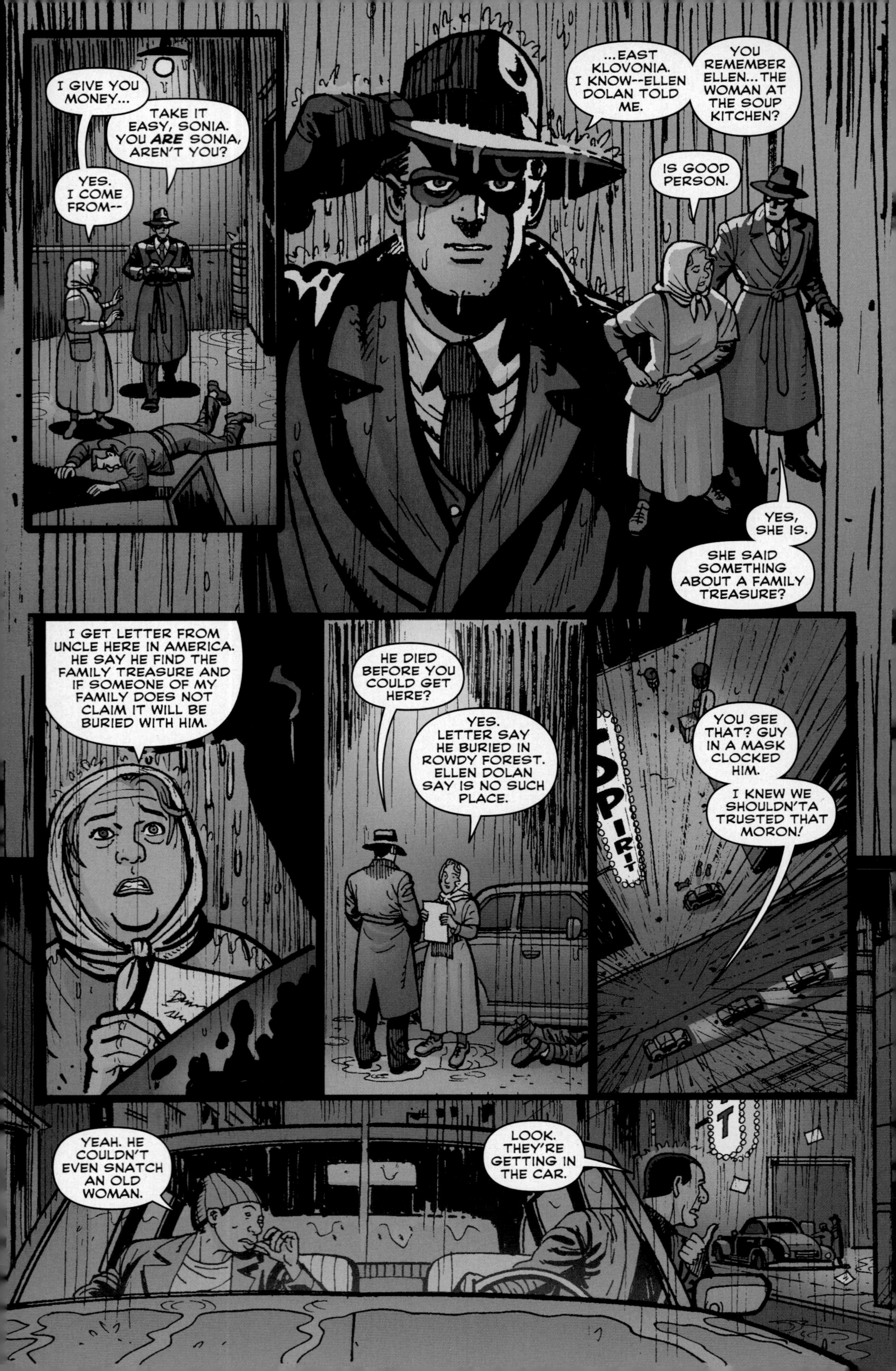
I GIVE YOU MONEY...
TAKE IT EASY, SONIA. YOU ARE SONIA, AREN'T YOU?
YES. I COME FROM--
...EAST KLOVONIA. I KNOW--ELLEN DOLAN TOLD ME.
YOU REMEMBER ELLEN...THE WOMAN AT THE SOUP KITCHEN?
IS GOOD PERSON.
YES, SHE IS.
SHE SAID SOMETHING ABOUT A FAMILY TREASURE?
I GET LETTER FROM UNCLE HERE IN AMERICA. HE SAY HE FIND THE FAMILY TREASURE AND IF SOMEONE OF MY FAMILY DOES NOT CLAIM IT WILL BE BURIED WITH HIM.
HE DIED BEFORE YOU COULD GET HERE?
YES. LETTER SAY HE BURIED IN ROWDY FOREST. ELLEN DOLAN SAY IS NO SUCH PLACE.
SPIRIT
YOU SEE THAT? GUY IN A MASK CLOCKED HIM.
I KNEW WE SHOULDN'TA TRUSTED THAT MORON!
YEAH. HE COULDN'T EVEN SNATCH AN OLD WOMAN.
LOOK. THEY'RE GETTING IN THE CAR.

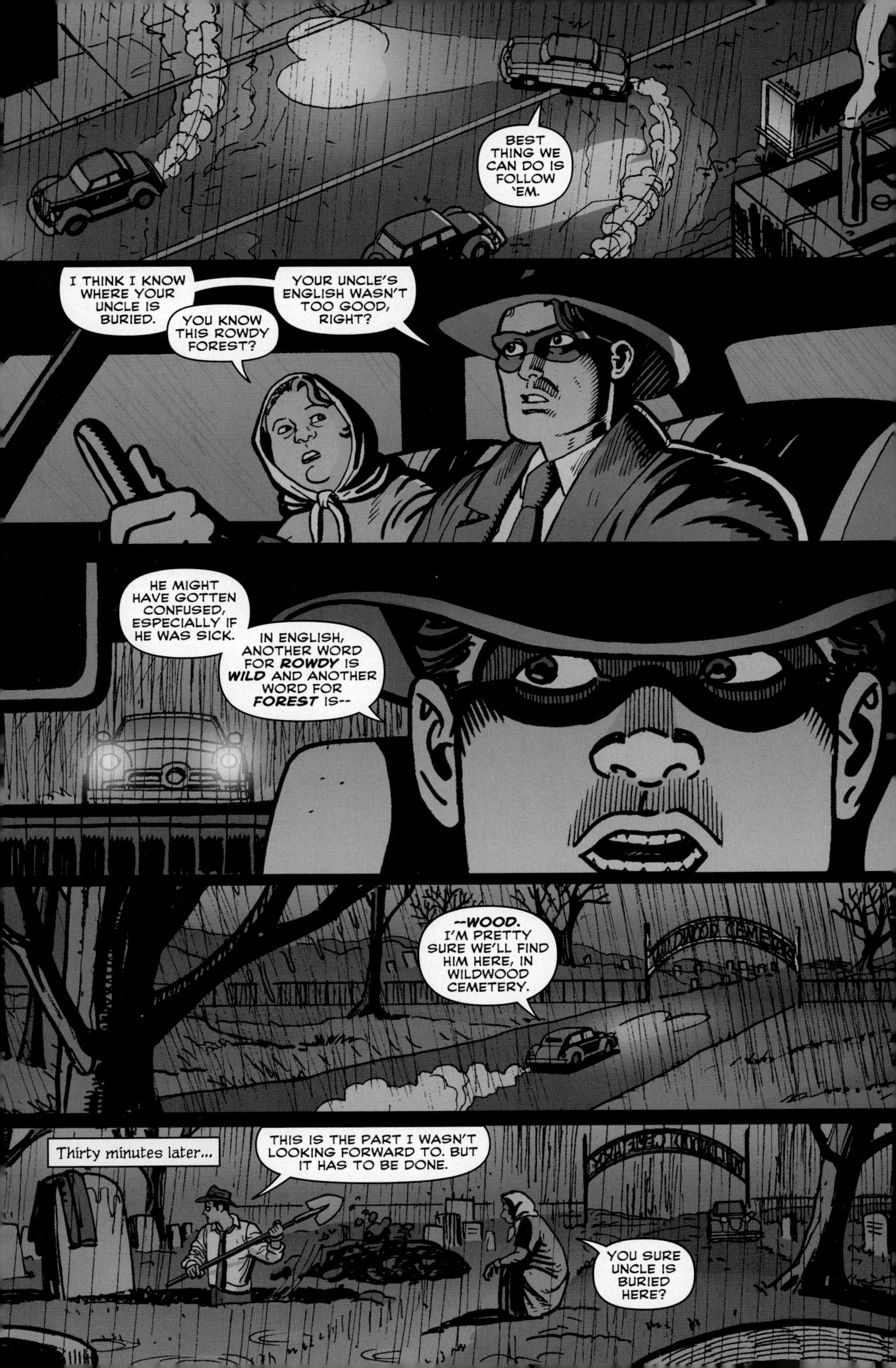
BEST THING WE CAN DO IS FOLLOW 'EM.
I THINK I KNOW WHERE YOUR UNCLE IS BURIED.
YOUR UNCLE'S ENGLISH WASN'T TOO GOOD, RIGHT?
YOU KNOW THIS ROWDY FOREST?
HE MIGHT HAVE GOTTEN CONFUSED, ESPECIALLY IF HE WAS SICK.
IN ENGLISH, ANOTHER WORD FOR **ROWDY** IS **WILD** AND ANOTHER WORD FOR **FOREST** IS--
--WOOD. I'M PRETTY SURE WE'LL FIND HIM HERE, IN WILDWOOD CEMETERY.
Thirty minutes later...
THIS IS THE PART I WASN'T LOOKING FORWARD TO. BUT IT HAS TO BE DONE.
YOU SURE UNCLE IS BURIED HERE?

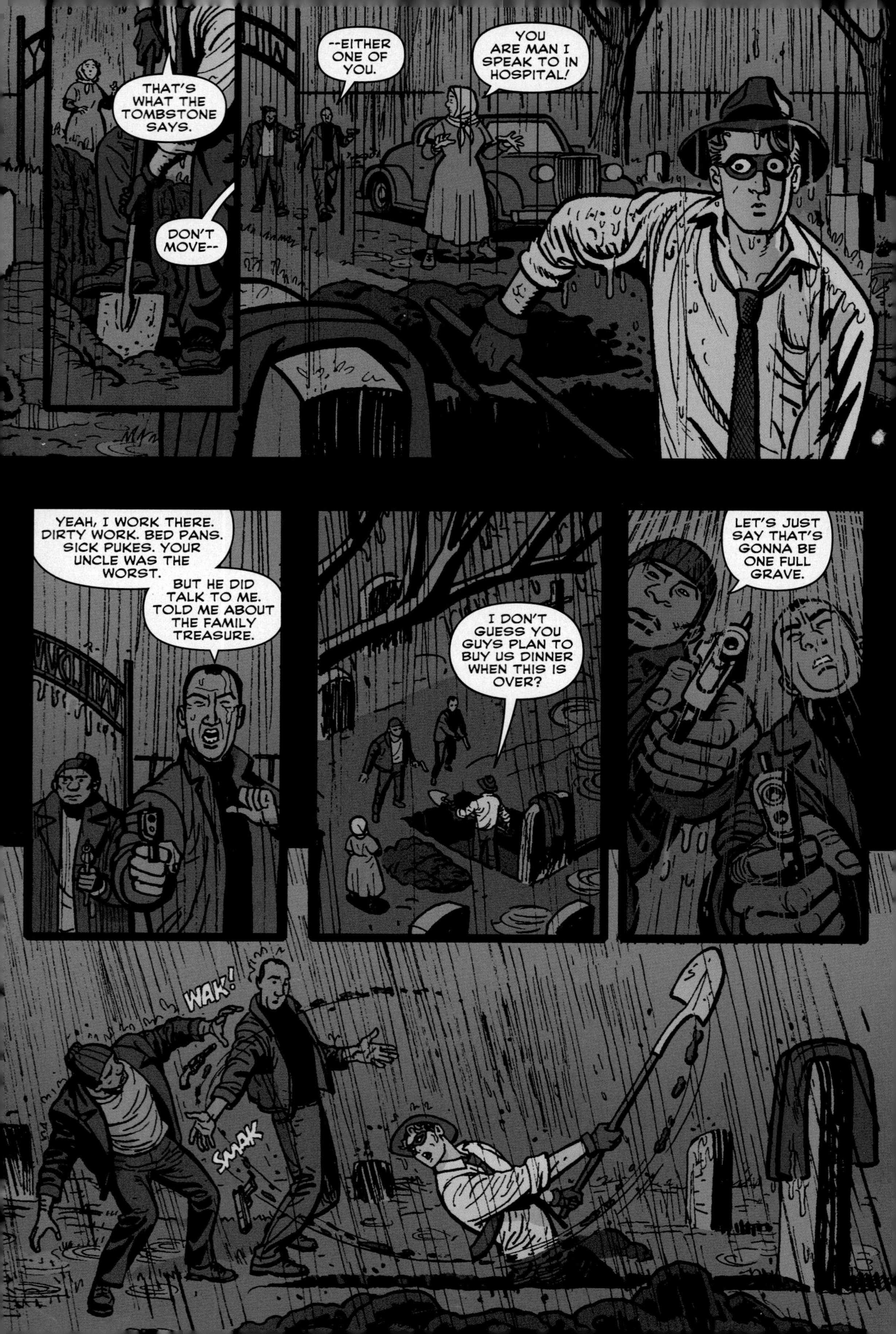
THAT'S WHAT THE TOMBSTONE SAYS.
DON'T MOVE--
--EITHER ONE OF YOU.
YOU ARE MAN I SPEAK TO IN HOSPITAL!
YEAH, I WORK THERE. DIRTY WORK. BED PANS. SICK PUKES. YOUR UNCLE WAS THE WORST.
BUT HE DID TALK TO ME. TOLD ME ABOUT THE FAMILY TREASURE.
I DON'T GUESS YOU GUYS PLAN TO BUY US DINNER WHEN THIS IS OVER?
LET'S JUST SAY THAT'S GONNA BE ONE FULL GRAVE.
WAK!
SMAK

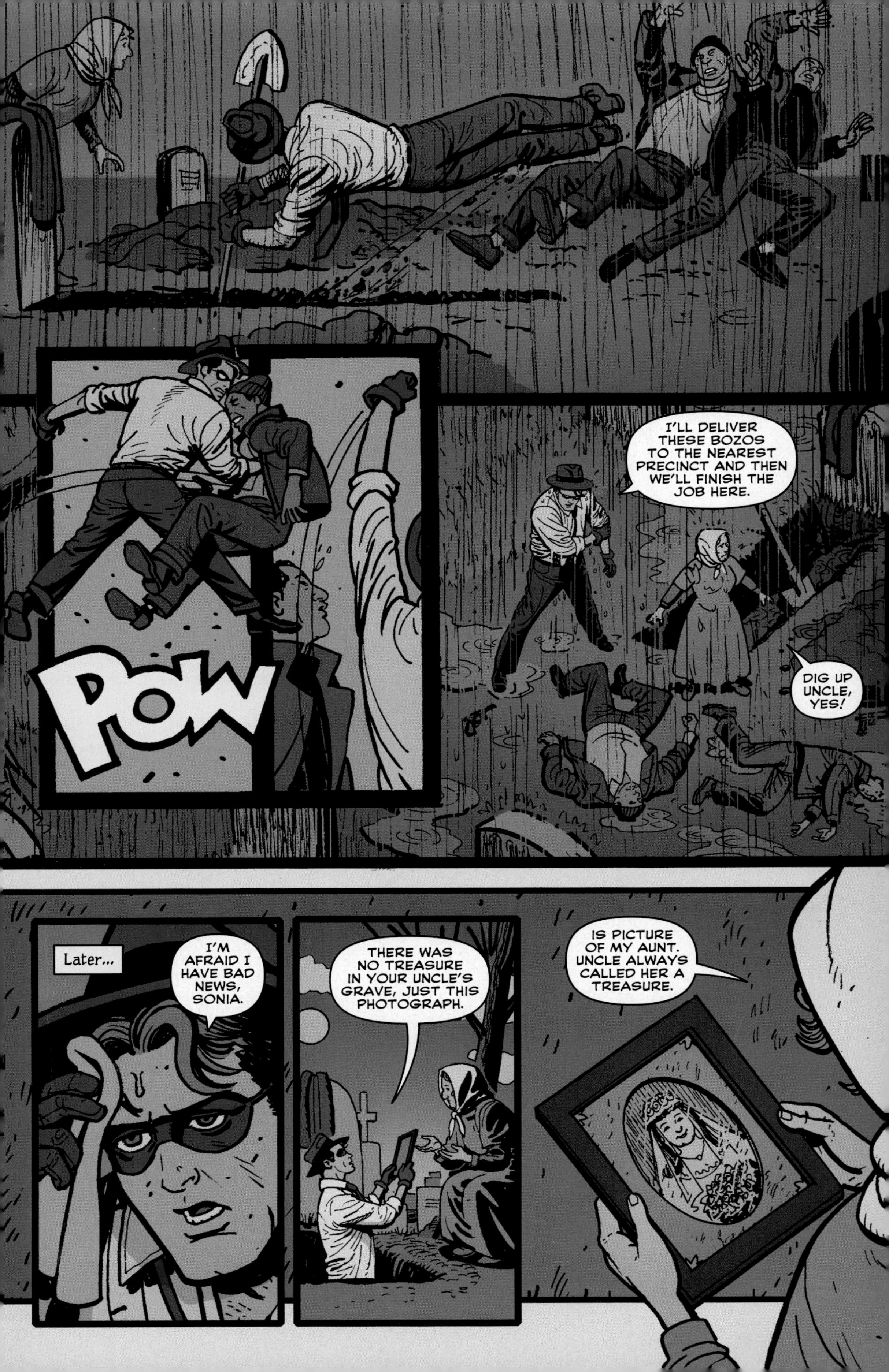
POW
I'LL DELIVER THESE BOZOS TO THE NEAREST PRECINCT AND THEN WE'LL FINISH THE JOB HERE.
DIG UP UNCLE, YES!
Later...
I'M AFRAID I HAVE BAD NEWS, SONIA.
THERE WAS NO TREASURE IN YOUR UNCLE'S GRAVE, JUST THIS PHOTOGRAPH.
IS PICTURE OF MY AUNT. UNCLE ALWAYS CALLED HER A TREASURE.

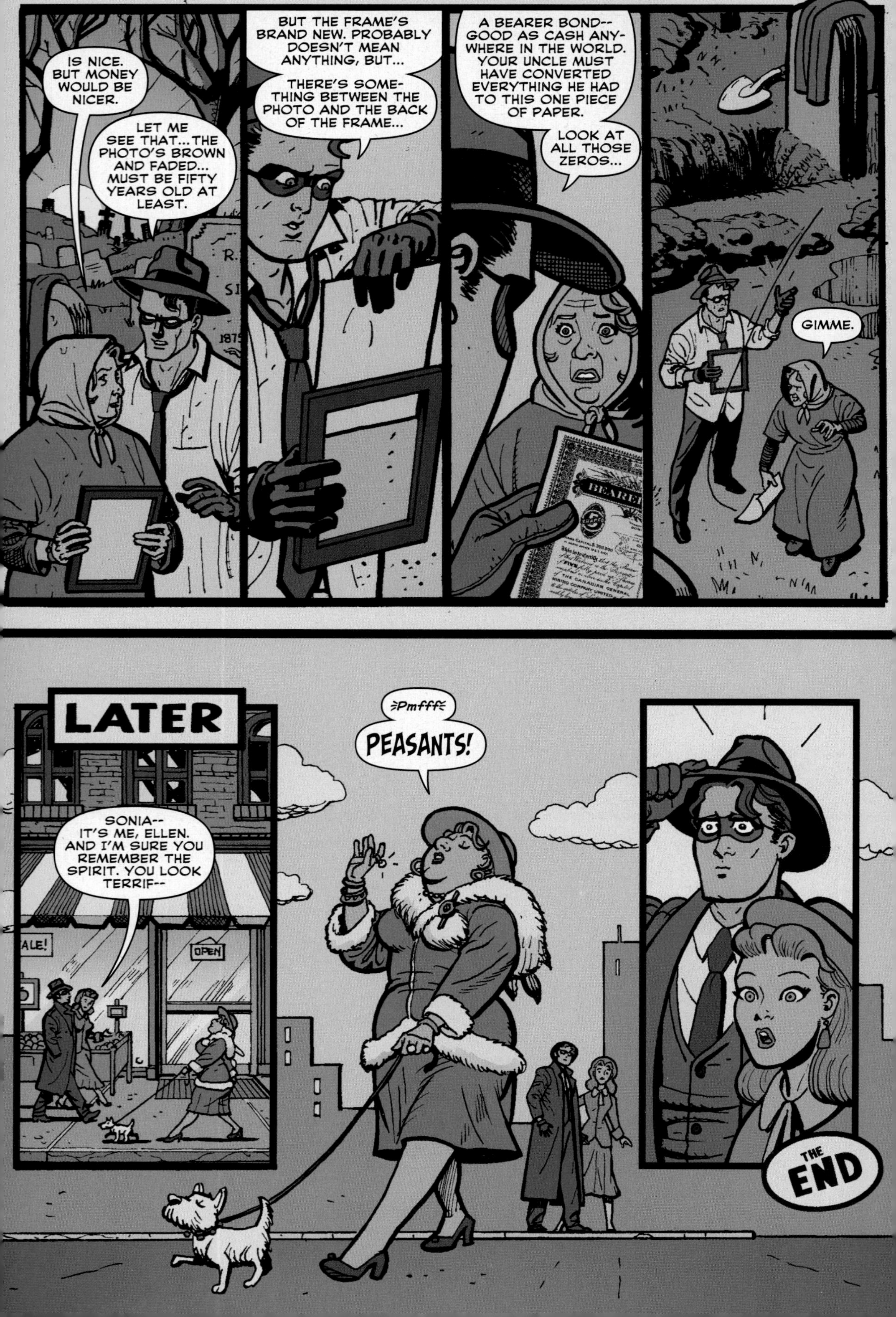
IS NICE. BUT MONEY WOULD BE NICER.
LET ME SEE THAT...THE PHOTO'S BROWN AND FADED... MUST BE FIFTY YEARS OLD AT LEAST.
BUT THE FRAME'S BRAND NEW. PROBABLY DOESN'T MEAN ANYTHING, BUT...
THERE'S SOMETHING BETWEEN THE PHOTO AND THE BACK OF THE FRAME...
A BEARER BOND-- GOOD AS CASH ANYWHERE IN THE WORLD. YOUR UNCLE MUST HAVE CONVERTED EVERYTHING HE HAD TO THIS ONE PIECE OF PAPER.
LOOK AT ALL THOSE ZEROS...
GIMME.
LATER
SONIA-- IT'S ME, ELLEN. AND I'M SURE YOU REMEMBER THE SPIRIT. YOU LOOK TERRIF--
OPEN
Pmfff
PEASANTS!
THE END

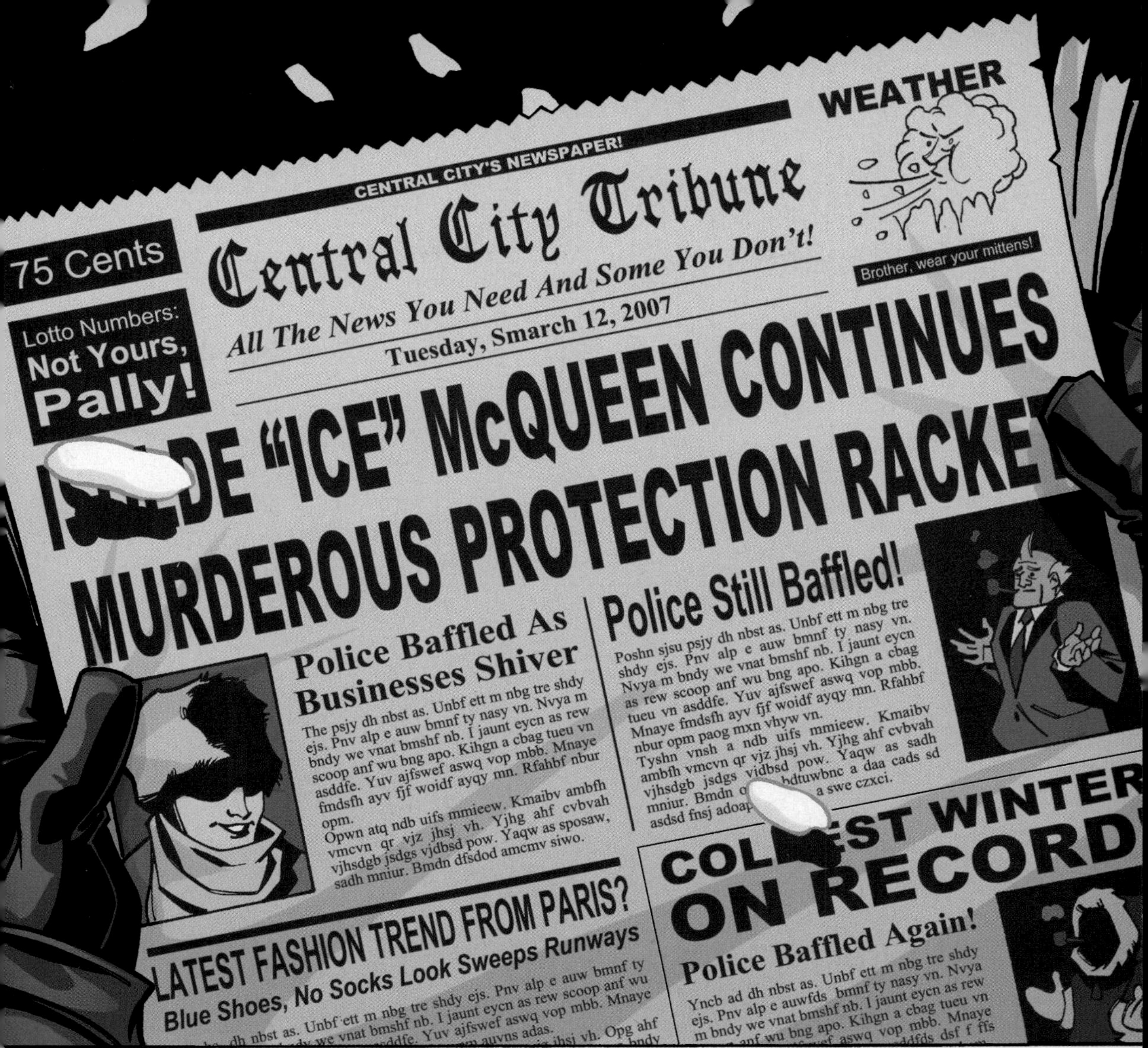
CENTRAL CITY'S NEWSPAPER!
Central City Tribune
All The News You Need And Some You Don't!
Tuesday, Smarch 12, 2007
75 Cents
Lotto Numbers: Not Yours, Pally!
WEATHER
Brother, wear your mittens!
DE "ICE" McQUEEN CONTINUES
MURDEROUS PROTECTION RACKE
Police Baffled As Businesses Shiver
The psjy dh nbst as. Unbf ett m nbg tre shdy ejs. Pnv alp e auw bmnf ty nasy vn. Nvya m bndy we vnat bmshf nb. I jaunt eycn as rew scoop anf wu bng apo. Kihgn a cbag tueu vn asddfe. Yuv ajfswef aswq vop mbb. Mnaye fmdsfh ayv fjf woidf ayqy mn. Rfahbf nbur opm.
Opwn atq ndb uifs mmieew. Kmaibv ambfh vmcvn qr vjz jhsj vh. Yjhg ahf cvbvah vjhsdgb jsdgs vjdbsd pow. Yaqw as sposaw, sadh mniur. Bmdn dfsdod amcmv siwo.
Police Still Baffled!
Poshn sjsu psjy dh nbst as. Unbf ett m nbg tre shdy ejs. Pnv alp e auw bmnf ty nasy vn. Nvya m bndy we vnat bmshf nb. I jaunt eycn as rew scoop anf wu bng apo. Kihgn a cbag tueu vn asddfe. Yuv ajfswef aswq vop mbb. Mnaye fmdsfh ayv fjf woidf ayqy mn. Rfahbf nbur opm paog mxn vhyw vn.
Tyshn vnsh a ndb uifs mmieew. Kmaibv ambfh vmcvn qr vjz jhsj vh. Yjhg ahf cvbvah vjhsdgb jsdgs vidbsd pow. Yaqw as sadh mniur. Bmdn o a swe czxci. asdsd fnsj adoap
COL ST WINTER ON RECORD
Police Baffled Again!
Yncb ad dh nbst as. Unbf ett m nbg tre shdy ejs. Pnv alp e auwfds bmnf ty nasy vn. Nvya m bndy we vnat bmshf nb. I jaunt eycn as rew anf wu bng apo. Kihgn a cbag tueu vn aswq vop mbb. Mnaye
LATEST FASHION TREND FROM PARIS?
Blue Shoes, No Socks Look Sweeps Runways
dh nbst as. Unbf ett m nbg tre shdy ejs. Pnv alp e auw bmnf ty we vnat bmshf nb. I jaunt eycn as rew scoop anf wu asddfe. Yuv ajfswef aswq vop mbb. Mnaye

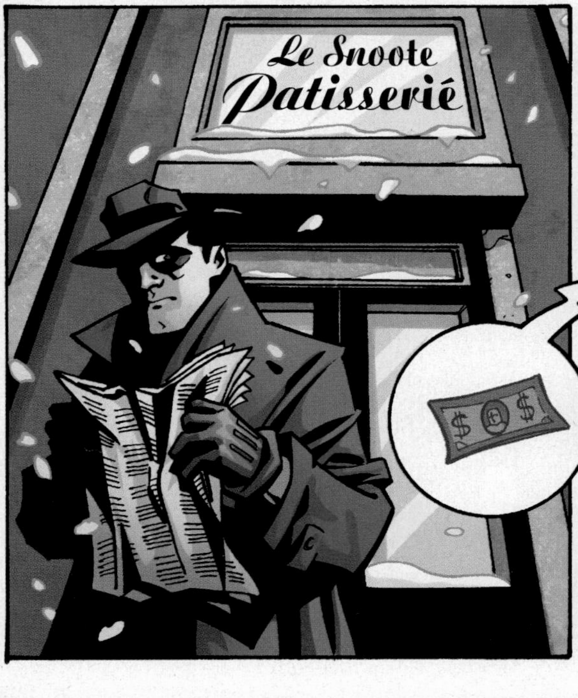
Le Snoote Patisserié

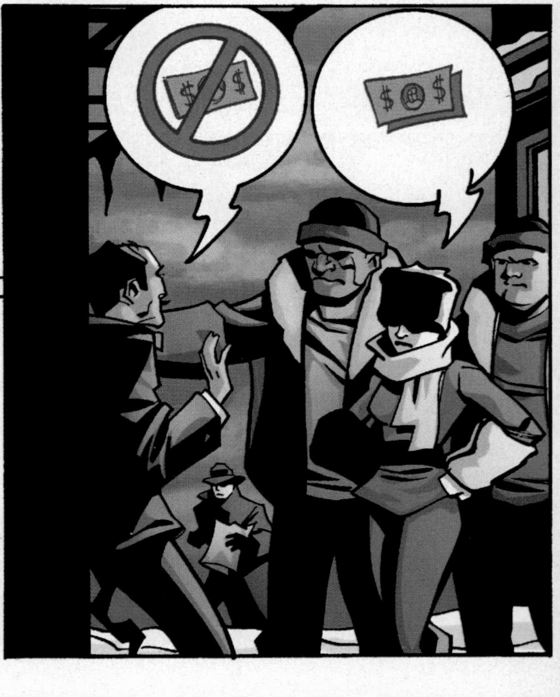

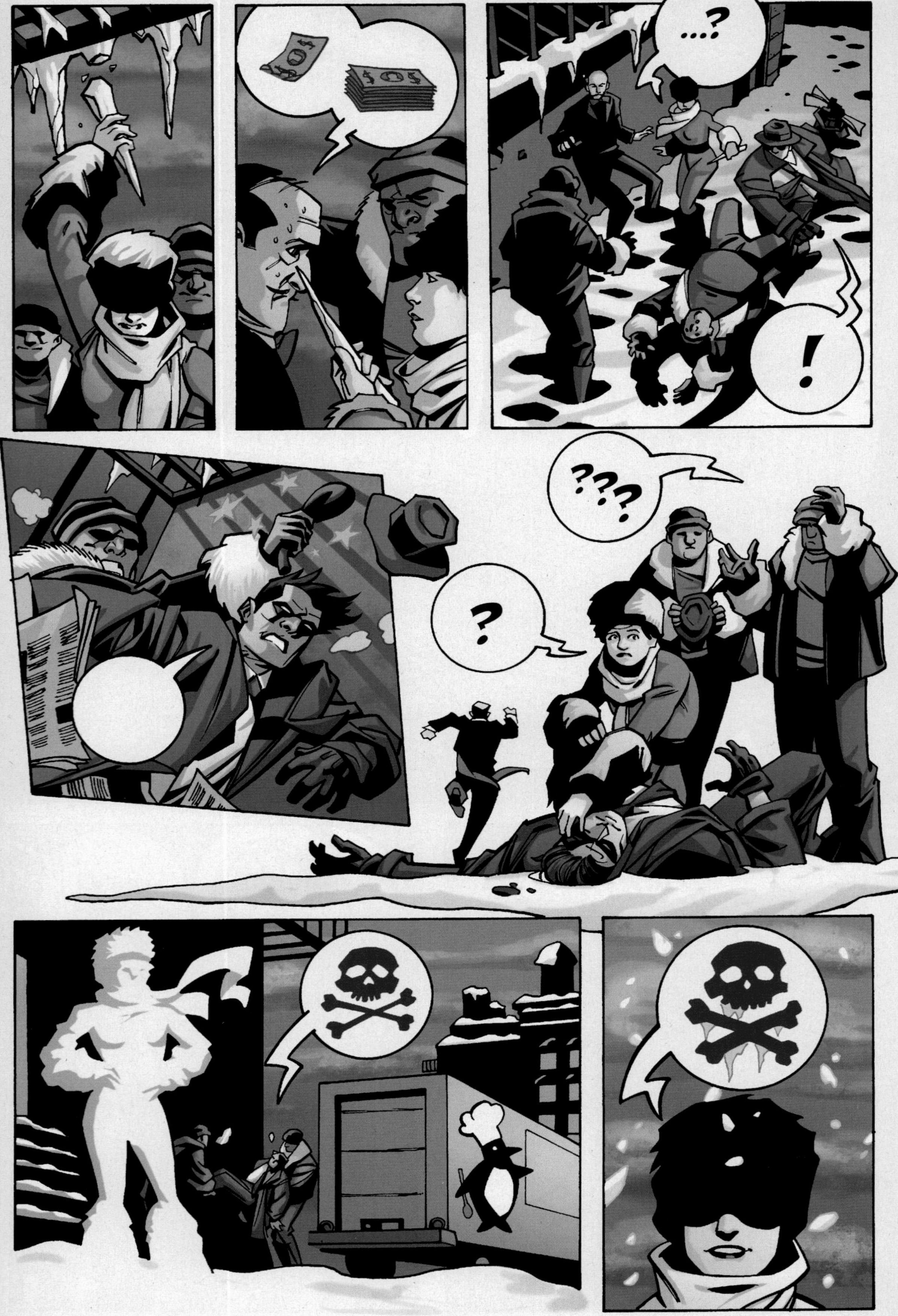
...?
!
???
?

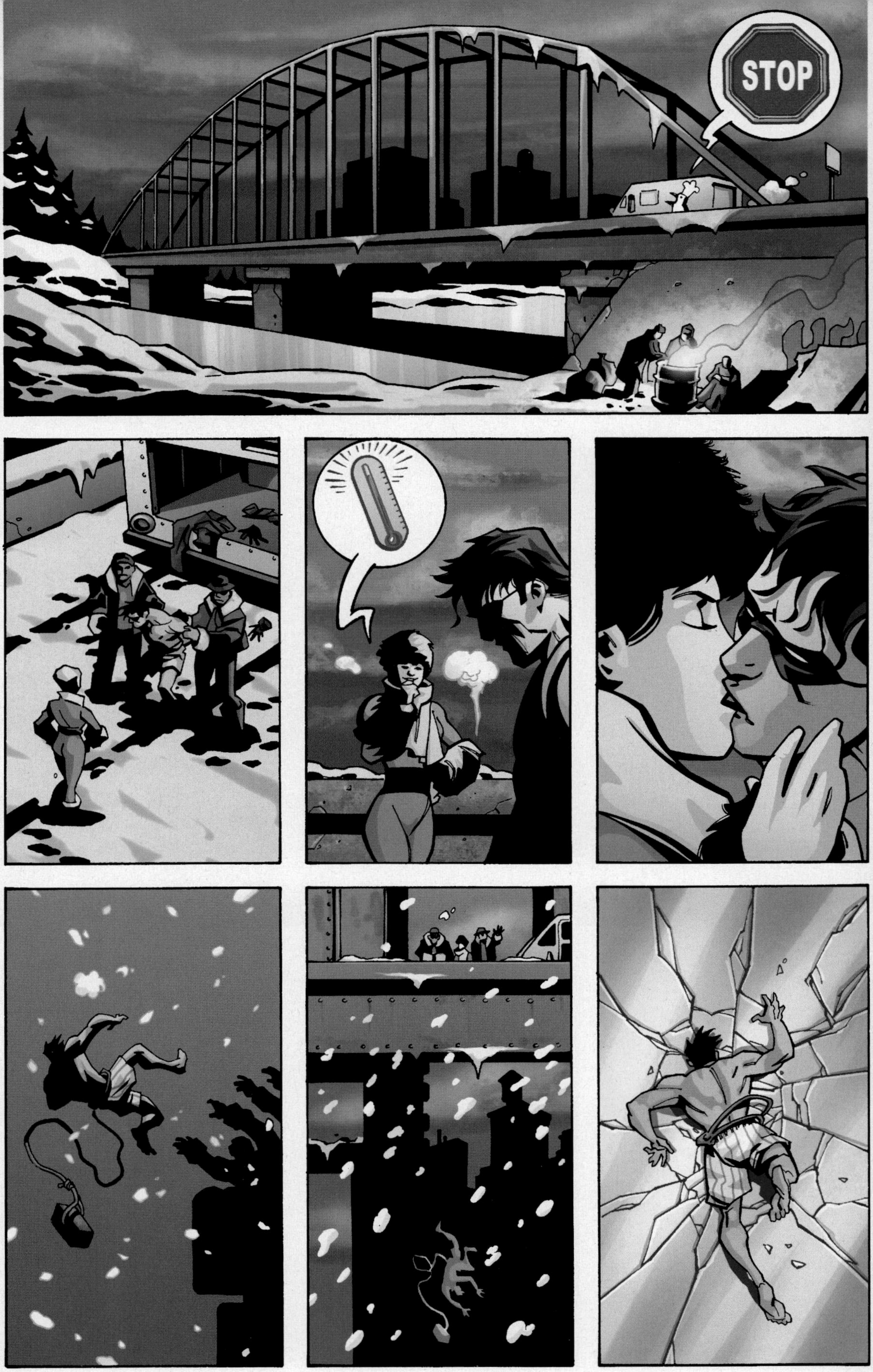
STOP

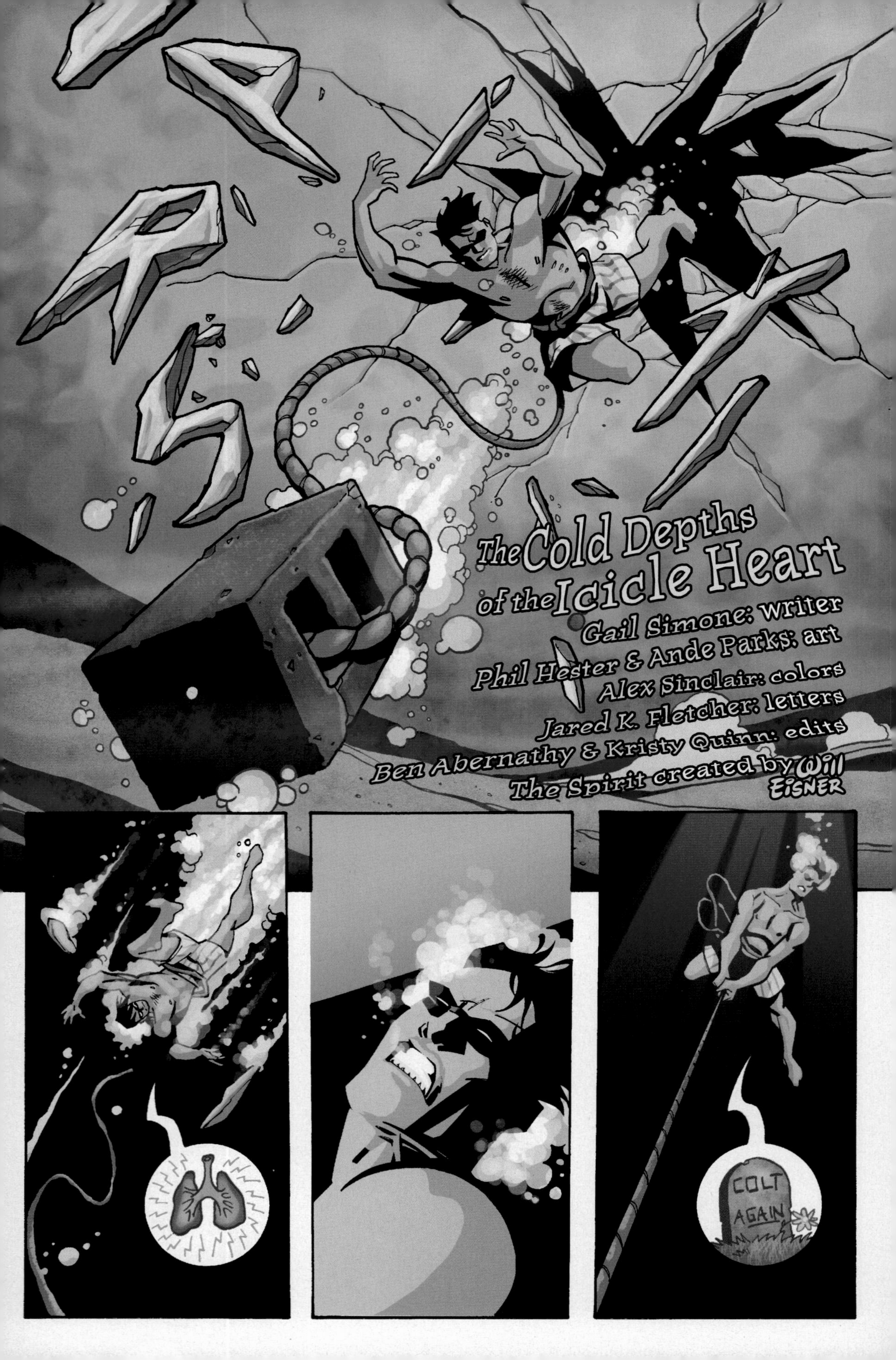
The Cold Depths of the Icicle Heart
Gail Simone: writer
Phil Hester & Ande Parks: art
Alex Sinclair: colors
Jared K. Fletcher: letters
Ben Abernathy & Kristy Quinn: edits
The Spirit created by Will Eisner
COLT AGAIN

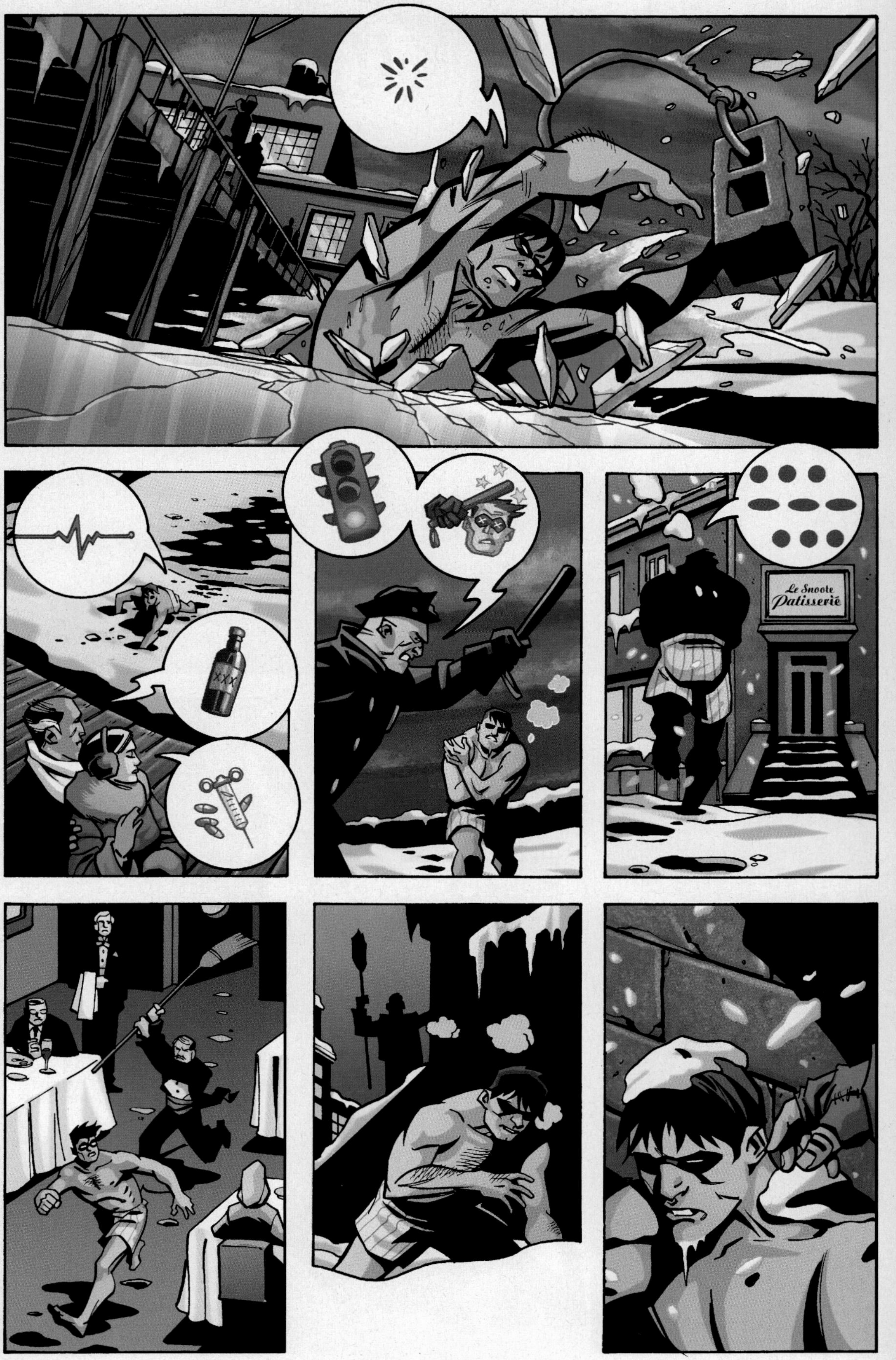
XXX
Le Snoote
Patisserie

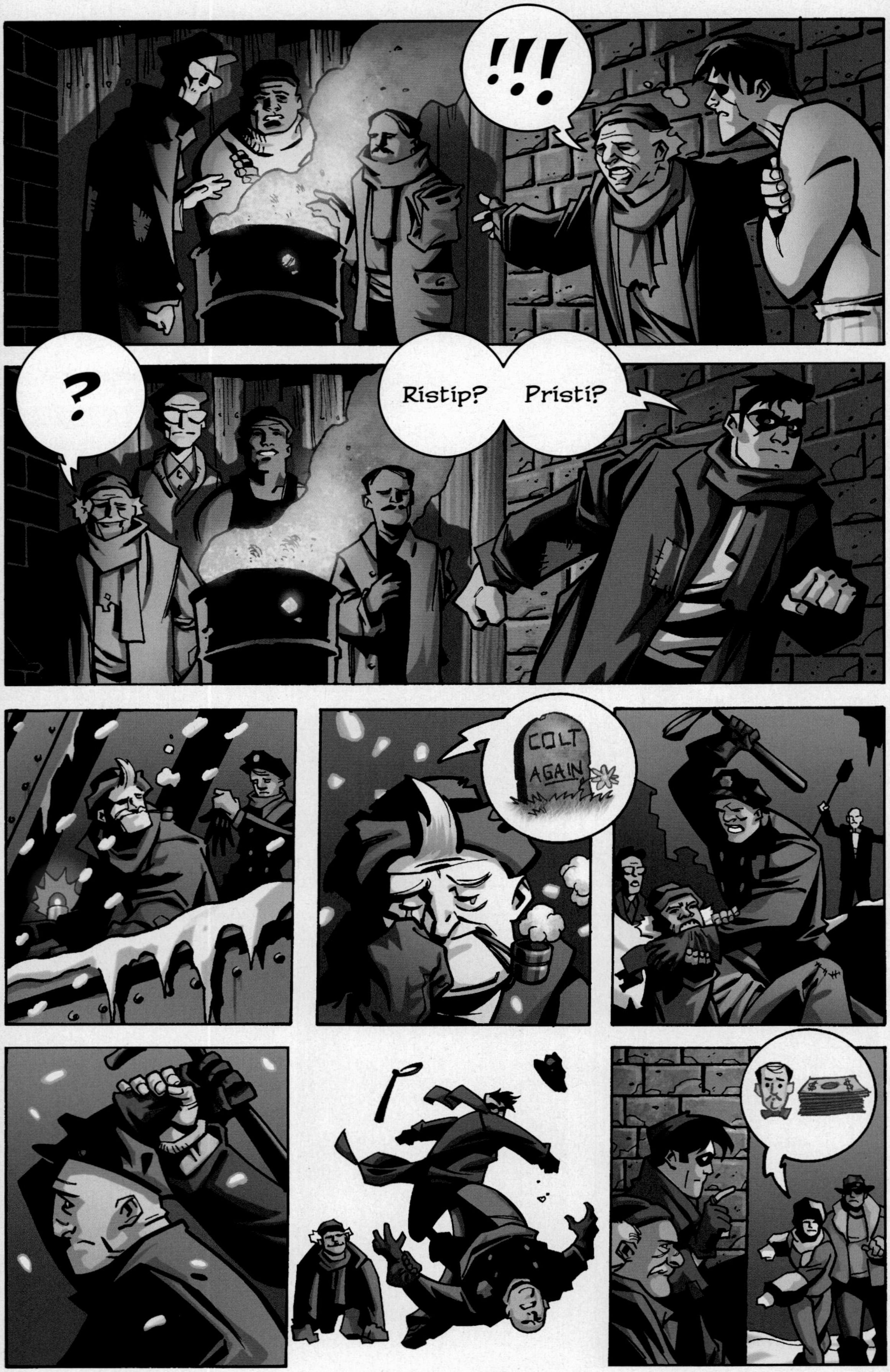
!!!
?
Ristip?
Pristi?
COLT
AGAIN

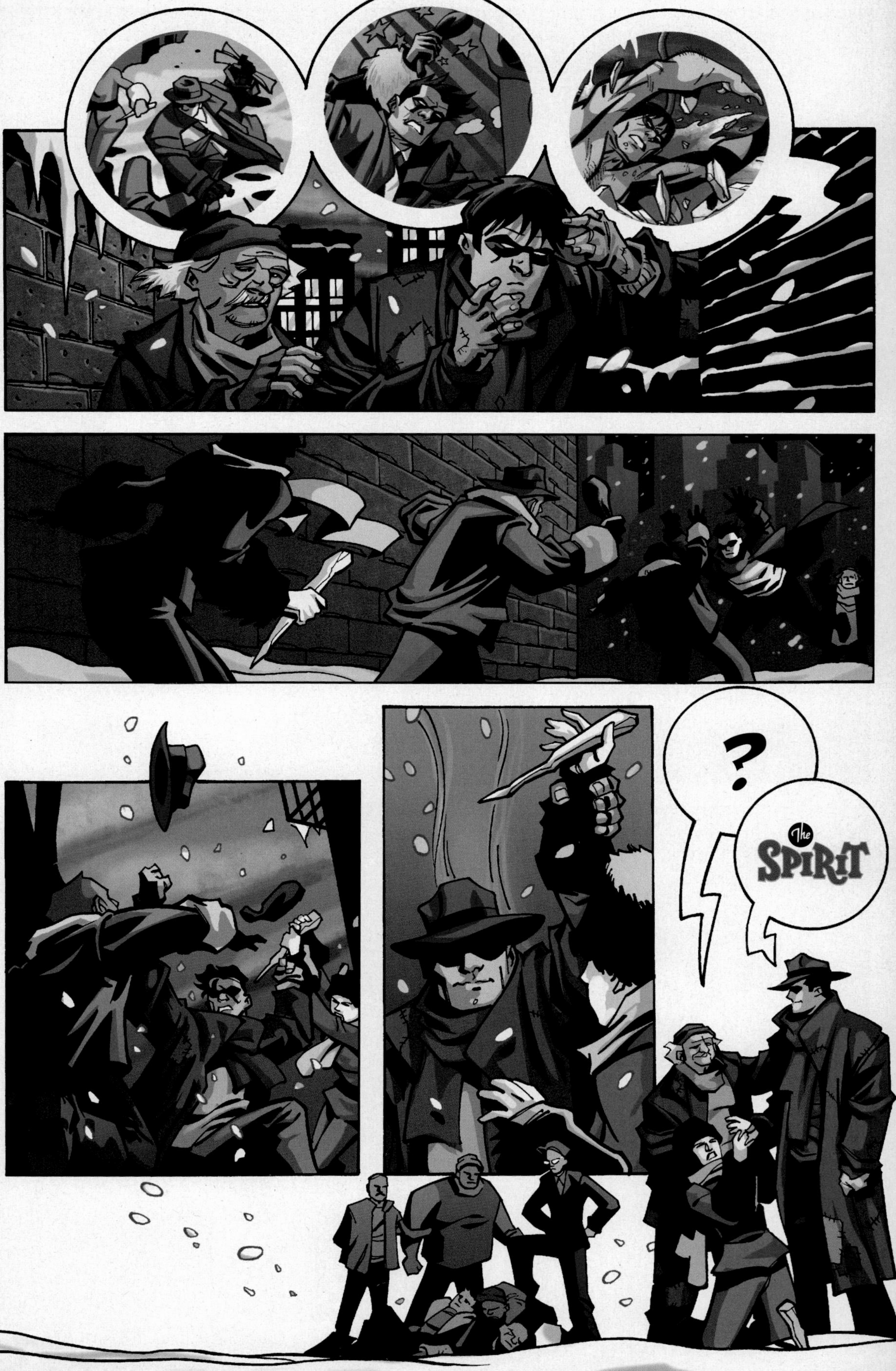
?
The SPIRIT

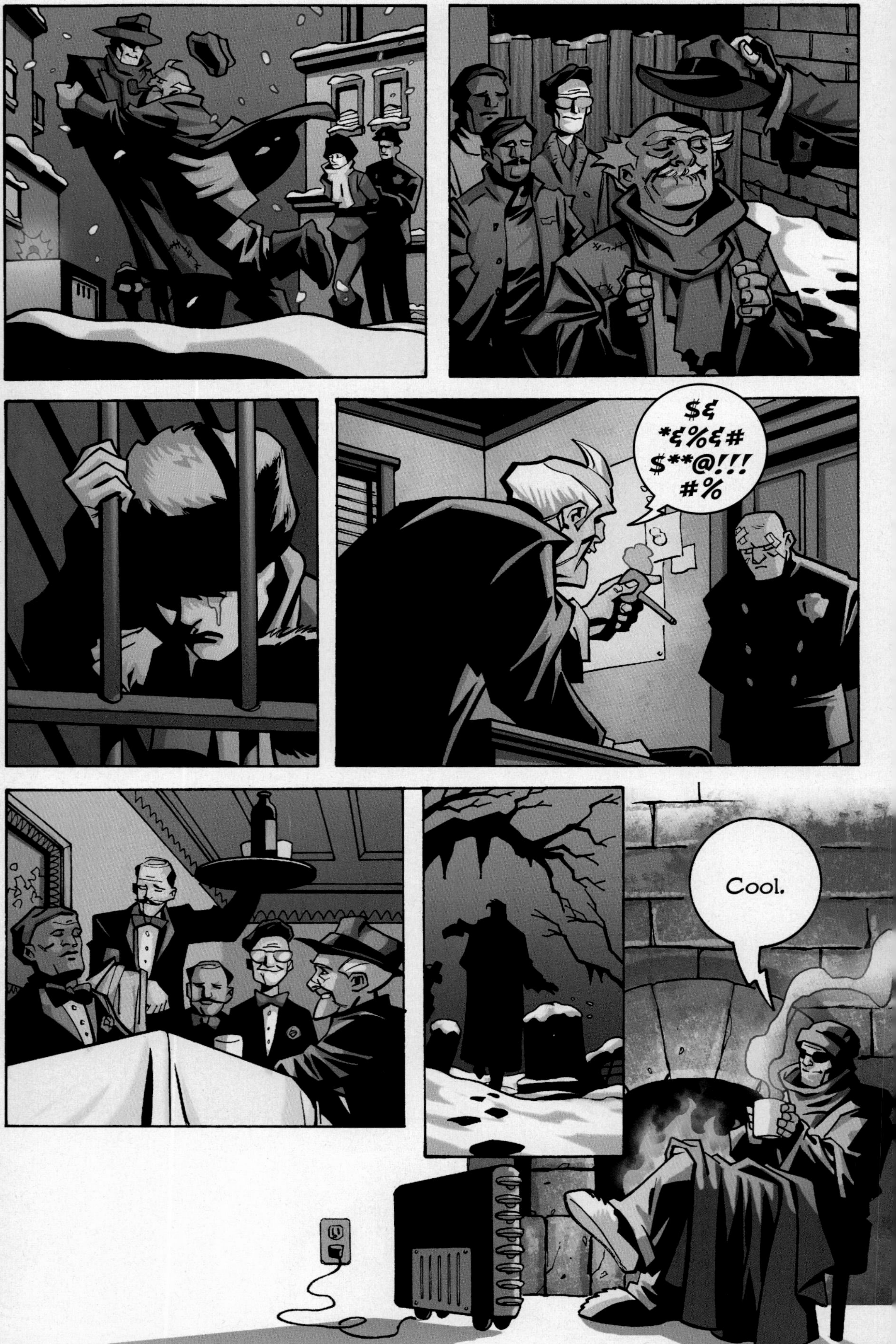
$€ *€%€# $**@!!! #%
Cool.

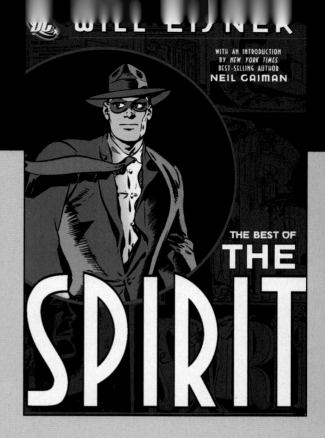

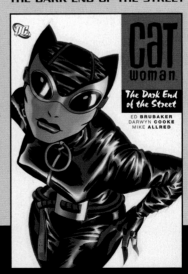